(De-)constructing Rape Culture and Victim Blaming Online

Text – Meaning – Context:
Cracow Studies in English Language, Literature and Culture

Edited by
Elżbieta Chrzanowska-Kluczewska
and Władysław Witalisz

Volume 21

PETER LANG

Berlin - Bruxelles - Chennai - Lausanne - New York - Oxford

Olga O'Toole

(De-)constructing Rape Culture and Victim Blaming Online

New Solutions and Critical Voices in Contemporary Literature and Language

PETER LANG

Berlin - Bruxelles - Chennai - Lausanne - New York - Oxford

Bibliographic Information published by the Deutsche Nationalbibliothek
The Deutsche Nationalbibliothek lists this publication in the Deutsche Nationalbibliografie; detailed bibliographic data is available in the internet at http://dnb.d-nb.de.

Library of Congress Cataloging-in-Publication Data
A CIP catalog record for this book has been applied for at the Library of Congress.

The publication was financially supported by the Faculty of Philology of the Jagiellonian University in Cracow.

ISSN 2191-1894
ISBN 978-3-631-92230-9 (Print)
E-ISBN 978-3-631-92237-8 (E-PDF)
E-ISBN 978-3-631-93588-0 (E-PUB)
DOI 10.3726/b22782

Published by Peter Lang GmbH, Berlin (Germany)
info@peterlang.com

This publication has been peer reviewed.

www.peterlang.com

Olga O'Toole

(De-)constructing Rape Culture and Victim Blaming Online

New Solutions and Critical Voices in Contemporary Literature and Language

PETER LANG

Berlin - Bruxelles - Chennai - Lausanne - New York - Oxford

Bibliographic Information published by the Deutsche Nationalbibliothek
The Deutsche Nationalbibliothek lists this publication in the Deutsche Nationalbibliografie; detailed bibliographic data is available in the internet at http://dnb.d-nb.de.

Library of Congress Cataloging-in-Publication Data
A CIP catalog record for this book has been applied for at the Library of Congress.

The publication was financially supported by the Faculty of Philology of the Jagiellonian University in Cracow.

ISSN 2191-1894
ISBN 978-3-631-92230-9 (Print)
E-ISBN 978-3-631-92237-8 (E-PDF)
E-ISBN 978-3-631-93588-0 (E-PUB)
DOI 10.3726/b22782

Published by Peter Lang GmbH, Berlin (Germany)
info@peterlang.com

This publication has been peer reviewed.

www.peterlang.com

Acknowledgements

I would like to extend my sincerest gratitude to everyone who has been a part of the process of the writing of this book, as well as to those who supported me over the years.

Above all, I would like to express my utmost gratitude to my thesis advisor, Professor Marta Dąbrowska for her continuous support as my wonderful academic advisor. Namely, I would like to extend my gratitude for her support of my study and related research, and for her patience, motivation, insight, and immense knowledge in sociolinguistics and discourse analysis. I would also like to thank the inspirational individuals, professors, researchers, and students that I have met along the way, many of whom shared their opinions, experiences, and thoughts on the project. I would also like to thank Professor Agnieszka Kiełkiewicz-Janowiak and Professor Andrzej Łyda, as well as my entire doctoral committee, without whom this project would not have been possible.

Finally, I cannot forget the support I received from my family, friends, and my partner, who ever so patiently accompanied me on the road to completing this work.

Table of contents

Introduction

Rape culture is a well-studied social phenomenon that also has embedded within it the practice of victim blaming, and both of these phenomena are present in American and Polish societies, especially within certain discourses. This specific social dynamic includes the practice of normalizing sexual violence and blaming rape victims for the crimes committed against their persons, thus strongly affecting and influencing the attitudes towards actors involved (cf. Chapter 1 for a comprehensive definition of rape culture). I highlight the view that in the online discourses presented in the specific genre of digital comments—which either directly or indirectly blame the victim—the product that is discursive secondary victimization emerges. As a result, the focus tends to be on how the presentation of the role of the victim highlights her as an actor who is seen as at least partially at fault for the crime committed against her.

As a social problem, sexual aggression has received much media attention over recent years, including the rise of the #metoo movement on an international scale in 2017 and the public and social persecution of perpetrators of sexual crime making headlines in the media, from social media, such as Facebook, Twitter, and Instagram, to official news websites. This increase in the vocality of women around the globe on the subject of abuse and harassment has been attributed to the growth of platforms for digital communication (Guha, 2020). Feminist activism online has resulted in various campaigns in the US, such as the SlutWalk movement, the Hollaback social campaign, and the #metoo movement (*ibid.*; Alaggia & Wang, 2020). In Poland, feminist organizations, such as Dziewuchy Dziewuchom, FemFund, Federa, and Feminoteka have been active both on- and offline in battling the stigma that victims of rape face in the country (Korolczuk et al., 2017). Even more recently, 2024 saw a change made to the definition of rape in the Polish legal system (Krytyka Polityczna, 2024).[1] Despite the efforts of such movements to eradicate ideas of victim blaming and its reproduction, however, the secondary victimization of those who have suffered rape still occurs, and stigmatization is still visible in various discourses, including in the media and regular talk and text.

The question of recognizing the problem and taking action against such forms of not only sexual, but also other highly gendered, aggression and crime has been

1 https://krytykapolityczna.pl/kraj/nowa-definicja-gwaltu-zacznie-obowiazywac-za-pol-roku-co-tak-naprawde-sie-zmienia/

manifested in many guises, ranging from public protest to a backlash of feminist groups against the legitimization of existing "normative views of female and male sexuality" (Ehrlich, 2001:1). Despite this fact, rape victims—or survivors—oftentimes do not find it an easy or feasible task to escape the social stigma attached to being the targets of sexual crime, and it is all the more alarming that women make up the majority of those affected (Wolitzky-Taylor et al., 2011; Yung, 2013, 2015). This has been previously investigated from a linguistic perspective in the literature concerning the discourse in legal language about rape, including the language of rape trials and the testimonies of victims and offenders (Ehrlich, 2001). This problem is also evident in the discourses of Internet users who make comments in publicly available discussions that may be found underneath articles about rape. This community has been found to draw on various linguistic strategies, namely that of implicitness in the evaluation of the social actors—namely the offender and the victim—involved in a sexual crime.

This work deals with the problem of sexual aggression in American and Polish cultures by looking at discourses of Internet users, namely those presented in digital comments. I aim to highlight where gender ideology is visible in discourse on sexual crime. Using Critical Discourse Analysis, my goal in this book is to point out that such discourses have a negative—even detrimental—effect on rape victims and the way that they are perceived overall, as the public nature of such comments entails that they are then read by different audiences.

By investigating the indirect evaluation of actors in such digital comments, it is possible to pinpoint more distinct mechanisms that lead to the claim implicit evaluation is used to express opinions both on the level of structure and socio-semantics in discourse. The nature of digital comments to be more conversational and informal in their register is reflected in the choice to investigate evaluation and the way that implicit evaluation can be seen in short comments, rather than in broader terms of evaluation in discourse (Martin & White, 2005; Hunston, 2011; Aijmer, 2015; Aijmer & Rühlemann, 2015; Millar & Hunston, 2015). By investigating the evaluative stance of authors' comments, what may be made more clear is how, by a variety in the choice of expression, the appraisal of social actors is made all the more covert, since direct negative expression of attitudes is rare. Such an investigation of the meaning behind comments of Internet users can demonstrate that victim blaming is carried out indirectly rather than directly, and as such spreads beliefs that a rape victim is at least partially to blame for having been raped. The cultural aspect of the analysis aims to present that, although victim blaming is present in both American and Polish CMC, strategies of indirectness in comments differ between the two cultures, reflecting cultural tendencies in language when faced with a taboo subject such as that of sexual crime.

The widespread underreporting of rape may, thus, be dealt with from a perspective that takes language as the basis both for the construction and maintenance of beliefs and stereotypes regarding the actors involved. Such an approach takes victim blaming as central to the perpetuation of harmful beliefs regarding rape and the actors involved, where negative attention is placed on the victim of the crime, even if the perpetrator is found guilty. *Victim blaming* places a victim (or survivor) of a crime in a position of culpability (iterating that she was even partially at fault for the crime committed against her), rather than placing full responsibility on the perpetrator. The United States Department of Justice has provided the statistics on the number of reported sexual assaults, estimating in 2007 that only 2% of victims who were incapacitated at the time of the crime reported being raped and that an alarming 13% of those physically forced report being raped, which has been deemed to still be of relevance today (Gray, 2017). Even more alarming are the statistics that predict the prevalence of rape, revealing an startling disparity between the sexual crime that takes place in men's and women's cases.

The National Sexual Violence Resource Center (2015: 1) states that "one in five women and 71 men will be raped at some point in their lives" and that "nearly one in 10 women has been raped by an intimate partner in her lifetime, including completed forced penetration, attempted forced penetration or alcohol/drug-facilitated completed penetration." The present work looks only at rape cases in which women are the victims, due to this alarming disparity.

The Polish statistics do not speak much differently on the problem of rape in Poland, as well as about the approach of rape victims and their access to proper aid from authorities. The most recent reports concerning the statistics on sexual assault date from 2014 (Raport „Przemoc wobec kobiet: badanie przeprowadzone w skali UE"[2]) and 2011 (Fundacja Feminoteka) for the EU and Poland, respectively. The report from 2014 states that in the EU, 33% of women experienced either physical or sexual violence against her person after the age of 15, that 22% of women were victims of physical or sexual violence by their partner, and that 5% of the women who partook in the study had been raped. The Polish report carried out by Feminoteka in 2011 states that very little is known about the scale of sexual aggression in Poland (Turecka, 2005; Borkowska & Płatek, 2011: 11). The report provides information from the year 2007, stating that 3% of respondents of a study carried out by OBOP (Ośrodek Badań Opinii Publicznych[3]) had been

2 Report: Violence against women: Research conducted in the EU
3 Center for research on public opinion (my translation)

the victim of some form of sexual assault, and that 1% had experienced being sexually assaulted by a family member. To my knowledge, more recent statistical research has not been carried out on the subject.

One reason for undertaking a study of the discursive representations of the motivations to view the victim as at fault for being raped is to underline the important role that public discourse plays in shaping and maintaining such beliefs, including attitudes towards actors in a rape case, especially where negative attitudes toward the victim are concerned. This perspective provides an opportunity to change the conversation on sexual assault, aggression, and rape, possibly creating space for a harsher approach within the criminal justice system towards those who commit such an insidious and criminal act. It has been argued that rape constitutes a type of social interaction with its scripts and that those scripts reflect or are seen in many cases as synonymous with normal cultural or sexual scripts, with the exception of sexual refusal (Ryan, 2011). The reason that I do not engage in an in-depth discuss on sexual aggression against men in this work, whether perpetrated by women or other men, is due to the above-stated information regarding the prevalence of sexual aggression against women by men (RAINN, online; Piotrowska & Synkiewicz, 2011: 117).[4] That is not to say that the subject is not equally important, however, it is unfortunately out of the scope of this work.

Although this book does not attend strictly to the structural linguistic aspects of discourse, which are entailed in traditional linguistic study, it does attempt to investigate what Foucault (1972: 49) deemed the "practices that systematically form the objects of which they speak." Thus, the work explores the linguistic representation of female rape victims in a cross-cultural analysis of the computer-mediated discourse (computer-mediated communication—CMC) on rape to demonstrate where gender and sexist ideologies are visible in discourse that maintains victim blaming present in rape case situations. In taking both American and Polish online discourses (CMC) as instances of attitude expressions, as made easier through the internet as a medium, i.e., via digital comments which can be found in the form of comments that often accompany articles on sites such as Facebook, tabloid sites and other fora, a window into the prevalence of victim

4 RAINN's website discloses that "sexual violence is notoriously difficult to measure, and there is no single source of data that provides a complete picture of the crime" (RAINN, online). Most of the data that make up the statistics regarding sexual assault on RAINN's site come from the *National Crime Victimization Survey* conducted by the Justice Department.

blaming in discourse may be provided and the magnitude of such a social problem shown.

In the chapters that follow, I delineate how discourses can be unpacked to reveal where power structures and underlying ideologies shape stereotypical interpretations of social situations. The work comprises four theoretical chapters and two separate analytical chapters, each of which focuses on a different aspect of the critical discourse analysis of digital comments. In Chapter 1, I name and describe in depth how critical discourse analysis, as a framework for the analysis of discourse that spreads ideology, provides tools adequate for the investigation of the foundations upon which victim blaming occurs on a regular basis, its genesis being in talk and text. The methodologies of investigation described include the representation of social actors on both levels of structure and socio-semantics as well as the investigation of linguistic pragmatics in CDA and the categories of analysis in social actor representation, as well as the question of linguistic choice and modality. These key aspects are described in detail, with examples provided for illustration. The subjects of evaluation in discourse and the appraisal that occurs through implicit evaluation are addressed from a pragma-linguistic perspective to show that digital comments about rape and the actors involved may be described from such a perspective. It is important to note that the subject of implicit evaluation is the main point of departure for the study conducted in this work (Chapters 6 and 7).

Chapter 2 deals more in depth with questions of ideology, how ideology as a phenomenon to be studied is interconnected with gender, and the normalization of patriarchal structure in many institutional, public and private settings. Notions of masculinity and femininity, as well as what constitutes them, are introduced here, and the idea of hypermasculinity defined as reproducing harmful patriarchal norms. In this chapter, I highlight how cultural sexual scripts, as related to gender ideologies, act rather universally (i.e., they are similar in both American and Polish cultures) and play a large role in the way that rape victims are viewed, as these scripts are largely responsible for the dissemination of rape myths present in the discourse on rape cases. In addition to this, sexual crime is defined, and the various typologies of rape also provided in the chapter.

In Chapter 3, the question of gender and sexuality in language, including previous linguistic studies in both American and Polish contexts is also addressed in depth, so as to provide the background for what linguistic aspects are seen here as affecting the perpetuating victim-blaming attitudes. This includes how communication and miscommunication have defined a standpoint perspective regarding who is to blame in cases of sexual crime. The chapter discusses the gender and language theories that make up the canon, including deficit theory, muted group theory, the difference approach to gendered communication, and, finally, dynamic theory. Gender representations that reflect ideologies of masculinity and femininity are also discussed where they partake in the forming of discourses about men and women. This includes phraseologies that refer to men and women, as well as semantic derogation and asymmetry, subjects which reflect negative discourses towards women. Finally, Chapter 3 covers the topic of language and sexuality and also describes the ways that discursive representations of genitalia and sexual intercourse reflect the ideologies that are discussed in Chapter 2.

Chapter 4 delineates the analysis of the Internet in linguistic study, presenting the idea of computer-mediated communication and within it, that of digital comments. The questions of genre, register and style are discussed in their relation to digital comments as a genre. Such an aspect is important in introducing the subject of online comments, which in the case of rape, could not exist without the points of reference that are the news sources on the subject discussed. The subject of online comments is then introduced, as well as that of anonymity in digital comments and its importance in leading to freer expression of blame attribution within the context of rape. This being said, the impact that such public sources have on collective attitudes is contended, since its widespread availability in the online sphere is what I argue to reproduce the discursive secondary victimization that emerges.

In Chapter 5, the aims, research questions and materials and methods used to carry out the analysis are presented. This chapter is laid separate from the two practical chapters, rather than embedded within their content, as the same methods of coding were applied to both tiers of the analysis and the same corpora (the AEC and the PC) were used to highlight evaluation in both structural and socio-semantic levels of the digital comments analyzed. An explanation of the program MaxQDA and how exactly the materials were coded and statistically analyzed is also provided in the chapter on methods and materials.

The theoretical chapters described above lead to the analysis of the two corpora collected, which consists of two chapters on the critical discourse analysis of the ways that discursive strategies in American and Polish digital comments which accompany articles about rape reflect predominantly negative attitudes towards victims. The first part of the analysis in Chapter 6 focuses on the way that the evaluation of actors is expressed within the structural elements of discourse, including how discursive strategies, such as negation and deontic or epistemic modality express evaluative stances towards the actors involved in a rape crime. Here, I take from van Leeuwen (1996, 2008), as well, focusing on the activation and/or passivation of actors and the ways that such strategies foreground or background actors, thus leading to the implication (through implicit evaluation) that one actor is more at fault than another.

Chapter 7, the final aspect of the practical analysis for the work, also focuses on the evaluation that lies in digital comments written by Internet users on the subject of rape, however in the socio-semantic aspects of such discourse. The analysis looks at how evaluation in the lexical representations of the victim, the offender, and the rape itself can provide insight into the meaning communicated by the writer where his or her stance is concerned. The subject of the representations of actors according to the social actors model is discussed in depth (van Leeuwen, 1996), including a focus on appraisement where metaphorical references are found (Chilton, 1996; Charteris-Black, 2004). Where the rape is concerned, the investigation of euphemization of the rape itself is seen as providing examples of sociocultural attitudes towards the crime and its actors. These aspects are also investigated as to what they reflect in the cultural sense, i.e., whether or not American and Polish discourses demonstrate any differences in the way socio-semantic representations of actors and events in rape come about.

I would also like to note that throughout the work I use the term *victim(s)* to refer to a woman or women who have been raped, rather than the counterpart *survivor(s)*. This is not because I disagree with the term, but rather, because both are problematic—not all victims want to be seen as survivors and not all survivors wish to be viewed as victims (Thompson 2000)—and the term survivor has as of late been deemed more objective and is used in contexts of the criminalization of sexual assault (SAKI 2015).

The purpose of such an analysis is to provide a full-bodied comparison of one kind of online discourse that is representative of the way that Internet users who make comments express evaluative attitudes (both positive and negative) towards actors in rape. The cultural aspect is of importance, as my main hypothesis purports that victim blaming is carried out through varying strategies in American online comments and Polish online comments. As the literature states that American culture is more indirect than Polish culture, where communication is concerned, it is of interest to seek out whether or not, given the nature of sexual crime, this remains the same for evaluation in anonymous online comments (Wierzbicka, 1985; Ogiermann, 2009). It is my hope that such an analysis will allow for conclusions to be made regarding the indirectness of the evaluation (as shown through the analysis of implicit evaluation) of actors involved in a rape and the link that such discourse has with taboo and what is considered unacceptable in American and Polish culture.

I have written this work with the hope of demonstrating the social weight of language, discourse, and cultural scripts and their reflection in the way that things are worded. These aspects of social expression in turn contribute to the construction of rape culture, as well as the reproduction of secondary victimization. The way that a community or society speaks on an issue shapes the values and what is upheld, illustrated and propagated by such societies. When examining the fact of persisting normalizations of the public persecution of victims of sexual crime, the discourse surrounding their role in the crime is pertinent in shaping the way that they are viewed. Although the situation of these victims is receiving increasingly more media attention, a highly embedded victim blaming is still present in both normal, everyday discourse, and in the discourse of the press. This work aims to describe the phenomenon, explaining where hegemony functions in maintaining the inferiority and lack of support towards victims of rape, and the fact that these phenomena are intrinsically linked with the linguistic representations of victims and perpetrators, distorting the perceptions regarding the actors involved and further victimizing those women who have been raped by men.

Chapter 1: Critical discourse analysis and the problem of rape

This chapter aims to explain the relevance of Critical Discourse Analysis (CDA) to the linguistic investigation of crime, specifically rape, as well as to delineate the approaches to CDA that are suitable for the analysis of a topic of such social significance. To be discussed in the pages that follow are the methodologies currently used in connection with tackling social issues, especially those that relate to discourses on gendered subjects. What is of interest here are those discourses about sexual aggression towards women and how actors are portrayed in such a way so as to perpetuate the problem of victim blaming within discursive aspects of social life. The justification of a discourse analysis approach to the subject of rape is that in any general investigation of sexual violence as a gender-based crime, in which women have been the victim in over 90% of cases in the United States and Poland (Koss, 1988, 1990; Borkowska & Płatek, 2011; Dutka, 2014; Chmura-Rutkowska, 2016), such an analysis acts as an attempt to help its eradication.

It can be argued that stereotypes regarding female sexuality as a taboo subject, which are related to normalized sexual scripts that promote male sexual dominance, are also at work in the maintenance of the blaming of women who have been raped, and that post-seventeenth century ideas regarding sexuality still apply to women today (Foucault, 1976; Cameron & Kulick, 2003). These ideologies are visible in evaluative discourse about rape, as such evaluation presents stances and attitudes.

Perspectives on sexuality today are said to be largely informed by the *repressive hypothesis*, which posits that human sexuality has been under repression over the past three hundred years at least (Foucault, 1976; Garton, 2014; Weeks, 2017), and largely creates a culture of shame around female sexuality in particular. The way of thinking about female sexuality as more passive and less naturally inclined than men's also contributes largely to what is referred to as attribution theory (cf. Chapter 2), a socio-psychological phenomenon that is at work in victim-blaming discourses (Grubb & Turner, 2012). Additionally, social attitudes that are reflected in discourse can point to various social attributions of blame when it comes to rape, by which are understood the beliefs regarding what it is that led a person to rape or be raped. Here, I aim to demonstrate how these discourses form the complex patterns of interdiscursivity within two cultural contexts, American and Polish, as discussed by Critical Discourse Analysis scholars, thus perpetuating an already-existing rape culture.

What is referred to as *rape culture*[5] instills into collective thought the belief that hegemonic masculine dominance is the norm, which in turn maintains the same thought that abides by notions of female submission and inferiority to men as a regular phenomenon. Such normalization of sexual violence also contributes to rape culture (Peters & Besley, 2019). Feminist Standpoint Theory, as well as other theories that take on the problem of the subjugation of women in other contexts of language and discourse, takes an analytical approach, the goal of which is to break down how any marginalized group suffers from the way that knowledge (i.e., knowledge as cultural capital (Bourdieu 1990)) is situated (cf. Chapter 2). There is a paradox surrounding rape, however—one that lies in the fact that it is a crime that occurs in alarmingly high numbers, and it is still believed by many to be an occurrence that takes place only under the most extreme circumstances or due to the fault of the victim (Brison, 2005). This idea goes hand in hand with the rape myths delineated in Chapter 2.

This chapter consists of a description of what is entailed in CDA, as well as the aspects that may be investigated to uncover ideologies within discourse. From the presentation of goals and main threads of research in CDA, I move on to the three smaller veins of research relevant to the presented study, including the representation of subjects as social actors (van Leeuwen, 1996, 2008), transitivity processes of verbs in Systemic Functional Linguistics (Halliday, 1985), the notion of evaluation in discourse and pragmalinguistic aspects of presupposition, implicit evaluation, and indirectness, all of which will be key in identifying attitudes in the two final practical chapters (cf. Chapters 6 and 7). Other, more marginal aspects, including investigating how multimodality and social semiotics impinge on social perception of issues like crime, are also briefly discussed.

Although I am aware of the many subcultures and communities of practice that exist in both the United States and Poland, I have, for the practical analysis, decided to examine the publicly available discourses of digital comments in the sphere of computer-mediated communication (cf. Chapter 4, Chapter 6 and Chapter 7), as well as the cultural schemata that are reflected within those discourses. It is important to note that all of the comments examined in chapters 6 and 7 followed a variety of news reports about rape. These types of texts

5 *Rape culture* is understood here as a complex set of beliefs that encourage male sexual aggression and support violence against women, additionally representative of a society in which violence is viewed as sexy and sexuality as violent. In a rape culture, women perceive a continuum of threatened violence that ranges from sexual remarks to sexual touching, to rape itself (Emilie Buchwald, 1994).

(i.e., news reports) are seen as inevitably tied to the discourses of digital comments presented in Chapters 6 and 7, thus acting as a discursive antecedent that informs public opinion.

This chapter presents the beginning of an argument that aims to make connections between sexist ideology, language, and the subjugation of women in discourses that normalize and proliferate the blaming of rape victims, in turn doing little to aid those who are subjected to sexual violence. It is the perpetuation of harmful beliefs about sexuality, rape, victims of rape and the perpetrators of sexual crime in both American and Polish cultures that place women at fault for the crime committed against them.

Defining discourse

Before explaining what Critical Discourse Analysis comprises, it is essential to examine what is understood by the term *discourse* and outline how it is used throughout this work. The terms *text* and *discourse* have been defined in many ways by scholars, and their usage throughout separate disciplines in the social sciences has demonstrated an array of their applicability (Wodak & Meyer, 2009). Text, in contrast with discourse, has been defined as "concrete oral utterances or written documents" (Wodak & Meyer, 2009: 6). Text has also been referred to in the literature as "written documents, pictures, films, advertisements, parades, plays, and other cultural products" (Boréus & Bergström, 2017: 5).

The focus in this work will not be on the term *text* as defined above, as any text analyzed and referred to in this case is considered a part of *discourse*, both physical (in the space that it occupies) and cultural (in the representations that it presents). Therefore, the term text will not be used except to discuss a specific text of interest, where necessary (i.e., concerning a specific comment about rape).

Discourse, in turn, may mean "anything from a historical monument, a *lieu de memoire*, a policy, a political strategy, narratives in a restricted or broad sense of the term, text, talk, a speech, topic-related conversation, to language per se" (Wodak & Meyer, 2009: 3). This concept has been described as social practice embodied in language use and other semiotic systems (i.e., images or music) (Boréus & Bergström, 2017: 6). In the way that the concept is understood by these authors, "notions such as racist discourse, gendered discourse, discourses on un/employment, media discourse, populist discourse, discourses of the past, and many more" can be found, which thus "stretch the meaning of discourse from a genre to a register or style, from a building to a political program" (Wodak & Meyer, 2009: 3).

Bloor and Bloor's (2007) taxonomy of discourse provides a presentation of how discourse has been defined, with six separate linguistic definitions:

1) discourse-1 is the highest unit of linguistic description; phonemes, morphemes, words, phrases, clauses, sentences, and texts are below;
2) discourse-2 is a sample of language usage, generally written to be spoken, that is, a speech;
3) discourse-3 refers to the communication expected in one situation context, alongside one field and register, such as the discourse of law or medicine;
4) discourse-4 is human interaction through any means, verbal and non-verbal;
5) discourse-5 is spoken interaction only;
6) discourse-6 stands for the whole communicative event.

(Bloor & Bloor, 2007: 6–7, after Tenorio, 2011: 184)

In Critical Discourse Analysis, discourse is not only representative of what it physically embodies, but it is, rather, viewed as shaping the world as we know it. A definition, taken from Fairclough and Wodak, become one of those most often used in understanding and communicating the meaning of the term discourse as applied in CDA.

> CDA sees discourse—language use in speech and writing—as a form of 'social practice'. Describing discourse as social practice implies a dialectal relationship between a particular discursive event and the situation(s), institution(s), and social structure(s), which frame it':
>
> The discursive event is shaped by them, but it also shapes them. That is, discourse is socially constitutive as well as socially conditioned—it constitutes situations, objects of knowledge, and the social identities of relationships between people and groups of people. It is constitutive both in the sense that it helps to sustain and reproduce the social status quo, and in the sense that it contributes to transforming it. Since discourse is so socially consequential, it gives rise to important issues of power. Discursive practices may have major ideological effects—that is, they can help produce and reproduce unequal power relations between (for instance) social classes, women and men, and ethnic/cultural majorities and minorities through the ways in which they represent things and position people.
>
> (Fairclough & Wodak, 1997: 258)

There are many other definitions and differentiations of the term discourse provided by various scholars within the circle of Critical Linguistics (Gee, 1999; Chilton, 2004; Gee, 2014, 2015). In this work, *discourse* is considered any text in context and denotes that language is a form of social practice with implications for societal perception of people and events.

This means that whatever language we come into contact with, be it in the news, in advertising or a textbook, our worldviews are shaped by underlying ideologies, which oftentimes remain biased. Hence, language reflects the perceived representations of phenomena in the world, and it is CDA that takes on the task of discovering where power is displayed to perpetuate certain ideologies, and what social positions and representations actors are placed into.

A brief overview of critical discourse analysis

There is little novelty in carrying out critical research on language, considering that much study conducted on influences of Marxist theory of language had its advent in the 1920s (Voloshinov, 1929/1973), and continued as an ever-more emerging phenomenon of language analysis in the 1970s. The main aim of CDA is to demonstrate that power relations are mediated through discourses, whether in the form of spoken or written text.

Critical Discourse Analysis, a field in linguistics that is also more broadly referred to as Critical Discourse Studies (Krzyżanowski, 2016), stems from the field of Critical Linguistics (CL) (Fairclough, 2001, 2017; Wodak & Meyer, 2009). There, CDA is defined as an area of linguistic study which "brings the critical tradition of social analysis into language studies and adds to critical social analysis a particular focus on discourse and on relations between discourse and other social elements (power relations, ideologies, institutions, social identities and so forth)" (Fairclough, 2001: 11). This entails that in any sociological work, the aspect which regards language should be taken into consideration as part of the equation, adding information of value to provide for a much wider scope of analysis on the whole (Gee, 2015; Krzyżanowski, 2016; Krzyżanowski & Forchtner, 2016).

The need to address discourses more directly in the realm of social study has been acknowledged within the various disciplines of social scientific research, including that of post-structuralist theory and feminist theory (Lazar, 2005: 4). Because CDA views language as a form of social practice, social behaviors, and expressions can be understood through its critical inquiry. There are several well-known tenets to what constitutes Critical Discourse Analysis, and they have been enumerated in the principles that underlie CDA:

1) CDA addresses social problems
2) power relations are discursive
3) discourse constitutes society and culture
4) discourse does ideological work
5) discourse is intertextual/historical
6) the link between text and society is indirect or 'mediated'
7) discourse analysis is interpretative and explanatory
8) discourse is a form of social action or social practice.

(Fairclough & Wodak, 1997: 271–280)

What is argued in using CDA is that, as a framework, it "necessitates the theoretical preoccupations of the analyst" (Chouliaraki & Fairclough, 1999: 7). Because CDA combines both linguistic and social scientific views on language, the idea of how social actors and agents, as well as attitudes of people, are captured within particular language usage (i.e., discourse) is the focus of the analysis. CDA has a long history, which includes its different schools and analytical methods that have constructed it as a tool and framework for the analysis of power structures. This means that any societal discursive product may be analyzed from a variety of perspectives that first germinate from a theoretical attractor and have since impacted a variety of frameworks of analysis (Wodak & Meyer, 2009; Fairclough, 2017). It is important to note that the selection of a framework through which to conduct a particular analysis is equally important to any hypothesis put forward. The question being investigating should, hence, be reflected in the way that a Critical Discourse Analysis is done.

The history of CDA

A development of discourse studies as a field and established in the 1980s by Norman Fairclough (1992, 2017), CDA is one of the most influential branches of discourse analysis that exists today (Blommaert & Bulcaen, 2000: 447; Chilton, 2005; Fairclough, 2017).[6] Critical Linguistics, however, was a school of critical theory and linguistics that came into existence in the 1970s at the University of East Anglia (Fowler et al. 1979; Krzyżanowski & Forchtner 2016). The school of CDA was formally initiated in the 1990s when, through the University of Amsterdam, Teun A. van Dijk, Norman Fairclough, Gunther Kress, Theo van Leeuwen, and Ruth Wodak met to discuss theories of discourse analysis (Wodak & Meyer, 2009: 3).

CDA began with the need for linguistic study to address the social issues that emerge from social discourses. The approach of the school of the University of East Anglia took much from Halliday's Systemic Functional Linguistics (SFL) (1985), stressing the importance of the social context in which language exists. The reason for such an interest in the SFL approach of Halliday was because, as a framework, it dealt not simply with smaller textual constituents and parts, like words and sentences, but with larger pieces of text, as well as collections of texts that come into a whole idea (Ahmadvand, 2011: 83). Other fields of linguistics that have aided in the formation of CDA are those of classical rhetoric, text linguistics,

6 also known as *discourse analysis* (DA)

pragmatics, sociolinguistics and applied linguistics (Wodak & Meyer, 2009: 2; Wodak, 2004). CDA's roots are not only in Critical Linguistics but also in the approaches introduced by the Frankfurt School of Social Research, since "critical theory is defined as a research perspective, which has basically a critical attitude towards society" (Langer, 1998: 3; Honneth, 2014; Allmer, 2015; Krzyżanowski & Forchtner, 2016).

The problem-oriented principles of CDA are visible in the varying schools and ways of carrying out Critical Discourse Analysis, which are divided by their propagators and include categorizations into five major approaches: dialectal-relational (Fairclough, 1992, 2001a; Fairclough & Fairclough, 2018), socio-cognitive (van Dijk, 1993; Abidi, 2015; van Dijk, 2017; Abidi 2021), discourse historical (Wodak, 1995, 2001a, 2001b; Wodak & Meyer, 2015), social actors (van Leeuwen, 1996, 2006, 2008) and the Foucauldian dispositive analysis (Jäger 2001a, 2001b; Jäger & Maier, 2009; Gottlieb, 2010; Raffnsøe et al., 2016; Reisigl, 2017). Each of the approaches named will be discussed in the sections to follow, for the sake of clarity.

Fairclough's dialectal-relational approach to CDA

The first approach to be described, pioneered by one of CDA's leading scholars, Norman Fairclough, entails the notion that language and ideas that exist on a social scale shape one another, thus communicating that "our language, which shapes our social identities and interactions, knowledge systems, and beliefs, is also shaped by them in turn" (Ahmadvand, 2011: 3–4). His is among the approaches to heavily utilize Halliday's SFL (1985) and Marxist theory in its analytical agenda.

Fairclough's (1992) approach to CDA is particularly relevant to the question of a serious social issue like rape. In investigating relationships between language and society or social thought, the goal of CDA is to unearth dominance, power and discrimination strategies that are manifested in language, making it the most suitable to examining how greater social and discursive contexts are related to their underlying linguistic components which shape them. This approach, as well as van Leeuwen's (1996, 2008) framework for the investigation of the representation of social actors to look at how ideologies shape agency will be applied to the analysis of rape.

The hegemonic practices located within existing discourses are, in part, what undergo analysis here, as CDA takes the constituents of language and analyses them, albeit not without ideology, in order to seek out the power mechanisms located within them. When taking a critical approach to discourse, it is first important to make cogent the distinctive framework of discourses contained within CDA. Fairclough's (1992, 2003) three-dimensional model is characterized by the following dimensions related to every discursive event: 1) discourse-as-text, 2) discourse-as-discursive-practice, and 3) discourse-as-social-practice.

The *discourse-as-text* dimension of CDA covers linguistic features and how concrete instances of discourse are organized. The second dimension, the *discourse-as-discursive-practice* dimension presents discourse as a phenomenon that is "produced, circulated, distributed and consumed by society" (Blommaert & Bulcaen, 2000: 448). The third dimension, *discourse-as-social-practice*, is embedded within the ideological effects and how hegemony manifests itself within surrounding discourses. Within the three-dimensional model, it is clear that a hierarchy of influences on social structure is formed, with the dimension itself being a mode of analysis of how social life and attitude are influenced by linguistic constituents that are bound together to create social meaning. Below is a reproduction of Fairclough's (2001) 3-D model (three-dimensional framework) of discourse and social practice.[7]

Figure 1 Reproduction of Fairclough's (2001: 21) three-dimensional framework

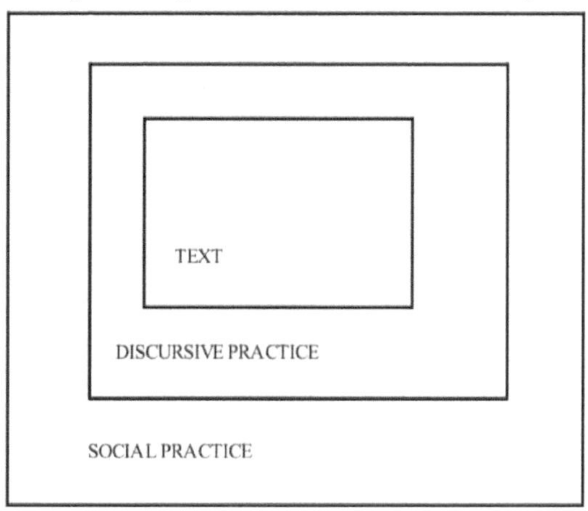

As illustrated in the figure above, text and discursive practice are embedded in social practice. Since the ideology-manifesting discourses in question here are discourses about rape in both American English and Polish, representing two separate cultural contexts, they will be investigated from the perspective of Fairclough's (*ibid.*) dialectal-relational approach to CDA. I iterate here that other dimensions

7 This reproduction was drawn in the MaxMaps application in MaxQDA (VERBI, 2019).

of analysis (i.e., the representations of social actors, analysis of presupposition and implicit evaluation (cf. van Leeuwen, 1996; Stalnaker et al., 1977; Grice 1975, 1989)) apply to Fairclough's (*ibid.*) model, as it is fitting for the contextual importance of ideology and its implications for discourse about rape victims.

Van Dijk's socio-cognitive model of CDA

Van Dijk's (1993, 1996) socio-cognitive model of CDA views critical language study as an interdisciplinary perspective on culture that utilizes various disciplines in the humanities to discover the underpinnings of power dynamics, especially that of socio-psychological dimensions. Van Dijk (1993, 1996, 1997, 1998) sees discourse as a communicative event that includes many aspects of communication from oral narrative to the semiotic signifiers of symbols and images.

The social actors involved or participating in analyzed discourses "rely upon collective frames of perception, i.e., *social representations*" (Wodak & Meyer, 2009: 25), thus drawing on social representation theory (Moscovici, 2000). Van Dijk (1993, 1998, 2017) sees social groups' representations as notions shared collectively by communities and social groups. Van Dijk's (ibid) approach to CDA states that discourse is largely the product of three major contexts: knowledge, attitudes and ideologies, and that discourses should be understood as reflective of the relationship between social situations, actions, actors and social structures.

Wodak's discourse-historical approach to CDA

The discourse-historical approach (DHA) to CDA (Wodak, 1995; Resigl & Wodak, 2001, 2009) makes connections between fields of action (Girnth, 1996), genres, discourses, and texts in order to pinpoint historical roles of discourse formation. DHA takes on the questions of the linguistic representations of "persons, objects, phenomena/events, processes and actions" (Reisigl & Wodak, 2009: 93), the characteristics of actors (*ibid.*), argumentation in text, and the perspectives from which nomination, attribution, and argumentation are expressed (*ibid.*), while taking into account the overarching historical context (*ibid.*: 95). The historical approach to CDA allows for the analyst to diachronically reconstruct and explain changes in discourses on subjects of investigation (*ibid.*).

Van Leeuwen's representation of social actors

Van Leeuwen's (1996, 2005, 2008, 2014) approach to CDA views discourse representations as based on what people do and how such actors are represented through language, taking from grand social theories such as that of Bourdieu (1991). The claim van Leeuwen (1996, 2008, 2014) makes is that the representations of individual actors in text are symbolic of larger discourses on social actors overall. This approach is further delineated in later parts of the chapter as it is one of the main analytical points used to investigate how rape and the actors involved are represented in online discourse.

Foucauldian dispositive analysis

The approach to discourse analysis taken by Jäger and Maier (2009) brings attention to a blind spot in Foucault's theory, namely concerning how discursive and non-discursive practices are mediated with manifestations (or objects). Foucault did not write out a methodology for conducting dispositive analysis (Caborn, 2007), however Jäger (2001; Jäger & Maier, 2009) has suggested putting to use the characteristics of the dispositive to conduct discourse analysis.

A term that is derived from French, a *dispositive* is a system that has been created for a specific purpose (Jäger & Maier, 2009). The notion of dispositive has been described by Foucault (1994: 299) as "a decidedly heterogeneous ensemble" of elements. The elements located within the dispositive are interconnected and interchangeable. In their approach, Jäger and Maier (*ibid.*) view Ernesto Laclau's (1980) social constructivism as representative of the dualism of discourse and social reality.

Semiotics and multimodality

The final and most recent thread of CDA is that of the investigation of semiotic devices in discourse, applying the social semiotic theory put forth by Kress and van Leeuwen (Hodge & Kress, 1988; Kress & van Leeuwen, 1996, 2001) to demonstrate that visual devices act just as strongly in creating discursive constructions as text. The model investigates semiotic practices that vary from the visual organization of text, image choice, positioning, color, and sound (including music) (Monelle, 2014).

Multimodal semiotics (Lemke, 2002, 2009; Michelson & Álvarez Valencia, 2016) and multimodal discourse analysis, which have emerged from semiotic production and consumption, are intrinsically linked to power strategies and hierarchies expressed through combined semiotic strategies. This is an aspect that has been viewed as pertinent in the critical analysis of gendered aspects of social life (Bulawka, 2013). Multimodality will not be analyzed and discussed in this work, except for the expansion on the subject as a part of CMC analysis in Chapter 4.

Feminist CDA

Since CDA aims to uncover "ways in which social structure impinges on discourse patterns, relations and models (in the form of power relations, ideological effects, and so forth), and in treating these relations as problematic" (Blommaert & Bulcaen, 2000: 447), the goal of the study is also to take on the task of proving how these factors encroach on women as a subject worthy of equal and adequate attention, specifically in the case of sexual aggression where sexual dominance is seen as being a quality prescribed stereotypically to men (Sanday, 1981; Carr & Van Deusen, 2004; Bates et al., 2019). For this work, the script of the submissive female sexual subject informs an unequal discourse that aids in the blaming of rape victims. It is important to mention this (feminist) vein of CDA, as it is relevant to the presented work. The references made to CDA in this work, however, will not explicitly be called feminist throughout, although the analysis may be considered to have a feminist agenda.

Feminist Critical Discourse Analysis studies not only explore "power relations between men and women," but also provides an investigation into the windings of gender and power and its constituents, making open contestation of dominant ideologies (Eckert, 1989: 253; Lazar, 2005: 2–3). Taking a CDA approach to discourse studies can reveal much about "the interconnections as well as particularities of discursive strategies employed in various forms of social oppression that can feed back into feminist strategies for social change" (Lazar, 2005: 5). Feminist CDA takes the CDA framework and applies it as a political perspective on the narrower category of gender on the spectrum of social stratification, which proves to be more revealing of certain dichotomies and the nuances of discourse practices that shape social structures.

Binding stereotypes that work against victims of rape, and which subsequently hinge on ideas of the supposedly inherent submissiveness of women (Wisłocka, 1978; Crawford, 1995; Sanchez & Kiefer, 2006; Zimmerman & Morrison, 2015) and their non-assertiveness not only in sexual areas of social life, but in everyday situations as well (Crawford, 1995; Lease, 2018), provide for the maintenance of victim blaming even when it is not necessarily obviously discernible from objective statements. Following the various methods encompassed by CDA does not go without criticism, and what must be kept in mind is the importance and overall goal of feminist work, which is to point out the systematic nature of discursive reproductions of gender ideologies (cf. Chapter 2).

> Although the prevailing gender ideology is hegemonic and is routinely exercised in a myriad of social practices, it is also contestable. The dialectal tension between structural permanences and the practical activity of people engaged in social practices (Chouliarki

> & Fairclough 1999), means that there are ruptures in the otherwise seamless and natural quality of gender ideology.
>
> (Lazar, 2005: 8)

The importance of taking an ideological perspective, such as a feminist one, is in marking where disparities exist and pointing out where they occur in institutionalized settings. The institutionalization of gender inequality, not only visible in discourse, is one such example of the pervasive nature of hegemonic patriarchal structures and their negative effect on people of all genders. This is particularly important when discussing the issue of rape in the social context. By applying such discourse analysis models to issues of immense social significance, one root of the issue may eventually come to be abolished. Some linguistic work has been done in the field of sexual crime, and, more recently, internet discourses on the subject of rape have come under investigation (Bou-Franch, 2016). This work aims to fill in the gaps, which are a comparison of American discourses with Polish discourses on the subject of sexual crime.

Summary of approaches to CDA

As presented in the various schools of CDA, Critical Discourse Studies focus on the intermingling of ideology with the different aspects of language which make up discourse (Wodak & Meyer, 2009). The approaches to CDA provided above are related to what Wodak and Meyer (2009: 20) call main theoretical attractors, including inspiration from Foucauldian (Foucault, 1975; Laclau, 1980; Mouffe, 2005) notions of power, Critical Theory (Mouzelis, 1995, 1997; Girnth, 1996), Marxist theory, Bourdieu's notion of *habitus*[8] (1991) and the Hallidayan (1985) perspective on language as social semiotic. Because CDA in itself does not constitute a methodology, what must be discussed is how it makes use of the ones that are offered within the framework to carry out its goal. This means that to categorize meaning and social actors, the analyst must be aware of semantics, metaphor and syntax (i.e., the case of the passive and active voice, transitivity and verbal processes), among other linguistic features viable in creating a representation. It is important to note here that the approach taken in this work is what Wodak and Meyer (2009: 22) have named a "detailed linguistic operationalization," because

---

8 Bourdieu's (1991) notion of *habitus* (related to the Aristotelian notion of *hexis* (Sachs, 1995)) discusses how social practice, habits, skills, dispositions, and behavior through mimesis and that it constitutes human nature, the formation of representation and identity (Bucholtz, 1999).

of its detailed corpus approach to the lexico-grammatical investigation of social actors and their socio-semantic representations.

Terminology used in CDA

Besides the term *discourse*, other terminology such as *text* and *context* are used to describe CDA as a research model. In addition to these terms, *power*, *hegemony*, *dominance*, *prejudice*, *representation*, and *ideology* also play a central role in describing or explaining CDA. These notions and the terminology used to describe them are important in delineating how societal structures and their cultural discourses may act as either oppressive towards or in favor of, certain social groups.

From a critical perspective, the relations between texts, their producers, and recipients are often characterized by an unequal distribution of power, such as the ones that arise in the face of racism, sexism, and homophobia, among other genres of discrimination. Gramsci's (1971) definition of power maintains that such unequal relations may be "enacted hegemonically through naturalizing ideologies as common sense rather than through sheer force" (Koller, 2009: 3).

Power, according to van Dijk (1996: 84) is "a property of relations between social groups, institutions or organizations" and therefore, in the context of CDA, "only social power, and not individual power, is considered." This is important in the field of CDA, because analyzing power, as opposed to the notion of hegemony, is imperative in observing the unequal relations that form via discourses. *Hegemony* as such "is the power or dominance that one social group holds over others" (Lull, 1995: 3), and has been studied in various contexts, including imperialism (Arrighi, 2005), political systems (Laclau & Mouffe, 2014), and language (Macedo et al., 2015).

The term hegemony itself is attributed to the social scientist Antonio Gramsci (1971), who worked towards broadening the theory of material Marxism, integrating it with the notion of *ideology*, which is understood here as cognitive structures that are collective and combine beliefs, values, social norms that include discursively formed norms and goals (cf. Chapter 2 for an expanded definition and relevance to the analysis of *gender ideology*).

Gramsci (1971: 12) defined hegemony as "spontaneous consent" to social situations, which is more passively accepted than in situations where power is demonstrated. Part of the second stream of research on notions of power, the Gramscian notion of *hegemony* may also be defined as describing "the mechanisms through which dominant groups in society succeed in persuading subordinate groups to accept the former's own moral, political and cultural values and institutions" (Simpson & Mayr, 2010: 3).

Gramsci (1971) viewed societal structure as inherently intertwined with "ideology-producing institutions in struggles over meaning and power" (Lull, 1995: 3). This notion is particularly significant to the present work, as well as to CDA on the whole, as it analyzes the processes that take place in creating unequal power structures of which many are unaware.

The notions of power and hegemony have been defined in order to understand exactly what is entailed by *dominance*, which is another term often used in describing the power structures under investigation through the application of CDA, marking how one social group dominates over another. Dominance is important in setting up the goals of CDA via the uncovering of how it takes place through discourse, which can be reflective of other ideologically tied notions, such as prejudice.

Prejudice is one of the human phenomena oftentimes discussed alongside discrimination and stereotyping (cf. Chapters 2 and 3), which describes a bias against a group or individual, based on individual experience or not (Allport, 1979; van Dijk, 1985; Kite & Whitley Jr. 2016). Fiske (1998: 375) describes prejudice as possessing "(1) some apparently automatic aspects, [and] (2) some socially pragmatic aspects both of which tend to sustain them."

Representation, as a notion in linguistics, will undergo discussion at much length throughout the work due to its role in reinforcing socially present ideologies and prejudices. Particularly, linguistic representation is of significance in investigating how social actors are understood in presentations of collective thought, since it considers the ways that written or spoken text produces the way human beings understand the world (Hill & Irvine, 1993; van Leeuwen, 2008; Park & Bucholtz, 2009). Apart from the above-mentioned concepts, there are other aspects of CDA that should be considered when looking at the power structures that lie within discourses, including how texts and discourses interact with other texts to influence social thought.

Intertextuality and interdiscursivity

Important to this work and the subsequent analyses (cf. Chapters 6 and 7) are the notions of *intertextuality* and *interdiscursivity*, which both relate to the reference and embedded knowledge of other texts that exist within analyzed texts. Wodak & Meyer (2009: 90) define *intertextuality* as the fact that "texts are linked to other texts, both in the past and the present" and that the connections are established "through references to the same events; by allusion or evocations; by transfer of main arguments from one text to the next, and so on." What Simpson and Mayr (2010: 54) refer to as *manifest intertextuality* is the practice of drawing on other texts in an overt manner, including quoting other people, organizations or institutions. What has hence been established is that discourses are always related in some way to other discourses, both those that were produced earlier and those that were produced at the time of the production of the text in question (Fairclough & Wodak, 1997). This may also be seen in Bakhtin's (1981) *heteroglossia*, which is the diversity of language varieties and languages within a single language as the manifestation or reflection of the varying ways that (culturally) one experiences, conceptualizes or evaluates the world (Bailey, 2007; Francis, 2012).

Interdiscursivity "signifies that discourses are linked to each other in various ways" (Simpson & Mayr, 2010: 54). Discourse is primarily topic-related (as in the case of this work, where "discourse on rape" is presented and analyzed), and as a result, a variety of subjects may derive from different discourses at various points (*ibid.*). Texts are "made up of heterogeneous elements or various discourse types, such as a mix of formal and informal language in a newspaper article" (Simpson & Mayr, 2010: 54). It is important to note that interdiscursivity is also responsible for constructing and reproducing representations in discourse.

Both intertextuality and interdiscursivity are pertinent to the analyses presented in Chapters 6 and 7, with intertextuality considered in Chapter 6, where the quoting of actors is concerned, and interdiscursivity considered in Chapter 7 with regard to the relationships between press and internet user discourses and gender role stereotyping, sexual scripts and rape myths as overarching discourses in the two cultures in question (cf. Chapter 2). They will not be referred to overtly as intertextual and interdiscursive practices throughout the analysis, but rather seen as such in their manifestations within more minute socio-semantic constituents.

Application of theory in this book

The terminology and models presented in the above sections aid in the analytical processes of this work, one of the aims of which is to uncover the unequal disparities that are at work in discourse about rape, functioning as representative of prejudiced or biased thinking about specific actors. In the sections which follow, I introduce the various veins of analysis (hence, the tools) that can be used in doing critical discourse analysis and delineate in depth those frameworks that are used to study the victim blaming of rape victims, as well as the representations of the actors involved and the act of rape itself within evaluative comments online.

Beginning with Systemic Functional Linguistics (Halliday, 1985), a framework that has largely influenced the work of van Leeuwen (1996, 2008) on the subject of social actors, and which is inherently tied to stance in discourse (in the analysis of social actors, this is expressed as appraisement), I discuss the categories that are used to investigate ideologically-based discourses as existing in evaluative language and then move onto the representation of social actors and the pragmatic aspects of the investigation of evaluative discourse and where it can be found. This includes, for one, the relationship of indirect speech acts with, as an intrinsic part of discourse, their evaluative use in discourse. In this book, the focus remains, more specifically, on the implicit types of evaluation in language, which indirectly targets the stance objects in question.

Evaluation in discourse

Linguists might agree that apart from the referential content that we communicate, to our interlocutors or those who read what we write, we also "give a more affective contour to what is said" (Carter, 2004: 11). This type of language expresses affect or subjective valuation of what is being discussed has been termed attitudinal by some (Jullian, 2008: 63). As mentioned above, however, I prefer to use the terms stance and evaluation to denote the language and discourse which express sentiment, attitudes, beliefs or valuations.

Evaluative language, as a context-dependent linguistic phenomenon, is amenable to investigation within the scope of the study of social phenomena and the action that surrounds them. This also assumes that, in grasping for an understanding of the social constructs that come about within discourses about a subject of social importance, including the impact of ideology and stereotype, evaluation arises as the outward expression of attitudes or beliefs regarding that subject. In the case of this work, that subject is rape and the actors that are involved. The type of evaluation studied here is related to the placing of blame onto one or both of the main actors.

Evaluative language and discourse have been defined as language that indexes the act of evaluation or the act of stance-taking (Martin & White, 2005; Du Bois, 2007; Hunston, 2011). The terms that have been subsumed under studies of evaluative expression through linguistic means include evaluation, stance(-taking), sentiment and appraisal, and thus *evaluation* is considered a "cover term" for the ones mentioned (Conrad & Biber, 2000; Hunston & Sinclair, 2000; Hunston & Thompson, 2000; Macken-Horarik, 2003; Du Bois, 2007). The terms were, for the most part, independently developed and, hence, are not synonymous, although they do share common ground (Góźdź-Roszkowski & Hunston, 2016: 131).

The language of evaluation "expresses an attitude towards a person, situation or other entity and is both subjective and located within a societal value-system" (Hunston, 2011: 1). Evaluation in language has also been described as subjective positioning towards an object that presents attitudinal stances or even change in topic (Du Bois, 2007; Góźdź-Roszkowski & Hunston, 2016).

The distinction between implicit and explicit evaluation has been made by Hunston (2011), with explicit evaluation being a more recognizable type of evaluating a subject (i.e., through lexical items that overtly connotate with positive or negative qualities) and implicitness being the type of evaluation that needs to be heavily deduced from the context, as well as from the shared knowledge of both writer and reader of a text. In other words, explicitness takes place when appraisement is indicated "explicitly," and implicitness takes place when appraisement occurs "implicitly" (Hunston, 2011; Millar & Hunston, 2015; Góźdź-Roszkowski & Hunston, 2016). More specifically, implicit evaluation has been studied in terms of its reflection of attitude and link to cognitive directionality of attitudes that are held by utterers (Vilar-Lluch, 2022), meaning that through cognitive associations, one can conclude that the implied meaning is that of making an evaluation or assessment. The notions of implicit and explicit evaluation are relevant to the work in that any indirectness in expression of stance on the subject of rape is considered implicit, and those discursive expressions which outwardly evaluate the object are considered explicit.

It is important to make note of the fact that evaluation does not take a concrete form in discourse and is expressed in different ways depending on the utterer, the context or the medium of communication (Hunston, 2011; Alba-Juez & Thompson, 2014; Góźdź-Roszkowski & Hunston, 2016). The linguistic tools that are described in the later parts of this chapter, ranging from transitivity processes to the representations of social actors contribute to the understanding of the various ways in which evaluation may be expressed. It is necessary to study evaluative discourse for several reasons, including that both speakers and writers indicate their attitudes as something of great social significance, including through means of speech acts of argumentation or persuasion. The move towards interactive aspects of linguistics rather than taking on a truth-value focus additionally highlights the necessity of undertaking such studies (*ibid.*). In this work, the aspect of evaluative discourse is highlighted and seen as an intrinsic part of the perpetuation of harmful ideologies about rape, the offenders and the victims involved in such a crime.

Stance and stancetaking

Biber et al. (1999) also use the term *stance* to denote the words and phrases which "inscribe an attitude or stance towards an entity in the text" (Góźdź-Roszkowski & Hunston, 2016: 133). In other words, stance refers to "the lexical and grammatical expression of an author's or speaker's attitudes, feelings, judgements and commitment concerning the propositional content of the message" (Biber & Finnegan, 1989: 93). This is the way that I see it be used in the context of negative or positive evaluation of objects of discussion.

What is known as *stance-taking* is derived from Conversation Analysis and denotes the act of taking a stance, which in turn denotes an attitude towards an object as expressed linguistically (either as an utterance or as text) (Du Bois, 2007).

Kinds of stance-taking include *affective* stance-taking and *epistemic* stance-taking. The first type denotes the type of stance-taking that occurs on an affective scale upon which a speaker (or writer) positions him- or herself. Such indexing of affective stance may be shown through the use of emotive adjectives or verbs (i.e., *glad* or *so glad*, as given by Du Bois (*ibid.*: 143)).

Epistemic stance-taking occurs when speakers (or writers) position themselves as knowledgeable or ignorant (*ibid.*). Du Bois (*ibid.*) illustrates this with examples of a speaker saying "I know" or "I don't know." As can be observed, Du Bois's (*ibid.*) categories are, in fact, more fitting for the context of conversational interaction, which is why they are not used in the analysis of this work (Chapters 6 and 7).

When studying stance, considering stance takers and stance objects is also important, as well as investigating the socio-cultural value ascribed to a subject in making utterances or writing about the objects of stance. *Stance takers* are the participants in discourse, i.e., those actors who express an evaluation, attitude or subjective position regarding a topic or an object (Du Bois, 2007; Bassiouney, 2015; Ruth-Hirrel & Wilcox, 2018). Not only spoken discourse may present stance, but also written forms and thus this framework can translate its usability into the sphere of online communication that is written, in which people interact with one another, as well as source texts that such communication accompanies.

The significance of stance takers, as presented in the literature, lies in the fact that the "participants derive memorable information about each other from stances taken, which they may retain as socially salient" (Du Bois, 2007: 149). This aspect encompasses the social indent that such stances have when it comes to interaction between participants in discourse.

The *object of stance*, on the other hand, is what a given stance taker is speaking about (*ibid.*: 147). As Du Bois (*ibid.*) states, "we need to know the referential object or target towards which the stance is being directed," i.e., the person being addressed or discussed or the subject being addressed or evaluated. The stance taker responds to other stance takers or the object of stance, linguistically expressing attitudes, feelings, judgement or commitment (Du Bois, 2007: 149; Jullian, 2008; Góźdź -Roszkowski & Hunston, 2016)

The stance objects in question in the analysis presented in this work are the social actors involved in the rape—the victim and the offender—and the event of rape itself. The evaluations of these objects can all be expressed through implicit or explicit evaluation, which is what I investigate specifically in the analyses presented in Chapters 6 and 7.

Systemic Functional Linguistics and appraisal

One of the main theoretical frameworks that aligns with critical linguistic analyses that is related to the subject of evaluation in discourse is known as Systemic Functional Linguistic analysis, which has been referred to as the approach that investigates how lexico-grammatical structures and semantic aspects of language create meaning (Martin, 2016). As a field, Systemic Functional Linguistics (Halliday, 1978, 1985, 1994, Thomson, 1996; Eggins, 2004; Matthiessen et al., 2010; Schleppegrell, 2004, 2013) views language as a "social semiotic" and looks at language as working on the two axes of *system* and *function*, and hence "the system of language is shaped by the function it serves" (Simpson & Mayr, 2010: 57). Since evaluation is one aspect constructed within the framework of Halliday's SFL, it is crucial to expand on the subject here. *Appraisal* offers the tools to systematically identify the interpersonal meanings of what speakers say and what writers write (Martin, 2000). Appraisal, being concerned with evaluation has been defined as "the kinds of attitudes that are negotiated in a text, the strength of the feelings involved and the ways in which values are sourced and readers aligned" (Martin & Rose, 2003: 22).

Within the framework of SFL, appraisal is modelled "in terms of systems which constitute sets of choices to impress attitude, emotion and evaluation in discourse" (Jullian 2008: 29). It is important to note that the SFL model has focused mainly on grammatical aspects, namely on Mood and Modality (modality will also be relevant to this work). Martin's (2000: 145) expansion of appraisal from Halliday's also accounts for "the semantic resources used to negotiate emotions, judgements and valuations, alongside resources for amplifying and engaging with these evaluations". Appraisal theory draws heavily on SFL's emphasis of the questions of meaning and choice (*ibid.*), forming the connection between that framework and the idea of appraisal as evaluative.

Appraisal has been considered "the most fully theorized view of evaluative language," (Martin & White, 2005, after Góźdź-Roszkowski & Hunston, 2016: 133). The term is used to denote the entire system of evaluation and incorporates three sub-systems (Góźdź-Roszkowski & Hunston, 2016), namely those of *attitude*, *engagement* and *graduation*.[9] Briefly, I would like to explain the three terms that have just been presented.

Attitude is viewed as made up of three subsystems (Jullian, 2008: 57), namely *affect*, *judgement*, and *appreciation*. Affect deals with the expression of emotions that the participants in discourse have, such as hate, fear, or love. Judgement works with regard to the expression of those evaluations concerning morality, ethics, truths, and capacities and appreciation concerns the aesthetic value of text, referring to those linguistic expressions which denote visual value (i.e., for texts, performances, natural phenomena, etc.). The use of linguistic devices such as *beautiful* or *stunning* fall under this category. Martin (2000: 147) notes that "affect can be taken as the basic system," because all three systems encode feelings.

The other two categories, engagement and graduation, are not as complex as the one described in the previous paragraph. Engagement makes a combination of resources of modality and the attributions of other models, as in *perhaps*, *I declare*, *obviously*. Graduation, as the last point, "congregates the resources involved in amplifying and mitigating meanings and evaluations through intensifiers" (such as very, really, sort of, somewhat), quantifiers and repetitions and analogy (through comparison, similes and metaphors) (Jullian, 2008: 57–8; Caldwell, 2009). The systems accounted for in the SFL approach present a different perspective on the category of evaluation, demonstrating that the study of evaluation or appraisal has been considered in various analytical frameworks that deal with attitude(s) towards an object of interest.

Because CDA is part of a long-standing tradition of the critique of language, it can be viewed from both a sociological perspective and linguistic perspective, with the linguistic perspective bringing "critical social science and linguistics (specifically, Systemic Functional Linguistics) together within a single theoretical and analytical framework, setting up dialogue between them" (Chouliaraki & Fairclough, 1999: 6). The sociological perspective applies grand social theories to the investigation of language. It is known that the "basic tenet of Systemic Functional Linguistics (SFL) is that language is a system of choices" (Fontaine et al. 2013: 1). The notion of choice in SFL has been described as important and when it comes to text or discourse, "we understand a continuous process of semantic choice. Text is meaning and meaning is choice" (Halliday, 1978: 137).

The notion of choice in the context of meaning and text is important when looking at the other linguistic aspects considered, as they are all related to it inherently, whether it has to do with semantic choice or grammatical choice. This choice

9 This is also called *amplification* (Martin, 1997; Jullian, 2008).

is described as taking place more paradigmatically than syntagmatically, meaning that the semantic features are placed at the core of discursive construction rather than the structural consequences entailed in syntagmatic relations (Bache, 2013: 72). For the analyses in this work, the Systemic Functional Linguistic perspective is considered where transitivity, more specifically the processes of verbs, is concerned.

The terms used for evaluation in this work

Since evaluation makes up the bedrock for the analysis here, I would like to make a point of distinguishing which terms will be used to indicate the evaluative quality of the digital comments that I propose contain harmful ideologies about rape. Of course, the general term used to refer to the positive or negative appraisal of actors and events will be referred to as simply *evaluation* and split into explicit and implicit types.

Implicit evaluation will be used to denote the evaluation which is not direct. Therefore, what is communicated by the users, i.e., the meaning behind the comments will be referred to as the *implied* meaning or as *implications* behind the text. *Explicit evaluation* will be used to denote the direct expression of stance that is either positive or negative.

The term *stance*, on the other hand, will be used to discuss the attitudes of the writers of digital comments in their linguistic form, in alignment with Biber et al.'s (1999) use of the term, which refers to the understood propositional content of what is uttered or expressed in writing.

The term appraisal is not used in the later chapters of this work, since in the analysis of the representation of social actors, the term *appraisement* as taken from van Leeuwen's (1996, 2005) typology denotes terms that add positive or negative value to actors in discourse.

Transitivity

Where discursive representations and reproduction of crime are concerned, one of the most investigated aspects in forming biases about the perpetrator and his/her fault is located within transitivity (Machin & Mayr, 2013). The linguistic model that deals with such, and has seen much application in CDA, is the *transitivity model* (Wodak & Meyer, 2009). It has been described as having "had an important bearing on the way gender issues in texts, especially media discourse, have been explored and understood in critical linguistics" (Simpson & Mayr, 2010: 65), and thus should be applied to this work.

As a grammatical concept, transitivity "is concerned with the semantic structure of clauses and refers, broadly, to who does what to whom, and how" (*ibid.*). Such an analysis, thus, "probes a clause to find out who are the actors, the acted upon and what processes are involved in that action" (*ibid.*). It is important to note, returning to Halliday (1985, 1994) and Systemic Functional Linguistics (Schleppegrell, 2013), that the critical approach views transitive patterns as markers of discursive choice, in that transitivity plays a key role in constructing meaning. Halliday's (1985) claim that linguistic forms carry with them certain significance that is chosen according to the circumstances of discourse is illustrative of the need for a critical linguistic approach to issues of aggression and criminal acts.

Within the analysis of transitivity, the roles of actors, as either agent or patient, are considered. In SFL, the agent is the doer of an action, whereas the patient is the actor to which or to whom something is done, therefore the receiver of an action (Schleppegrell, 2013). The analysis of agency helps iterate the importance of understanding how language is at the forefront of a somewhat collective or societal understanding, along with other forms of discursive reflections of ideology. In light of this, the processes that verbs represent, as presented in the transitivity model should be mentioned as they are enumerated in the literature on the subject. The transitivity processes in SFL include material processes, mental processes, behavior processes, verbal processes, relational processes and existential processes.

Material processes have been described as representing processes of *doing* and usually constitute concrete actions with material results (Simpson & Mayr, 2010; Ezzina, 2015). An example has been provided:

1) *The soldiers <u>killed</u> three insurgents* (Simpson & Mayr 2010: 66)

Material processes might also represent more abstract or metaphorical processes (Martinez 2001; Kondowe 2014; Ezzina 2015), such as the following (examples 2 and 3, respectively).

2) *The temperature <u>rose</u>.*[10]
3) *She <u>destroyed</u> his reputation.*

Mental processes have been described as processes of *sensing*, and include verbs of cognition (thinking, knowing and understanding), verbs of affection (i.e.,

10 The examples not cited within the chapter are my own.

affective) (such as liking, disliking and fearing), and verbs of perception (seeing, hearing and perceiving) (Martinez, 2001; Song, 2013).

4) *She liked the cake a lot.*
5) *The neighbor saw them.*
6) *Adam understood what he had said.*

Behavior processes are those that can be described as psychological or physical behavior, including verbs such as *watch, taste, stare, dream, breathe, cough, smile* and *laugh* (Simpson & Mayr, 2010; Song 2013; Ezzina, 2015).

7) *The couple stared at the vast ocean.*
8) *She smiled at the thought.*

Quite straightforwardly, verbal processes are those represented by the verb of "saying" and its synonyms. There are usually three participants in a verbal process: the *Sayer*, the *Receiver*, and the *Verbiage* (Martinez, 2001; Chen, 2005; Simpson & Mayr, 2010).

9) *The teacher said he would give the students homework.*
10) *Bitty shouted into the abyss.*

Relational processes refer to those "processes that encode meanings about states of being, where things are stated to exist in relation to other things" (Simpson & Mayr, 2010: 67) and they have been divided into three types: *intensive, possessive* and *circumstantial* (*ibid.*; Martin, 2012). An intensive relational process describes an equivalent relationship between constituents, where x = y (example 11).

11) *The house is beautiful.* (Simpson & Mayr, 2010: 67)

A possessive relational process describes the relationship between x and y, as described in examples 12 and 13, which both describe what an agent or actor has in his or her possession, taken from Simpson & Mayr (2010: 57):

12) *Nancy has a 1977 Chrysler Cordoba.*
13) *That cat-shaped mug is Meghan's.*

The nature of a circumstantial relationship is what can be described as being the "x is at/on/in/with" type (Matthiessen, 1999; Simpson & Mayr, 2010), and includes the following:

14) *The festival is on all weekend.*
15) *The sisters were in the house.*

There are two ways in which relational processes communicate the concept of being, namely, through *attribution* and *identification*. This has been described quite simply by Simpson & Mayr (2010: 67):

"(1) Attributive processes with the participant roles of *Carrier* and *Attribute*
(2) Identifying processes with the participant roles of *Identified/Token* and *Identifier/Value*"

The Carrier is always represented through the use of a noun or noun phrase, whereas the Attribute "expresses a quality, classification or a descriptive epithet" (*ibid.*).

16) *The United States* (Carrier) *has long been a symbol of freedom* (Attribute).
17) *The benefit of studying hard* (Carrier) *is obvious* (Attribute).

It is important to note that an attributive intensive property is not reversible, and therefore the order of lexical items in the clause cannot be switched around to maintain the same meaning.

Existential processes are the linguistic representation of an occurrence or something that exists, such as in sentences beginning with the *existential there* in the subject position (Simpson & Mayr, 2010; Thompson, 2013; Ezzina, 2015). Some examples would be:

18) *There was a party.*
19) *Was there anyone else there?*
20) *There weren't any reasons to say no.*

These processes usually use the verbs *to be, exist, arise*, or *occur*. Out of context, one might not see the tie to ideology, but once such instantiation of discourse is found within a setting, the implications may be further interpreted. If the above examples are considered, the statement that *there was a party* might have suggestive proposition for the reason an event might have occurred, for one.

The question of transitivity and choice (Halliday, 1985) is of importance to the work presented, because of its importance in applying van Leeuwen's (1995, 2008, 2013) taxonomy of the way in which social actors are represented in discourse. The question of transitivity has been embedded into the method for analyzing social actors, but is taken from SFL, since Halliday's (1985) view of language as social semiotic was expanded by van Leeuwen in the social actors framework (Norgaard, 2010).

Modality and negation

There are two other structural aspects of discourse that I focus on in the practical analysis besides the aspect of transitivity in Halliday's model of linguistic analysis.

The concepts of *modality* and *negation* have also been taken from Halliday's SFL (Halliday & Matthiessen, 2004), and both can be used to present what have been referred to in the literature as constructing alternative hypothetical situations within the context of attitudinal expression. Modality and negation may be used to express an evaluative stance without being too obvious, both modality and negation allow a speaker or writer to somewhat conceal any overt statement of judgement without being too open or overt about it. Within CDA, modality is described as encompassing units of language which express a speaker or writer's opinion, the use of modal adjectives and adverbials, as well as the occurrence of overt modal verbs like *may, might, can, could, shall, should, must* and *oughtto* (Nuyts, 2001; Machin & Mayr, 2012; Aijmer, 2015). It is seen as concerning the attitude of the speaker or writer or his or her confidence in a given proposition (Lillian, 2008: 2). Within linguistic analyses of the category, a differentiation between the types of modalities has been made, including their division into the distinct categories of *deontic* and *epistemic* modalities (Jesperson, 1924; Palmer, 1986).

Deontic modality refers to the necessity or obligation of an actor to do or not do something (in a particular way), i.e., what should or should not be done. According to Saeed (2003: 136), deontic modality conveys two types of social knowledge, namely that of obligation and permission, with the former concerned with what a person must or is obligated to do and the latter being concerned with the authority to permit an actor to do something. Examples have been provided below.

21) *You may leave.*
22) *Rafał is supposed to help me later.*
23) *The children must do their homework.*

Epistemic modality indicates possibility and prediction and acts as a reference to the certainty or uncertainty of a given proposition. This type of modality also points to the speaker or writer's assessment of the truth of a given proposition. This includes verbs such as *could, may,* or *might,* among others. Some examples have been provided.

24) *She may be in the house.*
25) *Ask Sara. She might know.*
26) *That cat could have been hurt.*

The role of modality in expressing evaluation lies in the fact that modality is used to express attitude and opinion in discourse, and thus presents evaluation in the meaning that is not explicitly stated in the discourse (Martin & White, 2005). In this work, I will focus on expressions of modality with reference to the actors that are involved in rape (cf. Chapter 6).

Negation also constructs hypothetical scenarios in discourse and reveals what the writer's point of view or attitude is on a subject. As a linguistic device which can express absence or deny a proposition, negation draws attention to a possibility of presence, suggesting that in the case of rape, any claims by the victim that something was present cannot be proven, thus cancelling the possibility for the rape to have actually happened. Negation is grammatically realized via the addition of a negative particle (*not, no* or *nie*) to a verb phrase, noun phrase or adjectival phrase (Jeffries, 2010a: 108, 2010b; Tabbert, 2015). In doing CDA, "the use of negation is a source of bias that reflects and transmits a speaker's prior assumptions about other people" (Beukeboom et al., 2010: 988). Furthermore, "negation is one possibility to trigger oppositional meaning beside antonymous sense relation" (Tabbert, 2015: 96), which contributes to its being a strategy to create sentences which contain implicit evaluation regarding, in this case, the actors in a rape. Some examples of negation have been provided.

27) *They <u>didn't try</u>.*
28) *The man is <u>not a liar</u>.*

In this work, the process of negation is focused on for its construction of alternative hypothetical situations as a means of expressing the evaluation of the situation of rape or the evaluation of the actors involved. This is considered a structural aspect of evaluative discourse and will be treated as such here.

Delineating the representations of social actors

In sociolinguistic study and CDA, the linguistic and multimodal representation of social actors is viewed as having a hand in their perception and representation. Much linguistic study has been carried out on such representations, in the context of newspapers (Fairclough, 1995; Teo, 2000; Wodak & Meyer, 2009) and textbooks (Sahragard & Davatharzadeh, 2010; Szpyra-Kozłowska, 2010; Davari & Moini, 2016), to name some examples.

Applying Halliday's Systemic Functional Linguistics to the investigation of how social actors are presented is also common in linguistic study (Cottle, 2000; Machin & Mayr, 2007; Simpson & Mayr, 2010; Tenorio, 2011). Van Leeuwen (1996, 2008) observed the roles of social actors in discourse, providing specific categories through which critical study may be carried out, namely *categorization*, *identification*, and *nomination* (van Leeuwen, 1996; 2008).

Machin & Mayr (2007), for one, conducted an analysis of the *Leicester Mercury* and its promotion of ethnic diversity by gathering a corpus of articles and gleaning from them the linguistic representation of social actors. Their investigation revealed that the *Mercury* was committed to positively evaluating people in minority communities and that the discourse present in its articles did much to reflect those values, combatting the anti-immigrant sentiment that pervaded Britain in 2001 (Machin & Mayr 2007). Their analysis utilized what is known as the *social actor model* (Wodak & Meyer 2009: 26). The categories presented above have been broken down even further in the paragraphs that follow.

The first larger category is *categorization,* which refers to the way that a social actor is linguistically categorized in discourse. The first subcategory, *functionalization*, denotes what a linguistic representation does or, more appropriately, what a linguistic form has an actor do, or presents an actor as doing (i.e., partaking in an action), whereas *identification* describes the phenomenon of how actors are presented, i.e., in the media.

The terms *inclusion* and *exclusion* maintain that social actors are at times purposefully omitted or backgrounded to serve a certain, oftentimes ideological, purpose. *Activation* and *passivation* refer to the grammatical processes that foreground or background certain social actors to bring attention to a specific actor as partaking in or carrying out a specific deed or action (Sahragard, 2016). It should be noted here that passivation refers to all processes that bring an actor to the background, where passivization related to the use of the passive voice. Actors who are *passivated* can undergo *subjection*, where they are made the subject of a clause or sentence, or they can become the object, such as in *beneficialization*, the process whereby an actor is presented as negatively or positively benefiting from a certain act (*ibid.*).

Nomination is typically carried out via the naming of actors, i.e., being used to denote an actor through processes of *formalization* (through the provision of only a person's surname), *semiformalization* (by providing a person's name and surname), or *informalization* (providing a given name only, for example, or another informal term used to refer to the actor) (*ibid.*). *Name obscuration* also occurs when an actor's name is hidden via the use of letters (*Mr. X*) or numbers.

What is known as *impersonalization* can be performed through processes, such as *abstraction* or *objectification*, in which social actors are denoted by a quality or abstract reference that is assigned to them. The process of *genericization* is somewhat related to the latter processes, as it occurs when actors are referred to as a class. *Collectivization,* however, occurs when certain social actors are referred to as groups by denoting them in the plural sense (plurality) through the use of a mass noun, for one (*ibid.*).

When it comes to evaluative processes of ascertaining negative associations or positive associations, van Leeuwen (*ibid.*) refers to the category of *appraisement*, which includes the subgroups *positive appraisement* and *negative appraisement*. Here, I will focus on how certain aspects of the taxonomy which have already been mentioned, such as connotation, and other categories that I have added, such as *metaphorical* reference, additionally subsume the attitude of the representation, be it positive or negative. This aspect will be especially important in the analysis of online user comments on the social actors in the rape, as well as the act of the rape.

Role allocation will also be explored in terms of transitivity (SFL), as there is more expansion on how activation and passivation take place from that perspective. Chapters 6 and 7 present the analysis of the linguistic constituents as representative of social actors within the context of rape cases. The representations analyzed here are viewed as reflecting attitudes (and ideologies cf. Chapter 2) towards the perpetrators, victims, and rape as a crime, itself.

In addition to elements taken from van Leeuwen's (*ibid.*) taxonomy of the representation of social actors, I have also drawn on Hunston (2011) and Bulawka (2013) for the broader category of *evaluation,* which is *appraisement* in van Leeuwen's terms, and have expanded the analytical categories to include *euphemization* and *neutralization* as a factor in the representation of the act of rape itself, which has been described here as an act, or broadly as a social activity, qualifying it as a social event for the study presented in Chapters 6 and 7 (Grant & Woodhams 2007). The reason behind such a differentiation is that similar processes occur in the representation of the rape itself, which is seen here as existing on the same plane/level as social actors and takes place on both a socio-pragmatic and socio-semantic level. This entails that negative and positive evaluation will be investigated as a part of blame attribution based on implicit evaluation on the structural and socio-semantic levels of discourse, presupposition (where rape myths are concerned), euphemization, metaphor, and naming strategies (for social actors) within the digital discourses analyzed.

Questions to ask about the features analyzed within CDA

The above sections have provided a toolbox to analyze language within the framework of Critical Discourse Analysis. Simpson and Mayr (2010) give readers a comprehensive list of strategies that help in conducting a critical analysis of crime-related text. Such stipulations formulate the basis of a preliminary investigation into the discourses that shape collective thought as such, especially in investigating vocabulary and grammar:

Vocabulary:[11]

a) Are there words in the text which are ideologically contested, such as sexist or racist terms?
b) Are there formal or informal words, or is there a mixture of the two?
c) What expressive values do the words have? How, for example, are evaluative words used?
d) What metaphors/idioms are used?

Grammar:

a) What types of verbs are used? For example, do the verbs describe activity or states?
b) Is agency (un)clear?
c) Are nominalizations used? That is, have some verbs been turned into nouns?
d) Are sentences active or passive?
e) Are there important features of modality? That is, are statements made directly and with certainty or are they toned down or 'hedged'?
f) Are the pronouns 'we' and 'you' used and if so, how?

(Simpson & Mayr, 2010: 110)

The above criteria are followed throughout the analysis of comments relevant to Chapters 6 and 7, to investigate how social actors are represented in CMC discourses on rape. It is important to note that the analysis of language through such means can be carried out on the material provided by various genres of Internet discourse. This includes digital comments, which constitute a specific register of their own, within the genre of digital comments in Internet genres (cf. Chapter 4; Biber & Egbert, 2018).

Pragmatics and CDA

Another one of the methods of conducting a critical analysis of the discourse of naturally occurring text or talk is through investigating its pragmatic aspects. Seeing language use as both seated within the framework of a psycho-social context and interaction, Critical Discourse Analysis and pragmatics may be combined to retrieve a deeper understanding of how ideologies manifest themselves on a linguistic level in discourses. Where rape is concerned, the pragmatic aspects have been investigated in the context of interviews as well as in the court setting, where questioning during a cross-examination occurred (Ehrlich, 2001).

As a field, *pragmatics* studies "language use in context" (Birner, 2013: 11) and is rule-governed, just as other linguistic disciplines are (such as syntax or semantics).

11 Here, the linguistic representation of social actors as seen by van Leeuwen (1996) provides a more comprehensive taxonomy to work by.

In other words, "pragmatics looks at such interpretive regularities and tries to make explicit the implicit knowledge that guides us in selecting interpretations" (*ibid.*: 12). There are four phenomena that Birner (2013: 11–12) says that pragmatics deals with, namely that it is: "a) non-literal, b) context-dependent, c) inferential, and/or d) not truth-conditional."

The context of this work concerns, in keeping with Fairclough's (2001) model, both the social and discursive contexts that surround the subject of the discussion of rape in the online sphere in two separate cultures, American and Polish. Here, discourse is seen as discourse practice. This means that the social context relates to the subject of rape and its actors and the beliefs and ideologies surrounding it, which then informs the discursive (and linguistic) context, as demonstrated here using the genre of digital comments as an example.[12]

As a part of the field of pragmatics, *pragmalinguistics* should be considered for the investigation of the evaluation (with emphasis on implicit evaluation) in discursive acts which take place in online spheres, especially in that of digital comments made by anonymous users. As a part of Critical Discourse Analysis, pragmatics may help to uncover the intended meaning behind what is said or written (i.e., in discourse). The point of interest in this study is that of evaluative discourse in digital comments, i.e., the expression of user attitudes as investigated in the evaluation present in their comments.

Pragmalinguistics

Because pragmatics may encompass all kinds of investigation of linguistic behavior, *pragmalinguistics* refers to one of the possible methodological approaches to pragmatic analysis (Marmaridou, 2011: 77). Pragmalinguistics "typically concerns the study of the particular resources that a given language provides for conveying pragmatic meaning (illocutionary and interpersonal)" (*ibid.*).

There has been a methodological distinction made between *pragmalinguistics* and *sociopragmatics*, as stated by Leech (1983) and Thomas (1983), which has been used widely in further work in pragmatics (cf. Culpeper, 2010; Holmes & King, 2017). *Pragmalinguistics* "marks the pragmatic turn in linguistic analysis and is broadly associated, or even identified, with sociolinguistics, stylistics, or text linguistics" (Marmaridou, 2011: 77). *Sociopragmatics* relates pragmatic meaning to the study of participant social distance, the pragmatics of identity formation (Leech 1983) or a language community's social rules, what is considered

12 The subject of the social context surrounding rape in both American and Polish cultures is described in Chapter 2.

appropriate or acceptable in terms of linguistic behavior (Marmaridou, 2011: 77). Because the focus of the present study is on aspects regarding how social thought and behavior are reflected in discourse, *pragmalinguistics* is of interest here, as well.

As a subdiscipline, pragmalinguistics focuses on sociological phenomena, such as communication and interaction or language as it works in various pragmatic settings. Sometimes called *pragmatic linguistics*, pragmalinguistics perceives linguistic action as determined by surrounding social conditions. For this work, the surrounding social conditions include the knowledge of journalists, writers, and internet users about rape, rape myths, and sexual scripts. Mey (1979: 11) articulates that "from a pragmatic viewpoint, the conditions for speaking and understanding, for 'production' and 'consumption' of language, cannot be divorced from the conditions of production and consumption in the society in general," and it is these conditions combined which take part in the production and interpretation of texts and form what is viewed here as a dynamic context (Marmaridou, 2011; Taguchi, 2018).

Speech acts and discourse

Speech acts have been defined by Austin (1962) as actions that are carried out when one makes an utterance (Cutting, 2008: 13). *Speech Act Theory* states that there are three levels of analysis when considering a speech act (*ibid.*): *locution* (where the act of saying something or making an utterance is known as *the locutionary act*), *illocution* (or *illocutionary force*, which is the aspect of what is done in uttering the words),[13] and finally, *perlocution* (the *perlocutionary effect*, which is how the hearer or receiver understands or interprets what has been uttered). In the study of speech acts, the intention of the speaker in making an utterance, as well as the recognition of the utterance and its interpretation under the conditions of that utterance play an important role (Sadock, 2004: 53).

The traditional classification of speech acts may be brought back to Searle (1976), who divided speech acts into five main classes: *declarations*, *representatives*, *commissives*, *directives*, and *expressives* (Searle, 1976; Cutting, 2008; Katz, 2015).

Declarations are those words and expressions that change the world just by being uttered, including *I bet*, *I declare*, and *I resign* (Searle, 1979; Cutting, 2008). *Representatives* are the acts in which the utterance states what the speaker

13 This concerns acts that may be considered the actual purpose of an utterance, such as "inviting", "ordering", "promising", "excusing" etc. (Searle 1979; Cutting 2008: 14).

believes to be true or to be the case, including "describing," "claiming," "insisting," or "predicting" (Searle, 1979; Cutting, 2008). *Commissives* are those acts in which the utterance commits a speaker to an action, including "promising," "offering," "threatening," and "vowing" (Searle, 1979; Cutting, 2008; Kissine, 2013). Commissives may be acts that commit a speaker to something in the future (Wielgosz, 2015).

Directives are those speech acts that aim to make a hearer carry out an act, such as "commanding", "requesting", "forbidding" and "suggesting" (Leech, 1980; Cutting, 2008; Flock & Geluykens, 2015). *Expressives* are speech acts in which the utterance states what the speaker feels, such as the act of "apologizing", "praising", "congratulating" and "regretting" (Cutting, 2008; Constant et al., 2009; Potts et al., 2009). Because they are related to the feelings of a speaker, the expression of opinions or attitudes which make up the category of expressives may also be considered as belonging to this category, which is an aspect of particular importance to the analysis of digital comments about rape.

Indirect speech acts

When what a speaker means is not actually expressed through the structure of the utterance but in the implied meaning, the speech act concerned is indirect. One might indirectly make a request by expressing a directive, such as *I'm dying for a cup of coffee* as an order for the speaker's interlocutor to go and get that cup of coffee. This constitutes an indirect speech act. In his work, Searle (1969, 1975, 1979) highlights that a speaker who uses a *direct speech act* wishes to communicate the literal meaning which the utterance expresses in the conventional sense. Where the phrase: *I'm going to the store* might be interpreted as a representation of reality, a fact, it might also be seen as an offer to purchase something for the person being addressed.

An *indirect speech act* communicates "a different meaning from the apparent surface meaning", thus "the form and function are not directly related," since the surface structure in a given context does not reflect what is meant by the speaker (Cutting, 2008: 17). For the purpose of this work, attitudes of internet users towards rape victims and perpetrators are investigated in terms of the way that such attitudes and beliefs are expressed, especially where victim blaming is present in the discourse. In this work, the implicit evaluation within discourse on rape is considered an adequate way of looking into how, overall, evaluative discourse may be determined. As the subject of sexual crime is rather specific, difficult in nature, and represents what can be considered a taboo subject (Wasilewski, 2010), it is necessary to consider where indirect means of discursive expression takes place in the illocution of an expression of opinion on the subject of rape, rape victims and perpetrators of rape, namely regarding who is at fault when it comes to the rape.

Evaluative speech acts

Just as various speech acts may express things that they do not explicitly state but must be discerned from the context of their utterance through means of understanding evaluation or stance, acts of evaluative expression have been viewed by some scholars as speech acts in their own right. Studies in pragmatics have also seen the variation in modes of expression of opinions as a possible point of difference between Anglo cultures and Polish culture (Gąsior, 2015). Wierzbicka (1985: 160) states that opinions are expressed with greater force in Polish, rendering more similarity to a statement of fact. She states that in Polish, opinions are not typically introduced by expressions such as *I believe*, *I think* or *in my opinion*. In English, "the difference between fact and opinions is usually expressed lexically, with opinions containing either expressions of modality, or appraisal lexis" (Eggins and Slade, 1997: 193–194). Wierzbicka (2003: 44) also claims that "in English, hedged opinions go hand in hand with hedged, indirect questions, suggestions or requests. People avoid making 'direct', forceful comments as they avoid asking 'direct', forceful questions or making 'direct', forceful requests" (*ibid.*). All of these contribute to how we understand the expression of opinion, more particularly negative opinion, from a cultural perspective (Prihodko, 2018; Tantucci & Wang, 2018).

I would like to additionally state here that the subject of evaluative speech acts relates to the former comments on evaluation in that they express evaluation as seen through the pragmatic lens. It is necessary, thus, to properly classify the expression of opinion where social issues are concerned, especially that of crime. The category of evaluative speech acts has been described in the literature as those speech acts that express attitudes, i.e., that something is good or bad (Genova, 1971). Prihodko (2018: 202) has defined evaluative speech acts in the following way:

> Considering the evaluative semantics expressed in the speaker's attitude as the concepts of "good / bad", the main types of evaluative speech acts include condemnation and approval, while other types, preserving this invariant meaning, can realize different illocutionary functions according to the intensity of the expressed evaluation or the degree of the perlocutionary influence on the addressee. The illocutionary force may not be conveyed explicitly by language means. It should be emphasized that the same propositional content in different communicative environments can represent different speech acts.
>
> (*ibid.*: 202)

Although relatively little work has been done on the subject of *evaluative speech acts*, for the purpose of the analysis, I have placed it into the category of *expressives*, since expressive speech acts concern the feelings of speakers (Kiklewicz, 2011; Prihodko, 2018). Here negative and positive attitudes, including heavy criticism of actors in social phenomena or social issues may be considered as belonging to the category. I believe that it is necessary to define an even narrower category—that of evaluation—in order to describe what takes place when expressing positive and negative attitudes towards something, in this case, a social issue.

Cutting's (2008: 15) examples of expressives present sentences containing speech acts that demonstrate what can be considered evaluative or of an appraising nature—this could be of social realities or cultural content—in their underlying meaning.

29) *A woman without a man is like a fish without a bicycle.* (Gloria Steinam)
30) *I've been poor and I've been rich—rich is better.* (Sophie Tucker)

Such evaluative expressives may occur in the form of proverbs or quotes which present an ideological assumption or opinion (as in examples 29 and 30 (Cutting, 2008: 15)) or are evaluative in their expression of negative attitudes which directly address other actors or the surrounding world. Each of the examples provided (above and below) belongs to the category of expressives and could also belong to the category of evaluative speech acts when interpreted even further, for their illocutionary force (Yong, 2011; Prihodko, 2018; Tantucci & Wang, 2018).[14] The examples that follow are my own:

31) *They should have known that something bad would happen.*
32) *It's nice to go to sleep at night knowing you're not such an idiot after all.*
33) *If I were him I would think twice.*

It should be kept in mind that, similarly to any other speech act, evaluative speech acts are context-dependent, and are found more often in social situations or in contexts in which reactions to texts occur (such as in a message board or comments section on the internet).[15] Both of the practical chapters deal with the evaluation of blame in the case of rape in the context of rape blame attribution

---

14 This deeper meaning is indicative of an attitude, and one that must be understood through inference.

15 In applying pragmatic analysis to CDA, it is important to note that both make up "approaches to studying language's relation to contextual background features" (Cutting, 2008: 2). The concepts of *narrow* and *broad context* must be considered. Information that is relative to a speaker's or writer's communicative intention lies within the scope of *broad context*.

(cf. Chapter 2), investigating negative and positive evaluations of actors through indirect means. To my knowledge, no cross-cultural comparison of American and Polish pragmatics in the discourse on rape has been investigated as of yet, and keeping in mind the way victim blaming and the maintenance of rape myths takes place discursively, it is important to understand the way context might determine that expression.

Presuppositions

Alongside implicit evaluation, presupposition is another phenomenon in pragmatics that can be described in the context of conducting analyses on the language that surrounds crime, such as rape. A *presupposition* is an element within a sentence that is "undeniable or non-negotiable" (Simpson & Mayr, 2010: 81), one that a speaker takes for granted before producing an utterance or text. Beaver (1996) maintained that it is difficult to reach a unanimous definition for presupposition that may be agreed upon by multiple scholars. One such definition may be considered in terms of semantic valuation and posits "that one sentence (semantically) presupposes another if the truth of the second is a condition for the semantic value of the first to be true or false" (*ibid.*: 2).

In considering that presuppositions concern speaker or writer attitudes towards an event or object, it must be kept in mind that "the majority of well-developed pragmatic theories concern the presuppositions not of a sentence (as in semantic theories) or of a speaker (as in Stalnaker's theory) but of an utterance" (Beaver, 1996: 2). He states that "one of the main insights of the last few decades of study of presupposition is that the phenomenon is heavily influenced by the dynamics of the interpretation process" (*ibid.*: 3). A rather adequate and simple definition, however, is the one put forth, i.e., that presuppositions "refer to propositions whose truth is taken for granted in the utterance of a linguistic expression" (Green, 1996: 72). Presuppositions are an important means of structuring information, and allow speakers and writers to insert or make an implicit assumption about the world (Sauerland, 2008). Presuppositions have previously been studied in the context of rape and its discursive representations (Ehrlich, 2001).

Analyzing rape within a CDA framework

The choice to analyze the subject of rape within a CDA framework was simple, as CDA provides the means to uncover ideologies in discourse and discourses about rape—as a gendered subject—are not bereft of them. The discursive and linguistic aspects of power structures present in cases of sexual aggression will be used to pinpoint where rape myths concerning actors and rape itself, as well as sexual scripts in heterosexual sexual contact, are present within the blaming discourse of user comments (for rape myths and sexual scripts cf. Chapter 2).

Beginning with West, Lazar, and Kramarae's (1997) discussion of tabloids and active and passive agents presented in the case of rape, linguistic studies have discovered its important role in indexing where exactly ideologies can be found in discursive action. In the case that a man is charged with sexual assault, "contradictory demands become an issue," where women are expected to help men "contain" their sexual urges, by way of not acting in a manner thought to provoke them (Cameron & Kulick, 2003: 34).

The subject of sexual agency and its genderedness has been examined from a linguistic perspective, for one, by Susan Ehrlich (1998, 2001). In her work, Ehrlich (*ibid.*) argues that legal discourses, through the use of a grammar of agency, discount the validity of the testimony of female victims by ignoring the perpetrator as an actor in the crime. Ehrlich (*ibid.*) brings attention to the fact that in rape trials, definitions of consent become significant in their validity, since oftentimes the evidence is discursive when presented with a lack of additional physical evidence of injury (Ehrlich, 2001; Cameron & Kulick, 2003).

There are also a number of papers on the pragmatic, semantic, and cultural meaning of the word *no* in sexual encounters (McConnell-Ginet, 1989; Frith, 1997; Kitzinger & Frith, 1999; Kulick, 2003). McConnell-Ginet (1989, 2011) observes that when a woman says *no* in the situation of a sexual encounter, her statement takes on a perceived meaning of *maybe* or *keep trying.*[16] She claims that, because of the socially informed ambiguous nature of the word *no*, women are faced with the possibility of their noncompliance not being understood as categorical refusal. This subject has been revisited in other works that discuss the subject of language and sexual consent (Cameron, 2006; Kiesling, 2019). The idea that a woman is incapable of knowing what she really wants, not only discredits her as an autonomous actor, but also explains away why it is that so much sexual violence has been found to take place against women.

Ehrlich's (2001) analysis of the grammar of the plaintiff, defense attorney, prosecuting attorney and the defendant himself is another example of how sexual refusal becomes an ideological tangle of what words, actions and expressions should be interpreted in what way. She draws attention to the way in which the grammatical strategy of the defendant, Matt, and his lawyers "reverses usual assumptions about gender and sexual agency" (Cameron & Kulick, 2003: 35).

16 Also referred to in the literature as *token no* or *token refusal.*

Through the use of the pronoun *we* and passive constructions, what Matt and his lawyers did was they transposed the agency from not being fully his, but as belonging to both parties of the case. It turned out that the majority of the questions posed by the defense attorney were aimed at interrogating why the female plaintiff did not assert agency in the situation and why she did not resist Matt by using force. He was eventually acquitted on one charge in court and, consequentially, not expelled from university (Ehrlich, 2001).

Ehrlich (*ibid.*) also discusses the idea of consent that weighs heavily on the discussion surrounding acquaintance rape trial she analyzes. Ideas of consent revolve greatly around how it is defined. In the early 1990s, Antioch College in the state of Ohio was faced with changing the way that rape is addressed by forming a new sexual consent policy. The policy stated that consent to a sexual encounter would be implied not by the lack of *no*, but by the presence of *yes*. This made so that with every act performed in a sexual encounter, "the request for consent would have to be specific for each act" (Cameron & Kulick, 2003: 36).

As a spokesperson explained to the press:

> The request for consent must be specific for each act…if you want to take off her blouse, you have to ask. If you want to touch her breast, you have to ask. If you want to move your hand down to her genitals, you have to ask. If you want to put your finger inside of her, you have to ask.
>
> (Cameron & Kulick, 2003: 32)

Although the policy was later criticized for its approach to sexuality that was seen as oppressive of what is natural, it constitutes one of the first insights into the way that consent was defined in the United States. Additionally, automatic assumptions concerning agency are visible in the discourse of requesting consent from a female (passively) sexual actor, providing an illustration of presuppositions regarding heterosexual sexual encounters (Cameron & Kulick, 2003: 39).

The representation of social actors and the representation of rape

The representation of social actors makes up a major part of the practical analysis in the final chapters of the work. Some work has been done on the ways that actors are named in the media in criminal case descriptions.

A study by Ulrike Tabbert (2016), who investigates newspaper representations of crime and the actors involved, including the naming strategies of alleged criminals and victims that she had collected from English and German newspaper reports. Her work is investigated from a corpus-linguistic perspective, and although it does not name van Leeuwen's (2008) model as the basis for the linguistic analysis, it discusses the most common naming strategies for actors involved in serious criminal cases, including rape within the framework provided by Jeffries (2010) from a stylistics perspective. The author has shown that in various crime reports found in newspapers, there is a linguistic constructivism at play where the actors and events are concerned and that it occurs within the discourses (Tabbert, 2016, 2017).

Pragmalinguistics and discourses on rape

Relatively little work has been done on the pragmalinguistic aspects of discourse on rape (Woodhams & Grant, 2006; Johnson, 2018). One such study that focuses on pragmatics is that of Susan Ehrlich (2001, 2005), who investigated the implicature within questions aimed at the victim of a rape in the courtroom setting, to demonstrate how social inequalities may impact the interpretation of utterances. Ehrlich (2001) adequately demonstrates how it is that presuppositions play a role in shaping the way that rape victims are viewed in a court room setting and what ideologically based assumptions are seated in and build the grounds upon which victim blaming occurs even in an institutional setting such as the legal one (*ibid.*).

Ehrlich (*ibid.*) considers the notion of the "reasonable person's" or "reasonable woman's"[17] perspectives in informing the dominant discourses which (re)circulate in the discourses and "talk" on sexual assault and rape. She draws attention to the way that certain norms regarding what happens in intimate situations inform the way that societies think about the actors in assaults (*ibid.*). The discourses on rape and sexual assault possess a cultural weight of "a sexist and androcentric belief-system" that informs and authorizes misinterpretations of what happens or should happen in sexual situations (*ibid.*: 148).

Another pragmatic study related to rape concerned the investigation of rape and murder threats directed at Caroline Criado-Perez on the online platform Twitter (Hardaker & McGlashan, 2015). The paper investigated the increasingly

17 The *reasonable woman's perspective* derives from the terminology of *reasonable person* pertaining to the courts of the United States and Canada, in which behaviors are assessed to be generally harmful or offensive, and thus punishable by court of law (Ehrlich, 2004: 138). The reasonable person is a representative of community norms and leads to what some feminist legal scholars have deemed to be the generalizability of "a reasonable person's experience" (*ibid.*). It is argued that because men and women experience sexual advances differently, the reasonable person's approach does not allow for fair judgment. This in turn has led to the introduction of the "reasonable woman" standard (*Ellison v. Brady* 1991).

prominent phenomenon of rape threats that are made through the use of social network sites, investigating language in context to see how such threats are carried out in the linguistic sense (*ibid.*).

As for the present work, where pragmatics is concerned, the question of implicit evaluation will be important to the overall investigation of the assumptions that lie behind the comments (cf. Chapters 6 and 7) regarding who is at fault in rape, as well as to demonstrate the victim blaming is still pervasive in the discourses on rape. This investigation has in mind the addition of a new dimension to the analysis of discourses on sexual crime, its offenders and victims.

Conclusions

Having presented the various approaches to CDA and the nexus of discourse and language in contributing to evaluative discourse, it is my hope that it is clear what critical analyses of discourse can offer in dealing with or analyzing the problem of sexual crime. The chapter that follows presents the sociological knowledge on sexuality and rape, which informs the discourses analyzed in the final two chapters of the work. It is crucial to understand the significance of gendered stereotypes and scripts in the discussion of the intricate connections between discourses and the perception of rape in a cultural context. Seeing that discourse is a window into social behaviors and beliefs (Jäger & Maier, 2009), it constitutes one of the most accessible ways of dissecting how harmful ideologies come to light.

These nodes create the intersections of a complex web created by the adherence to cultural norms instilled by ideologically ensued action. The analyses presented in the final chapters, through the investigation of the representation of social actors, the transitivity processes in which they are involved, and the implied meaning of internet user comments, conveyed through implicit evaluation, will demonstrate how engrained in social norms are attitudes that intrinsically place blame or partial blame on the victims of sexual crime. On the cusp of implementing new standards of looking at the situation of rape victims, of course, from a western and privileged perspective, it is necessary to recognize the fundamental connections language makes in the contingencies of a continuing negative attitude towards the role of the victim blaming in changes in attitude towards assault victims. The investigation of attitudes looks into the presence of stereotyping and how victim blaming occurs in CMC in both American and Polish contexts (cf. Chapter 6 and Chapter 7).

The linguistic aspects of investigating the media are described in Chapter 4, where a definition of how digital comments are defined in this work is provided. These chapters will lead to the practical analysis, which is a Critical

Discourse Analysis of the ways that discursive media communication strategies in both American and Polish discourses maintain and reproduce rape myths and stereotypes about women and men as sexual actors (Piotrowska & Synkiewicz, 2011: 5) and also perpetuate the victim blaming which stems from it, thus causing the focus of the blame for rape to remain on the victim, rather than the offender.

Chapter 2: Implications for rape The intersection of ideology, gender and sexuality

Having discussed Critical Discourse Analysis and the way the framework will be applied to investigating discourses on rape, it is necessary to touch on the broader sociological aspects that surround, shape and maintain the reproduction of victim blaming, representations of the perpetrator and victim, as well as the representations of rape itself. The theoretical background to those aspects, which subsequently inform the discourses of interest is a critical part of understanding the goal of such an analysis (van Dijk, 2001), which is to show where and how victim blaming occurs in American and Polish discourses. In general, discourses are culturally dependent (van Dijk, 2015). Thus the social and cultural implications regarding the ways that gender, sexuality, and the crime of rape itself are understood in the United States and Poland must also be delineated.

In Eastern European cultures, including in Poland, *gender* is a word that has been attributed a negative ideological standing (Parker et al., 2009; Korolczuk, 2014; Korolczuk & Graff, 2017).[18] This may be set against the way that gender as a construct is approached in the United States, which does not necessarily see gender itself as ideological (Korolczuk, 2014), but rather that gender has ideologies attached to it. This fact accounts for one of the primary inspirations for the presented project, as issues of sexuality and sexual assault are intrinsically tied to how gender and gender roles are understood (McDermot et al., 2015). This chapter aims to provide a window into understanding ideologies and stereotypes that are related to gender in the binary sense since a gender binary of men and women or masculinity and femininity dominates in both cultures. Considering that rape is a gender-based sexual crime (Brison, 2006), major issues surrounding gender and sexuality are also described in this chapter.

In this chapter, rape is discussed from the two cultural perspectives analyzed. The theories of secondary victimization and attribution theory are also introduced, as they are relevant to the question of victim blaming. The final discourse analysis (cf. Chapters 6 and 7) will attempt to make sense of the nexus of victim blaming, ideologies, and rape myths, as well as the sexual scripts that are borne

18 Judith Butler (2024), in her most recent work, *Who's Afraid of Gender?*, claims that wariness surrounding the word "gender" has now reached the United States (*ibid.*: 3–4).

from them. It must be noted that, for the sake of space, only the most pertinent sociological aspects are discussed here, by which I mean the ones that inform representations and reflection of ideologies in public discourses about the heterosexual rape of women by men, as opposed to the heterosexual rape of men by women or cases of homosexual rape.

Ideology

It must first be said that the notion of *ideology* is crucial to understanding how ideas inform the way human beings construct social realities based on what is communicated to them through their surroundings and the contexts they find themselves in. As mentioned in Chapter 1, ideology is one of the underlying questions for conducting Critical Discourse Analysis, and hence it is important to provide an in-depth definition. The beginnings of theorizing ideology have their roots in de Tracy's (1796) use of the term, which upheld that ideology is a system of beliefs of people in a community. He called ideology "a science of ideas" (after Kennedy, 1979: 353), naming the societal beliefs which determine systems of thinking, and from which stereotypical imagery is born. In his book entitled *Ideology: An Introduction*, Eagleton (1949) presents a list of definitions of *ideology:*

a) The process of production of meanings, signs and values in social life
b) A body of ideas characteristic of a particular social group or class
c) Ideas which help to legitimate a dominant political power
d) False ideas which help to legitimate a dominant political power
e) Systematically distorted communication
f) That which offers a position for a subject
g) Forms of thought motivated by social interest
h) Identity thinking
i) Socially necessary illusion (…)

(Terry Eagleton, 1949: 1–2)

The list goes on to provide more, however, for the sake of space the enumerations have been limited to the ones that reflect the definitions of ideology used. This work draws on van Dijk's (1998) explanation and understanding of the term. Van Dijk (1998: 116) emphasizes that there are "no private, personal ideologies" and that ideologies are systems of belief which are "*socially shared* by the members of a *collectivity* of social actors" (*ibid.*).

Woolard and Schieffelin (1994: 58) state that "the term ideology reminds analysts that cultural frames have social histories and signals a commitment to address the relevance of power relations to the nature of cultural forms," which means that ideology in and of itself, as a social factor embedded in collective belief, should not be undermined in any kind of social study. When investigating ideology, as an elusive concept in the social sciences (Ehrlich, 2001: 65), the diversity of ideological frameworks and ideological-discursive formation (IDF) (Fairclough 1995) are what put these beliefs into practice. If a dominant ideological frame co-occurs with an ideology that might be considered secondary, it is almost natural for the dominant frame to be naturalized and "accepted as commonsensical" (Ehrlich, 2001: 65). This demonstrates that it is, therefore, important to recognize how dominant ideologies might obstruct more marginalized ones, such as the way that patriarchal ideologies in many ways obstruct feminist ideologies (Sultana, 2010; Miller, 2013; Christ, 2016).

Ideologies that impinge on social thought come in many shades and under many names. The main focus throughout the work will be on the following three ideologies, the first of which is *patriarchal ideology,*[19] which shapes the many times hibernating and encumbering idea that men are innately superior to women (Tyson, 2006). The second, *gender ideology,*[20] refers to "attitudes regarding the appropriate roles, rights and responsibilities of women and men in society" (Kroska, 2007: 1). *Feminist ideology*[21] aims to argue that inequalities between men and women do not take place in their own right, but rather exist as a result of the long-standing oppression of women and the mutually assumed notion that they are an inferior sex (on a gender binary rather than continuum) (Tyson, 2006). These ideologies are highlighted, since the goal of the work is to uncover discourses that reproduce gender inequalities in which women are viewed as inferior. Investigating where ideologies are at work in discourse is a major part of CDA (cf. Chapter 1) and makes up the basis of the delineation of the reproduction and maintenance of power structures in social life. In looking at ideologies in a work such as this one, it is also essential to introduce the definitions and understandings

---

19 In terms of the ideologies surrounding gender as a social construction, there are several that have been named as propagating gendered stereotypes and ideas. The first, which Tyson (2006) constitutes as a major factor owing to the inequality between men and women in her in-depth discussion of critical theory, is *patriarchal ideology*. From this, Tyson (2006: 87) claims that many women are forced to recover, referring even to herself as a "recovering patriarchal woman" to emphasize the detrimental effect that patriarchal ideologies have on societal expectations of both men and women, which we oftentimes find ourselves caught up in.

20 *Gender ideologies* are also prevalently known as *gender role ideologies*

21 Within feminist ideologies, branches of feminism can be found, including *transnational feminism* and *materialist feminism.*

of the terms sex and gender, including how they are seated in biology and culture. Linguistic ideologies are introduced in the chapter which follows (cf. Chapter 3).

Differentiating sex and gender

To understand the overarching gender ideologies that are related to understandings of human sexuality in varying social and cultural contexts, it is necessary to first discuss *sex* and *gender* and how these terms are understood throughout this work, especially where expectations about men's and women's behavior are concerned. The term *sex* is used to refer to biological sex, as understood by anthropologists and sociologists who began work in the social construction of sex and gender. According to Oakley (1985: 16), sex is "a word that refers to biological differences between men and women: the visible difference in genitalia, the related difference in procreative function." Gender is a "matter of culture" (*ibid.*; Marecek et al., 2004; Sheppard & Mayo, 2013), however, and hence it is a social construction, in line with social constructivist theory,[22] which has established that gender is "constantly created and re-created out of human interaction, out of social life, and is the texture and order of that social life" (Lorber & Farrell, 1991: 112).

Unger (1979) stated the need to differentiate between what distinguishes biology from behavior. In some of the seminal works on gender, Sherif (1982) also considered gender "a scheme for the social categorization of individuals" (after Wiedeman, 1990: 15). Brannon (2016: 12) points out that while distinctions between sex and gender have been elusive, "those who use the term *gender* often intend to emphasize the social nature of differences between men and women." Hence, throughout this work, gender refers to the cultural construct of gender, including how such constructs shape the ideologies and stereotypes that inform discourses (Marecek & Crawford, 2004).

Ideology and gender essentialism

The ongoing debate regarding the germination of gendered constructs polarizes those that support an essentialist leaning toward the understanding of gender and

---

22 *Social constructionism* or *social constructionist theory* came about with Berger and Luckmann's (1966) book *The Social Construction of Reality*, and was further developed upon the tenets of major social scientists (i.e.,, Anthony Giddens and Michel Foucault) as the idea that reality and the way it is perceived is a social construct rather than an individual one, in other words, it can be considered as the reconstruction of subjective reality by outside factors.

those who refute essentialism, maintaining that gender is for the most part a social construct (Witt, 2011). The notion of *essentialism* itself lies in foundations of a more biological nature, with its bearings grounded in the Aristotelian definition of essentialism as properties that make something what it is, and without which it would not be that kind of thing (Matthews, 1990).[23] Essentialism accounts for observation-based definitions, and argues that, where gender is concerned, men and women are fundamentally different. What has been criticized in essentialist leanings, however, is where social constructions are concerned.

In Crawford's (1995: 8–9) criticism of biological-based views on gender, she remarks that "essentialism conceptualizes gender as a set of properties residing in one's personality, self-concepts, or traits. Gender is something women and men have or are." In opening up a venue for linguistics to take on the notion of essentialism as a restrictive concept, Crawford (*ibid.*) maintains the argument that women are stereotyped against the plain ideological ideals that work against them by prescribing cooperative and unassertive behavior to their being as an instinctive quality.

It must be made clear that for ideologies to exist, essentialist leanings first create notions of what natural and recurring states define an object or being. In the case of gender, internal and persistent attributes might be considered what was previously referred to as an internal (hence innate) female characteristic, such as that of the quality of unassertiveness (Tyson, 2006: 109–111). What might be prescribed as essential to the maintenance of masculinity, for one, are traits of dominance and aggression, which, in turn, produce the common notion that a man without such traits is "a sissy" or "not masculine", and therefore not a real man.

Crawford (1995: 8) writes that "the sex difference approach is an *essentialist* approach, [which] views gender as a fundamental, essential part of an individual," and that taking such an approach to gender reproduces the myth that women are the weaker and subordinate sex (Rossi, 2021). The common view on gender as an essential construct has its basis in gender ideology, a term that was brought about in the research conducted on gender in the United States in the 1980s and 1990s (Butler, 1993). It is in this work that I aim to show how gender as a social construct impacts the way that actors in rape cases are seen.

---

23 Aristotle's idea of essentialism was among the first to put forth the idea that "some of the attributes of a thing (quite independently of the language in which the thing is referred to, if at all) may be essential to the thing and others accidental" (Quine, 1966: 173–174). What has been referred to as "Aristotelian essentialism" (ibid; Matthews, 1990) presents the idea that things are defined by the essential parts that constitute their make-up.

A brief history of research on gender

Gender was first discussed as a concept in the social sciences in the 1970s, with the various ground-breaking sociological works of Ann Oakley (1972). Her work was preceded by the anthropological studies on sex differences by Margaret Mead (1949), which have been considered a pivotal transformation for gender studies overall. The shift from what was originally termed *sex roles* to that of gender came with Oakley's 1972 book entitled *Sex, Gender, and Society* (Dahlerup, 2015). In her work, the idea of sex roles referred to the roles prescribed to individuals of a certain sex (male or female), making up what we currently recognize to be *gender roles* (Lindsey, 2015; Eisand, 2019).

1980s and 1990s also saw much research on gender branching out to other social sciences, including psychology and linguistics (cf. Chapter 3). The psychological aspects have been considered, where Talbot (1998: 11) defines gender as "not biological, but psychosocial" and a phenomenon that "should always be considered in the context of social relations between people." This emphasis places at the forefront the malleable nature with which gender socially precedes sex on a cultural continuum. Understanding gender—and how it has been deemed by many scholars as belonging to a class of social constructs—is not only necessary to the psychological understanding of men and women, but also to the notion that patriarchal societal structure is universal (Lorber & Farrell, 1991; Skrla, 2000; Connell, 2003; Gorley et al., 2003; Brown, 2012).

Gender, of course, does not limit itself to just men and women. Although the focus of the analysis regards a binary approach to gender discourses on the rape of women by men and the way discourse reflects harmful ideologies, the importance and prevalence of other gender categories must be acknowledged, so as not to undermine or erase them. Studies on the transgender community, including non-binary individuals (Monro, 2019), have given way to the view of gender as a spectrum (Monro, 2005; Tharp, 2016; Zimman et al., 2014) and have paved the way for an even more diverse discipline that is gender studies.[24]

The performative nature of gender

In her most famous work, *The Second Sex*, de Beauvoir (1949) stated that gender is not something that one is born with, but something that is acquired through

24 Lavender linguistics is a burgeoning field of research that focuses its attention on the prominence of language as it is broadly defined, in the lives of gay, lesbian, bisexual, and transgendered people (Leap, 2015; Smith, 2019).

"practice". Her claim that "one is not born a woman, one becomes one" led the world and feminist theory into the social constructionist view of gender as performative. West and Zimmerman (1987: 126) described the means through which gender as a construct is performed, meaning that gender is "an accomplishment, an achieved property of situated conduct." They emphasize, however, that our attention moves from the individual to the interaction that takes place within a societal web. Those authors (*ibid.*) made use of Goffman's (1976) idea of *gender display*[25] to discuss what happens in the performance of gender, with the focus being "on behavioral aspects of being a man or a woman" (West & Zimmerman, 1987: 127).

With performative theory now widespread in the discussion of gender studies (Bieńkowska, 2012; Plata, 2012; Meyerhoff, 2015), sex has been viewed as too binary a construct by the social sciences and thus, gender—being viewed as a social construct—more readily fits the discourse on the fluidity and spectrum-nature of gender. Butler's (1991, 1993) claim that "gender is an impersonation" reflects well what West and Zimmerman (1987) stated in their expansion of performative theory that, as humans, we are bound by the constructs of society to play a role, a gender role. Most often the choice of role means that those who make that choice are impersonating ideals unnatural to human beings, hence their being performed (Butler, 1992).

Butler (1993: 5) resumes her position on gender by saying it is "in no way a stable identity or locus of agency from which various acts proceed" and that gender is rather "an identity tenuously constituted in time." She views gender as performative in the same way that West and Zimmerman (1987) do, i.e., as "instituted through a *stylized repetition of acts* (…) instituted through the stylization of the body and, hence, must be understood as the mundane way in which bodily gestures, movements and enactments of various kinds constitute the illusion of an abiding gendered self" (Butler, 1988: 519). Not only through language, as West and Zimmerman (1987) emphasize, is gender played out, but also through everyday behavior and the enactment of ideologically prescribed *gendered* behavior.

In addition to the above, the idea of gender performativity has been claimed to perpetuate patriarchal ideologies. Butler (1993: 5) expresses the view that nothing is left of sex after it has "assumed its social character as gender." Here,

25 Goffman's (1976) notion of *gender display* sees imagery surrounding gender which communicates cultural understandings of gender at a mere glance. The idea is used to describe the effects that advertising has on body image, through visual definitions of beauty norms and depictions of parenting, education and intimate relations, to provide some examples.

she prescribes interaction as being necessary to the manipulation and formation of gender as a social construct, on the basis of associations with biological sex. Gender thus becomes an entity that absorbs sex entirely. What the idea of gender performativity aims to show is that gender is a fluid concept, and not something to be prescribed to an entity or being on the basis of presumed essentialist characteristics that are observed.

Important studies on gender in the West

In addition to Butler (1990), other important work on gender in the western context which still stands today is that of Sandra L. Bem (1974). With the Bem Sex Role Inventory (from here, referred to as the BSRI), Bem (1981) aimed to create an inventory of behavior and roles usually prescribed to both men and women. It was until the 1960s that men and women were considered fundamentally polar opposites, and what the BSRI (Bem, 1981) measured was the ideas of gender roles that people had. She discovered that in many cases, both stereotypically male and female characteristics were found in men and women, thus popularizing the idea of *psychological androgyny* in modern-day studies of gender, psychology, and sociology (Titkow, 2007: 31). This type of androgyny has been defined as "strongly endorsing both stereotypically feminine and masculine attributes within the same individual" (Dean & Tate, 2017: 643).

The BSRI (Bem, 1974, 1981) was developed to gauge gender role perceptions, meaning that each respondent fills out accordingly how he or she views him- or herself according to the psychology of masculinity and femininity on a scale. Bem (*ibid.*) demonstrated that certain characteristics prescribed to each sex are shared. She did so by measuring the prevalence of androgyny in individuals. The study led to dispute among psychologists and social scientists as to the actual validity of the BSRI (Holt & Ellis, 1998). Spence, Helmreich and Stapp (1975), for one, criticized the scoring scale of the Bem Sex Role Inventory. Although the BSRI is still relied on in some gender research today (Titkow, 2007), it has gone widely out of use in measuring masculinity and femininity.

Following Bem (1974, 1981, 2008), in the late 1980s and 1990s, Judith Butler (1988, 1990, 1993) launched a discussion on the performative nature of gender (McRobbie, 2013). Her works include "Performative Acts and Gender Constitution" (1988), an essay in which Butler first proposed her theory of *gender performativity,* as well as *Gender Trouble: Feminism and the Subversion of Identity* (1990), in which she critically discussed the theories of philosophers and psychologists and herself theorized gender, sex and sexuality as performative, among other titles well known in academic circles.[26] The theory of the performative nature of gender follows social constructivist theory, which maintains the idea that being born a man or woman does not determine one's behavior, and that behavior is the result of gendered socialization (*ibid.*).

The ideas of masculinity and femininity, two key notions underlying culture and the presentation of ideals, have been around for ages and still permeate through social institutions and the way they function. Such notions work to perpetuate a patriarchal structured society which set men at the forefront of discourse, leaving women in subjugated roles.[27] Other significant studies on gender will be discussed where the linguistic research on gender is concerned (cf. Chapter 3).

Important studies on gender in Poland

Although the first studies on gender have their origins in the West, they have also made their way under the academic eyes of Polish sociologists, psychologists, anthropologists and linguists alike (Slany et al., 2011; Krzaklewska et al., 2016). Polish studies on gender made headway after the fall of communism in the 1990s, a pillar of which was to bring attention to gender equality issues (*ibid.*; Graff, 2014). The literature on the socio-cultural understanding of gender (Polish: *płeć kulturowa*) draws on pivotal studies from the West, including Bem (*ibid.*, 1974; Titkow, 2007) and Butler (1990, 1993, 2004, 2024).

In the second half of the twentieth century, Polish research on gender was preoccupied with discussion on the meaning and value of women's experiences (Slany et al., 2011: 8). Parallel to the research on women in the United States of the time, gender studies in Poland concerned the ways that women are socially situated and how they are culturally constructed (*ibid.*). Much of the research has been related to changes in women's experience in the working world (Grajek, 2003; Titkow, 2007), women in politics (Fuszara, 2011), inequalities in the university setting (the glass ceiling effect) (Titkow 2003), care-taking roles of women (Titkow, 2007), and violence against women, sexual and domestic (Kwiatkowska, 1998). The research on gender in Poland has focused on the position of Polish

26 Other titles of Butler's work include *Imitation and Gender Insubordination* (1990), *Bodies That Matter: On the Discursive Limits of Sex* (1993), *Excitable Speech: A Politics of the Performative* (1997), *Undoing Gender* (2004), and *Giving an Account of Oneself* (2005), and, most recently, *Who's Afraid of Gender* (2024).

27 For the purpose of this work, this pertains to sexual scripts and men's and women's roles in heteronormative sexual interaction, which I argue impacts the way that rape victims and offenders are perceived.

women and the role of representations of women in maintaining stereotypes based in Catholic ideological regard of women (Bulawka, 2015).

In Polish studies on gender, masculinity was only studied in depth later at the start of the twenty-first century, whereas in the United States, men's studies entered the academic arena in the 1970s (Mrozik, 2010; Slany et al., 2011). In Poland, studies on gender have taken on a highly feminist standpoint (Mrozik, 2010) with the promotion of gender equality in mind. More recently, Polish research on gender has focused on the LGBTQ+ community and the reproduction of homophobia in social discourse (Kowalska, 2008; Slany, 2008). Both the American and Polish cultural contexts are strongly tied to ideologies related to gender and in turn sexuality and sexual script.

Ideology, stereotype, and gender

It has been argued that the push for male and female equality is a rather new phenomenon, emerging from the centuries-old "masculinist community of practice" (Talbot, 2010: 187). Because women have historically been placed on the backburner in the public sphere, their marginalization has been, in a sense, naturalized. Talbot (*ibid.*) provides examples of the masculinist nature of parliament and the British House of Commons, which have been in existence that way since the fourteenth century. The entrance of women into politics only boomed towards the end of the twentieth century.

Instead of simply reproducing naturalized gender differences, what ideological prescriptions for masculine and feminine behavior do is sustain the hegemonic patriarchal structure that we are used to experiencing in society today. Gender ideology prescribes certain roles to men and women in a gender binary system. The fact that a strong patriarchal ideology is pervasive in society (in both the United States and Poland) can be argued by the fact that it does not belong to individual perceptions of the world, but is in fact located in the structure of society, and in an underlying factor for why gender seems to be at the forefront of many social issues (Lazar, 2005: 8).

As Thompson et al. (1992: 576) rightfully point out, "the array of beliefs and attitudes individuals hold about men, women, and gender relations do not make up a single tidy set." This means that there is more than just the simplified beliefs that concern what should constitute gender and gender behavior. What is here referred to on an opposing scale as *masculinity ideology* and *femininity ideology* comprises not simply a physical trait or a certain social role prescribed to *being* male or female, but "interlocking sets of practices, norms, beliefs, and mandates" that work together to create what one can utilize in performativity, for example

(Tolman et al., 2015: 3). These ideologies are strongly linked to stereotyping (Talbot, 2008).

In general, *stereotyping* is the act of "simplification, reduction, and naturalization" and is a practice that has been defined as one that maintains "social order" (Talbot, 2008: 471). Within the typology of stereotypes, *gender stereotypes* simplify behaviors and thinking of men and women, which affects the way that people think about and define men and women according to prescribed gender norms (Deaux & Kite, 1993; Talbot, 2008; Ellemers, 2018).

If gender is a construct of "hierarchical and complementary ideologies" (Tolman et al. 2015: 1), the concepts that make up femininity and masculinity are crucial in understanding how ideology and the gender stereotypes that derive from them remain in the mindset of binary socialization. The consequences of such thinking are doubtlessly easy to comprehend, with a chain-like reaction occurring between the existence of long-lived ideologies and stereotypes expressed through discursive and multi-modal production.

What must be kept in mind in discussing the ideologies and stereotypes which surround gender is the fact that one gender ideology or stereotype is in need of the other in order to exist, and that "as a *process*, gender creates the social differences that define 'woman' and 'man'" (Lorber, 1994: 60). It is impossible, then, to discuss male or masculine standards without considering to some degree, how it compares to existing ideologies of feminine behavior or characteristics (Thompson et al., 1992: 577). It must be stressed that the descriptions of gender ideologies provided are not exhaustive, but have to be limited to the most culturally dominant examples for the sake of space. Throughout the work I will refer to gender stereotypes within the category of gender ideologies.

Masculinity

What it means to be masculine, or male, and feminine, or female, has been scrutinized in psychoanalytic theory (Freud, 1927), cognitive-developmental theory (Kohlberg, 1966), as well as in direct reinforcement (Weitzman et al., 1972) and modeling (Mischel, 1973) learning theories. As the dominating subgroup of the gender dyad, the male comes first, and being female often comes second to the dominating category of *masculinity* (Talbot, 2008).

As far as the terminology in studies of men and masculinity is concerned, many authors have attempted to clarify related concepts, but have not come to a universal consensus (Deaux, 1984, 1993; Gentile, 1993; Good & Mintz, 1993; Mintz & O'Neil, 1990; Pleck et al., 1993; Unger & Crawford, 1993). What these authors do point out, however, is the importance of distinguishing *sex-based characteristics (maleness)* from *psychologically-based conceptions of masculinity* (Good & Sherrod in Unger, 2001: 202), which means differentiating between what is considered biologically essential in constituting maleness, and the social constructionist model of what constitutes masculinity.[28] When discussing the conception (social, psychological) of masculinity, a variety of terms have been used, including: masculine gender roles, attitudes towards the male role, conceptions of masculinity, and masculine ideologies (Good & Sherrod, 2001: 202). For the sake of consistency, I will most often refer to these ideas as pertaining to ideology (here more specifically as *masculine ideology*), since ideology is what we are utilizing to define the nature and basis of social thought processes regarding gender.

According to David and Brannon's (*ibid.* 1976, after Kahn, 2009: 55) *blueprint for manhood*, four major masculine themes that men "struggle with to maintain their 'gender role'" exist, namely (1) no sissy stuff (i.e., antifemininity), (2) be a big wheel (gaining status and achievement), (3) the sturdy oak (being inexpressive and independent), and (4) give 'em hell (remaining adventurous and, at the same time, aggressive) (cf. Kilmartin, 1994 for more detail). Abiding by the tenants these themes present, they argue that masculinity is almost guaranteed. What *no sissy stuff* presents is the idea of tough maleness and the rejection of anything that might be considered feminine (or the antithesis of male) in the least. The theme to *be a big wheel* plays on the idea that men's focus in life should be on gaining a high status and high degree of social achievement. And *the sturdy oak* places restrictions on the male emotional reaction to any situation, maintaining the pervasive idea that emotional intelligence and gaining emotional capital is not in the best interests of a masculine man. The final theme, *give 'em hell*, reiterates the tendency to associate masculine nature with aggression, and, in turn, with power and adventure. David and Brannon's (1976) theory not only places the stereotypical values of manhood in the forefront of being male, but also reinforces their importance and what they mean for *masculinity*, and even *hypermasculinity*.

Thompson et al. (1992: 576) argue that some aspects of David and Brannon's (1976) theory (the Brannon masculinity scale), which is a blend of the *trait* and *normative* approaches to gender prescription, make sense, especially from the normative or socially constructed perspective on gender. They decide to view the normative approach as being more valid as a result of its basis in the social constructionist model. Thompson and Pleck's multidimensional Male Role Norms

---

28 I distinguish between the ideas of maleness and masculinity, as do Good and Sherrod (2001: 202) to maintain the clarity of difference between the biological and the social aspects of "being male".

Scale (1986) before that, was formulated to a large extent on the basis of David and Brannon's 1976 "blueprint for manhood", so it is only natural that the consequence of thinking remains in the frame of a normative, or psycho-social approach. Why the normative approach is more reliable than the trait approach, when it comes to gender, is tied to what was said earlier about gender performativity and the social regard, rather than biological regard, of femininity and masculinity.

In a more recent review of masculine ideologies, Thompson and Bennett (2015) reanalyze Thompson and Pleck's (1992, 1995) review of masculinity measures. They conclude that ideologies and the measures used to determine them have either faded out in the last twenty years or that different ones now apply. It is not, however, the measures that are important to us here, but rather what it is that makes up the ideologies of masculinity. For example, the fact that masculinity is associated with "a degree of mastery over one's environment, the display of avid interest in sports, competitiveness, independence, being strong/tough, suppressing feelings, and aggressive/dominant control of relationships" (Ward 2005: 496).

What is essential is to underline the ideologies of masculinity that exist and juxtapose them against ideologies that concern femininity. By looking at how masculine and feminine ideologies differ from one another, it will be easier to arrive at a conclusion as to why it is that women remain a minority and why many times the justice system, even, works against them.

Hypermasculinity and the reproduction of harmful ideologies

Studied by psychologists since the 1920s, hypermasculinity can be defined as the exaggeration and distortion of masculine traits that exist across the span of masculine ideology (Glass, 1984). The phenomenon, also commonly referred to in literature as *machismo*, takes the tenets discussed earlier and combines them with hegemonic ideals.[29] Hypermasculinity is oftentimes associated not only with men as assertive, active figures, dominant in the social sphere but also with dominance as a trait, present in displays of an "assertion of power and dominance often through physically and sexually aggressive behaviors" (Ward, 2005: 496). This is particularly important when considering scripts for male sexual behavior and explanations of rape. The role of hegemony in creating the notion of not just hypermasculinity, but even trickling its way into masculinity in general, plays

29 Also known in sociological terms as *hegemonic masculinity* (Connell and Messerschmidt, 2005: 832), and "understood as the pattern of practice (i.e., things done, not just a set of role expectations or an identity) that allowed men's domination over women to continue"

a role quite detrimental to the empowerment of women in a highly patriarchal ideological system (Talbot, 2008).

Even upon arriving at the assumption that masculine and feminine ideologies exist as entities simultaneously connected and ruling one another out, one automatically consigns to the formation of gender stereotypes on such a basis. Of course, this may be argued as something unavoidable in a world where we many times function in a way that places gender difference in the forefront of dividing groups of people, making decisions, or even gaining social capital. This is where it is important to consider why the existence of such a dichotomy remains seen to be true in the eyes of at least most highly developed societies in the world. Not only for the sake of description should attention be brought to the way that men and women are perceived to psychologically and socially differ, but also for the sake of demonstrating that women are, in fact, still subject to (subconscious) repression via the work of ideology in creating what are believed to be proper gender roles. These ideologies are considered similar in both the American and Polish contexts (Kluczyńska & Wojnicka, 2015).

Femininity

Whereas masculine ideologies of the West present themselves to be rooted in hegemonic patriarchal masculine ideals, femininity is said to have undergone change, leaving the male in a somewhat static position (Thompson et al., 1992). Although agreeably, feminine ideologies have evolved over the years (Kimmel, 2000; Davis & Greenstein, 2009: 87–88), there still exists the maintenance of certain ideas of women and their behaviors as pertains to what is common and right. Just as hypermasculinity as a masculine ideology that society has us believe should be the goal towards which the male gender is driven, so femininity, in turn, is an idealization of the perfect woman and what she should represent, or even the definition of "woman".

From women in aprons (Oliver, 1974) to a mix of ideas on women and their increasing inclination to join the workforce while simultaneously acting the role of the nurturer in the family context (Caldwell, 2006), ideology concerning women has, in fact, changed, but this does not necessarily mean that the reigning subordinate position of women overall has vanished. Definitions of femininity have been known to act in oppressive and repressive ways for women residing in patriarchal societies, and differ from culture to culture (Kimmel, 2000; Kluckhohn & Anthony, 2000). It is important to look to symbolic archetypes and semiotic representations of dominant gender ideologies to properly grasp views of femininity in both American and Polish cultures.

In the United States, dominant gender ideologies regarding the behavior and comportment of women have greatly concerned docility and appearance, which are ideas not dissimilar from those considered more universal (Kimmel, 2000). The dominating femininity ideology lies in passivity, where women are expected to possess a high ability to maintain social relationships, present excess emphasis on appearance, and act as caretakers. Tolman et al. (2015: 3) make it clear that these are expectations that women are subjected to on a day-to-day basis:

> Femininity ideology comprises qualities girls are to enact, including being responsive and caring, avoiding conflict and anger, preserving relationships, curbing hunger (for food, sex), having and maintaining a body that conforms with particular standards of beauty, and not expressing sexuality.
>
> (Tolman et al., 2015: 3)

It is for this reason that women suffer stereotyping which defines them according to demureness, purity and passivity (Talbot, 2008). As long as these ideologies continue to reign within culture (and in western society, in particular), they will continue to build and uphold a gender hierarchy which reproduces the subordinate position of the female as a gender (Rubin, 1984; Kiesling, 2019). Even in the view that gender "ideals capture what is considered most desirable in men and women and include both physical and personality characteristics" (Berdahl, 2007: 426), women are considered most desirable when they fit a set of ideals that includes "modesty, deference, and warmth" (*ibid.*), as well as the physical ideal of the thin, model-type female that the media emphasizes as the ideal (Grabe et al., 2008).

Polish femininity ideologies differ slightly from those in the United States, adding more dimensions of a culturally specific nature to the discussion of the perception of women. Dominating ideologies regarding women in Poland place them in care-taking roles, which include their presentation as the mother figure in the family who is responsible for the weight of the family (Titkow, 2007). This is reflected in the "myth of the Polish mother" (Bulawka, 2013: 43), which has placed women in a role of martyrdom, where she sacrifices herself and her own happiness for her family, hence deepening the ideology of the Polish woman as a caretaker (Szwajcowska, 2006; Bulawka, 2013; Rogowska, 2018). The Polish mother's deep religiosity is also symbolic of Catholic behavior, and what feminist scholars refer to as symbolic oppression (Porter, 2005).[30] Women's sexuality is also impacted by

30 It is argued that national and religious underpinnings of the myth of the Polish mother (Matka Polka), combined, have strong associations with the Virgin Mary. According to Porter (2005: 160) "the Matka Polka image and the Marian cult shared an emphasis

this religious dimension, which stresses sexual innocence and virginity as a virtue (Raszewska-Żurek, 2011; Bulawka, 2013).

The care-taking role is also reflected in the Marian cult that has marked Poland's long period of devotion to the Mother Mary in Polish Catholicism (Szwajcowska, 2006; Bulawka, 2013), representing the divine virtue of good Catholic behavior (*ibid.*). What Bulawka (2013: 42) has called "Mary the Exemplar" has significant implications for gender norms in Polish culture.

According to the Polish Marian ideology[31] femininity is "reduced to motherhood, relegating women to activities tightly linked to the domestic sphere of hearth and home" (*ibid.*: 42). This tie between what is viewed as Catholic virtuous behavior of women celebrates women as "obedient," "faithful," "simple," passive," and "pure" (Środa, 2007: 611), at the same time acting as a propagator for the virgin-mother archetype.

The relationship of stereotype to ideology is that ideology, as a larger and more encompassing notion, takes stereotype under its wing and validates it in mainstream beliefs that exist in culture. Although not to be recognized as universal, on the whole, existing stereotypes say that "men are stereotyped as independent, agentic, and goal-oriented; women are stereotyped as interdependent, communal and oriented toward others" (Cuddy et al., 2010: 3). It is argued that gender stereotypes are at work in every culture, but this does not happen on the same level or to the same degree when workings of ideologies on a more subconscious level (Spence & Helmreich, 1978; Eagly & Steffen, 1984; Eagleton, 2014).

The cultural nature of gender stereotypes

Cuddy et al. (2010) argue that gender stereotypes are not to be considered universal, but rather cultural and that the male is seen as the embodiment of a given culture and its ideals (Hofstede, 1980; Cuddy et al., 2008, 2010). On a level that considers intercultural difference, the value of male independence as opposed to female passivity and interdependence is said to have its basis in cultural value in general (Cuddy et al., 2010: 12), which means that if a culture is found to value independence as a general trait (value), the male (as the embodiment of that culture) will be found as the idealized representation of that culture's values, i.e., he will be viewed as independent. This idea will be further discussed in terms of the

on suffering and pain, with portraits of grieving mothers echoing pietas of an earlier time."

31 This ideology is referred to by Porter (2005: 160) and Bulawka (*ibid.*: 41–42) as "the Marian cult."

formation of representations through discourse (cf. Chapter 3) and their implication for actors through representations by social perceivers (i.e., Internet users).

Although it is difficult to generalize for both the American and Polish contexts, the focus on language narrows the window through which stereotypes and stereotypical thinking may be viewed. In discussing gender ideologies and stereotypes, and their link to discourses on sexual crime, it is of course necessary to examine the question of sexuality.

Sexuality

The above sections discussed gender ideologies and introduced the concept of the social constructionist approach to gender. Sexuality, also considered here a social construct, is demarcated by the views on how one defines it, in this case when tied to gender and gendered scripts reflected in the perception of roles in heterosexual sexual interaction.

In his seminal work, *The Transformation of Intimacy*, Giddens (1992: 2) veered towards a new definition of what he called "plastic sexuality", which talks about how human sexuality can be molded to suit the identity of the individual being.[32] He quoted Foucault's (1986) explanation of sexuality and that "sexuality should not be understood only as a drive which social forces have to contain, [but] rather, 'it is an especially dense transfer point for relations of power,' something which can be harnessed as a focus of control through the very energy which, infused with power, it generates" (Foucault 1986 after Giddens, 1992: 18). And so it goes that Foucault's theory's contrasts with Giddens's, and produces a rift between understandings of the nature and implications of sexuality on society. Whereas Foucault looks at power from a lens skeptical of the positive nurturing of society's sexiness, Giddens (*ibid.*: 1) claims a revolution has come about.

Giddens (1992: 19) claims that, contrarily to Foucault's comparison of discourses on sexuality to Catholic confessionals, "sex is not driven underground in modern civilization" but rather "it becomes part of a great sermon, replacing the more ancient tradition of theological preaching" (*ibid.*). Hence, in Giddens' (*ibid.*) eyes, the bearings of culture on sexuality have not placed limitations on it, as was common practice in prior eras but have aided it to grow and promulgate throughout society. However, although this is partially true, Giddens (*ibid.*) does not take into account the sexual repression that occurs in other European or more "Westernized societies",

32 Giddens (1992: 27) states that within the frame of *plastic sexuality* subjects such as the availability of contraception to women and men (in the form of pills and condoms, for example) allow for full sexual autonomy to take place.

such as in Europe today (Sauerteig, 2009; Mosse, 2020). I do not wish to argue with Giddens' (*ibid.*) claims that we have taken great steps in the sexual revolution, for even in the late 1980s and early 1990s, a change was seen in attitudes towards sexuality, including more social openness (Rubin, 1990), but the revolutionizing turn did not have such a positive effect on the sexual perception or treatment of women.

Other explanations of the term sexuality include that it is "a short-hand term referring to same-sex (homosexual) versus other-sex (heterosexual) erotic preference, particularly where that becomes a basis for some ratified social identity such as 'gay man' or 'lesbian'" (Cameron & Kulick, 2003: 7). In short, however, sexuality can be defined as an "umbrella term" (Milani, 2017: 404), which "encompasses both sexual identity and erotic" (Queen, 2014: 204). Although much of the research on language and sexuality focuses on the aspect of sexual identity, the field cannot be limited to such (Kulick, 2000: 272).

The dimensions of heterosexual sexuality and perceptions of sexual roles are as much tied to sexual identity as they are to eroticism. This approach demonstrates where predisposition to stereotypical thinking encroaches on the public naming of actors in sexual relations. There do exist sexist stereotypical differences between male and female sexuality in the heteronormative binary perspective, which is the most pertinent to the discussion of the rape of women by men.

One of the key ties between gender and sexuality lies in the fact that certain scripts are ascribed to men and women in heteronormative contexts, namely sexual scripts. Cameron (2005: 484) brings to light the changing nature of approaches to gender and sexuality, emphasizing the now-default social constructionist approach to gender studies that came with the second wave of feminism (or what she calls "modern").

Cameron (*ibid.*: 484) highlights the differences between the second and third ("postmodern") waves in feminism and their descriptions of gender and its socialization, stating that while in the second wave, gender was grounded in sex, the third wave sees gender as "produced in specific contexts and 'communities of practice', in relation to social arrangements" and that the patterns are not necessarily "universal", as previously assumed. Gendered constructs become sexual constructs in ideologies that subsume heteronormative thought on where gendered roles in sexual interaction are concerned.

Sexual script theory

Although Giddens (1992: 1) has claimed a sexual revolution where the relaxation of attitudes is concerned, it is important to bear in mind that cultural scripts greatly determine stereotypes and ideologies about gender roles in sexual interaction. Sexual script theory is predominantly associated with the work of Gagnon and Simon (1973, 1984, 1986), and has been used as a method of qualifying the sequences present in sexual encounters, the gendered sexual interaction that takes place in heterosexual sexual interaction, flirting between heterosexual pairs and members of the LGBTQ+ community, as well as in explaining and analyzing rape. As can be read in the literature, *sexual cultural scripts* are not synonymous with actual sexual behavior (*ibid.*). These are, as Simon and Gagnon (1984: 53) put it, a means of seeing how "the enactment of virtually all roles must either directly or indirectly reflect the contents of appropriate cultural scenarios. These cultural scenarios are rarely entirely predictive of actual behavior, and they are generally too abstract to be applied in all circumstances."

What sexual script theorists (cf. Simon & Gagnon, 1986) argue is that cultural norms regarding sexuality provide social information about the behaviors of people in romantic and sexual relationships (Seabrook et al., 2017). Sexual script theory is attractive to social research because it presents the perception of sexual encounters and situations as being *learned* rather than innate or related to biology (Frith & Kitzinger, 2001: 210). Because "scripts are involved in learning the meaning of internal states, organizing the sequencing of specifically sexual acts, decoding novel situations, setting the limits on sexual responses and linking meanings from nonsexual aspects of life to specifically sexual experience" (Gagnon & Simon, 1973: 17), they must be considered in the way that they shape discourses on sexuality.

If sexuality is considered a mechanism of social control over the female body—in a similar way to that of the one via which advertising in the fashion industry functions, in the sense that it acts as a panoptic mechanism of control over the women's body (Berger, 1972; Acker, 2000; Majer, 2016)—the question of teaching to abstain from sexual intercourse also plays a role in structuring the way sexual experience is learned and perceived.

It is sexual scripts that are responsible for certain perceptions of sexuality and what it is that constitutes a sexual encounter. Frith and Kitzinger (2001: 210) state that "according to the theory, these culturally available scripts are adapted by individuals to particular interpersonal contexts and are also modified and internalized as 'intrapsychic scripts.'" Sexual scripts that we are used to sexually abiding by, implicate that female sexuality is taboo (Masters et al., 1995; Stephens & Phillips, 2003; Markle, 2008). These ideas contribute to internalized notions that tend towards women and girls not exploring their sexuality and also work as scripts that are followed as being thought of as proper or right (Cameron & Kulick, 2003: 34). The fact that these scripts are so socially and culturally engrained makes them difficult to abolish, thus making the argument against them, as well as against consciousness-raising on the subject of women's sexuality and sexual aggression as being more subversive all the more pertinent.

Sexual scripts are important in understanding why rape victim blaming occurs, and why the problem of sexual crime is oftentimes not treated with the severity that it should be (Ryan, 2011). The male aggression that is associated with masculinity is derived from western scripts regarding male sexuality (Simon & Gagnon, 1986; Kulick, 2000; Frith & Kitzinger, 2001). Because scripts are seen as offering a metaphor to conceptualize the ways humans produce behavior in social life, it becomes obvious that such human-made notions help us to file away certain acts and behaviors, thus making them easier to understand and explain (Wiederman, 2015: 7).

Giddens (1992) states that it is abnormal for the literature that is targeted at male readers to mention the aspect of love as a crucial component in discussions of intimacy, thus male sexuality tends towards a bias which leaves the male image as bereft of emotional attachment to the object of desire. Apart from this, Giddens (*ibid.*: 15) states that the question of gender in the case of male sexuality was also rarely brought up as part of an entire sexual makeup, leaving behind only room for "digression" on the intricate state of male sexuality.

In much of the literature regarding male sexuality, a consensus has been reached that gender roles play an extensive role in the formulation of sexual identities (Kowalski & Scheitle, 2020). Where moving away from essentialist assumptions has gained dominance in the sphere of social study on sexuality, social constructionism has made headway and become the domineering window into modern analyses of sex (Philaretou & Allen, 2001; Parker & Gagnon 2013). Male sexuality has, in particular, been investigated from the point of view of power structure and dominance theories that attempt to demolish the essentialist leanings towards male sexual dominance as having to do with the beginning of heterosexual sexual act as beginning with erection and ending in ejaculation (Philaretou & Allen, 2001: 303). This fact has bearings on the sexual behavior of men, and what they expect from themselves in situations of sexual encounter:

> Essentialist sexual scripting is responsible for generating considerable sexual anxiety in those men who pursue the idealized and unrealistic masculine standard of ultimate male sexual performance and satisfaction—only to find themselves relegated to constant sexual anxiety and deprivation. This also affects those females who actualize their sexual desires by going against essentialist female prescriptions for sexual prudence and containment
>
> (*ibid.*: 304)

Male sexuality is, in effect, a socially constructed notion derived from culturally engrained ideas that men are inherently slaves to their sexuality. This provides for ideas which force men into thinking of any other type of sexual behavior as going against the grain of masculine sexuality. Female sexuality on the other hand, as stated in previous chapter, abides by rules which place women into submissive roles of the docile other in stereotypical situations of sexual encounter (Brannon, 2002).

Many of the studies on masculinity and sexuality carried out over the decades have contested the nature of male dominance and aggression in sexuality (Sanday, 1981; Dworkin, & O'Sullivan, 2005; Kimmel, 2007; Murray, 2018). This, however, also places expectations on men where sexual performance is concerned, as they are more likely expected to perform sexually than women (Barlow, 1986; Fergus et al., 2002; Young & Penhollow, 2004; Groes-Green, 2009). The question is, then, how do expectations of male sexual performance impact the social expectations regarding male sexuality on the whole, and do they?

Pryor (1987) brought attention to the gravity of sexual harassment as a social issue, with three studies that demonstrated male proclivities towards the sexual harassment of women and its correlations with the acceptance of men as sexually aggressive subjects. The research of the 1980s created the cusp of studies on the nature of sexual harassment, with discoveries that, among others, 95% of women in the US navy experienced some form of sexual harassment (Reily, 1980; LeardMann et al., 2013).

The knowledge of what scripts surround male sexuality, here viewed as universal to both of the cultural contexts discussed in this work, aids in the understanding of how victim blaming in the case of the female victim of rape is linguistically formed.

Although Foucault (1980, 1985, 1986) claimed that there is much repression tied to female sexuality, derived from attitudes of the nineteenth century, Giddens (*ibid.*, 1992; Cook, 2005) argued that the sexual revolution of his time brought about abundant change. He argues that there is a difference in female attitudes to sex which have accompanied the introduction and more prevalent use of contraception, for one. This allowed women's fear of becoming pregnant and the naturally subsequent fear of death at childbirth, to wane, and for women to take control of their sexuality, leaving room for sexual liberation and emancipation in the discourse of the time (Giddens, 1992: 42; Hekma & Giami, 2014).

Nonetheless, the question of the subordination of women is one that revolves around, and is intertwined with, sexuality, for the division of gender roles has as much repercussion on female sexuality as it does on opportunities in the social and career-oriented sphere. Even the question of women's sexuality after the sexual revolution began to revolve around the female being unable to easily reach orgasm, contrary to men, which explains the socially situated and perceived need for a woman to fake an orgasm on account of her partner's ego.

As far as cultural scripts are concerned, one pattern that is reproduced is the one that says that "women who initiate courtship are seen as sexually available, whereas men who fail to pursue courtship opportunities are questioned about their masculinity and/or sexual orientation" (Seal & Erhardt, 2003: 375).

> But if by believing that women are by nature less violent, we reinforce the sex roles that have held women down for so long, then perhaps it is time to dare to admit that some of the sex-role mythology is in fact true and to insist that the qualities attributed to women (specifically empathy, nurturance and cooperativeness) be affirmed as human qualities capable of cultivation by men even if denied them by nature.
>
> (Gearhart, 1982: 271)

Gearhart (*ibid.*) claims that it is difficult to turn away from the fact that expectations of men and women are explained away by the belief in nurture, rather than nature. This claim facilitates the discussion of the multifaceted phenomenon of human sexuality. With the introduction of common ideologies regarding sexuality as beholden to social constructionism, a change has come about, propelled by the many movements all over the world that exist to combat stereotypes which keep gender in the rigid confines of limitation.

When it comes to female docility in sexual relationships, a woman's virginity is still seen as a kind of capital in maintaining a romantic relationship with a man into marriage (Abraham, 2002). Although, as Giddens (1992) points out, chastity is not as common a practice among women as it once was, and men also express approval at a woman's having had sexual experience as enriching of the relationship, virginity is still somewhat of a commodity.

The literature has shown that stereotypes regarding female sexuality are very much still alive and that "girls are [still] careful to guard their virginity and 'honor', as, according to some of them 'anything can happen' before marriage" (Abraham, 2002: 367). This type of sexual behavior contrasts greatly with another image of women in heterosexual relationships, that of the initiator of sexual contact and the sexually experienced woman, which Giddens (1992) described as a more common occurrence among women in the twentieth century.

Numerous studies have shown that the sexual dynamics discussed result "from the passivity women can experience through being positioned in a discourse of heterosexual feminine sexuality in general," meaning that the modern discourses on sex declare women as more passive actors (Gavey & McPhillips, 1999: 349).

Heterosexual scripts and adherence to gender stereotypes

It has been argued that in modern society, and with the dawn of social constructionist theory, "our view of male power has grown out of research on young people's accounts of their sexuality and heterosexual practices" (Holland et al., 1998: 1). The male sexual role is one that has not seen much change in terms of media representation and is a subject that has been under feminist investigation since the 1970s (Edwards, 1987). According to script theory, men experience more social pressure to dominate in sexual interaction than do women (Holland et al., 1998). The theory that revolves around the social construction of sexuality posits that sexual knowledge is gendered, gender paradigms control notions of sexual dominance, power and control and that real-life sexual beliefs and practices are embedded in patriarchal perspectives about sex (*ibid.*).

When viewing heterosexual sexual scripts, which constitute the most socially engrained scripts in today's sexual culture, one can perceive the gap in stereotypical sexual roles. This stereotypical approach to sexuality, and what is considered feminine or masculine where cultural pressures are concerned, has much to do with the socially engrained, perceived role of women in heterosexual sexual relationships.

To illustrate this fact, Gavey and McPhillips (1999) carried out a study on women's assertiveness and condom application in contexts of sexual intercourse. They discovered that in heterosexual sexual encounters, women who were usually "assertive and committed to sexual equality" have a tendency to passively express the "initiation of condom use" (*ibid.*: 349–350; Brodsky, 2017). The issue here is that women's passivity is taken to be so matter-of-fact that even the discourses which normalize attitudes that eventually act in a victim-blaming manner go unnoticed in the trenches of their structure. Of course, understandings of sexuality are culturally conditioned, and this work being a cultural comparison of the United States and Poland, the background of sexuality in both cultures must be given.

Sexual scripts and communication

One approach to the role of sexual scripts in sexual assault is that "sexual scripts that position men as the aggressors and women as reluctant, passive recipients of sexual activity encourage divergent communication patterns in sexual encounters" (Muehlenhard & Rodgers, 1998: 444). In the case of women's behavior in sexual settings, it is said that "the traditional sexual script perpetuates the belief that women's refusals of sexual advances are often insincere and need not be taken seriously" (*ibid.*).

Because sexual communication is "indirect, subtle, complex, and shaped by gendered norms for interaction, genuine miscommunication does take place" (Crawford, 1995: 108), however, this approach to the linguistic aspect of gendered interaction and understanding is here viewed as an approach which simply explains away the issue. Although miscommunication theory does make an attempt to highlight gendered issues surrounding the question of rape, by attributing language and communication style differences to the occurrence of rape, the male and female binary retains its structured power (cf. Chapter 3 for more on the linguistic theory of miscommunication where it accounts for the explanation of rape).The sexual behavior of women as it is portrayed and interpreted as naturally or traditionally submissive is a result of learned behavior rather than innate (Ward, 2002, 2003). This can also be seen as reflected in the language which is used to understand situations of sexual encounters (within this, provision of consent or lack thereof, and rape). These scripts are also considered similar in both the United States and Poland, on the basis of the rather universal nature of sexual scripts in developing societies (Gagnon & Simon, 2017).

Sexuality in the United States

Although it may be claimed that many questions of sexuality are universal, the reason for choosing the western context is that the rape cases which are subject to analysis are, in large part, cases that reside in the U.S. (with the other half being Polish cases). The discussion above concerns the sexual revolution of the West, however, for the purpose of the discussion presented, a comparison needs to be made between the American and Polish contexts (i.e., in Chapter 4).

The western context is known for being overly-saturated with sex, whether in cinema, television, advertising, or pictographic and semiotic representation (Tyler, 2011; Gagnon & Simon, 2017). Sexuality studies in the disciplines of sociology and psychology have dealt with a plethora of subjects in the US context, including queerness and its many faces (Gamson & Moon, 2004; Andrucki & Elder, 2007; Alberti & Back Danielsson, 2014; Worthen, 2021), geography (Hubbard et al., 2015), the intersectionality of race, feminism, sexuality and polyamory (Crenshaw, 1989, 1991; Noël, 2006; Nash, 2014), among others. Of course, it is important to highlight the importance of feminist work done in the field of sexuality studies.

Where much feminist work in sexuality studies looks at the more passive and submissive roles that women are placed in, it is important to remember that such an approach is also dictated by ideological (and gendered) attitudes to sexuality. Although it has been discovered that many of the cultural scripts that place women in a role leading to subversive attitudes towards sexuality—which can be read as breaking out of a shell of repression—this is not universal to all cultural contexts. As stated earlier, the aims of this work regard the demonstration of how binding sexist and patriarchal ideologies are in their cultural enactment in American and Polish settings (Bartky, 1997); it goes without saying that although I believe such discourses to be dominant, I acknowledge that they are not universal.

Sexuality in Poland

The academic attention that the question of sexuality has received in Poland is on the rise, however from the perspective of the social sciences, it is also inspired by western studies (Slany et al., 2011). Public attitudes towards sexuality, however, still remain partially reluctant to enter the more open discussion that the West has brought in (Kościańska, 2017). Recent papers have been written on the significance of sexuality in the pre-war and post-war periods, including gay and lesbian movements of the times (Graff, 2006; Chetaille, 2016), demonstrating the view of an increasing necessity to discuss the various topics encompassed by the umbrella term that is "sexuality".

Negative sexuality (meaning that sexuality is not considered part of national or personal identity) is described by some as the passive demeanor of Poles towards sexuality (Płonecka, 2017). Kościańska (2017: 84–87) discusses the bias surrounding perceptions of the negative effects of masturbation among men and boys; this is an example of how such issues related to sex are "severely inhibited by strong taboos surrounding sex and sexuality in Poland" (*ibid.*: 146). This has also been discussed as a prelude to the necessity for a more enhanced sexual education program in Poland (Graff & Korolczuk, 2017), as the sexual education received by most Poles in that respect differs greatly from that of many (but not all) students in the United States (*ibid.*).

From sex to sexual crime

The main preoccupation of the traditional feminist movement, with concern to sex, had to do with the high rate of sexual crime committed against women, as well as the will of political parties and regimes to control female sexuality and reproductive rights through the axing of rights to safe abortion. Sexology has been criticized by feminist activists and scholars for failing to recognize the risk-related aspects of sex (Tiefer, 1994; Heise, 1995; Irvine, 2005; Machin & Thornborrow, 2006). This side of sex and sexuality is what a majority of heterosexual women are faced with, pertaining to detrimental social problems like as abuse, rape, Sexually Transmitted Infections (STIs), unwanted pregnancy and/or humiliation (Irvine,

2005). The literature additionally points out that "none of the breakthrough studies that first documented the pervasiveness of non-consensual sex came from mainstream research," meaning that it was not necessarily made available to the general public (Heise, 2007: 276). This leaves little real room to actually combat the issue.

The necessity of studying sexual crime from a linguistic perspective is not required only in the context of the far West, but also in Europe, as it should be considered a universal issue seated in the normalization of hegemonic discourses in cultures that demonstrate a cognitive bias against subjects of sexuality. This is why the analytical aspects of the work focus on the subject of sexual assault and the linguistic representations which are within the discursive practices that make up much of its social structuring (cf. Chapter 3).

Important aspects of sexual crime

The following sections will discuss the definition of rape, the idea of the age of consent, rape typologies, hegemony as it relates to sexual aggression in particular, as well as the rape myths that have so far been enumerated in the literature (Burt & Albin, 1981; Burt, 1980, 1998; Bohner et al. 2002; Franiuk et al., 2008; Łyś, 2015).

Another point worth mentioning, being one that is referred to in legal definitions of rape and other forms of sexual assault or aggression, is that of the *age of consent.*[33]The age of consent is defined in the legal dictionary as "the age at which a person may marry without parental approval" and "the age at which a female is legally capable of agreeing to sexual intercourse, so that a male who engages in sex with her cannot be prosecuted for Statutory Rape" (*West's Encyclopedia of American Law*, 2nd ed. 2005: accessed online).

The age of consent varies from country to country, and state by state in the United States, ranging from the age of 12 to the age of 19, with the age of consent at 16 the most commonly acknowledged legal age of consent (Sutherland, 2003). The close-in-age exemption, which is commonly known as "Romeo and Juliet laws" in the US, is taken into account when two partners are close in age and one of them is under the legal age of consent. In Poland, there has been no close-in-age exemption law put into effect (*ibid.*). The age of consent in Poland is currently 15 (Dziewanowska, 2014).

Rape in the context of the United States

Early nineteenth-century definitions of rape were such that the crime did not work in favor of married women or women of color (Freedman, 2012). The definition

33 Polish: *wiek zgody*

of rape provided then was "(1) the carnal knowledge of a woman by a man when achieved by force and against her will by a man who was not her husband, (2) any sexual activity with a child under age ten" (Kalinski, 2016: online).[34] These definitions saw women as property, essentially objectifying them. Even at the dawn of the sexual revolution, it was men who wanted sex, and women who gave it (Cameron & Kulick, 2003; Gavey, 2005: 1), continuing the stream of passivity on the part of the female. When the need for attention towards sexual liberation and non-committal sexual interaction came around, a new "era of sexual permissiveness" (*ibid.*) occurred and the idea that "a woman should never turn down her husband on appropriate occasions simply because she has no yearning for sex" (Eichenlaub, 1961; *ibid.*) began to recede in popularity.

It is important to acknowledge both the prevalence and the pervasive nature of the problem, and that it has an effect on women and men of all race, color, background, sexual orientation and social class. The work of feminist scholars such as Dworkin (1987) and MacKinnon (1983, 2016) are historically at the forefront of a shifting approach to women's sexuality and the war on rape. As a result, more attention has been drawn to the subtleties involved in acknowledging the grand scale of the issue of sexual assault and sexual harassment against women in various disciplines, as well as in culture. In the US, an updated definition of rape has been provided by the Department of Justice, as of January 6, 2012:

> The penetration, no matter how slight, of the vagina or anus with any body part or object, or oral penetration by a sex organ of another person, without the consent of the victim.
>
> (Source: https://www.justice.gov/archives/opa/blog/updated-definition-rape)[35]

The definition previously provided, and which had not been changed or modified since the year 1927, was considered outdated and much too narrow, as it only considered the penetration of a female victim by a male perpetrator[36] as constituting the act of rape (The United States Department of Justice: online). The 1970s saw the criminalization of marital rape in the United States, ending with its being a penal offense in all fifty states by 1993, and most states differed in the ways that marital and non-marital rape were penalized (Russell 1990; Bergen, 1996; Bennice & Resick, 2003). Marital rape exemption, which provides "legal immunity to a

34 http://gender.stanford.edu/news/2016/changing-definitions-rape-and-citizenship

35 Accessed on 8/11/2017, 7:18pm

36 "The carnal knowledge of a female, forcibly and against her will" (Department of Justice: online)

man who forcibly sexually assaults his wife" has been legally recognized in some cultures and countries (Pracher, 1981: 717).

Acquaintance rape in the United States

Acknowledging date rape and acquaintance rape as valid in light of sexual assault consciousness-raising was a game changer in the movement for women's rights and equality. Koss's (1988) work provided an even broader definition of rape, which constitutes the first national study on that kind of sexual assault. Even so, victims of acquaintance rape are more likely to be blamed than victims of rape committed by a stranger (Pollard, 1992). The reason for my singling out date rape here is that it has been seen as a wide-spread social problem in the United States for several decades now, but has received much less attention in Poland. Much of the reports on rape in the United States discuss this problem specifically, and this is where much of the victim blaming occurs (Masser et al., 2010).

Sampson (2003) has provided a list of different kinds of acquaintance rape, including *date rape, rape in a non-party/non-date situation, party rape,* and *rape by a former or current intimate* partner, as well as rape by a person known to the victim. The Legal Information Institute provides the following definition for acquaintance rape against women, as of June 2020:

> the phenomenon where the woman was forced to have sexual intercourse by a male acquaintance during a voluntary social engagement. It is not a new phenomenon. In fact, more than half of all rapes are committed by male relatives, current or former husbands, boyfriends, or lovers. During a date-rape trial, the biggest dispute is whether the alleged victim has actually consented. Therefore, evidence of prior sexual conduct between the alleged victim and the accused is especially important.
>
> Several drugs are considered "date rape" drugs. One powerful and potent drug is Rohypnol. This drug is not legally manufactured or approved for use in the United States. Another commonly used date rape drug is Gamma-Hydroxybutyrate (GHB). It is also illegal in the United States. Ketamine, or "Special K," "OK," "KO," "Super K," "Vitamin K," "Kid Rock," and "Kit Kat." is legally sold as a veterinary sedative or hospital anesthesia. Evidence of date rape drugs in the victim's system would have been powerful evidence of the defendant's guilt.
>
> (https://www.law.cornell.edu/wex/date_rape)

Many times, this type of rape goes unreported, it is because cultural rape scripts make it difficult to recognize certain situations, causing the questioning of the validity of violation on the part of the victim (Turchik et al., 2009; Raphael, 2013: 101–123). The existence of websites such as falserapesociety.com, also insinuative of disregard of the validity of a woman's claim to having been raped, represents a discourse of public doubt concerning a rape victim's credibility. The media plays an evident role in the maintenance of the belief that many rape claims are false, with columns published on why it is that those who "cry rape" should not always be believed (Raphael, 2013: 114–115).

The subject of acquaintance rape is of extreme importance in the American literature on rape, and has been tied to the question of sexual consent (Lyden, 2007; Friedman & Valenti, 2008; Jozkowski & Peterson, 2013; Willis & Jozkowski, 2019). One such research project attempted to determine what exactly correlates with attitudes to sexual consent and acquaintance rape. Humphreys' (2004, 2007) studies of sexual consent among college students have demonstrated a need for a more comprehensive discussion on what constitutes sexual consent.[37]

Rape in the Polish context

Some work has been done with regard to defining and typing different kinds of rape in the Polish context, namely by Sabat (2013).[38] The author (*ibid.*) provides a typology of rape, however, she fails to recognize date rape as a separate category of rape among those listed, despite the fact that date rape is present in typologies of rape by other researchers in the field (Cowan, 2000). Sabat's (2013) typology includes but is not limited to, the following types of rape: incestuous rape, gang rape, rape while sleeping, rape by sodomization, and rape during war.

As a category within the typology of rape, marital rape was first widely recognized in Poland in the year 1997 (Dąbrowska, Z., 2001). Since then, the unlawful initiation of sexual activity against a woman's will by her husband has been the subject of much discussion (*ibid.*). Other definitions within the same typology, including incestuous rape, gang rape, isolated rape, and war rape,[39] have been provided, however, they will not be discussed in depth here.

---

37 In his paper, Humphreys (2007: 310) has revealed the complex nature of sexual consent in heterosexual sexual interaction and how data constituents, such as gender and relationship history, influenced the interpretation of sexual consent in the three vignettes he provided. In none of the vignettes did the woman verbally express sexual refusal, i.e., by saying "no", but rather gave signals, such as "unenthusiastically kissing" her partner back. The respondents were to provide answers whether or not they believe that the actors consented to sexual activity, and whether or not the indications were clear.

38 This includes the organizing of the conference *Kobieta...Bezpieczna*, which covers issues of aggression against women in Poland.

39 Polish: *gwałt kazirodczy, gwałt zbiorowy, gwałt indywidualny* and *gwałt wojenny*.

One salient difference between the American and Polish contexts is the fact that there is yet more research to be done on the subject of acquaintance rape in any setting (Piotrowska & Synkiewicz, 2011; Szczucki, 2011). The research on acquaintance rape (more commonly known as date rape) has garnered much attention in the United States, but lacks in-depth discussion in the cultural contexts of Eastern Europe. However, the fact that the issue of sexual violence against women itself, in both the American and Polish cultural contexts, is seeing increasing recognition speaks volumes about the way it is regarded on the whole.

The Polish linguistic perspective of sexual aggression and its construction has not received as much attention in the literature as in the context of the United States. Piotrowska and Synkiewicz (2011: 12) highlight the estimated number of rapes that go unreported, approximating the numbers to be similar to those represented in studies carried out in the context of Canada (*ibid.*).

In March 2021 Poland's Left-Wing Party "Lewica" put forth a project demanding that the aspect of sexual refusal that does not include physical force be taken into the equation. The current legal definition of rape in the Polish executive penal code[40] is as follows:

> Whoever, by force, illegal threat or deceit subjects another person to sexual intercourse shall be subject to the penalty of the deprivation of liberty for a term of between 2 and 12 years.
>
> *Legal provisions on protection orders*
> See Criminal Code, Articles 39 and 41a
>
> *Legal Source*
> Criminal Code, Article 197
>
> ***Observations***
> *Special circumstances of rape (in the same legal provision):*
>
> If the perpetrator, in the manner specified in § 1, makes another person submit to other sexual act or to perform such an act, he shall be subject to the penalty of the deprivation of liberty for a term of between 6 months and 8 years.
>
> If the perpetrator commits the rape 1) in common with another person, 2) against a minor under 15 years of age, 3) against an ascendant, descendant, or a person being adopted, or brother or sister, he shall be subject to the penalty of deprivation of liberty for a minimum term of 3 years.

40 Kodeks karny wykonawczy

If the perpetrator of the crime specified in § 1—3 acts with particular cruelty, he shall be subject to the penalty of deprivation of liberty for a minimum term of 5 years.[41]

(Translation by the European Institute for Gender)

Twelve studies on sexual victimization in Poland have been identified, with 10 of them on the sexual victimization of both men and women (Łukaszek, 2013).[42] Two studies regarding victimization have been carried out on women only (Gruszczyńska, 2007; Czapska et al., 2012). Other studies discuss myths surrounding rape in the context of Poland, including those regarding prostitution and the culturally-seated and sex work-phobic notion that a female prostitute may not be raped because rape is many times assumed to be automatically written into her contract (Welskop, 2009).

In addition to this research, Kwiatkowska (1998, 2013) investigated correlations between aggression and gender stereotypes, and in later work scrutinized biased and gendered notions in language with regard to gendered domestic violence in the Polish context. Her work (*ibid.*) has shown that a cultural dichotomy of gender stereotypes abides by the social stereotype that "if women are not ladies, then they must be sluts. If men are not gentlemen, then they must be brutes" (Kwiatkowska, A., 2013: 5). Such a paradoxical split is visible in the sexual scripts that have become rather illegible in social discourse through the embedding and normalization of such dichotomies that do collateral damage which goes uncommented

41 Art. 197 (SOURCE: http://eige.europa.eu)
§ 1. Kto przemocą, groźbą bezprawną lub podstępem doprowadza inną osobę do obcowania płciowego, podlega karze pozbawienia wolności od lat 2 do 12.
§ 2. Jeżeli sprawca, w sposób określony w § 1, doprowadza inną osobę do poddania się innej czynności seksualnej albo wykonania takiej czynności, podlega karze pozbawienia wolności od 6 miesięcy do lat 8.
§ 3. Jeżeli sprawca dopuszcza się zgwałcenia:
wspólnie z inną osobą,
wobec małoletniego poniżej lat 15,
wobec wstępnego, zstępnego, przysposobionego, przysposabiającego, brata lub siostry, podlega karze pozbawienia wolności na czas nie krótszy od lat 3.
§ 4. Jeśli sprawca czynu określonego w § 1–3 działa ze szczególnym okrucieństwem, podlega karze pozbawienia wolności na czas nie krótszy od lat 5.

42 The research here discussed was carried out on cis-men and cis-women, not on individuals belonging to the Polish transgender population (Dębski, 2011; Public Opinion Research Center [Centrum Badania Opinii Społecznej], 2007; Doroszewicz & Forbes, 2008; Dünkel et al., 2006; Gutkowska, 2011; The Institute of Health Psychology [Instytut Psychologii Zdrowia] 2011; Izdebski, 2012; Krahé et al., 2015; Tomaszewska & Krahé, 2018)

in many cases. The discussion of rape culture as a derivative of stereotyping is nothing new in the field of feminist discourse, but little has been said of the direct effect that discourses that reproduce stereotypes have on integrated ideologically based, collective social thinking (van Dijk 1998; 2006).

Kościańska's (2014, 2021) work has focused on expert discourse in sexology and its focus on socio-cultural differences between men and women. She (*ibid.*) brings attention to gender stereotypes and their influence on the way that (hetero)-sexual encounters are seen. In her anthropological analysis, she concentrates on how the victims of rape are perceived in the expert eye and finds that there is a binary that occurs. The first approach is that of rape as a monstrous crime, which should be addressed as soon as it happens, and the second addresses the perception of the victim as inducing her own rape—i.e., as being at fault in some way (*ibid.*: 156–157).

Kwiatkowska (2013: 4) confirms that stereotypes about gender are still held to a high degree in Polish society and culture, even today (Kościańska, 2015). She (*ibid.*) claims the following:

> [T]he idealized image (mostly held by women) of men as respectable family fathers and gentlemen, and the equally idealized image (mostly held by men) of women as caring mothers and elegant ladies is the reason why domestic violence is seen only in circumstances where these ideals are not met, namely in marginalized environments and among people who are less educated and relatively poor.

It is made clear that it is the link between patriarchal gender ideologies and ideas about violence towards women that does not bring attention to the severity of the problem of male violence against women.

Understanding hegemony in the case of sexual aggression in the United States

In the study of feminist work theory, by taking Henley's (1975) *Standpoint Theory* perspective into account, patriarchal norms reveal the marginalization of women, as well as their limited access to knowledge as cultural and linguistic capital (Bourdieu, 1986; Simpson & Mayr, 2010). With that in mind, recognizing the hegemonic sources present in patriarchal systems is important in feminist analyses, as they argue that any kind of female marginalization is caused by dominant patriarchal ideologies. *Hegemony*, which is control by consent rather than control by force (Gramsci, 1971), makes for an even more tedious task of bringing attention to the existence of patriarchal norms (Wetherell & Edley, 1999).

Hegemony—or rather the concept of hegemonic masculinity—works on the bases of hierarchies that are socially bound and maintained through media messages more than through any other means, and can easily be applied to the context of sexuality. When considering the predominance of patriarchy and the way that it backgrounds institutionalized and collective thought, the fact that "male dominance is sexual" begins to come full circle with the realities of any form of sexual aggression (MacKinnon, 1989: 315).

What MacKinnon (1989: 316) clarifies as being a blurred line over which male aggression transgresses in its supposedly natural dominance over women is that "the male sexual role (…) centers on aggressive intrusion on those with less power." Her discussion of male sexual aggression sees it as a phenomenon socialized through the existence and promotion of pornographic material which promotes the aggressive behavior that places women in a sexually inferior position. This sexual inferiority felt by many women, she argues, is wrought with distress and instills fear in them. This is an issue that brings to light the problematic nature of patriarchal structures in society. There has been a link made throughout scholarly feminist work that recognizes a correlation between pornography and *hegemonic masculinity* as a structure (Peterson, 2015).

Hegemonic masculinity, a term first proposed by Connell (1982, 1983, 1986, 2005), is a concept based in patriarchal thought, which promotes the hyper-masculine male as a power source, as encompassing an ideal masculinity, and is thought by feminist scholars to be at work in the subordination of women. The notion of hegemonic masculinity was developed in the 1970s and discussed as idealized in the United States (Connell & Messerschmidt, 2005; Nylund, 2007). Because hegemony is linked to power through ideologies and institutionalized thought, it is more subtle in its work, which is where CDA becomes a useful tool in picking out where hierarchies in gendered discourse (both overt and covert) take place.

Some studies, which have shown that hegemonic masculinity is specifically linked to sexual aggression, demonstrate that the socialization of a certain kind of masculinity advocates and even pressurizes boys and men to act in a more sexually aggravated manner to be perceived as a "real man" (Cowburn & Dominelli, 2003; Robinson, 2006). Robinson's (2006) paper explores the relationship between ideas of dominant masculinities and adolescent male tendencies towards sexually aggressive behavior aimed at female peers. It was pointed out there that not only is there an obvious link between a heterosexual, hegemonic masculine structure, popularity in schools and sexual harassment, but that sexual harassment is an integral tool in normalizing hegemonic masculinity and creating "hegemonic heterosexual masculine identities" (*ibid.*: 19).

Hegemonic discourse: Polish society and violence as related to gender stereotypes

The prevalence of violence is usually underestimated, as Kwiatkowska (2013) points out in her paper, and in the case of domestic violence, alcohol abuse is often found to be the blame (*ibid.*; Roszak 2008). In studying family violence in Poland, Kwiatkowska (1998: 129) found that "violence is determined by culturally and socially learned cognitive schemata such as gender stereotypes," adding that stereotypes of hegemonic masculinity are particularly salient in Polish culture and the discourse that reflects it.

Much empirical study has been carried out on violence in Poland, as well as its liaison with gendered relations (male and female—particularly in the context of male violence towards women as gendered violence), as well as its tie to stereotypical ideals of masculinity (machismo) in Poland (Makara-Studzińska et al., 2005; Nowakowska 2008; Sygit & Ossowski, 2008; Chmura-Rutkowska, 2012; Kwiatkowska, 2013; Zalewska, 2013; Kościańska, 2015). The studies carried out on the correlation between gender, violence and/or aggression have shown the prevalence of male violence over female violence be it physical or sexual (*ibid.*).

Such cultural aspects are important in determining the cause of beliefs surrounding violence and aggression. Ideologies surrounding violence and blame in criminal situations have been attributed to several theories that deal with the issue, namely victim blaming, secondary victimization, and attribution theory.

Victim blaming, secondary victimization and attribution theory

One of the key notions tied to acts of negative perceptions of victims of a rape (in this case, female victims) is what Williams (1984: 67) termed *secondary victimization*, in which a victim of the primary experience of rape "can be further victimized by negative and judgmental reactions following the rape incident, which may prompt feelings of guilt or shame *on the part of the victims*" regarding their role in the crime (*ibid.*). This notion is important in understanding how such victimization arises discursively (cf. Chapters 6 and 7).

Another theory which takes social biases into consideration is *attribution theory*, which has looked into attributions of rape victims by others and shown that women who are the victim of a rape tend to be judged by others as being responsible for what happened to them (Grubb & Turner 2012).

Attribution in attribution theory "relates to the way that individuals allocate or attribute responsibility to individual actors within a scenario" (*ibid.*: 444). What research has shown is that such processes of attributing blame or sympathizing with a victim in a crime are influenced by various cognitive and motivational biases which in turn result in an interpretation of the event that tends to be less factual in nature. It is believed that attribution is impacted by cultural and personal differences (Maddux & Yuki, 2006).

Although acquaintance rape has been discovered to generate higher levels of blame attribution (Personn et al., 2018), the question of where victim blaming occurs is of general importance to this work, considering all types of rape to investigate the way that victim blaming takes place in the American and Polish cultural contexts on a discursive basis. Blame attribution in the case of rape has been predominantly linked with aggressively sexist attitudes (*ibid.*). On the whole, attribution theory has provided researchers with a basis to investigate the way that victims of a crime are socially perceived, in this case, the victims of rape and will be used as a guiding theoretical frame for the critical linguistic investigation of victim blaming in this work, as it forms the cusp of where the boundaries of evaluative discursive behaviors are (cf. Chapters 6 and 7).

Rape myths

Surrounding the problem of sexual aggression are certain socially-influenced discourses that tend to be false assumptions and have a tendency of placing the victim of such a crime as being to blame. In some cultures, rape is justified as a natural consequence of the provocative behavior of a woman and strong male sexual desire, which is a claim that draws on the common rape myth that women provoke men to rape them (Burt, 1980). In short, *rape myths* "are generalized and false beliefs about sexual assault that trivialize a sexual assault or suggest that a sexual assault did not occur" (Franiuk et al., 2008: 288). Many scholars studying gender and sexual aggression claim that "these notions also diminish the different dimensions of the realities of sexual aggression" (*ibid.*).

Such ideas build the foundation of discourses that perpetuate the idea that a victim of rape is at fault for the crime committed against her. Kościańska (2015: 169), for example, draws attention to the fact that analyses of the discourse in newspapers confirm that the provocation rape myth is one of the most prevalent, in which the female victim is exacted as the perpetrator. She also brings about claims made by famous Polish sexologists, citing authors Wisłocka and Lew-Starowicz that act as further evidence of the even professional discourses that keep rape myths in the circle of public belief (Kościańska, 2016).

In discussing consent, Lew-Starowicz (1988: 83) states that in the case of silence, a lack of refusal should naturally be read as consent and comments the unclear nature of sexual situations and whether or not they are consensual in practice. He says that "passive permission [is given] when a woman does not have any desire for the [sexual] act, but does not physically resist, which is then understood as consent"[43] and that "this type of permission raises the most doubt in a court of law. Another issue is the problem of permission in the case of gang rape, when the victim consented to have sex with one partner, but did not consent to have sex with others"[44] (Lew-Starowicz, 1988: 83). This claim, however, does not account for the linguistic understanding of the complexity of sexual consent and how it is read (cf. Chapter 3), where silence does not always mean that sexual intercourse is wanted or consensual.

(1980) famous study also pointed to a number of existing rape myths when it comes to women, and is still used as a reference in current studies on rape myth acceptance (RMA) (Frese et al., 2004; Peterson & Muehlenhard, 2004; Suarez & Gadalla, 2010). The rape myths listed by Burt (1980: 217) include "only bad girls get raped," "any healthy woman can resist a rapist if she really wants to," "women ask to be raped," "they 'cry rape' when they've been jilted or have something to cover up," "rape is about sex," and that "rapists are self-starved or insane." Much of the literature argues that these rape myths are still prominent in today's understanding of rape and what factors lead to it (Frese et al., 2004; Peterson & Muehlenhard, 2004; Franiuk et al., 2008; Suarez & Gadalla, 2010), and I argue that such rape myths are also present in the discourses that represent actors in rape in digital comments.

It is important to note the role that discursive practices, including grammars of agency or non-agency, play in the maintenance of this kind of collective thought. Franiuk et al. (2008) examined the prevalence of rape myths in newspaper headlines as a way of retrieving information about attitudes people have about rape. They found that media sources work to cement existing notions that a sexually active woman, with a history of multiple sexual partners, for example, should not be altogether believed when claiming having been sexually assaulted or violated.

The importance of rape myths in the present analysis, as well as to the area of linguistic study regarding rape is in investigating rape myths as a part of the

43 „przyzwolenie bierne, kiedy kobieta nie pragnie aktu, ale nie stawia oporu, co jest rozumiane jako zgodę" (Lew-Starowicz, 1988: 83). (The translation in the text is my own).

44 „Ten rodzaj przyzwolenia budzi najwięcej wątpliwości w rozprawach sądowych. Innym problemem jest sprawa przyzwolenia w aktach gwałtu zbiorowego, kiedy ofiara wyraziła zgodę na akt z jednym partnerem, ale nie wyraziła na akt z innymi." (Lew-Starowicz, 1988: 83). (The translation in the text is my own).

discourse which presupposes the acceptance of such rape myths, as well as in the implicit evaluation presented in the comments made regarding the actors. Rape myths are considered universal in the literature on the subject (Kaim, 2004; Oh & Neville, 2004; Kahlor & Morrison, 2007; Piotrowska & Synakiewicz, 2011).

Correlations between rape myths and sexual aggression in males

Malamuth and Check (1980, 1983, 1985) carried out a series of investigative studies on the correlation between men's watching of violent pornography and their belief in rape myths. Although the results of most of the studies were quite inconclusive, the conclusions that Malamuth and Check (1985) reached leaned more towards claims that supported the correlation of viewing violent pornography with the normalization of rape culture.

Naturalistic approaches, which adhere to the essentialist explanation of sexual behaviors, tend towards biological reasoning for sexual aggression in men (*ibid.*; Hanna, 1999). Malamuth (1986: 954) enumerated several correlates present in his findings and illustrated a more naturalistic approach to sexual aggression in males, which included a desire for "dominance", "hostility towards women", "antisocial personality characteristics/psychoticism", as well as "sexual experience." These were all described as essentialist in character, rather than learned expressions of sexuality.

The question of male sexual aggression and its correlates have additionally been investigated in the case of date rape (*acquaintance rape*), where findings have shown that sexually aggressive men were read as being more prone to committing sexually coercive acts, and referred to studies in which it was discovered that sexual coercion of women by men is linked to feelings of hostility towards women (Lackie & Anton, 1997). The issue of male aggression and cultural acceptance of male violence and aggression as more essentialist than culturally stemmed has to do with the ignorance regarding perceptions of masculinity and their hand in male sexual violence.[45] These ideas are still very relevant today and have been described as such in the current literature, with the context of social media making way for new categories of analysis on the issue (Rentschler, 2014; Suzuki, 2014; Keller et al., 2018; Mendes et al., 2018).

45 See Katz's *The Macho Paradox* (2006) for an expansion.

Conclusions

The notions found within this chapter have presented how gender and sexuality are viewed, and how their representations are highly dependent on one another and the scripts that accompany them. It is not without reason that the social expectations of women and men have been enumerated from a sociological overview. The gender norms and stereotypes that have been discussed throughout the chapter have great implications for the perception of rape victims, especially where the perception of women as passive actors and men as domineering are concerned. The expectations of men and women in heteronormative sexual situations, which arise from ideologies and stereotypes, are largely responsible for the discursive representation of the individuals in a situation of rape.

The reference to sexuality also draws largely on cultural and social stereotypes, including what sexual scripts ascertain as being appropriate of men and women as social actors in the realm of heterosexual sexual interactions. It is crucial to bear in mind that these scripts are also present, however not always, in the discourses on the subject of sexual aggression/assault and the actors involved, and that they contribute to blame attribution (the focus here being on rape victim blaming).

The linguistic perspective of gender and sexuality ranges from theories regarding the communication of men and women (as well as people of other genders) to discursive representations of gender and sexuality. Language plays a very important and salient role in reproducing the gender ideologies discussed in this chapter, contributing to stereotypes of gender and sexuality. The chapter that follows takes into account and discusses in depth what language has to do with both gender and sexuality and the maintenance of hegemonic patriarchal ideologies. This forms the basis of what the final analyses in chapters 6 and 7 aim to expand, in the way that discourses are most active in the maintenance of harmful ideologies regarding rape victims and offenders in such a crime, because gender and sexuality ideologies pervade social life through discourse. How they are constructed through the discursive reproduction and maintenance of gender ideologies and gender stereotypes determines how actors are perceived.

Chapter 3: Implications for discourse The intersection of ideology, gender and sexuality

Considering the social significance of the discussion of gender, sexuality, and rape as presented in the previous chapter, I would like to highlight the importance of such a discussion on the subject of gender and ideologies in discourse and how such notions impact knowledge and beliefs about social actors. The remainder of the work draws attention to the role of such discourses in informing society about what aspects of human interaction and sexuality lead to the rape of women by men, therefore making it pertinent to consider the linguistic bases, grounding, and foundations that underpin them.

Sapir and Whorf's (1921) theory of linguistic relativity views language as a determiner of cultural thought and understanding of the world. Although their theory has been criticized, its importance in modern linguistic study remains, including in questions of language and gender and their relation to society (Clarke et al., 1984; Livia & Hall, 1997; Goddard & Patterson, 2000; Crawford 2001). When trying to uncover the discursive aspects surrounding aggressive behavior and crime, in particular sexual aggression and sexual crime, it is essential to take note of the fact that ideology and stereotyping present ideas that stigmatize social groups (cf. Chapter 2). The question of how these two constructs remain a constant encumbrance on strategies of social scripting (in this case those that are gendered) should be sought out from a linguistic perspective.

This chapter investigates gender ideologies in language and discourse, and hence their pervasiveness in American and Polish cultures, and considers language and gender theories, gender categorization, as well as language and sexuality (including sexual scripts that dominate discourse regarding both gender and sexuality in a social context (Kiesling, 2011)). After the introduction of ideologies related to language, what will be discussed are the ways that existing language and gender theory (genderlect theory), and language and sexuality theories, are framed in a system of ideological beliefs concerning what constitutes "men's language", what constitutes "women's language" (upon the assumption that they exist as valid linguistic categorizations) and how these prescriptions additionally perpetuate existing stereotypes (discursive or otherwise) which normalize sexual aggression towards women, as well as the ideas that women's perceived behaviors play a role in undermining their claim of having been raped. Both English and Polish are described from the perspective of language, gender and sexuality, including the research carried out by multiple authors on the subject of euphemisms, phraseology and overall linguistic representations of sexuality and sexual intercourse.

Linguistic ideology

This work does not simply concern *ideology* (cf. Chapter 2, but rather discusses a specific type of ideology that tends to permeate everyday life, from what is heard to what is read. Linguistic ideology, language ideology, or the ideology of language (Woolard & Schieffelin, 1994: 56) become a subset under the umbrella of ideology. Defining *linguistic ideology* (akin to *language ideologies*), however, is a challenge in itself, for it is not something that has been discussed by many social scientists or linguists as of yet (Woolard, 1992; Irvine et al., 2009), and is a notion which does not simply adhere to societal boundaries, but rather surpasses them (Woolard & Schieffelin, 1994). Why language ideologies cannot be equated with folk-linguistic stereotypes is obvious once the fact that it is not individual attitudes or beliefs that are taken into consideration, but rather a societal push for the certain normative constructs that become ingrained in everyday thought.

The idea of language ideology as a "mediating link between social structures and forms of talk" (*ibid.*: 55) is crucial in finding its definition, for the role that these types of ideologies play is just as pertinent to surrounding ideology as any other. Just as Cameron (2003: 447) herself remarks, "it is worth commenting briefly on the definition of language ideologies in terms of *representations* of language rather than (…) beliefs or attitudes relating to it." Feminist perspectives on language provide us with one of the more salient examples of language ideology, similarly to the way that studies of language and ethnicity have (Fought, 2006). When it comes to minority and marginalized groups, the investigation of the beliefs surrounding their "language systems", or ways of talk, provides a window into how language ideologies shape the way such groups are perceived and construed.

As an example, despite the fact that movements for the wider acceptance for the African American Vernacular are becoming a more widespread phenomenon, AAVE is still thought to be representative of a less intellectually capable minority group (Rickford, 2016). The same can be said of language ideologies concerning gender, with "women's language" (Lakoff, 1975; Holmes, 1984, 1997; Goldstein, 2011) being the language of the lesser of the sexes.

What began with Jespersen's (1922: 246) categorization of women as "shrinking from coarse and vulgar expressions," as well as maintaining a preference for "refined and (in certain spheres) veiled and indirect expressions" (*ibid.*) has only moved on to other limited representations of women in the form of linguistic and discursive expression, such as what has been studied in the existing notion of sexist language (McConnell-Ginet, 1984; Wodak, 1989; Goddard & Patterson, 2000; Parks, 2004) (cf. 3.3).

Therefore, when approaching the subject of how language ideology is defined, we are not simply speaking of beliefs about language, but also the ways in which societal expectations shape how people, or a group of people (social or otherwise) talk or are conditioned to talk. This is important in understanding the overall construction of beliefs regarding certain groups, namely the beliefs and stereotypes concerning minority groups, encompassing women, for their social subordination to men remains omnipresent in interaction. It is thus important to begin with the first studies on language and gender, which sought to point out the differences between men's and women's speech, with some writers and scholars claiming those differences to be natural, and others stating that they are the result of cultural conditioning or socialization.

Discursive aspects of ideology

Of course, the linguistic aspects of ideology do not only concern the way people talk or how they interact with one another (Kiesling, 2019). Another important point to consider on the subject is that of how language, and more particularly discourse, reproduce existing ideologies (cf. Chapter 1).

Van Dijk's (2001: 11) work in CDA has highlighted the role that discourse plays in spreading ideologies:

> That is, ideologies may influence the ways social attitudes are expressed in discourse structures. The same ideology, however, may influence the way whites construct themselves and blacks as participants in conversation, how they define the interaction, and what knowledge, beliefs or aims are activated during conversation. These typical context features may in turn show up at all levels of discourse, e.g., in intonation, sentence syntax, lexical selection, topicalization or implicitness, among many other properties of talk.

The sections of this chapter which present the discursive representations of gender and sexuality are strictly related to this issue. This includes subjects such as sexist language, semantic derogation of gendered terms, and the discursive representation of gender ideologies and sexuality. The uncovering of ideologies in discourse was also mentioned in Chapter 1, however, the presented chapter takes a more detailed perspective of where those gendered ideologies manifest themselves in English and Polish language and discourse, which is understood as the linguistic representations of reality as semiotic.

Overview of research on language and gender in English

Before embarking on a discussion on the way discourse about gender or sexuality relate to attitudes about rape, it is crucial to enumerate the ways that language and gender have been studied. In discussing the relationship between gender ideology and language, it is crucial to tie all of these ideas to the implications placed on the gender-related aspect. A link to the different belief systems that affect culturally conditioned perceptions of gender has been covered in the existing theories of language and gender in sociolinguistic study.

The beginnings of language and gender studies in sociolinguistics began with Otto Jespersen's (1922) book, which claimed women to be irrelevant in the social sphere and explained differences in language as belonging to women's inferiority, however it was officially Lakoff (1975) who was the first to have described linguistic differences as related to gender (Kiesling, 2019). In a similar vein to Lakoff's (*ibid.*) approach, Spender (1980) attempted to explain the inferiority of women's language to men's, but made rather erroneous and generalized claims which lacked evidence that women's language differed from that of men's in that expressions, words and the image of women's experiences (including childbirth) would take on new meanings if women were provided the opportunity to express themselves. Spender's (*ibid.*) work, although heavily criticized for lacking evidence for her claims (Black & Coward 1981), marked a rise in feminist scholarly expression in linguistics and opened a door to more open discussion and in-depth research on the subject.

Linguists, as well as scholars from other disciplines, began to take an interest in the gendered aspects of words, including those denoting occupations (Irigaray, 1993). They also showed an interest in the androcentrism of prescriptive grammar (Bodine, 1975; MacKay, 1980; Zuber & Reed, 1993). In the 1980s and 1990s, sexist language and discourse saw much discussion on both sides of the issue, with some writers claiming its non-existence (Hofstader,[46] 1985) and others advocating that such discriminatory language must be done away with (Miller & Swift, 1980; Doyle, 1995).[47]

The first experts in language and gender research maintained a focus on how women's language differs from men's language. Linguistics has seen several shifts

46 Here it should be noted that William Satire used the alias Douglas Hofstader in authoring his papers (Cameron 1998).

47 Not all of those involved in the 1980s and 1990s discussions on sexist language were linguists; many of them were not, representing disciplines such as sociology and psychology (Cameron & Kulick 2003; Kiesling 2019).

from *deficit theory* (Lakoff, 1975) to *dominance theory* (Zimmerman & West, 1975) to *difference theory* (Maltz & Borker, 1982; Tannen, 1990), among other *genderlect theories* or *theories of gender communication*. These include theories such as Wood and Harding's (1991) *standpoint theory* and the theory proposed by Edwin and Shirley Ardener (1975), which was then furthered by Kramarae (1981) to apply to a specifically gendered communication model, *muted group theory* and *dynamic/performative* theory (Butler, 1990; Coates, 2004).

Of course, on top of such trends in the research, language, and identity studies that look at gender identities have been conducted on an equally large scale. Eckert (1996) investigated the correlation of changes in vowel patterns among adolescent girls and their belonging to the subculture of heterosexual female adolescence. Using women's or men's language and relying on language stereotypes to construct one's gender identity has also undergone much investigation and analysis (Besnier, 2005; McConnell-Ginet, 2005; Camp, 2009; McConnell-Ginet, 2011).

Litosseliti (2006: 24) calls the study of language and gender "feminist linguistics," as it is "interested in identifying, demystifying and resisting the ways in which language is used, together with social practices, to reflect and sustain gender division and inequalities in society." Each of the theories has been enumerated in the following sections, and the question of sexist language and sexist discourse follows, in order to illustrate other aspects of study on language, gender and gendered ideology present in language. A description of the most significant theories and studies is necessary to achieve a holistic view of the field of language and gender, as well as to later tie it to the study of language and sexuality.

Deficit theory

Every theory on gender communication indicates underpinnings of sex-difference as either based in and completely reflecting patriarchal ideologies (cf. Chapter 2), or as reproducing them. *Deficit theory* has persevered ever since, attributing gender inequality to language and its persistent existence in a patriarchal matrix. Lakoff (1975) argued that women's and men's differences in speech/communication skills are due to the fact that women's language (i.e., women's assumed natural communication style) seems to be deficient by default, undermining women on the whole and thus forcing them into a position of having to use men's language when they wish to be taken seriously (Kiesling, 2019: 36–37). What Lakoff (*ibid.*) described as women's language is characterized by a broader array of vocabulary on topics that are considered less worldly, such as home décor and fashion (i.e., displaying a greater variety of color terms such as *mauve* or *fuchsia*, where men might simply—and stereotypically—use the term *purple*).

Other features of women's language include the greater tendency for women to use hedging devices, question tags and rising intonation at the end of affirmatives (Lakoff, 1975; Holmes, 1984; Swann, 2000; Kiesling, 2019). In addition to the interactional aspects of language, Lakoff also claimed that language about women (what Kiesling (*ibid.*: 37)) calls categorization aspects) demonstrated sexist leanings in that there are visible inequalities in the way that men and women are referred to on the whole. For example, she described the reference to women as *ladies* as highly euphemistic (Lakoff, 1975; Kiesling, 2019), including its use in the modifier position (as in *lady doctor*).

The theories put forth by Lakoff (1975) have been heavily criticized for their prescription of feminine language that perceives passivity as natural and inherent to women and thus a language which naturally hinders their ability to communicate and negatively impacts their social standing. In making such claims, Lakoff (*ibid.*) was among the first to not only exaggerate the popular notion of the existence of a gender binary, but also call women's speech styles inevitably bound to leading women to their own plundering unless a "masculine" alternative is adopted. In addition to this, the lack of empirical data to support the claims has been stated to weaken her position, which presented "only the language of an assumed White, middle-to-upper class, heterosexual, cisgendered woman" (Kiesling, 2019: 39).

Muted group theory

On further theoretical grounds, *muted group theory* (Ardener & Ardener, 1975; Kramarae,1981) discusses the idea of the mutedness of certain social groups, especially the muting of women in society (Wall & Leary, 1999; Cowan, 2007). This comes into contrast with the silence or silencing of certain marginalized groups, placing emphasis on the fact that the idea of mutedness pertains to cases when social groups cannot properly articulate their ideas and opinions. In Kramarae's (1981) view, this has much to do with the perceived differences in communication styles between men and women, and that male societal dominance is a leading factor in creating the quite visible differences between men's and women's communication styles.

> The language of a particular culture does not serve all its speakers equally, for not all speakers contribute in an equal fashion to its formulation. Women (as well as members of other non-dominant groups) are not as free or as able as men are to say what they wish, because the words and the norms for their use have been formulated by the dominant group, men.
>
> (Kramarae 1981: 1)

This theory is important in its relevance to the question of language and gender because it highlights the fact that in the face of inequalities in patriarchal societies, women do not have equal linguistic opportunity since language is posited here as being man made. Therefore, the language one speaks does not serve all its users equally.

Dominance theory

As opposed to deficit theory, *dominance theory* views women's inferior position in society as a result of men's domination of women, including in interaction. In addition to the fact that the theory views women as linguistically powerless, it also states that social structures of dominance are reflected in the idea that men linguistically dominate women (O'Barr & Atkins, 1980; Zimmerman & West, 1987).

In their work, O'Barr and Atkins (*ibid.*) investigated language in the courtroom, looking in particular at the speech of witnesses on the stand during a hearing. With the goal of investigating possible biases in such a legal setting, they investigated the influence of gendered speech styles and the impressions that those styles made on listeners. The authors (*ibid.*) concluded that, while the features of what Lakoff (1975) had termed women's language were more prevalent in women's speech than men's, "the tendency for more women to speak powerless language and for men to speak less of it is due (…) to the greater tendency of women to occupy relatively powerless social positions" (O'Barr & Atkins, 2005: 458).

Similarly, in the research carried out by Zimmerman and West (1985) on the theory of dominance, concerning gendered speech styles, interruptions were studied and found to take place on the part of men, more often than that of women. This was attributed to the view of the female group as being subordinate to the male group. Again, through their theory, an asymmetry in speech between the sexes was observed, and utilized to support the feminist critique of language that patriarchal dominating ideologies are visible even in everyday interaction. Spender (1980) also presented the work on *dominance theory* with her theory of man-made language, which claimed that language works to disadvantage women, contributing to their being literally and symbolically silenced.

Difference approach

In their 1982 work, Maltz and Borker (*ibid.*) explained gender differences in conversation as a type of *cultural difference* (the approach is sometimes referred to as the "cultural difference approach" (Kiesling 2019: 44)), rather than a question of power differences (as posited in the two theories explained above—the deficit and dominance approaches).

Tannen (1990) worked in a similar vein, expanding on what has also been called "the difference framework" or "the difference model" (Talbot, 2010: 99). This model moved away from the view that women's and men's interaction styles are seated in men's power and women's powerlessness, but rather took on a hypothesis that women inherently possess different communication styles than men. Talbot (*ibid.*) summarizes the difference approach in linguistics in the following way:

> As people are growing up, so the story goes, girls and boys spend their time in subcultures with different social organizations. Children learn the rules for friendly interaction from their peers, not from adults. They grow up in gender-specific cultures. The difference model, then, depends on a 'two cultures' account of male and female socialization. […] Behaviours that have previously been perceived as men's efforts to dominate women in interaction is reinterpreted as a 'cross-cultural' phenomenon, a result of mismatches in what men and women expect interaction to be like.

Best known for her *genderlect theory*, Tannen (1986, 1990, 1994) claims that women's and men's "languages" are neither based in deficit nor in men's largely dominating conversational stature, but rather in the fact that men's and women's communication goals and strategies are inherently different. She claimed that due to differences in communication needs and aims, women and men are bound to find difficulties in completely understanding one another.

Women's language, for one, is characterized by the communication needs to build rapport with others, thus displaying verbal features and strategies, such as cooperative overlaps, private speaking, asking questions (to build rapport), and nonverbal strategies, such as head-nodding or maintaining eye contact with interlocutors (Tannen, 1990). This leads to the description of women's language and women's communication style as private, as opposed to men's, which has been described as public (*ibid.*).

Men's communication, in Tannen's (*ibid.*) view, on the other hand, is characterized by a need to dominate and challenge, to garner the attention and respect of interlocutors, as well as to demonstrate dominance. In Tannen's (*ibid.*) theory, men's talk is thus described as "public." This supports the theory that men are more likely to interrupt in interaction than women (Holmes, 1995). Crawford's (1995) criticism of the theory draws on its tendency to essentialize behavior normally associated with men and women as social groups. Such a perspective on linguistic behavior is seen, from the socio-cultural perspective, as learned rather than innate. Difference theory is important to the work with regard to any myths that might occur which hinge upon the subject of miscommunication (*ibid.*).

Dynamic theory in language and gender

Performative theory, as part of the study of how human beings construct and present themselves, was explained in the section about theories posited by Judith Butler (1999; cf. Chapter 2). Social constructionist approaches, however, also carry over into the sphere of language and gender (Coates, 2004; Sunderland, 2006); most researchers now adopt a dynamic approach to looking at language and gender (*ibid.*).

Such a theory has been called the *dynamic approach* to language and gender because of the emphasis it places on the "dynamic aspects of interaction" (Coates, 2004: 6) of language and gender relations. Because "gender identity is seen as a social construct rather than a given social category," (*ibid.*) the linguistic ways of expressing gender must also be seen as a way of "doing gender" (*ibid.*). Studies of language and identity, for one, are examples of how the dynamic approach has been considered (Bucholtz, 2002). Where computer-mediated communication (cf. Chapter 4) is concerned, investigations of whether CMC is used differently by men and women to express gender identity (one's own identity and that of other users, both present and absent) has been investigated in the vein of the approach (Herring, 1996). In another study, Bucholtz (2002) looked through the lens of dynamic performativity at the ways that Greek identity was expressed by young women in a chat room.

The importance of gender and language theory

What these different gender and language theories demonstrate is the ways in which both overt and covert sexist leanings attribute themselves to language. The dialogues of such theories aim to bring attention to the sexist tendencies that shape societal and cultural thought by emphasizing that a relationship between linguistic usage and thinking (by making cognitive associations) regarding gender exists. Language and gender theory is an essential illustration of the way that sex and gender differences are perceived in the societal sense. The cognitive dissonance created by the chasm between collective thought (cf. Chapter 2) and the actualities of gender (where women are, in actuality, equal to men) is one that persists in its problematic leanings. As pertains to this work, the fact of focusing on the differences between men and women and the ways that they communicate (whether it be as different cultures or as having weaker styles of speech, or a weaker social position in the world) draws attention to the binary approach to issues of language and gender. Some of these theories have been used to explain those issues strictly related to the thesis, as well: that of miscommunication between the sexes as a cause for rape.

The theoretical issues put forth by Anglo-Saxon scholars, however, are not the only ones that have been presented by scholars focusing on linguistically discernible differences between men and women. The representation of men and women (and now, people of other genders) in discourse has also given much attention in the field. This does not simply include the perspectives discussed in Chapter 1, but also refers to expressions which are heavily gendered and are seen by many scholars as perpetuating stereotypes. Such stereotyping also takes place on a discursive level, which reproduces ideologies in the form of linguistic and discursive representations. This is a very broad subject, and so will be discussed only within the length of several pages in this chapter, as the literature is extensive. It is also important to note here that, as the above-mentioned theories in language and gender are seated in Anglo-Saxon cultural contexts, specific reference to Polish research on language and gender is made later in the chapter.

Gender representations in English discourse

The research scopes on language and gender do not only take talk and interaction into consideration, as issues of inequality in language, where gender is concerned, also deal with the issue of gender representation from a lexical (semantic), or phraseological viewpoint in English linguistics (Zafarovna, 2016). This categorization of gender representation includes linguistic categorization through grammatical gender in various languages, figurative language that is related to or representative of gender (such as metaphor, the naming of parts—such as body parts—and insults), as well as the categories of binarity and pronouns (Kiesling, 2019). Other research has discussed the semantic derogation of terms that refer to women (Goddard & Patterson, 2000; Kieltyka, 2005; Kochman-Haładyj, 2007), and this aspect will be discussed in more depth later in this chapter.

I maintain here that it is rather the categorizing discourses related to gender which reflect ideologies that have broad social relevance and serious implications in situations like rape, more so than the gender theories regarding talk and interaction. Although, as presented above, stereotypical views about gender interaction keep women in a subordinate social position, the linguistic elements that reproduce harmful ideologies that have a bearing on perception are discursive ones (Curzan, 2003; Kitzinger, 2005). This means that the semantic roles of discourse, which will be discussed separately, have implications for current meanings and the value of those actors and subjects related to certain terms and expressions. The same can be said of phraseological descriptions of men and women in general (Kochman-Haładyj, 2007; Zafaranova, 2016; Willis & Jozkowski, 2018;

Kochman-Haładyj, 2020). It has been shown in the literature regarding gender and phraseology that proverbs and phraseological expressions also tend to be marked for gender or present gendered ideologies (Benedito, 2000; *ibid.*). It must be kept in mind that there is no room to provide the entirety of what phraseological expressions and working metaphors express and show in both English and Polish, and therefore only some examples are provided in this chapter to illustrate the imbalance that exists in representations of men and women.

Some examples of expressions in English that pertain to or refer to women are those related to appearance and beauty ideals, via which beauty is something seen as an ideal that women should strive to attain, such as in the examples provided by Zafaranova (2016: 1505):

1) *have roses in one's cheeks*
2) *a slick chick*
3) *hot stuff*

This is accompanied by other notions that are related to gender, gender stereotypes, and ideology in discourse, including the position of women as weaker than men (Nasrullaeva, 2016: 74):

4) *the softer sex*
5) *the weaker sex*

Some of the expressions that describe men that are named in the older literature include ones that place men in positions of power, physical dominance, and greater social importance than women (Saporta, 1974: 1). These expressions are still known today and thus maintain their relevance in the context of gendered expressions:

6) *Man the boats*
7) *A man's home is his castle*
8) *Oh man!*

Other phraseological units with component of masculinity characterize men through marking them as positive or through neutral expression, such as those used to describe traits of honesty, as provided by Nasrullaeva (2016: 74–75):

9) *square John*
10) *a man of his word*

Goddard and Patterson (2000: 88) provide a list of expressions used in everyday English, which are tied to gender stereotypes and speech. Such examples express the view that women should not use profane language and that it is not feminine to do so, that women are so-called "gossips", and that when men converse, it is on worldly topics and that men's speech is more aggressive, thus making such aggression in speech acceptable. I have changed the order given in Goddard and Patterson to show how expressions about women's speech categorically differ from men's. The first list shows examples of how women's behavior in talk and interaction are described, abiding by stereotypes (cf. Chapter 2).

11) *Nice girls don't swear*
12) *Talking in a lady-like way*
13) *Talking like a woman*
14) *She's got a mouth like a fishwife*
15) *Women's talk*
16) *Girl talk*

Examples of expressions that construe men as aggressive or dominating actors in conversation are as such (Goddard & Patterson, 2000: 88):

17) *Swearing like a trooper*
18) *Men's talk*
19) *Bloke'ish talk*
20) *Laddish talk*

Even earlier works, such as Saporta's (1974) paper, support linguistic phenomena that have not lost their relevance in the discussion of sexism in language. The author brings attention to expressions which are more overtly and mildly sexist to illustrate that surrounding cultural behaviors and associations give rise to sexist thinking.

Saporta (1974) also brought attention to the fact that sexism exists on many levels when it comes to expressions, including in the areas of semantics and syntax. The list of gendered expressions in phraseology may be expanded, but it has been made clear in the literature on the subject that the asymmetry in expressions construes women as the weaker sex, and places focus on their physical attraction and relationship to men, whereas men are represented as being domineering, powerful and honest (Eveline, 2005; Nasrullaeva, 2016). The same can be said of the Polish linguistic context, which presents even more asymmetry, as Polish is a language that inflects for gender.

Language and gender research in Polish

Much of the research on language and gender in the Polish context cites the research mentioned above in the sections regarding English studies on language and gender, and expands on issues of grammatical differences in inflection, for example (Koniuszaniec & Błaszkowska, 2003). In order to demonstrate that asymmetries exist where gender and language are concerned in both English and Polish, some scholars have taken the traditional English studies on language and gender and applied similar research methods to the Polish language (Handke 1990).

Among prominent Polish language and gender scholars in Poland are Karwatowska and Szpyra-Kozłowska (2010; Szpyra-Kozłowska, 2021a, 2021b), Kiełkiewicz-Janowiak (1992, 2006, 2019), as well as Handke (1992, 1994, 1995a, 1995b, 2006) and Krysiak (2020). Karwatowska and Szpyra-Kozłowska (*ibid.*) investigated the androcentricity of the Polish language in first and last names, the semantic derogation of lexical items referring to women, grammatical gender asymmetry, the invisibility of women in discourse and youth language where the issue of gender asymmetry is concerned (*ibid.*; Szpyra-Kozłowska, 2021a). Handke's (1992, 1994) work consists of the investigation of gendered attitudes towards language, including women's style of talk and Polish women's attitudes towards profanity. More recently, Szpyra-Kozłowska's (2021) collection of essays demonstrates novelties and developments in language differences where gender is concerned, including the phenomenon of creating male forms of traditionally women-associated nouns (i.e., *prostytut* 'male prostitute' or *kosmetyk* 'male cosmetologist'), the influence of Anglo-Saxon culture present in loan words (i.e., *metrosexual*). Other works concern the discursive representations of men and women, with a focus on negative (stereotypical) representations of women (Krzyżanowska, 2012; Bulawka, 2013; Stoch, 2015; Zabrzewska, 2020).

The studies of discursive representations in Polish have covered aspects of language including grammatical gender and feminine forms (*feminatywy*) of women's occupations and naming where gender is concerned, as well as newer discursive representations which overstep traditional gender norms or reinforce already-existing stereotypes (Stępień, 2018; Kiełkiewicz-Janowiak, 2019; Szpyra-Kozłowska, 2019, 2021a, 2021b; Krysiak & Małocha-Krupa, 2020). Other studies have investigated gender from the perspective of both Discourse Analysis and Critical Discourse Analysis (Bulawka, 2013; Krzyżanowska, 2018), and look into the ways that gender representations spread ideologies about gender.

The section which follows deals with the question of grammatical gender, an important aspect in the field of Polish linguistics and gender, which has been described as contributing greatly to the gender inequality in Polish culture.

Grammatical and lexical gender in Polish studies

One important aspect of language and gender studies that is not as strongly or noticeably present in English (barring the feminist language reform's promotion of more linguistic equality, such as in the use of pronouns), is the grammatical gender highly salient in Polish. The Polish language inflects for what Miemietz (1997: 31) calls "grammatical sex" and "natural sex" (referred to as "biological sex" in other literature), on the level of nouns, adjectives, pronouns and verbs, when referring to a third party. Miemietz (*ibid.*) puts the Polish language and gender inflection into perspective in a few words:

> Whoever speaks Polish as a native language…would meet the idea of sex-differentiated modes of expression with a shrug of the shoulders, as the special distinct forms for women and men are omnipresent in the Polish language. It is nearly impossible to engage in conversation in Polish without constantly referring to one's own sex and that of the interlocutor by means of special grammatical morphemes. The same holds true when a third party becomes the subject of discussion: information about the sex is repeatedly provided by means of grammatical structures
>
> (Miemietz, 1997: 31)

Research that has been conducted on the grammatical and lexical gender in Polish concerns many different aspects, and has been given increasingly more attention from a research perspective. In their book, Karwatowska and Szpyra-Kozłowska (2005) analyze and describe the gendered grammatical asymmetry present in Polish. The authors compiled a corpus taken from dictionaries, texts and surveys. They investigate the way that Polish society is chock-a-block with patriarchal underpinnings, therefore creating more space for sexist and androcentric linguistic tendencies. They investigate the asymmetry in which women suffer negative stereotyping and a lack of representation in questions of virginity, promiscuity, sex, marriage, loyalty within a relationship, and infidelity, calling into question how lexicology and phraseology have perpetuated the "Polish gender axiology" (Rejter, 2013: 12).[48]

Kępińska's (2006) work focuses more strictly on grammar, highlighting the asymmetries that exist in masculine and non-masculine gender inflection (Rejter, 2013: 12). The author takes an individual look at verbs, pronouns, adjectives, nominals and nouns, and investigates them from a historical perspective. Besides the highly descriptive view that Kępińska's (*ibid.*) work

48 My translation

presents, part of it looks at the influences of cultural and cognitive linguistics on the language and gender paradigm. She additionally takes note of the fact that linguistic categories mirror what is present in the extralinguistic world (Kępińska, 2006: 306).

Another important work on language and gender is Łaziński's (2006) book, which describes the asymmetry present in the Polish honorific system, comparing it with other languages. In the book, he highlights grammatical asymmetry in Polish where gender is concerned, looking at and describing its historical roots, as well as the socially tiered nature of unequal linguistic and discursive representation (*ibid.*).

As a part of grammatical gender, lexical and referential gender have also been discussed in the literature (Koniuszaniec & Błaszkowska, 2003; Haertle, 2017). It has been noted that masculine forms dominate the Polish language not only for grammatical inflection but also where neutral collective forms of nouns take on a masculinized bias, comprising both male and female reference on the masculine base form, as in *bratostwo* ('brother and his wife'), from *brat* ('brother') or *ambasadorstwo* ('ambassador and his wife'), from the Polish *ambasador* (Koniuszaniec & Błaszkowska, 2003: 263).

As Koniuszaniec and Błaszkowska (2003: 264) have pointed out in their work, "the male gender is also decidedly favoured in word formation" in Polish, as feminine personal nouns derive from masculine forms through suffixation like *-ka*, *-ini/yni* or *-a*, as well as by adding suffixes like *-owa*, *-aczka*, *-ina/yna*, *-ówna* and *-anka* (however more rarely). This has also been investigated and discussed by Szpyra-Kozłowska (2021a). Such derivational processes result in word pairs that are semantically asymmetrical with the feminine term typically denoting a relationship of some kind to a male, whereas the masculine term denotes an individual or the agent of some profession or function (*ibid.*). In addition to the grammatical and lexical asymmetries that have been pointed out, word order, proper names, and generic masculine forms have also been pointed to in order to demonstrate the imbalance. These aspects highlight the gender asymmetry in the Polish language, as well as the discursive aspects of gender visible in phraseological expressions.

Gender representations in Polish discourse

One important aspect of this work, previously mentioned, is the analysis of linguistic gender representations in online discourses. There are fewer works than the ones in English linguistics which take the Polish language gender media representations under scrutiny, but those which have been done are comprehensive and in-depth. Others related to the discursive representations of gender have to do with phraseological representations of gender in Polish (Krawczyk-Tyrpa, 2001; Puda-Blokesz, 2016).

When it comes to the media representations of gender in Polish, the focus has been on discursive representation in sports (Jakubowska, 2012), as well as the language of advertising surrounding consumerist culture as it relates to gender (Krzyżanowska, 2014). The work on gendered representations in the Polish press by Bulawka (2013) is an example of pioneering work in Polish linguistic study and CDA in particular.

In her book, *Gender Representations in the Polish Press: A Feminist Critical Discourse Study*, Bulawka (2013) looks at the various ways that Polish women are presented in the media. She examines Polish archetypal femininities, their origins and dissects how religion and mythology play a role in reinforcing stereotypical images of Polish women (*ibid.*: 35). Bulawka's (*ibid.*) focus remains mostly on the aftermath of the Polish political elections of 2006 and 2007, and continues her discussion of women's presentation in the Polish media by deconstructing the semantic features present in the discourse on the "widely appointed" female MPs. She draws attention to how female political actors fall prey to "possessivation, impersonalization and appreciation" (*ibid.*), all of which strategies construct a method for sexualizing women in media discourse. The author moves on to analyze highly gendered "military metaphors in conceptualizing professional identities of three leading female politicians" (*ibid.*) and claims that although this change advocates for the inclusion of women in the political sphere, by bringing masculinized constructs into discourse on female power adverse effects may occur through a "disruption of schematic gendered behavior" (*ibid.*: 37). The final part of her book deals strictly with the representation of female MPs as "differently gendered subjects" (*ibid.*). By looking at lexical and collocational patterns, she investigates constructions of women as adhering to traditional ideals of femininity and powerlessness (*ibid.*). These stereotypical ideas are also visible in Polish phraseology, although less research has been done with relation to this particular context, as compared to English.

The existing literature on gendered phraseological expressions has focused on mythological references that present archetypal discursive construction of women and men (Puda-Blokesz, 2016). There is a juxtaposition shown that mythological figures of strength and power are discursively associated with those masculine figures, such as in the following examples (*ibid.*: 210–211):

21) *herkulesowa siła* ('herculean strength')
22) *tytan pracy* ('titan of work')
23) *zły jak furia* ('angry as fury')

These mythological representations, although gendered in their form and meaning (based on their stereotypical value) are used to refer to both women and men (*ibid.*). Here it may be noted that strength and work are associated with a masculine god, and therefore with masculinity, whereas anger (hence instability in emotions) is related to goddesses, working inherently as a representation of femininity. These are only some of the examples, however for the sake of space, there is no room for more.

Concerning the linguistic behavior of men and women, Wolański (2013) notes that vulgar expressions, for one, are heavily associated with men, and have been illustrated in the following expressions (Wolański 2013: 68):

24) *kląć jak szewc* ('swear like a cobbler')
25) *kląć jak marynarz* ('swear like a sailor')

As Wolański states, these were both "traditionally male professions" (2013: 68) and therefore are phraseologically associated with men. The act of profanity or swearing is also associated more often with men than women, as Wolański (2013) writes in his paper.

Coinciding with Szpyra-Kozłowska and Karwatowska's (2004) statement that in Polish it is very easy to cross the line that differentiates a woman from a "slut," Wolański's (2013) study on the use of the word *kurwa* (one of the most commonly used swear terms in the Polish language that equates to 'whore' in English) illustrates the gender differences in the use of the word and how it is used, i.e., in what context. Not only does he describe how the word *kurwa* is used, and in what instances, but also discusses the prevalence of the use of the word and by whom. The importance of mentioning this particular taboo word, as Wolański (*ibid.*: 70) calls it, is the sexual connotations that are attached to it, rendered from its primal meaning of 'whore' or 'prostitute' in Polish, as mentioned above.

Linguistic sexism

The notion of *sexist language* or *linguistic sexism* is one that has notably been argued over by theorists for decades (Gastil, 1990; Ross, 1996; Wareing, 1999; Goddard & Patterson, 2000; Pauwels, 2003). Whether or not language works to uphold the superior status of men over women can be seen in the work of many linguists and other social theorists. Sexist language tends towards a language system and function that is gender exclusive in practice, with English, for one, sustaining the subordination of women through a wide variety of linguistic elements. From the use of the generic *he* to the notion of *semantic derogation* or *pejoration* of terms that refer to women, sexist language is visible from everyday discourse to overt sexist comments regarding women (Lei 2006). By looking into the issue of language and gender, one can come to see the relationship between language and gender, and gender ideology as such.

The way that linguistic sexism is linked to gender ideology is quite obvious, in that the interpretation we take here states that certain linguistic features are inherently reflective of collective thought. Martyna (1983: 26–27) brings attention to a 1971 *Newsweek* article, in which "pronoun envy" is discussed. What Martyna (*ibid.*) calls "the linguists' claim" is that pronouns are simply grammatical features, whereas the "students' claim" is that the use of generic *he/man* is reflective of a societal sexism, which through the perpetual use of generic *he/man* is maintained. This, Tyson (2006: 83–84) argues, is something that is viewed as knit-picking on the part of the feminist community, for one, but does have merit in its reflection of the way in which women are societally *marked* and, in turn, marginalized on many planes.

When it is said that women speak differently than men, and that they must strive towards a language more similar to that of the language used by men (Lakoff, 1975), an interplay between ruling ideologies and the pre-existing marked identity of even being a woman is foregrounded. It is a taxing phenomenon, but one that is present in the re-construction of the idea of the minority, that things that are marked are things that happen to be regarded widely as "other." If men's speech is what is considered to be the unmarked, or normal, linguistic phenomenon (with the same going for the markedness of styles prescribed to groups of ethnic minorities (Hill, 1999; Chun, 2004, 2009), for one), then women's speech is marked, since it is considered lacking the positive characteristics that men's language has. Markedness is a theoretical notion that is also present in studies of language and gender (Andrews, 1990; Barrett, 1998; Bale et al., 2011).

In the markedness model, the argument that male forms of nouns are unmarked and, therefore, neutral, places the female forms in a position of "marked" status, denoting an irregularity of such female forms. As part of the study of sexist language, in markedness theory, where gender is concerned, forms such as *actor/actress* or *prince/princess* present grammatical gender to refer to the trait of being male or female, as marked linguistically (Kiesling,

2019; Sprouse et al., 2021). In earlier linguistic observations about gender, Lakoff (1975) also drew attention to the fact that many terms for women are marked since they are made longer through the use of diminutive forms. The stance on the sexist language of such forms lies in the fact that they are seen as a reflection of social inequalities between men and women, where men are seen as representative of groups, excluding exceptions such as certain occupations (nurse, teacher, etc.).

Although much research has been conducted on sexist language, sexist discourses, and sexist expressions, there is only room enough to discuss some of the findings. Mills (2008) is one of the better-known scholars in the field of semantics to focus on sexist language and in her book *Language and Sexism* she points out the way that sexism oftentimes breeds hate speech, how semantic processes have changed neutral words into negative ones about women, as well as indirect sexism in language. This phenomenon is called semantic derogation, and has been known to pertain to language about women (*ibid.*; Goddard & Patterson, 2000).

Semantic derogation and its relationship to gender ideology

The notion of *semantic derogation* is particularly important in the discussion of the way linguistic sexism and the fact that the ideology surrounding it, as such, is manifested in language. This is because of how ideas surrounding women and their perceived subordinate societal position are reflected in the linguistic references to them. Semantic derogation is when "a perfectly innocent term designating a girl or woman may begin with neutral or even positive connotations, but gradually it acquires negative implications, at first perhaps only slightly disparaging, but after a period of time becoming abusive and ending as a sexual slur" (Schulz, 1975: 65; Kiełtyka, 2005). This concept is important in understanding the weight that linguistic construal carries in its semanticity, where gender is concerned.

Semantic derogation in English

Stanley's (1977) collective work provides a list of words describing both men and women who are considered "sexually available", and in that she discovered that more terms that described women as sexually available had acquired a negative connotation than those which referred to men. Lei (2006: 89) points to the fact that "North American English has no fewer than 220 words for a sexually promiscuous woman, but only twenty for sexually promiscuous men, and London school children had a rich vocabulary of insult terms for girls, all related to sexual behavior, but very few specifically for boys." Some examples of semantically derogatory terms in English include "pussy, ho, slut, bitch, cunt, bimbo, thot, ratchet, broad" (Ray, 2016: 11). These labels, of course, refer directly to a woman's sexuality or genitalia as inherently negative, whereas men's genitalia is usually rarely referred to in such a way. The studies on semantic derogation of lexical items that refer to sexuality have shown that a negative connotation is more easily attributed to discourse on women (Sutton, 1995).

It has been argued that the semantic derogation of terms regarding women and their sexuality is not accidental, but connected to the ideologies regarding femininity and masculinity discussed in Chapter 2 and that this has consequences for the perception and the discursive construction of women (Pauwels, 2003).

Semantic derogation in Polish

The subject of semantic derogation has also been discussed in descriptions of the Polish linguistic representations of women (Jaworski, 1989; Kochman-Haładyj, 2007; Szpyra-Kozłowska, 2021), although not to the extent that it has in the literature on English linguistics. As Karwatowska and Szpyra-Kozłowska (2010) write, the Polish language also presents a semantic derogation of terms referring to women, similarly to the cases in English. Some examples of terms that have undergone the pejoration process in Polish are *dziwka* ('slut'/ 'prosititute'), *kurwa* ('slut'/ 'prostitute'), and even *panienka* ('maiden'/ 'unmarried girl'/ 'young girl') or *dziewucha* ('girl' in augmentative) (*ibid.*: 48–49) in given contexts where they take on negative meaning. Such linguistic asymmetry is reflected in that almost all cultures of developed areas of the world display gender inequalities on at least some level (Kochman-Haładyj, 2010: 137).

Other forms of linguistic asymmetry, as mentioned in the previous sections of this work (i.e., grammatical and lexical gender), are more prevalent than semantic derogation in the Polish language, as shown in the Polish studies on gender and language (Anusiewicz & Handke, 1994; Szpyra-Kozłowska, 2005; Karwatowska & Szpyra-Kozłowska, 2010). In the Polish literature, linguistic asymmetry has been claimed to show the most salient instances of gender in the discursive sense (*ibid.*). Why it is important to acknowledge such asymmetries in the representations of men and women is to fully understand how ideologies are maintained through the discourses that both produce and reproduce them (Krawczyk-Tyrpa, 1999).

The circle of stereotyping

Akin to Noelle-Neumann's (1974) *spiral of silence,*[49] the theory that is called the "circle of stereotyping" explains how stereotypes are upheld and perpetuated through discourses, collective thought, and adhering to expected action. This circle of stereotyping may also be compared to what is known in social psychology and sociology as the mechanism of the *self-fulfilling prophecy*. This term was originally coined by Merton (1948: 477) as "a false definition of the situation evoking a new behavior which makes the originally false conception come true."

The maps which are presented in the sections that follow (Figures 1–3) are loosely based on the circle of stereotyping, however, first the linguistic aspect of gendered language ideology must be factored into the equation in order to properly describe what language and discourse have to do with the hypothesis.

The closed circle of gendered language ideology

Because gender ideology may be considered a major contributor, with patriarchal ideologies backing it as being arguably the most dominant gender ideology (Lazar, 2005, 2007), to the upholding and maintaining of stereotypes that surround the subject of women, the intricate elements that lie within the framework of creating such stereotypes must be taken into consideration. Having discussed, in part, the way in which ideologies regarding the subordinate position of women manifest themselves in English and Polish, it is clear that the linguistic aspect is not independent from the ideological one. The same way that these specific

49 The German political scientist Elisabeth Noelle-Neumann (1974) proposed a theory which explains the succumbing or adherence to social expectations instilled in a society. Her theory has been broken down into a series of hypotheses, some of which are as follows: 1) most people are afraid of social isolation 2) therefore people constantly observe other people's behavior in order to find out which opinions and behaviors are met with approval or rejection in the public sphere 3) mass media may have a decisive influence on the formation of public opinion. If the media repeatedly (in a "cumulative" way) and concordantly (in a "consonant" way) support one side in a public controversy, this side will stand a significantly higher chance of finishing the spiral-of-silence process as winner 4) public opinion stabilizes and integrates society because conflicts will be resolved through spirals of silence in favor of one opinion. This is what is referred to as the integration function of public opinion. (Source: http://noelle-neumann.de/scientific-work/spiral-of-silence/)

ideologies are seen to be manifested in other settings, such as that of politics and the workplace, they only work to confirm what is already suspected when it comes to the beliefs surrounding a reactionary system that acts more against than for the emancipation of women.

It is here that I aim to illustrate the step-by-step processes by which we observe the influence of gender ideology on the perception of women and men through language, with women taking the brunt of negative and oppressive discursive representation where sexuality is concerned. In the analysis, I will show how, in practice, gendered ideologies are reflected in the act of victim blaming in both English and Polish contexts. By demonstrating the relationship that gender ideologies have with behavior based in traditional gendered roles, I go on to explain how this has implications for the language that women are claimed to use (that being the discourse that abides by the archetypal and stereotypical ideas of women's behavior (Lazar, 2005: 7–8)), as well as the discourse concerning women, present in cultures that function in patriarchal gender ideologies.

Gendered language ideology's relationship to gender stereotype

Considering that stereotypes exist as a "part of our cultural knowledge" (Kiełkiewicz-Janowiak & Pawelczyk, 2006: 349), it is important to consider how they vary according to culture. When one allows thoughts about the stereotypes relating to gender to be expressed discursively (cf. Chapter 2), he or she is taking part in the (re)production[50] of gender ideologies through language and discourse, which tend to produce what is considered a norm, as long as it is strong enough to be upheld in the collective sense. How this is so visible is due to the evidence that exists in different discourses that regard gender, which are, simply put, "ideology in a linguistic form" (Pichler & Preece, 2011: 99). As Pichler and Preece (*ibid.*) point out, even the discourse in advertisements tells women how they should feel about their bodies and what kind of behavior they should strive for to be perceived as more feminine.

The same may be said of the linguistic and discursive reproductions of ideologies surrounding gender and the representations of roles prescribed to men and women in a binary manner through such reproduction and their depiction in text and talk.

---

50 This idea of (re)production of ideology is a reference to figure 1 (this chapter).

Figure 2 Map illustrating ideology's relationship to language

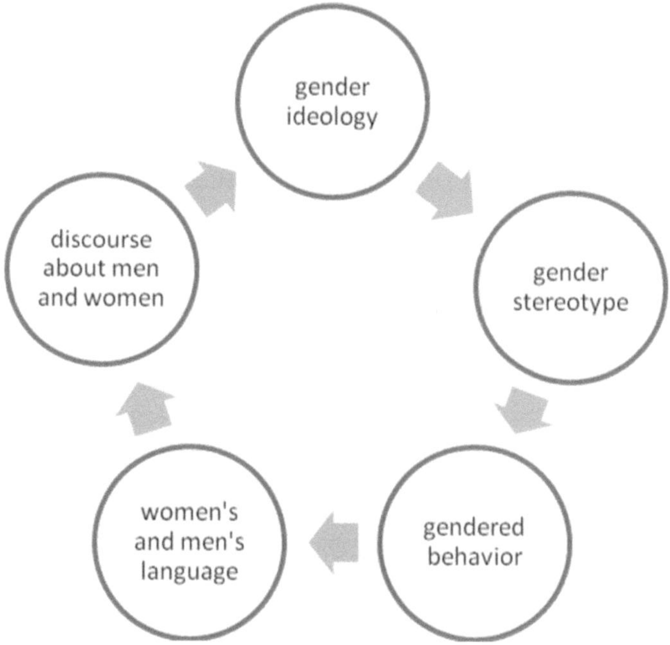

The purpose of the map presented in Figure 2 is to illustrate the way that gender ideology, as presented through linguistic means, intrinsically leads back to itself. The circular effect that ideologies have (as demonstrated above) causes a chain of reproduction that takes place in great part via discursive means. Because the work concerns those ideologies that are related to gender, it is gender ideologies that are named, which then impact the way that women and men perceive themselves and others, which is represented above as the reproduction of gender stereotypes as germinating from ideologies. When social actors abide by stereotypes through their reproduction, by prescribing gendered behaviors as innate or essentialist to men and women, gendered stereotypes take on an embodied form. This embodiment also includes the notion of gendered language (men's language and women's language). This essentialist approach to men's and women's behavior in turn leads to the talk about men and women, which is presented as discourse about gender and is the focus of the final two chapters of this work (cf. Chapter 6 and Chapter 7).

Gender stereotypes and their relationship to women's behavior and speech

As mentioned earlier, Goddard and Patterson (2000: 88) provide examples of discursive expectations of women and men expressing ideological thought regarding gender norms.[51] One of the chapters in their book (Chapter 5: "Gender and speech styles") discusses well-known expressions in societal (collective) discourse used to talk about what could be considered the norm for a "women's language." What they refer to as "culturally embedded ideas on gender and talk" (Goddard and Patterson, 2000: 88) can also be thought of along the lines of cultural gendered language ideology.

The United Nations Human Rights Office of the High Commissioner defines gender stereotype as "a generalized view or preconception about attributes, or characteristics that are or ought to be possessed by women and men or the roles that are or should be performed by men and women" (*ibid.*, 2014: 1). What gender stereotypes say about collective regard of women and men pertains to beliefs about their psychological traits and characteristics, as well as to the idea of gender roles, which tend to be quite weak in their pertinence to modern realities (Brannon, 2004: 161). With female stereotypes based in the nineteenth-century ideals of The Cult of True Womanhood, which emphasized a woman's *piety*, *purity*, *submissiveness*, and *domesticity*, one does not have to look far to see that it still bears great influence on thought concerning women and women's behavior today (Brannon, 2004). The same pertains to stereotypes of men, which seem, for the most part to be based in Brannon's (1976) components of modern masculinity[52] (cf. Chapter 2).

In Steele and Aronson's 1995 study, what they found was that "negative stereotypes affect those who are part of the stereotyped groups" (Brannon, 2004: 159) and called the situation *stereotype threat* due to the tendency such negative stereotypes to threaten the "performance and self concept" (*ibid.*). The stereotypical portrayal of women found in the media (Furnham et al. 2000; Goddard & Patterson, 2000; Kumari, 2018) is particularly detrimental to their overall social perception. The same is true of language and discourse.

It is easy to see how stereotypes regarding women, from a psychological and behavioral standpoint might have implications on their speech and the speech prescribed to them, as well as the discourse about them. Keeping in mind that

---

51 What I mean by *discursive expectations of women* are the representations of women that present themselves in discourse, be them of a nature regarding behavior, or of a linguistic one.

52 No sissy stuff, the big wheel, the sturdy oak, give 'em hell

what we say shapes our realities, it is easy to see the intricate (sometimes indiscernible) connections that are formed between what we say about women, their speech, their behavior, and how they are, as a result, represented in the public sphere.

Because women's behavior was perceived as including any actions taken to attain a certain ideal (done under societal pressure), so was the speech used by them, and unfortunately, in much of the existing discourse regarding women, this is still visible on a large scale (Pichler & Preece, 1999: 99). Due to the fact that being "girly" or "girlish" (*ibid.*) is portrayed by the media and advertising industry as a desirable quality, so is the idea of "girlish speech", which has made way for the practice of differentiating between men's and women's style of talk.

The same may not exactly be said of gender and linguistic interaction in Polish. A study carried out by Kiełkiewicz-Janowiak and Pawelczyk (2006) showed that gender and interaction stereotypes are culturally relevant. The results of their study proved that most stereotypical gendered communication styles pertain to speakers of English and not Polish, thus being dependent on culture, rather than universal (cf. Tannen, 1994). For the case of Polish, the stereotypes that were confirmed by the attitudes of Polish men and women were that women tend to interrupt more to provide personal opinion on a subject, whereas men's communication was found to be fact-oriented and use vulgar language more often (*ibid.*).

Stereotypes as influencing women's behavior

Studies have shown how the perpetuation of a thin body as being an ideal for females has proven a great risk in being a cause of bulimia and anorexia nervosa in females (Myers & Biocca, 1992; Botta, 1999). Although the same can be said for idealizations of a certain male physique (Barlett et al., 2008; Majer, 2016), the effect certain stereotypes have on women seems to be at large on the social scale when one thinks about the patriarchal ideologies which European and western societies reflect (cf. Chapter 3).

Exposure to gender stereotypes begins at a very young age, with introduction to them sometimes coming in the form of reading material for children (children's books) (Taylor, 2003). This linguistic rite of passage into a reality where gender stereotypes are presented as normal and self-evident existence in the world is quite blatant in its show of the actual social constructionist nature of gender (Lorber, 1997: 83–9; Holmes, 2007). Martin and Little (1990) also looked into the development of gender stereotypes, and found that even at the age of three, children begin to display signs of gender stereotyping (2004: 164).

Figure 3, which is presented below, demonstrates how gender ideology as reproduced in language more specifically affects the way that women are both constructed and perceived via discursive means. Similarly to Figure 2, the ideas (and ideologies) regarding gender norms related to women impact the discourses which then work to reproduce them, hence circular representation.

Figure 3 Ideas of women's behavior on its own as influencing discourse

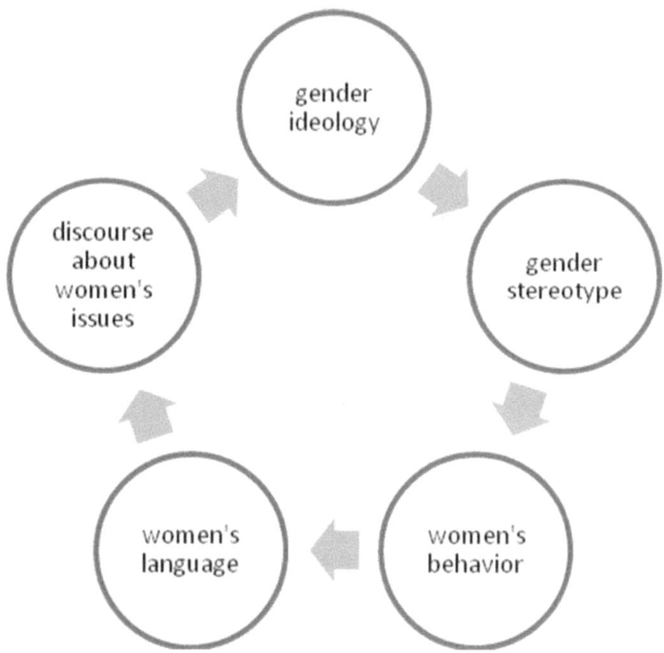

It is important to remember that stereotypes work to (re)produce ideas and ideals regarding women's behavior, which is highly visible in the discourse that concerns women (Lazar, 2005). Keeping in mind that the phenomenon of language can be equally allocated into the behavior bubble, one can see how the social constructionist perspective of language and gender is overt in its undertakings. Lazar (2005: 12) states that:

> Social constructionist approaches emphasize the on-going, iterative and active accomplishment of gender (along with other identities) in and through discourse (West, Lazar and Kramarae, 1997). Accomplishment suggests that people, through their linguistic (and non-linguistic behavior), produce rather than reflect a priori identities as 'women' and 'men' in particular historical and cultural locations, although the produced identities often get viewed as 'natural', imminent and transhistorical.

In the map below (Figure 4), women's behavior also encompasses the way that they speak, since linguistic behaviors are also seen as learned behaviors that come from culture, deriving from the socio-cultural norms that form them.

Figure 4 Women's behavior as including linguistic behavior

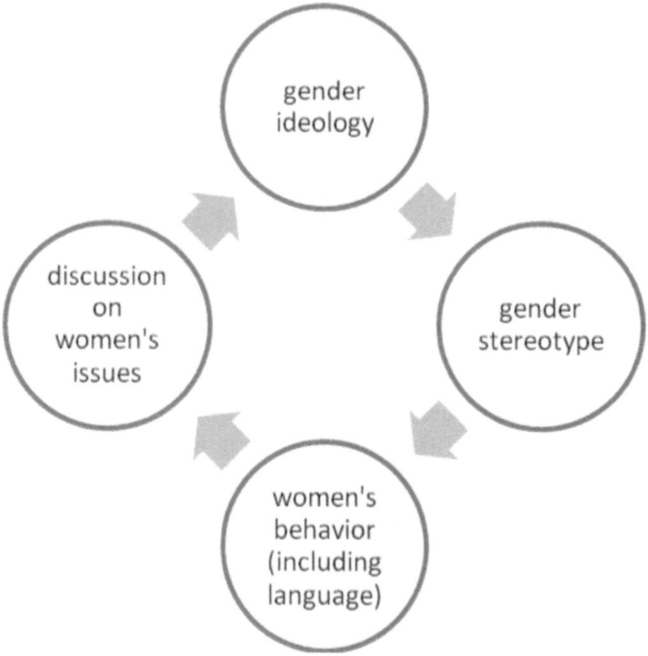

Since the idea of *women's language/girl talk* exists, its implications—along with behavior stereotypes—on the linguistic and alternative modes of their depiction are quite visible in the public sphere (Talbot, 2010: 184). As was mentioned in Chapter 2, Butler (1990, 2011) correlated Austin's (1962) idea of performativity with gender and called it what is known as *gender performativity*. In her book, she cites Wittig (1981) with regard to the collective body as reflective of ideological patterns pertaining to gender and sexuality.

> The task for women, Wittig argues, is to assume the position of the authoritative, speaking subject—which is in some sense their ontologically grounded "right"—and to overthrow both the category of sex and the system of compulsory heterosexuality that is its origin. Language (…) is a set of acts, repeated over time, that produce reality-effects that are eventually misperceived as "facts". Collectively considered, the repeated practice of

> naming sexual difference has created this appearance of natural division. The "naming" of sex as an act of domination and compulsion, an institutionalized performative that creates and legislates social reality by requiring the discursive/ perceptual construction of bodies in accord with principles of sexual difference.
>
> (Butler, 1990: 115)

Because ideology is linked with stereotype—and because these ideas are ever present in the media and discourse—the act of conformity to prescribed gender roles was something that was found in both US and Spanish populations (Sanchez-Lopez et al., 2009; Steinfeldt et al., 2011). The fact that conforming to gender stereotypes happens as a result of the media's influence in most cases, some media (such as beauty campaigns, like Dove (2015) and recent body positivity trends on Instagram or TikTok) have taken it upon themselves to change the objectifying image of women often presented in advertising (McCleary, 2014). However optimistic this seems, ideologies are difficult to overcome, as they are deeply ingrained in societal thought (Tyson, 2006) (cf. Chapter 2).

Public creation and reflected representation

As is shown in the next constituent of the map (Figure 3), the link between women's behavior and the discourse which takes place on the subject of women in the public sphere is both discursive and cultural. Because the public sphere is readily available to everyone, the connections that take place in the discursive interaction between the public and the media have space to materialize in the discourse of individuals, be it public or private. It is because of the underlying sexism which exists in gendered remarks that language is based on and seated in patriarchal ideology (Kiesling, 2019; cf. Chapter 2). From the notion of silencing (Talbot, 2010: 185) to the presence of sexist language in phraseology of both English and Polish (Goddard & Patterson 2001; Krawczyk-Tyrpa, 2001; Puda-Blokesz, 2016), the marginalization of women's societal standing is visible in many aspects (Bulawka, 2013).

Whether it is instructions on appropriate behavior for the feminine individual or social ritual such as beauty practices, women's oppression comes in many symbolic forms (Brownmiller, 1984; Gamson, 1997; Jeffreys, 2005; Kang, 2010). From a linguistic perspective it is necessary to take a social constructionist approach, supported by the methodology of discourse analysis, in order to shed light on the mechanisms used in creating an image of women that presents them as having little power within social structures.

Mechanisms of social control which meld the private sphere with the public have been known to be likened to mechanisms such as the Panopticon (Foucault,

1979; Duncan, 1994). This metaphor holds that social systems and society work as a kind of prison in which one is always subject to being watched by the watchman, and, in turn he monitors his own behavior. Just as Majer (2016) states the relevance of this to the ever-present male gaze, she maintains that with the evolution of masculinities, Panopticon ideology is relevant to media depictions of males (Majer, 2016), as well. This metaphor (of *panopticism*)[53] was applied by Foucault (1979) to express and emphasize the nature and implications of notions of social control. In his book *Discipline and Punish* (*ibid.*), he takes the social theorist Jeremy Bentham's prison model (thought up in the eighteenth century, but never constructed during his lifetime) and uses it as a metaphor for modern "disciplinary" societies. From there, it has been used in reference to the "big brother" nature of the invisible hold of technology on societies in the modern sense.

Masculinity and femininity under the eye of society

Majer (2016) also refers to the ideology behind the Panopticon theory to describe the constant pressure for one to monitor his or her corporeal outward appearance. The existing discourses on masculinity and femininity alike are illustrative of the socially-induced pressure the everyday person puts on him- or herself to attain the so-called ideal. This forces the woman, in the case of beauty culture, to strive to minimize herself by squeezing herself into a smaller invisible space (Bartky, 1988; Jeffreys, 2005). The discourses I am talking of can be found in text, both long and short, located in media discourse, which is readily available to a greater public.

In their analysis of the connotations that accompany certain works, Goddard and Patterson (2000: 32) draw attention to "terms describing personality traits, such as 'chatty' or 'aggressive', can often be seen to fall into certain predictable patterns when used to describe the sexes." We can view the prescription of social roles as not simply sexist descriptors, but forms of ideologically-based social control.[54] Not only do they bring our attention to questions such as the way that sexist

53 *Panopticism* is the metaphor used to refer to social control of which many are aware, yet unaware, where "he who is subjected to a field of visibility, and who knows it, assumes responsibility for the constraints of power; he makes them play spontaneously upon himself; he inscribes in himself the power relation in which he simultaneously plays both roles; he becomes the principle of his own subjection" (Foucault, 1979: 202–203)

54 *Informal means of social control*, by which individuals are driven to follow and abide by societal norms (Black, 1976). The metaphor of the prison system is, in essence, appropriate to the issue of patriarchal ideology and the array of social control over the female (body, self-awareness, consciousness).

language overtly distinguishes females as being the weaker sex on lexical grounds, but also to the way in which many labels utilize prescriptive tactics to form certain representations of women in their discourse.

In another analysis of the English language, Lopez Rodriguez (2007) discusses metaphorical representations of women in popular magazines aimed at a younger female audience, namely those of *Glamour* and *Cosmopolitan*. In the same vein, Bulawka (2013) discusses the archetypal representations of women found in the political texts of Polish media outlets, and draws attention to the way in which female archetypes upon which stereotypes are drawn place women into categories that deem them suitable to certain roles and bars them symbolically from the participation of their own empowerment, even if they are political actors (cf. Chapter 2).

This aspect is important in the conversation on sexual aggression and sexual scripts, for one may consider panoptic mechanisms equally present in sexual interactions or the way that survivors or victims of sexual assault speak about their experiences. This particular aspect, however, is not part of the presented study and will not be discussed in depth. It is important, however, to consider that gendered ideologies and the way social perceptions are reflected in discourse are telling of the collective, ideologically, and that they lead to the cognitive processes present in the discourses that construct ideas and identities regarding the self and others.

English linguistic perspectives on sexuality

The linguistic work on language, gender and sexuality is quite expansive, and one cannot talk about language and sexuality without first discussing the issue of language and gender (cf. Chapter 2. Butler's (1990) theory of performativity plays just as much into the question of linguistic performativity, where sexuality is seen as reflected in gendered performance. Where women constitute the marked gender in a gendered binary normative society, the language used to refer to women has equal implications on the way a woman is viewed in a sexual context.

Much of the literature surrounding the question of sexuality, gender and identity focuses on sexual orientation, sexual preferences and marginalized sexual identities, as well as the construction of sexuality (Bucholtz, 2004). The linguistic research which accompanies such study focuses on how these "marked identities" are formed from a linguistic aspect, namely regarding what linguistic features are used to mark identities of those who belong to communities of sexual minorities or otherness.

Studies on language, gender and sexuality also encompass the study of the language used by sexual minorities, including gay and lesbian discourse (Morgan & Wood, 1995; Leap, 1996; Cameron & Kulick, 2003; Msibi, 2013; Leap, 2015). The study of gay and lesbian language is related to sexual scripts, as much so as it is to phonological aspects of, for example, the use of breathy voice and raised intonations in gay men's speech (Leap, 1996; Cameron & Kulick, 2013). From a phonological perspective, Hall's (1995) equally ground-breaking paper on the language of phone-sex operators examined the use of suprasegmental features and lexical items considered markers of femininity that are usually seen as non-empowering features of language in the context of the provisioning of services in the sex industry.

Other research on English linguistic perspectives of sexuality concerns the question of language and sexual crime. A section for each of the cultures will present this particular subject, as the subject of language and sexual crime, which is later presented, is central to this work.

Polish linguistic perspectives on sexuality

Not as much study has been strictly done on the aspect of sexuality in the Polish language in comparison to the linguistic study that has been carried out on the subject of English, similarly to the way that studies on gender and language are limited in the Polish literature (Kiełkiewicz-Janowiak, 2019). Some studies do not focus strictly on the issues surrounding the subject of sexuality, itself, but rather make up part of a whole study, such as the research carried out on the different dimensions of taboo in phraseological study, which demonstrates the overall taboo character of sexuality in Poland (Krawczyk-Tyrpa, 2001; Wiśniewska, 2010; Dembowska, 2013; Dec-Pietrowska & Papryczka, 2016).

Wiśniewska's (2010) study on the contemporary use of the word *sex* proved the taboo nature of sexuality that has proliferated throughout Polish society, as well as an interpretation of the dual nature of sex and love. What she found was that "the primacy of sexuality is just as unsafe for society as ignorance regarding one's own body, experience and behavior."[55] This in itself is a demonstration of how the issue of sexuality is both silenced and seen as being interconnected with the concept of love, making bodily autonomy almost invisible in Polish discourse. Although

55 My translation of the Polish text: „Okazuje się, że prymat seksualności jest równie niebezpieczny dla społeczeństwa jak niewiedza, dotycząca własnego ciała, przeżyć i zachowań" (Wiśniewska, 2010: 204)

Wiśniewska (*ibid.*) was against the radical changes in approaching the notion of sex, her analysis still demonstrates cultural and social attitudes towards sexuality.

Karwatowska (2010) has carried out some studies on the language of young people, and in doing so, first touched on the lexicographical aspects of the word *seks* ('sex') i the Polish language. She described that up until 1908, when the word *seksualny* ('sexual') was defined as having to do with the biological sex of a person, it was finally provided a more adequate and encompassing definition in the fourth volume of *The Polish Dictionary*, which added to it the sphere of attraction and intimacy.[56] The aim of Karwatowska's (*ibid.*) parallel study and analysis was to look at the way that young people over the age of 16 view the noun *seks* (2010: 134).

When it comes to feminist activism in areas of linguistic concern, the issue of the female forms of occupational titles is one that comes to the forefront of a list of debatable issues seen in the Polish language (Dąbrowska, M., 2008). The work of Karwatowska and Szpyra-Kozłowska (2010; Szpyra-Kozłowska, 2021), which has attracted the attention of many scholars in the field of gender studies in Poland, describes the semantic asymmetry present in terms that refer to men and women's sexual roles, thus illustrating where gender and sexuality intersect, stating that men have more dominant sexual roles.

Defining sex

As mentioned in Chapter 2, definitions of sex and what is in fact considered sexual intercourse fall into the field of study of language and sexuality. As Cameron & Kulick (2003) describe in their book, definitions of sex are not necessarily straightforward, either, taking into consideration, more specifically, the Lewinsky-Clinton scandal of the 1990s. This propelled a discussion on what it means to have "sexual relations", sparking a debate on the subject of oral sex, touching and sexual stimulation that does not include penetration.

---

56 In summary, Karwatowska discusses how Wiśniewska (2010) draws attention to the fact that only in the 1908 edition of the *Dictionary of the Polish Language* does the word *seksualny* 'sexual' appear, with a brief explanation as: "gendered or having to do with gender (or biological sex)" (Karwatowska, 2010: 134–135). But it is when editor Witold Doroszewski presents a definition of the work in *the Dictionary of the Polish Language* that seven structures all related to *seks* ('sex') come out, including those having to do with gender, attraction, sex-appeal, sexualism, sexual, to do something in a sexual manner, and sexology. The Polish dictionary as edited by Szyczak makes note of three terms, namely *seks* ('sex'), attraction and traits which attract the opposite sex (*ibid.*).

Cameron and Kulick (2003: 3) provide an example of a questionnaire carried out by two researchers at the Kinsey Institute for Research in Sex, Gender and Reproduction in 1991. The goal was to attempt to describe how university students would define sexual intercourse.

> Would you say you 'had sex' with someone if the most intimate behavior that you engaged in was . . . (mark yes or no for each behavior):
>
> (a) a person had oral (mouth) contact with your breasts or nipples?
> (b) you touched, fondled, or manually stimulated a person's genitals?
> (c) you had oral (mouth) contact with a person's breasts or nipples?
> (d) penile-vaginal intercourse (penis in vagina)?
> (e) you touched, fondled, or manually stimulated a person's breasts or nipples?
> (f) a person had oral (mouth) contact with your genitals?
> (g) you had oral (mouth) contact with a person's genitals?
> (h) deep kissing (French or tongue kissing)?
> (i) penile-anal intercourse (penis in anus [rectum])?
> (j) a person touched, fondled, or manually stimulated your breasts or nipples?
> (k) a person touched, fondled, or manually stimulated your genitals
>
> (*ibid.*)

The results were interesting, as they indicated that "60% of the respondents would not say that they 'had sex' with someone if the most intimate behavior engaged in was oral-genital contact" (*ibid.*: 3). This is just one of the studies which focus on different understanding of sex, and one of the only ones that looks at different understandings of sex and sexuality from a standpoint of definitions (McPhillips, Braun & Gavey, 2001; Wynn et al., 2010; Sewell & Strassberg, 2015).

Another study (McPhillips, Braun & Gavey 2001) discusses the "coital imperative", investigating how much of the way that individuals define heterosexual sex is defined by its existence in a sexual situation. McPhillips, Braun, and Gavey found that "a "coital imperative", [...] makes it unthinkable that mature heterosexuals could have sex without having intercourse" (*ibid.*: 229). The results of their study on 15 New Zealand men and 15 New Zealand women of European (Pakeha) descent show that intercourse, here defined as the coital imperative itself, was thought to be necessary to be able to define what constitutes "heterosex" (*ibid.*: 238–239).

Language and discourse constitute some of the clearest reflections of attitudes towards socially significant issues, including ones that raise feelings of discomfort, uncertainty or shame. In many cultures, including both American and Polish cultures, the sphere of sexuality is considered taboo, as well as the language used to describe it (Krótki, 2014).

Taboo in discourse

It is known that "taboos arise out of social constraints on the individual's behaviour where it can cause discomfort, harm or injury" (Allan & Burridge, 2006). Taboos that have been considered more or less universal among cultures include bodily functions of sex and excretion, genitalia and women's breasts, illness and death, words believed to be blasphemous, income, salary, among others (Gao, 2013: 2310-1).

According to Wardhaugh (2000: 234), *taboo* is the prohibition or avoidance of behavior that is believed to be harmful to a society's members in that it would cause anxiety, embarrassment, or shame. Thus, where language is concerned, saying certain things should be avoided or certain objects can be referred to only in certain circumstances, by certain people, or expressed euphemistically (Gao, 2013). *The Routledge Dictionary of Language and Linguistics* (2000: 1173) states that a taboo word is a term that is avoided for religious, political or sexual reasons and is usually replaced by a euphemism, which will be the focus of any expressions of socially taboo subjects in this work, namely that of "rape".

Among existing taboos are those which impinge on moral status or standing, thus placing at risk the person to which it pertains. This includes the sphere of sexuality (including the organs one relates to sex), which is one of the subjects considered in the literature on taboo (Allan & Burridge, 2006), and of most importance of such topics where taboo is relevant to the work. Taboo subjects have been known to be expressed through various forms of politeness and impoliteness, including dysphemistic and euphemistic means (*ibid.*). The reason for mentioning taboo and language in this chapter is that when a subject is treated as taboo (such as is the case with sexuality), the repercussions are visible in cultural discourses that are related to the subject (such as with rape). This tabooization of sexuality has led to the tabooization of rape and its reflections in discourse (such as the linguistic constituents which reflect tabooization) must be investigated in how it leads to victim blaming.

Sexuality is one of the social categories which fall under the subject of taboo, which is visible in the discourse on the subject in the English language. Although the taboo status of sexuality in English has slightly changed, there are certain aspects of sexuality that remain hushed, including the sexuality of people with disabilities (Duguay, 2011). Rosewarne (2013) has illustrated the wide array of taboos around sexuality in American culture, highlighting that homoeroticism and gay sex, as well as the act of performing oral sex are made highly taboo (*ibid.*; cf. Chapter 1; Chapter 2). The subject of euphemization is brought up in the work with reference to female sanitary pads and periods (i.e., the expression of *feminine hygiene*), as well as the male penile erection.

As an example, the act of masturbation, which has been referred to through biblical euphemisms as *onanism* for one, varies between euphemism and dysphemism as pertains to the ways of its expression (Allan & Burridge, 2006). What is included in the study of taboo expression in language is how exactly it is that euphemism and dysphemism are expressed: whether through metaphorical expression or the renaming of an object (for example, in the language to discuss sex in English, some euphemistic expressions include "do the deed" or "do the nasty" (Crespo-Fernandez, 2008: 103–104)).

There is an extensive list of the subjects related to sexuality that are perceived as taboo, including ones related to gender identity, the sexual infidelity of women, masturbation, sexually transmitted infections, rape, and the question of sexual intercourse between people of the same sex (or gender) (Allan & Burridge, 2006: 145). Rosewarne (2013: 71) provides some examples of euphemistic expressions that are used to talk about rape, stating that "while news reports readily use euphemisms to discuss rape (*indecent assault*, *carnal knowledge*, *attack*, and *abuse*, for example) the use of euphemism by victims is particularly relevant for this section, highlighting some of the psychological underpinnings of euphemism use." The use of euphemistic expression to talk about rape is discussed at length in the practical part of this work (cf. Chapter 6 and Chapter 7). It must be kept in mind that subjects, such as sexual consent, are also constrained by taboos (Allan & Burridge, 2006; Beres, 2007; Rosewarne, 2013).

Taboo, the body and sexuality in Polish

The literature on the subject has shown that the sphere of sexuality is also among the most taboo in Polish culture (Melosik, 1996; Wasilewski, 2010; Smoter, 2013; Loch, 2015; Gorajska et al., 2018). Of the topics related to sexuality, body parts, and more specifically genitalia, are among the subjects referred to by means of euphemization, mainly through lexical metaphorical substitution (Dąbrowska A., 2008; Żurowski, 2014). The domination of gendered construals of sexuality is also visible in the Polish research, including the binary division of women into the categories of "virgins" and "vamps" (i.e., "porządne" and "ladacznice"), which are categories that exist in the English language context as well (Drapalska-Grochowicz, 2018: 36). The array of dysphemistic expressions which denote female sexuality in particular displays negative construals as dominant ones (*ibid.*).

Although little work has been carried out regarding the discursive representations of sexuality, and what they reflect in culture, the literature that does exist demonstrates the taboo nature of sexuality in the surrounding Polish context (Żurowski, 2014). This can be seen in the two subjects that will be further discussed in the sections to follow, namely the naming of genitalia and expressions for sexual intercourse. I have chosen only these select semantic fields because they are seated within the discussion of sexuality in culture and also capture the binary polarization that exists within discourses about men's and women's sexualities.

Discursive representations of genitalia

Research concerning the discursive representations of genitalia has been linked to taboo positioning of the physical aspects of reproductive and sexual health, as well as to the social-constructivist implications they have for both women and men, with a specific focus on the negative impact that it has on women's perceptions of themselves and others (Braun & Kitzinger, 2001; Braun & Wilkinson, 2001; Fernández Martín, 2010; Wójcik, 2015). It is important to understand that the body is here seen as both a social construction and a material object, and that prevailing discourses greatly impact the attitudes of receivers to the sexual subjects that are both directly and recursively a part of them. The following sections describe discursive representations of genitalia, which are reflective of perceptions of human sexuality on the whole, namely heteronormative sexual practices.

Discursive representations of genitalia in English

Other studies that fall under the category of language and sexuality include Braun and Kitzinger's (2001) paper on women's linguistic reference to their own vaginas and the discursive relationship between vaginal shape or size and culture. Studies on the way people name the vagina and penis focus on the semantics which reflects attitudes towards female and male sexuality and genitals (in the binary sense) (Braun & Kitzinger, 2001; Potts, 2001; Zimman, 2014; McLaren & Gatwiri, 2016).

In the aforementioned study carried out by Braun and Kitzinger (2001), there was a correlation found between vaginal size and feelings of security in a sexual relationship. The narratives of the participants in the study demonstrated how patriarchal ideology creates feelings among women that dictate to them an inherent need to sexually please men, which was greatly viewed as being related to the literal, physical tightness of the vagina. This differs greatly from prevailing cultural discourses on penis size, in which physical largeness is viewed and constructed as desirable in the West, for one, although this might not be universal (McKee, 2004; Ostberg, 2010).

Another study which investigates the linguistic representations or semanticity of terms for genitalia was conducted by Fernández Martín (2010), in which she deconstructs the reflection that words for female genitalia reflect societal standpoints on women and their sexuality (read as sexual inferiority). She states that "words for women's genitalia are mostly perceived as receptacles" and that the terms used "emphasize the passive role women adopt in sexual intercourse" (*ibid.*: 77). Her study considers both English and Spanish lexical items, making for a comparative study. What she discovered was that many terms describing women's genitalia simply reinforce women's roles in pleasuring men. Some examples are provided (Fernández Martín, 2010: 77):

26) *box (jelly-, tool)*
27) *hole' (cheese-, glory-, slam-, stimey)*
28) *honeypot, muff*

Other examples include selected examples of the ones provided by Braun and Kitzinger (2010: 148), who found that the most frequently used terms were the following:

29) *cunt*
30) *fanny*
31) *pussy*

Although there are few papers describing the semantics of the discursive representations of the vagina, the results are very telling of social attitudes in general. In another work, Braun and Kitzinger (2010) discovered that overall linguistic reference to genitalia tends to be euphemistic or metaphorical (for both male and female biological genitalia), yet vaginas are represented as receptacles and abjections, highlighting the role of the vagina as a passive receptacle for male pleasure (*ibid.*). The discussion about female passivity in sexuality can be seen as correlating with the representations of the corporal aspects.

To provide a cultural comparison, Fernandez Martin (2010) provides examples from Spanish, which refer to the vagina as "places for men to hide" (*ibid.*), relating a kind of universality in the conceptualizations surrounding female sexuality. Her work points out what Mills discovered about the English language's treatment of female genitalia as taboo, reflected in how Mills (1995: 104) calls attention to the fact that these words somewhat "bridge the gap between the formal words for female genitalia associated with medicine and science, like 'vagina' and 'vulva', and the most colloquial, glossed in dictionaries as 'taboo' and 'offensive'."

Romaine (1990, 2003) discovered that linguistic terms and representations of men's genitalia suffer quite the opposite. Romaine (*ibid.*) divided metaphorical representations of penises into two categories. It is stated in the literature that "those belonging to the first group have to do with the idea that male erections and orgasms are uncontrollable," with representations utilizing terms for penetration which are associated with weapons, tools, and wild animals, for one (Fernández Martín, 2010: 78). The examples include words such as the following (Romaine, 1990; Fernández Martín, 2010):

32) *drill*
33) *chopper*
34) *hose*
35) *pipe*
36) *snake*

The second group was described as containing terms related to war metaphors and mythical names, with the following examples (Fernández Martín, 2010):

37) *sword*
38) *gun*
39) *meatspear*
40) *beef bayonet*
41) *King Kong*

Additionally, linguistic reference to physiological processes that are related to male sexuality, including erections, have been noted to be expressed in the following euphemistic ways, as examples (Rosewarne, 2013: 67), including "big boost of confidence, natural male enhancement, living large, and a generous swelling of pride." What is important to highlight in this is that size is again seen as a valor where male sexuality is concerned, as opposed to the smaller size that is seen as more desirable where vaginas are concerned (Braun & Kitzinger, 2001).

The differences in connotations between men's and women's genitalia is simultaneously alarming and telling of the associations they have with the male and female sexuality described in the previous chapter and have been referred to here in order to clarify just how entrenched these scripts are in culture, language and discourse. The same may be said of Polish discursive construals of genitalia.

Discursive representations of genitalia in Polish

The Polish terms for genitalia have also been subject to investigation, from historical, cultural and linguistic perspectives (Lewinson, 1999; Jagielski & Morstin-Popławska, 2009; Karwatowska, 2010; Karwatowska et al., 2014a/ 2014b; Broszko 2017; Pacuła, 2020). Karwatowska (2010: 136–137) names the most common terms for male and female genitalia as used by high school students. There was a greater variety of terms used for the vagina (examples 42–46) than for the penis (examples 47 and 48):

42) *cipa/cipeczka* ('cunt')
43) *łechtaczka* ('clitoris')
44) *pochwa* ('vulva')
45) *szparka* ('gap')
46) *wagina* ('vagina')

The terms used for the penis in her study included the following (*ibid.*):

47) *penis* ('penis')
48) *prącie* ('penis')

In her analysis, Broszko (2017) similarly enumerates the different categorizations of terms denoting genitalia, describing references to the vagina and penis in categories of medical terms, colloquially, through the use of vulgar expressions, and poetically, thus providing a broader overview of the semantic fields for genitalia. This further explains the connotations that are met in the view of discourses on sexuality. The categorized terms for the vagina are as follows (*ibid.*):

49) Medical/anatomical expression: *pochwa* ('vulva')
Colloquial expressions: *kuśka* ('cunt')
Vulgar expressions: *cipa, piczka* ('cunt')
Poetic expressions: *ogród rozkoszy, grota Kupidyna* ('pleasure garden'; 'Cupid's lair')
Expressions used to describe genitalia to children: *sisiorek* ('wee wee')

The categorized terms for the penis are the following (Broszko 2017; Pacuła 2020):

50) Medical/anatomical expression: *prącie* ('penis')
Colloquial expressions: *członek, interes* ('member')
Vulgar expressions: *kutas* ('dick')
Poetic expressions: none listed
Expressions used to describe genitalia to children: *sisiorek* ('wee wee')

More interesting are the euphemisms used to refer to the vagina and phallus. The ones denoting the vagina include *muszelka*, *brzoskwinia*, *norka*, *guziczek*" ('shell,' 'peach,' 'hole', 'button') as examples, and *kij*, *pała*, *koń*, *miecz*, *ptaszek* ('stick,' 'chump,' 'horse,' 'sword,' 'bird') denote the penis (Broszko 2017: 39). Broszko (*ibid.*) makes a connection between the use of euphemistic expressions for genitalia and the taboo surrounding them.

The connection with ideology throughout the discourses on male and female genitalia speaks to the socio-cultural views of human, heteronormative sexuality.

Not only do these expressions tend to be highly euphemistic, communicating strategies of expressions for taboo subjects, but they present an asymmetry of power where men's and women's sexual agency is concerned. It becomes clear, from the examples provided above, that male sexuality (even with reference to male biology) is built on power, linking to it metaphors of war and monstrosity, whereas the euphemistic expression that represents female genitalia evidently construes women's sexuality as demure or passive through its allusions to sweetness and the vagina as a receptacle. This is true of both American and Polish cultures, meaning that although this asymmetry is cultural, it is more or less universal.

Discursive representations of sexual intercourse in English

In her paper, Fernández Martín (2010) also provides some of the terms used to describe sexual intercourse, emphasizing the passive linguistic presentation of female sexuality, as well as the brutality of which sex is often described (Ehrlich, 2001; Fernández Martín, 2010).

The beginnings of study on discursive representations of sexual intercourse were in the 1970s, with descriptions of the usage of terms for sexual intercourse by men and women (Walsh & Leonard, 1974). Manning (1997) also analyzed the grammatical structure of verbs which denote intimate acts, both sexual and romantic, and created a large corpus of words taken from British and American English to illustrate the diversity (Clark, 2012). Some of the verbs named were *kiss, hug, caress, fondle* and *shag,* or *make love* (Manning, 1997).

When strictly speaking of verbs which denote sexual intercourse, some of the examples enumerated in the by Cameron (1985) and Ehrlich and King (1994) included:

51) *fuck*
52) *screw*
53) *lay*

More recently, Ehrlich (2001) points to the fact that most of the verbs describing sexual intercourse focus on men as active in heterosexual intercourse and women as the passive reciprocator of the sexual act upon them. Ehrlich and King (1994: 60) poignantly state that if penetration were described from a female perspective, it would "be more appropriately encoded as *enclosure, surrounding,* or *engulfing.*" This deconstruction of the discursive embodiment of sexual intercourse shows precisely the unequal allocation of roles in heterosexual sex.

Other studies on verbs and expressions which refer to sexual intercourse have to do with the denotations of gay sex in English, usually referring to pejorative slang terms meant to harm or create negative representations of homosexual men.

The use of the word *fuck*, analyzed from the critical view of fuck as a metaphor and which aimed to provide an explanation for why the expression "fuck you," still constitutes an offensive retort in the English language. It has additionally been described as a symbol of male sexual aggression (Hobbs, 2013). What was discovered was the symbolic nature of the degradation and transformation of the person on the receiving end of such a retort into a female receiver of sodomization (Gass, 1978: 50).

Discursive representations of sexual intercourse in Polish

Some of the research concerning names for sexual intercourse includes naming heterosexual intercourse, although few such studies have been carried out, and also naming sexual intercourse between gay men (Karwatowska, 2010; Rejtar, 2013; Krótki, 2014). Some of the verbs denoting sexual intercourse in Polish follow, as cited by Karwatowska (2010: 137):

54) Neutral: *kopulacja* ('copulation'), *oddanie się* ('surrender'), *stosunek (płciowy)* ('intercourse'), *współżycie* ('intercourse')[57]
Vulgar: *bzykanie/bzykanko, dupczenie, jebanko, pieprzyć się, ruchanie/ruchańsko* ('fucking')[58]
Slang terms: *bara bara, jazda* ('a ride'), *ostra jazda bez trzymanki* ('riding with no reins'), *szybki lopez* ('a quickie'), *zaliczenie* ('home run')[59]

Krótki's (2014) analysis of euphemisms denoting sexual intercourse draws on the concept of sex as a taboo subject and the fact that today's euphemistic expressions for sexual intercourse are extensions of historical euphemisms taken from the Bible and other older sources. She includes some of the following examples of modern euphemistic expressions:

55) *robić to* ('to do it')
56) *o tych sprawach* ('about those things')[60]

---

57 These examples, provided by Karwatowska (2010), are more equivalent to the English term 'intercourse' or the meaning simply 'to have sex'
58 The examples provided under vulgar expressions may be considered the equivalent of the English terms *fucking* or *screwing*
59 The examples of slang terms have been translated into the closest equivalents in English (my translations)
60 Examples taken from Krótki (2014: 143)

She then cites older examples, some of which are as such:

57) *rzecz* ('thing'/ 'it')
58) *swą rzecz odbywać* ('to do one's deed')[61]

Other works citing euphemistic expressions for sexual intercourse have been written, including an analysis of expressions in legal language (Leśnik, 2011).

Rejter (2013) has also listed expressions for sexual intercourse between gay men, including the following (not all examples are listed):

59) *bawić się cwelem* ('play with the pansy')
60) *brać górą* ('take the top')
61) *lecieć w tyłek* ('take it in the ass')
62) *masowanie rury* ('massaging the pipe')
63) *pierdolenie w czarne oczko//czekoladowe oczko* ('screwing the black/chocolate hole')

The negative and jocular semantic weight that these expressions contribute to the presentation of homosexual sex is attributes to the negative connotations that are given to the act of homosexual sexual intercourse on the whole, especially considering an omnipresent negative sentiment felt and expressed in the current Polish political climate (Kulpa, 2020). These expressions have been listed in order to illustrate the broad spectrum of linguistic analysis and corpus building with regard to issues of sexuality. The following will focus more on the sphere of the heterosexual market where representations of heterosexual sexualities are concerned, as that is the focus of the analysis.

Deflowering the maiden: The languages of virginity loss in English and Polish

Yet another example of socially constructed asymmetries that are discursive is that of the concept of virginity, which has been argued to be upheld by patriarchal norms and discourses. As has been pointed out, men who marry virgins are viewed in many cultures as more respectable since women's virginity is of value, presenting sexual cultural capital and thus enhances the status of her marital partner (Schlegel, 1991: 731). The question of virginity as a social construct will not be discussed in depth in this work, for the sake of space, but delineated briefly in order to tie it to the aspects of sexuality that have enforced it as a social construct (Carpenter, 2001; 2011). The phraseological descriptions of virginity loss have mostly to do with a young woman's loss of her virginity, the semantic weight of

61 *Ibid.*

which describes the cultural capital that virginity seems to carry with it (Irigaray, 1997; Carpenter, 2011).

In the context of the English language, expressions which draw on the symbolic representation of women in the metaphorical sense may be located in discourse. This is seen in expressions such as *deflowering*, which draws on the popular representation of female chastity as valuable and beautiful (Carpenter, 2001; Kelly, 2010). In opposition to this, male virginity has been described as an encumbrance in the negative sense, and pressure put on boys and men to lose their virginity as soon as they reach an appropriate age (*ibid.*).

Semantic studies concerning the issue of cultural obsession with the chaste female was carried out in the African context (more specifically, Zambia) by the African Regional Sexuality Resource Center in collaboration with Health Systems Trust, South Africa and The University of Fort Hare (2014). These examples are partially taken from Anna Dąbrowska's (1998) *Dictionary of Polish Euphemisms.*

64) *Pozbawić wieńca* ('to do away with the wreath')[62]

The question of virginity is important in the discussion on sexuality and its social construction since many feminist scholars have highlighted that as a notion it also falls under such terms (Carpenter, 2001, 2011). This can be found true with regard to various cultural contexts, which in turn exemplifies how universal the high value of female virginity is (Lightfoot-Klein, 1989; Kambarami, 2014).

Of those contexts, the African one has been highlighted in the discussion of the various forms of the symbolic oppression of women in the context of sexual freedom, marital freedom, and religious pressure to adhere to traditional notions of femininity (Damasus & Okoro, 2020). Kambarami (2006: 1) declares that "it is only appropriate that we continue to assess how culture continues to impact negatively on feminine sexuality despite all efforts that have been made to minimize its impact by challenging the status quo," which brings to light the severity of culture's impact on societal thought (cf. Chapter 2). This can and should be considered from a linguistic perspective in other cultural contexts as well, including those of Poland and the United States, shown in the analysis (cf. Chapters 6 and 7).

It is important to discuss this aspect of sexual scripting, as virginity has come to be argued as a social and cultural concept, largely dictated by the discourse

62 The meaning of this is literally *to do away with the wreath* (as in a flower crown), the English equivalent of which is *to deflower*, as stated earlier. This allusion to flowers in both languages additionally demonstrates the construction of women and femininity in the realm of things that are beautiful, as well as maintains the image of female sexuality as a prized, beautiful object that should be saved until due time.

which surrounds female sexuality. The capital placed on virginity as a notion is also what ascribes attributes of innocence, passivity, and docile femininity to female sexuality.

Since this work focuses on the social construction of gender within the sphere of sexuality, and describes it as having repercussions in the way that female victims of rape are viewed in society, it is crucial to mention the aspect. In a similar way to that of the gender ideologies concerning the roles of men and women in society, as well as expectations of traits and behavioral stereotypes related to rape, the constructs surrounding female and male sexuality also play a role in the perception of actors in rape. The sections that follow discuss the discursive investigations of sexual crime, which makes up the epicenter of the work. Here I ask that the reader consider the asymmetries in discourse presented above in its juxtapositions with the way that societies view social actors involved in sexual assault, for it is my claim that sexual assault, being a highly gendered subject is not without influence from the various social constructions of gender, including the way sexuality and gender are related.

English linguistics aspects of sexual crime

As mentioned in Chapter 1, the discursive representations of heteronormative sexual actors in intercourse have seen much study in the English context, especially where passivity and active partaking in the act of sex are concerned. The question of assertiveness and saying *no* is equally important in the construction of social actors, which I argue is a result of the different linguistic aspects surrounding male and female (in this case, especially female) heterosexual sexualities. Serious linguistic interest in cases of sexual assault began in the 1990s, with the investigation of the discourse of the court. Norma Mendoza-Denton's article, "Pregnant Pauses: Silence and Authority in the Anita Hill–Clarence Thomas Hearings" (1995), brought to light the linguistically relevant language aspects of Justice Clarence Thomas's hearings, as well as the rise in concerns about sexual harassment in the United States (more of the English linguistic studies on language and sexual crime are outlined below).

The aspect of language and sexual crime is being stated here, since it is the objective of this work to demonstrate how various discourses on rape, in their status as public discourses, perpetuate the harmful ideologies that have been so far presented in this work. Any attitudes surrounding sexuality, including those negative ones, additionally play a role in how the subjects of sexual crime are perceived, hence the importance of engaging in further discussion of linguistic perspectives of sexual crime.

English and sexual crime

Although much of the linguistic perspective on sexual crime was enumerated in Chapter 1, it is important to mention in this chapter too, as research on language and sexuality has embraced the study of language and sexual aggression as one of its pillar subjects. Aside from the more technical and erotic aspects of sexuality, the issue of sexual crime is also covered in the field discussed (Ehrlich, 2001; Cameron & Kulick, 2003; Thornborrow, 2014). Multiple studies have been conducted on the area of sexual crime from a linguistic perspective, including the tackling of the issues of rape trial protocol (Ponterotto, 2007), child sexual abuse (O'Keeffe & Breen, 2007), and the discourses of sexual coercion (Ehrlich, 2007). Milani's (2015) volume of articles on issues in language, gender, and sexuality in South Africa also focuses on the discourses which reproduce skewed and biased images of rape victims in widely read public media (Krige & Oostendorp, 2015: 7–23) (cf. Chapter 1).

> If the subjects of the passive construction are being harmed, presumably the subjects of the active construction are doing harm, and, indeed, we do conceive of these subjects in precisely the same way. Suppose one is angry at someone and wishes to express malevolence as forcefully as possible without actually committing an act of physical violence. If one is inclined to be vulgar one can make the sign of the erect male cock by clenching one's fist while raising one's middle finger, or by clenching one's fist and raising one's arm and shouting such things as 'screw you,' 'up yours,' or 'fuck you.' In other words, one of the strongest possible ways of telling someone that you wish to harm him is to tell him to assume the female sexual role relative to you.
>
> (Baker, 1974: 178)

Although the above source is quite outdated, the information presented is still relevant. Research and analyses which have been conducted on the sexual aspects of the English language focus on the beliefs that some sexual activities are "considered good (versus bad) and normal (versus deviant) sexual activities" and how it is that "identities are historically and socioculturally situated" (Milani, 2017: 404). Much other work has been written regarding the linguistics of sexual aggression such as rape, molestation and other forms of sexual assault and has been published by leading scholars in the field (Ehrlich, 2003; Cotterill, 2007; Bou-Franch, 2016) (cf. Chapter 1). This perspective is important in understanding western approaches to sexuality and its implications on other sexual cultures.

Some of the earliest English linguistic studies on sexual crime dealt with the discourse of the press, as a way of illustrating the power of utilizing the passive voice in representing social actors, and foregrounding those actors within an event (in this case, the crime of rape) (Henley & Miller, 1995). This topic has been dealt with in numerous works as illustrative of the "expression of perceived responsibility of the victim" (Bohner, 2001: 515), thus contributing to the discursive secondary victimization of the rape victim (cf. Chapter 2). Although this aspect concerning the linguistic representation of rape victims has already been investigated, it will also be considered here in the cross-cultural understanding.

Where discourse studies are concerned, some research has been carried out in relation to investigating the discourses that surround language and crime. Anderson and Doherty (2008) investigated the categories of metaphor that arise in the talk and text which describe the problem of sexual crime, and what they discovered was namely that investigations in Critical Discourse Analysis could uncover the underlying problems that reproduce harmful stereotypes of victims in rape in English. These stereotypes are of course derived in the general rather cliché and metaphorical expressions that represent women (*ibid.*: 109).

Overall, English linguistic perspectives have done quite a lot to enrich the field, taking on various perspectives on the surrounding discourses. Not as much may be said of the investigation of discourses on rape in Polish, however, thus making such a cross-cultural discourse analysis as the one presented in this work necessary for the further understanding of social and cultural domains which differentiate perceptions (cf. Chapter 6 & Chapter 7).

Polish linguistic aspects of sexual crime

As mentioned above, relatively little investigation of the linguistic aspects of sexual crime has been carried out in the Polish context, especially where various media discourses are concerned. Any of the research that has been carried out on language and sexual assault in Poland comes from sociological views rather than linguistic ones (Kościańska, 2019). The comparative aspect of the work will demonstrate where ideologies are present in the Polish discourses on rape, and that victim blaming is a phenomenon that occurs in many discursive forms in Polish. To my knowledge, no more linguistic studies on the subject of rape have been conducted, hence the disparities between the research on the American and Polish contexts and the necessity to carry out such a study.

Circling back to ideology

Considering that Western gender ideologies are deeply rooted in biblical representation, especially in the belief that women are passive, delinquent, promiscuous, or the epitome of a saintly woman, therefore chaste, humble, and gentle (Kowalska, 2010; Bulawka, 2013), it is no surprise that those ideologies have remained within language and discourse. The ideas of women and men present in today's portrayals have not strayed much from the detrimental dichotomy of the dominant male and submissive female, despite the many efforts that have been made (Jeffreys, 2005). Since the dawn of representations of women and men in written media (cf. Chapter 2), language has aided in upholding the ideologically based images of men and women.

What existing sexist language does is create a foundation for the omnipresent beliefs that women truly are less capable than men. This can be brought back to the ignorance of expression found in the sexist discourse of women's magazines which also work to keep women in so-called archetypal and stereotyping boxes (Nowak, 2012; Bulawka, 2013). Hence the claim that these expressions are not only presentations of ideological beliefs concerning women, but they are also viable to be seen as cognitive metaphors of women (Lakoff & Johnson, 1980). The same can be said of sexuality and the passivity attributed to women both linguistically (Crawford, 1995) and sexually (Ehrlich, 2001; Fernández Martín, 2010).

Because the linguistic aspects are linked to the cognitive ones (Varela et al., 1993), the way in which women (and men) are discursively presented must be seen as linked, then, to the images that language forms representations in the minds of its speakers. By discursively construing certain presentations of women and men in the media, ideologically-based values are not only upheld but reinforced, making it difficult to surpass them to introduce other notions that might play a more empowering role in the lives of those that they target (Franiuk et al., 2008; Bulawka, 2013; Tabbert, 2016).

Conclusions

Although, arguably, the language one chooses to use is a marker of identity (Gumperz, 1997), it is difficult to ignore the role that discourse plays in the construction of ideals to be prescribed and thought of as necessary to be attained by certain social groups. What we see in the linguistic phenomena described is an example of the manifestation of patriarchal and sexist gender ideologies which presents themselves in the English and Polish.

More specifically, in Polish, the existence of differences in linguistic reference to gender and in discourse is even more difficult to deny, as grammatical gender makes its mark on the inflections of the parts of speech of a sentence, rendering it omnipresent even in everyday speech. This arguably essentializes gender, which has been claimed to be (at least in part) reflective of the ideologies present in Polish society and embedded within Polish discourse (Koniuszaniec & Błaszkowska, 2003; Karwatowska & Szpyra-Kozłowska, 2010).

Sexuality also has extremely significant implications for society and culture and is, without a doubt, one phenomenon that modern, more western(-ized) cultures have been preoccupied with for centuries. Critical studies have begun to tackle the meaning of sexuality and how its understandings impact ideologies in situations of sexual harassment and assault. The intermingling of the political with the private goes back to Habermas' (1989) concepts of the melding of the private and the public spheres (Calhoun, 1993; Benson, 2009). Thus, when considering the language and discourse surrounding sexuality, it is important to think about how social perspectives influence discourses. Since rape is a crime of a sexual nature, the broader narrative of sexuality as presented in this chapter is needed to locate ideologies in discourse, so as to properly demarcate the blurred lines that are found in both public and private discourses surrounding the issue.

The relevance of this chapter to the entire work lies mainly in the subject matter, which concerns issues in language and gender, as well as issues in language and sexuality. It is important to note, however that both the linguistic behaviors of social groups (including gendered groups), as well as their discursive representation in different contexts both impinge on and are present in discourses on the subjects which concern them, including rape.

In the practical analysis (cf. Chapter 6 and Chapter 7), I aim to demonstrate that women and men who are the actors in rape are discursively kept in positions that reproduce the presented scripts, myths and stereotypes (cf. Chapter 2 and Chapter 3). The dissonance and asymmetry of discursive representations of men and women in discourses that are heteronormative and discuss sexuality work to further the beliefs that women are to blame for their own rape. Discourses are here seen as highly reflective of societal attitudes and must be discussed in the context of rape. Before this is done, however, an overview of the media that will be subject to analysis must be discussed as well (cf. Chapter 4).

Chapter 4: Critical discourse analysis and digital comments in computer-mediated communication

Computer-mediated communication has aided in the redistribution of information and the dissemination of public opinion in both traditional and non-traditional forms, including that of reporting incidents that occur not only on a mass scale, but also situations of a great social gravity, through traditional websites, the blogosphere, public forum or social media, among others. Issues ranging "from climate change to the war on terror, financial meltdowns to forced migrations, pandemics to world poverty and humanitarian disasters to the denial of human rights" are ones which "represent the dark side of our globalized planet" (Allen & Thorsen, 2009: ix). The importance of covering these issues from various discursive perspectives provides a wider scope for the understanding of its social and cultural capital in the provision of information within critical discourse studies, especially. Crime, rape in particular, is one such social problem that is discussed in the online sphere and, and with rape being intrinsically tied to human sexuality, gives rise to a cacophony of opinionated discourses on the subject, related to taboo, blame attribution and also opinions about how rape may be defined (cf. Chapter 1).

Digital comments regarding issues related to rape will be investigated in this work, with both Chapter 6 and Chapter 7 concerning the discourse of Internet users in comments concerning various types and more specific cases of rape. The goal of this chapter is to characterize digital comments and define how the content located within them, which in this work arise as a result of longer informative texts such as news reports, is an adequate reflection of opinion formation and dissemination by discursive means (i.e., being evaluative in their meaning). Because they are different in their form and the discursive style communicated, I claim that the discourse of digital comments (cf. Chapters 5, 6 and 7) delivers much more ideologically-laden messages and opinions than the press articles on rape which they accompany, hence projecting victim-blaming attitudes through both direct and indirect discursive means. News reporting genres, on the other hand, are what give rise to these opinions through their presentations of rape in the first place and therefore must also be discussed in the chapter. The focus of the work, however, remains on digital comments.

Within the vein of Critical Discourse Analysis, the genre of digital comments provides a window into the ways that important social issues and problems, such as crime, may be presented in the media. In the following sections, I will consider computer-mediated communication as a field and then move on to describe the status of digital comments within the realm of genre, register and style. The question of investigating this particular type of discourses within the framework of CDA will be described, along with other key aspects of analyzing such a genre as digital comments.

Computer-mediated communication

The digitized sphere of communication has undergone extensive study since the 1980s (Fano, 1984; Rafaelli, 1988), taking off in the 1990s and 2000s in more interdisciplinary areas, including psychology, sociology and linguistics (Spears & Lea, 1992; Walther, 1995, 1996; Baron, 2008; Golka, 2008; Crystal, 2011; Davison 2012; Herring 2013; Kerr & Hiltz 2013; Thurlow 2018; Dainas & Herring, 2021). The field has more recently developed into the area of mobile communication (Herring, 2013; Deumert, 2014; Danesi, 2016; Pérez-Sabater, 2019; Campbell 2020).

Levinson (2009) provides a historical perspective on what he calls *new new media* (cf. Web 2.0), through which he discusses the dawn of YouTube, Twitter, Wikipedia and other forms of a constantly transforming and developing Internet culture (Tannen & Trester, 2013; Walther & Whitty, 2021). The social aspects of life, which are heavily intertwined with the everyday lives of those residing in technologically developed countries, has as much to do with language as social discourses do (cf. Chapter 1; Deumert, 2014). One can say that computer-mediated forms of communication act as a channel for the mediation of talk and public discussion. The linguistic perspective of CMC has been analyzed so that CMC, as a concept, has become a part of sociolinguistic study (Herring, 1996; Kress 2003; Herring, 2005, 2013; Deumert, 2014; Procházka, 2016; Blommaert, 2018; Thurlow, 2018). Prior to making such distinctions, the concept of CMC should be defined.

Definitions of computer-mediated communication

In their book, *Computer-mediated Communication*, Thurlow, Lengel and Thomas (2004) make use of the metaphor of fractals to demonstrate the patterned and continuous nature of communication processing online. The Internet is a tool and platform which influences identities, relationships and communities, and this is done through the communicative function that it plays (*ibid.*). Just as Thurlow et al. state, technically, CMC has been in existence for many years (Thurlow et al., 2004: 14), however the CMC as we know it has instated an interest on the part of scholars, not only due to its important role in society and understanding behaviors (*ibid.*: 15). One of the first definitions provided in their book was originally provided by Santoro (1995: 11), namely that CMC "can encompass virtually all computer uses including such diverse applications as statistical programs, remote-sensing systems, and financial modeling programs, all which fit within the concept of human communication."

CMC also goes by other names, including digital discourse, new media or digital communication, however no clear distinction has been made with regard to the various terms (Herring, 2013; Bou-Franch & Blitvich, 2019). The subjects of and approaches to studying computer-mediated communication have varied since their dawn, but it is clear that they revolve around the medium of communicating and range in focus from the subject of the medium itself to the subject of the users of such media.

In her earlier work, Herring (1996: 1) stated that "CMC is communication that takes place between human beings via the instrumentality of computers." More specifically it "can be classified into text, audio, audio/video, and multi-media-based formats" (Zhou et al. 2004: 81) and divided into *synchronous CMC*, which includes instant messaging and has "minimal delays between message transmissions" (*ibid.*) and *asynchronous CMC*, such as email for one, which "allows people to respond to incoming messages at their convenience" (*ibid.*: 82). CMC can be both text-based and asynchronous, making it *text-based asynchronous CMC* (Zhou et al. 2004; Johnson 2006; Baron 2008).

Yet again, these differences have been blurred in more recent scholarship (Herring, 2013) and the definition of CMC expanded (Herring et al., 2009; Żebrowska, 2012). Herring (2013: 5) states that "CMC itself has been undergoing a shift, from occurrence in stand-alone clients such as emailers and instant messaging programs to juxtaposition with other content, often of an information or entertainment nature, in converged media platforms, where it is typically secondary, by design, to other information or entertainment-related activities." She (*ibid.*) refers to the phenomenon of convergent media communication (CMCMC), which is common on Web 2.0 sites, including text comments, text and video responses to video material, such as YouTube videos, text messaging on mobile phones or text and voice chat while during online games (Thurlow & Brown, 2008). It is called convergent because it "converges" text with text, rather than text with another mode of communication (Herring, 2013: 5; Herring, 2019; Fu & Lai, 2020).

Moreover, Herring's (2013) discussion of three different genres of discourse in CMC and CMD (Computer-mediated Discourse) names familiar, reconfigured, and emergent discourses as existent within the classification of CMC. In Herring's classification of the three types of discourses presented in CMC study, the term *discourse familiar* is used to suggest continuities in (as opposed to copies of earlier) discourse phenomena. These so-called familiar patterns are assumed to have manifested continuously on the Internet from the 1990s until the present, however not necessarily on the same web sites (*ibid.*). What she calls *reconfigured discourse* is used to emphasize the reshaping and reusing of various discourse phenomena that takes place in online environments, i.e., the status update functions on Facebook or Twitter (Herring, 2013: 11; Fu & Lai, 2020), which first appeared in the online sphere in the 1990s. Reconfigured discourse are, in short, the reproduction of earlier online practices. The term *emergent discourse*, on the other hand, is preserved by Herring (*ibid.*) from Crowston and Williams (2000), describing the phenomenon that occurs when "new web genres and discourse phenomena can equally well be said to emerge—that is, to become evident where previously there was no general awareness of their existence" (Herring, 2013: 8). These three differentiations of discourse types in CMC or CMD research are important when considering any study of discourse practice online.

What will also be important in discussing how information dissemination takes place and the way that digital comments apply to such an idea of the functions of CMC is its evolution throughout the years. This is to say that "computer-mediated communication begins with the Internet, but also emerges from a long line of mediated communication technologies such as the printing press, the telegraph, radio, the telephone, and television" (Thorne, 2008: 1). The dawn of the Internet and the birth of social media sites, including the concepts of Web 2.0 and Web 3.0 should also be discussed.

Web 2.0 and Web 3.0

In recent developments and deliberation on the subject, Internet and media scholars have tackled the notion of the progression of the Web and what it encompasses as a field of study and a part of modern life. This includes analyses of the growth and spread of social networking sites and mobile technologies as well as analysis of the participation of users that belong to what is known as Web 3.0.

Before the dawn of Web 3.0, Web 2.0 began the Internet trend of interactivity between web users (O'Reilly, 2009). Web 2.0 is what is known at the "second phase in the Web's evolution" and is "also called the wisdom Web, people-centric Web, participative Web, and read/write Web" due to its more interactive and collaborative nature (Murugesan, 2007: 34). The importance of the change that the Web has undergone lies in the dynamic and interactive tools that it provides to its users. Not only has Web 2.0 been described as a collection of new technologies, what is also emphasized in the literature is that it causes the spread of social trends which develop at rapid rates (O'Reilly, 2009).

Web 3.0 has marked the evolution from a simply interactive Internet to one of higher user engagement and focus on individual expression (Hendler, 2011). Because the web is in an evolving state, it has been provided a name separate from Web 2.0, seeing as Hendler (*ibid.*: 111) states that "we can thus essentially view Web 3.0 as Semantic Web technologies integrated into, or powering, large-scale Web applications." When it comes to the discussion of CMC and language, understanding that the web of things has a great impact on society as a whole makes for the relevance of the discussion of web types within a linguistic context.

The beginnings of social media channels in Web 2.0 gave rise to sites such as Myspace and Flickr, which then transformed into currently trending sites such as Facebook and YouTube (Murugesan, 2007: 34). Web 3.0 differs from Web 2.0 in that it is more interactive and uses algorithms to adjust to users as well as locate on a chain-basis what a user might be searching for.

Both the concepts of Web 2.0 and Web 3.0 are important in conducting an analysis of digital comments present in online forums. Both types of Web allow for interaction online, with Web 3.0 emphasizing the importance of user interaction in an even more refined and intricate manner. In this chapter, I discuss how user interaction through digital comments provides more room for the expression of evaluation of social issues. The notion of digital comments is encompassed within the linguistic notions of register, genre and style, some of which are intrinsic aspects of the analysis of discourses of the online media.

One-to-one and one-to-many in CMC

Yet another important aspect of studies in CMC is the consideration of *one-to-one communication* and *one-to-many communication*. As Baron (2004: 398, 2008) informs, the former consists of online communication that takes place between two people and the latter in which "one person's message is broadcast to multiple potential interlocutors." She describes synchronous one-to-one communication as including chat such as IM or Facebook's Messenger and asynchronous one-to-one communication as e-mail or texting on mobile phones. Modern communication has provided us with mobile communication online via the use of applications on handheld smartphones. Synchronous types include one-to-many communication chat, MUDs and conferencing via computers, whereas the asynchronous type includes newsgroups and comment sites (Tong & Walther, 2011). This work concerns one-to-many communication, stressing the public nature of comments made online.

Linguistic aspects of CMC

Both the ubiquitous and voluminous nature of CMC makes it important to linguistic study and it is crucial to bear in mind the relevance of language to society in such a context. Besides the fact that variation and change can be seen in computer-mediated communication, where structure and lexicon are even concerned, "the digital nature of CMC also facilitates recording both the content and context of human interaction" (Paollilo, 2015: 50), which includes the reflection of social attitudes in text. Interaction as a subject in CMC will be discussed more in full later in this chapter (cf. Chapter 4). It is necessary to undertake further linguistic study of the various discourses that are present in the online sphere, which make up a large part of the widely investigated linguistics of CMC.

Herring (2001, 2002, 2003, 2004, 2013, 2017, 2018, 2021), as one of the first to conduct in-depth analyses and work on the linguistic aspects of computer-mediated communication, has laid the foundations for furthering such work on the strictly language and discourse-based aspects of the interdisciplinary field that are CMC studies. The description of linguistic trends in CMC began in the 1980s (Herring, 2000) and has continued on in the contemporary linguistic analyses of today (Herring, 2005; Vincent, 2009; Perez-Sabater, 2013; Sowa, 2018). The 1990s saw a booming advent in the linguistic research concerning Internet communication, including looking at "electronic language" as a new variety of English (Collot & Belmore, 1996), the functional differences between face-to-face and Internet-based interactions (Grzenia, 2006; Antheunis et al., 2020), the way that group dynamics function in email forum (Korenman & Wyatt, 1996; Coduto 2020), and more (cf. Herring, 1996; Baron, 2008; Crystal, 2011). Other aspects, such as politeness and impoliteness in CMC have also been investigated from a linguistic perspective (Locher, 2010), as well as the linguistic aspects of text messaging (Thurlow & Brown, 2003; Ling, 2005; Crystal, 2008; Baker, 2010; Rafi, 2010; Bell & Gibson, 2011; Deumert, 2014; Seals, 2021).

The importance of linguistic study in the interdisciplinary outlook on CMC is indisputable, as Tarsiero (2004: 983) states:

> In recent years, linguistics has been challenged by the advent of the "new media" whose sensory channel permutations are so high and whose sociological and psychological characteristics are so complicated and intertwined that they stress the very concept of "media discourse"

As far as the sociolinguistics of CMC is concerned, Androutsopoulos (2006: 419) underlines the "the move from the 'language of CMC' to socially situated computer-mediated discourse," stating that studying CMC in a sociolinguistic context sheds light on the importance of linguistic variability in forming communities and shaping online social identities. When looking at linguistic trends in online communication as reflective of the practices of building these identities, Androutsopoulos (*ibid.*) agrees with Crystal's (2001) claim that there will be a future interest vested in so-called "network societies" (Castells, 2004; Castells, 2011; Anderson, 2014; Deumert, 2014; Danesi, 2016).

This linguistic approach to online discourses can also be utilized within the framework of CDA. As mentioned above, much of the current linguistic and discourse analysis concerns some aspect of computer-mediated communication, especially considering the relationship societies have with Internet communication through social media, making it increasingly possible to view how discourse is tied to attitudes, ideologies, and communities (Androutsopoulos, 2006; Deumert, 2014). Taking again into consideration the weight and significance of social media on the dissemination of information today, it is no surprise that CMC has had such an impact on the research concerning language and discourse today.

The research regarding online discourse(s), where ideologies are concerned, includes looking into the spread of hate speech within the context of nationalist sentiments (Posteguillo, 2003; Brown 2009) and other far-right movements (Atton, 2006), illness support groups (Gonzales 2005), financial crises (Kelsey, 2014), political discussions online (Camaj & Santana, 2015; Freelon, 2015), anti-immigrant discourses (Bloch et al., 2020), as well as subjects of multilingualism and affordances (Deumert, 2014). What has seen relatively little study is the way social problems are presented in discourse through the analytical lens of the investigation of the representation of social actors, and the question of implicit evaluation with regard to subjects of a criminal nature. These are issues that are inseparable from the overall discourses which are linked to social problems presented in online media (Bou-Franch, 2013; Herring, 2016; Lavin, 2020). What should also be highlighted as important in building the already existing literature on the subject of language in CMC is that it forms a good basis upon which to conduct critical analyses of discourse, in this case that of representations of rape and the attitudes which they reflect.

New media discourse

The language that is found in digital comments, as mentioned above, has been referred to as *new media language* or *new media discourse* (Thurlow, 2007; Thurlow

& Mroczek, 2011; Lee, 2014; Tannen, 2013). New media discourse has been defined as the presence of oral communication strategies in written communication, usually in the context of social media (Herbig et al., 2015). It is characterized by its informal style and can be found in the majority of social media sites and applications of today.

Tannen (2013: 99) provides examples from where new media discourse can be located, i.e., in email, on social media sites such as Facebook, Reddit or X, in instant messaging or text message exchanges. Tannen and Trester (2013: x) suggest that the application of conventions like capitalization, repetition, punctuation that has an emphatic purpose, as well as the speed of reply make up new media analogs. The concept of new media discourse is important in its relevance to the status of digital comments and their being on the cusp of written and spoken communication.

Register, genre and style analysis

The investigation of language used in various texts, including those located online, may undergo three broader categories of analysis: those of *register*, *genre* and *style* (Biber & Conrad, 2009). This aspect is important to the work and must be described in order to understand how digital comments function as a genre (or sub-genre (Biber & Egbert, 2018)) of their own. The study of how samples of text vary from one another and the ways that they can be compartmentalized into categorizations belongs to the method of how we can differentiate the various texts that we come across in our daily experience. Biber and Conrad (*ibid.*: 1) highlight the various roles that text may play in the life of a reader and language user:

> Written language also plays a very important role in daily life for many people. Students usually produce many kinds of writing: notes during class sessions, written assignments, term papers, and possibly numerous text messages and/or e-mail messages. But similar to spoken language, most people read more than they write. In fact, many people read even more different kinds of texts than they listen to: newspaper articles, editorials, novels, e-mail messages, blogs, text messages, letters and ads in the mail, magazine articles, ads in magazines, textbooks, research articles, course syllabi, and other written assignments or handouts.

All of the aforementioned text types can be described with regard to register, genre and style, which differ in their textual focus, linguistic characteristics and the distribution of such, as well as in the interpretations of those perspectives.

Register

CDA investigates the ways in which varying discursive and linguistic aspects of talk and text are mediated through power dynamics (cf. Chapter 1). In addition to specific aspects of discourse analyzed in CDA, such as the representation of social actors, *register* is also seen by the framework as a power-structured phenomenon manifested in grammar. This notion is a regular and fixed pattern of both vocabulary and grammar, and is defined according to its function (i.e., the use to which language may be put in a given context) (Biber & Conrad, 2009; Simpson & Mayr, 2010). Generally speaking, a register of a language is a variety "associated with a particular situation of use (including particular communicative purposes)" and includes three main components, named by Conrad and Biber (*ibid.*: 6) in their seminal work: the situational context, the linguistic features, and the functional relationships between those two components. Thus, a register demonstrates "what a speaker or writer is doing with language at a given moment" (Simpson & Mayr, 2010: 57).

Within register analysis, three contextual variables have been defined, namely the *field*, *tenor*, and *mode* (Halliday, 1985). The *field* refers to the topic, setting and the purpose of a given interaction, the *tenor* relates to the relationship between the participants present in the interaction, and the *mode* refers to the medium of communication (i.e., whether it is relayed in spoken form, written form or visually) (*ibid.*).

As Halliday and Hasan (1985) state, the register of a text is, in relation to the meaning that is being conveyed, as follows:

> It can be defined as a configuration of meanings that are typically associated with a particular configuration of field, mode and tenor. But since it is a configuration of meanings, a register must also, of course, include the expressions, the lexico-grammatical and phonological features, that typically accompany to REALISE these meanings.
>
> (*ibid.*: 89)

The importance of register lies in the fact that it comes in a variety of forms and constitutes a phenomenon that infiltrates the day-to-day of communication from active interaction to the passive observation of signs, symbols, as well as linguistic and non-linguistic messages. What is considered in the field as existing next to the investigation of register is the phenomenon of genre, which has been described as a higher level than register (Chilton, 1985; Fowler & Marshall, 1985; Simpson & Mayr, 2010). The question of register in this study falls under the relevance of the types of text that are investigated, which are the digital comments written by anonymous Internet users, which have an informal style (cf. Chapter 4). As stated by Biber and Conrad (2009: 2) "any text sample of any type can be analyzed from a register perspective," and thus the main perspective of the analysis (cf. Chapter 6 and Chapter 7) looks at register, since the function of the lexico-grammatical features is under investigation. The related term, genre, however, must also be defined, at least in short.

Genre

As a term, *genre* has been defined by Biber and Conrad (2009: 2) as similar to the register perspective of language analysis and includes "the description of the purposes and situational context of a text variety." Since a genre is a complete text, from beginning to end, an example of genre could include a conventional letter and the way it begins and ends (*ibid.*). The focus of a genre analysis looks at linguistic characteristics that include specialized expressions that make a genre, rhetorical organization and formatting. The features investigated are usually conventionally associated with a genre, and often not analyzed as having functional value, as opposed to a register analysis.

This specific genre, which are the complete texts that constitute digital comments contain a combination of conversational and written styles and has been preliminarily classified in other works tackling the issue of the status of digital comments as a genre or subgenre (Shchipitsina, 2015).

In the present study, register rather than genre will be highlighted with regard to its relation with computer-mediated communication, since it is the selected parts of discourse analyzed that are of interest. There will be one main register relevant to the analysis: that of digital comments, which are more conversational and informal in the style which they present than more formal genres of written discourse, such as news reporting discourse (Dias Oliva, 2020).

Style

Put briefly, *style* is similar to the register perspective where the linguistic focus is concerned, as it analyzes "the use of core linguistic features that are distributed throughout text samples from a variety" (Biber & Conrad, 2009: 2). In contrast with the register perspective, however, the use of linguistic features is not functionally motivated by the context in which it is located, yet the features presented are reflective of aesthetic preferences (ones which are usually associated with particular authors of a text or historical periods).

Joos (1976) also classified style into five distinct categories that should be enumerated. He argued that the five styles were namely the following: frozen style, formal style, consultative style, casual style, and intimate style. Frozen style is the language that is used in more formal settings, such as in contexts of ceremony or in palaces during events that would call for a manner of expression tied by conventions that represent tradition, whereas formal style is defined by the language used in situations considered more serious, such as a lecture or a sermon. Consultative style is semiformal speech that is used when, for instance, talking to a stranger. Casual style is that which is used for conversation in which interlocutors feel more relaxed and in conversation, i.e., in a classroom with peers. The final style, intimate style, is said to be reserved for communicating with families, partners and close friends.

Sociolinguistic works on the subject of style have touched on both talk and text of individual language users. In his work, Coupland (2007: ix) draws attention to Labov's (1972) studies on speaker's individual style, and how variation also accounts for differences in talking and writing based on the interlocutors one is interacting with, as well as the context of speaking or writing. He emphasizes the role of the context in which one finds oneself as influencing the style that someone takes on.

The question of open and closed sites must also be addressed in order to clarify the interaction that may or may not take part on a site, particularly important to the aspect of this work, which deals with digital comments by Internet users. In traditional news dissemination, letters were the main fashion through which readers could express their views on issues publicly (Tunstall, 1977). At present, newspaper sites are open to providing interactive features with which their audiences can express their views or take part in debates, both asynchronously or synchronously (Greer & Mensing, 2006; Thurman, 2007). A site may be "open" if it allows users to share through commenting, posting, and uploading files (referred to as content in some literature (Deuze, 2003)) without any filtering, as well as monitoring or intervention. These are the types of sites from which the comments analyzed in Chapters 6 and 7 have been taken.

Closed participatory communication in online media, such as news sources or blogs, may be defined as a site that allows its users to participate but restricts their communicative acts through moderation and control (Sherrick & Hoewe, 2018). There was monitoring in some of the sites used for the analysis in Chapters 6 and 7. Both of these types of sites are integral to the analysis of participation in discussions that are presented by the media through digital comments (Deuze, 2003). For this reason, I consider online discourse that are led by media outlets as informing and facilitating the spread of ideologies on social issues, such as sexual crime.

Digital comments

What are referred to throughout this work as *digital comments* have been described by Shanahan (2017) as online comments which are associated with the expression of attitudes, both negative (O'Sullivan & Flanagin, 2003) and positive (Hurrell, 2005). This notion, of course, falls within the study of computer-mediated communication and digital discourse described in this chapter. Pascual (2020) sees the comments which interact with the material preceding it (including articles, blog posts or informational sites) as a genre in their own right.

Writing comments on the news is a pastime in which not many invest a great amount of time, however it is important to bear in mind that aside from "heavy users" of comment options, there are those users who comment once or twice, or even 10 times, and will most likely never write a comment on the subject again (Ruiz et al., 2011; Ksiazek & Springer, 2018: 476). This means that the type of person who writes digital comments can be considered to belong to a community of comment writers. It is important not to generalize the content found in digital comments to entire populations. Digital comments have been described as public deliberation, interactive in nature, as a result of the quality of discussion that occurs in such spaces (Barnes, 2015).

Register of digital comments

The register of digital comments, which differentiates them even from other texts found online (Biber & Egbert, 2018) is the fact that they are usually written in informal language that is similar to spoken language. Biber and Egbert (*ibid.*: 15) provide the differentiation for the subgenre *interactive discussion register* (or sub-register), based on its being of interactive quality despite its being in written form. They classify the general register of interactive discussion into three types, including discussion forum, the Q&A forum and reader responses (*ibid.*: 17). The one that the work here is concerned with is that of reader responses, which is of course being referred to in the work as digital comments.

The features of the register of interactive discussion, which includes reader responses (akin to the digital comments described in the chapter), as enumerated by Biber and Egbert (*ibid.*) are listed as follows:

- present tense verbs
- first-person pronouns
- conditional subordinators
- mental verbs
- contractions
- abbreviations
- *that*-deletion
- activity verbs
- modals of prediction
- second-person pronouns

- discourse particles
- modals of possibility
- adverbs of time
- Certainty adverbs

The features of discourse enumerated above demonstrate that there is affect and personal opinion located within the comments, including the use of mental verbs, the first person, modals of prediction, and conditional subordinators. Some features, such as contraction, *that*-deletion, abbreviations, and discourse particles indicate more conversational qualities of the comments.

It is important to note what has been described in the literature as less common for the register of comments, in addition to what is a usual phenomenon within them. Biber and Egbert (2018: 198) provide a list of more uncommon features in the register of interactive discussion, including the passive voice, nominalization, premodifying nouns, adjectives and common nouns.

Although not all of these features will be interpreted and analyzed for their evaluative quality, it is important to describe the characteristics of digital comments as a register which belongs to the broader classification of online registers. What also characterizes the register of digital comments is the tendency for errors or mistakes (such as orthographic errors) to be found within the texts. For this reason, examples used to illustrate the points of analysis in Chapters 6 and 7 are left unmodified from their original form, including the errors in spelling and grammar.

In discussing the register of digital comments, it is necessary to discuss the relevant field, tenor, and mode. In this study, the field, which is the subject matter of the text, is rape and its actors. The tenor, relevantly, relates to the "personal relationships between the individuals involved in an activity" (Nunan, 2008: 58). Here, the lack of a relationship between those writing the comments impinges on the form in which the communication takes place. Their anonymity also leads them to use more of a conversational tone in writing comments. The mode, which is the third register variable, and refers to the channel of communication, is written, but, as stated earlier, balances between the forms of written and spoken communication (Biber & Egbert, 2015).

Digital comments as a genre

As stated in the section on genre, the focus on digital comments in this work remains on digital comments as a register, rather than a genre. It is, however, important to highlight here that the form of a digital comment is not clear-cut (McNiell, 2005; Mok & Chen, 2021).

Shchipitsina (2015) notes that the variety of internet genres available distinguishes comments as a genre rather than a subgenre because of the role that they have in online communication and how they differ from other genres in online interaction. She states that comments "are short utterances of the users about the source text" (*ibid.*: 532), and it is also worth noting that they are located under the source text to which they refer or in an online forum where space is provided to users to express themselves in short texts. A digital comment can range from 11 to 414 words (Rösner & Kramer, 2016: 8). A digital comment is usually accompanied by a handle that is either the name of the user, a pseudonym or the term "guest" or "anonymous" (*ibid.*). These features classify the genre of the digital comment.

Style of digital comments

As concerns the present study, style is considered where the lexico-grammatical choices of authors are concerned, especially those of authors of digital comments (Rösner & Kramer, 2016). The style analyzed, in accordance with the five categories of style, belongs to that of casual style, since it encompasses more informal and conversational language presented above (Joos, 1976). Because the comments range from anonymous to semi-anonymous, the informality is no surprise and has been subsumed within lexical features, as well as grammatical features.

Digital comments and diversity

As Carpenter (2010: 1064) describes, "the presence of online [comments] in the marketplace may add to the diversity of information that citizens have access to when making decisions related to the betterment of their community or their life," and it is for this reason that participation in discussion about the news has gained so much attention in the context of an increasing turn towards democracy in the media. What such participation in discussion of subjects disseminated in the news does is bring forth an accessible range and variety of opinion into the new sphere. This includes the fact that any person can distribute information freely on the web. Hence the claim that accuracy is brought about through a more diversified community, aided with tools provided by the Internet (Carpenter, 2010; Muller et al., 2012; Beam et al., 2018).

The democratic nature of digital comments

Whereas on one end of the spectrum professional, traditional journalisms act as one-sided productions of news, the proliferation of information has taken a turn into a more participatory form. The question of public political knowledge is often raised in the discussion of the nature of online user generated content

(Kaufhold et al., 2010: 515). Because news media provide wide-spread access to information, formal education now merely exists as only one of the means of having access to information, be it news or otherwise (*ibid.*: 515–6).

Technology's aid in the electronic distribution of media online acts as "hybrid potential for democratization and control" (Chouliaraki, 2010: 227). This, in turn, provides for what Bou-Franch (2013: 6) informs us is the *polylogal* (or multiparty) nature of the data, which in essence means that participation in the provision and comment of news is open to any reader or journalist, professional or citizen. This multiparty property of participation in discussions about the news online provides for its democratization in that it performs as a door to a platform in which different opinions may be expressed.

Anonymity and digital comments

Because the question of anonymity pertains to the final chapters of the analysis in this work, its relationship to opinionated discourse and the presentation of certain ideas and ideologies is pertinent in the discussion about discourse and rape culture. The final chapters of this work aim to demonstrate that anonymity encourages the spread of harmful sexist ideologies regarding rape, where victim blaming is more evident.

Since the birth of the printing press, authors have been known to conceal their identities, especially when expressing opinions that might be viewed as unpopular (Reader, 2021). Anonymity is the state of being unidentifiable and has been defined by Wallace (1999: 24) as "when others are unable to relate a given feature of the person to other characteristics." The aspect of semi-anonymity in online comments has been said to be of similar status, but takes place in contexts where a user may use his or her real identity or a fake one (Dąbrowska, M., 2014; Hosseinmardi, 2014).

Herring (2013:11) points out that "anonymity is a major theme that runs through gender and CMC research, where it (or its close relative, pseudonymity) is often claimed to promote gender equality." She states that this proposition is problematic, because anonymity in online communication may encourage greater participation on the part of female Internet users. In contrast, others claim that it causes a reduction in social accountability, making it easier for harassment to take place, and for users to engage in hostile or aggressive acts and communication, as well as the posting of "open and uninhibited content" (*ibid.*). Research has claimed that their styles of interaction and the content of their messages might reveal the gender of a given user (Donath, 1999; Baron, 2008; Herring & Stroeger, 2014; Dąbrowska M., 2014). That, however, is not the focus of this work.

This aspect of gendered communication as reflected in styles of interaction will not be taken into consideration for the work, as the subject of investigation is the overall manifestation of victim blaming in the discourse of Internet users, as well as the way the phenomenon is communicated in the linguistic contexts of American English and Polish communication online.

CMC can facilitate a type of anonymity that has been "noted as being both potentially beneficial and detrimental to individuals and society," and the harm that anonymous users may cause in the discourses that they produce has been noted to cause "others online distress without repercussion" (Hardaker & McGlashan, 2016: 82–3). Although this subject has been discussed in the context of rape threats, the subject of anonymity is important to this book, for what is under investigation is the specific spread of ideologies and attitudinal polarization that takes place in the online sphere on the subject of rape.

Anonymity where digital comments are concerned is considered proliferative of ideologies which reflect collective thought, because "users may experience a sense of disinhibition such that they become willing to express opinions online that they would never voice if they knew that those opinions could be attributed to them offline" (*ibid.*). The high degree of anonymity allowed in computer-mediated discourse is said to offer a greater circumference of allowance for behavior online that would be considered socially unacceptable, which in turn breeds negative online behaviors such as flaming or trolling (Douglas & McGarty, 2001). This also includes the expression of negative attitudes in discourse, such as victim blaming in comments (cf. Chapter 6 and Chapter 7). The comments investigated are either anonymous or signed under pseudonyms, thus all comments are treated as anonymous and not investigated in correlation with the gender of the users.

The question of interaction

It has come to be observed that "the unique Internet attributes of interactivity and multimedia are forcing significant evolutions in journalistic culture as the basic mission of the reporter has evolved for the digital world" (Robinson, 2006: 59). This means that both journalism and interaction have become more intrinsically involved in information dissemination processes, in both the spread of news and reactions to it. It also leaves room for social responsibility on the part of "laypeople" to voice their opinions regarding issues and problems they are faced with via the interactive nature of news dissemination and consumption (Kline & Burnstein, 2005). Richardson and Stanyer (2011) have drawn attention to the fact that reader opinion is more easily shared because news is publicly available on the internet.

Although relatively new, online reading and commenting forums have become increasingly ubiquitous as accompanying online newspapers (Johnson, 2008; Stanyer, 2009; Bruce, 2010; Levy & Adam, 2018), accounting for the open sites previously discussed. By the year 2010, among over 150 of the most-read U.S. newspapers, 92 percent of them allowed for online comments to be made by readers (Santana, 2011). This is a phenomenon that has recently change, as an increasing number of "news outlets engage in the moderation of [...] comments" (Naab et al., 2021: 567).

Biber and Egbert (2018) also note the interactive quality of digital comments (however in their book they relate specifically to the category of discussion forum and reader responses). They (*ibid.*: 15–17) draw attention to the fact that digital comments belong to a genre that is interactive, hence falling into what they call "oral-involved", because such comments are oral in nature, due to the fact that responses in comments often represent users responding to other users or to the source text itself (in our case, the source text is the article about rape).

Here, interaction with the media is seen through the ability that lay people have to post comments online regarding things they are presented in various news reporting sites. The Internet users who are behind the digital comments analyzed, for the most part, are not interacting with each other, but are rather interacting with the author of the article and the subject therein presented. It is important to bear in mind that, in the case of the digital comments analyzed in this work, the Internet users making comments are also interacting with the subject of rape by expressing attitudes on the subject.

One goal of critical discourse analysis is to uncover the ways in which the media creates and propagates certain representations of the world (Fairclough, 2013). In order to properly understand where ideologies may be found in the various discourses mentioned so far, a critical stance should be taken. The critical analysis of the media and also online media is nothing new in sociolinguistic study and has been carried out for the last few decades (Fought, 2004; Stamou, 2013; Blommaert, 2014; Rymes & Leone, 2014; Heller et al., 2017). This work aims to expand on the role of online discourses in spreading negative blame attribution and re-victimizing victims of rape. It is, hence, crucial to discuss the various ways that the expressing evaluation in online media may be investigated from a CDA perspective.

Digital comments, discourse analysis and rape

The allowance for commentary of online content contributes to the participatory nature of the internet and sharing in news media, making it one of the many layers in which this kind of participation takes place along the continuum "from making comments on a news article to submitting full-length stories" (Lewis, Kaufhold & Lasorsa, 2010: 4). Because digital comments are user-centered, any type of means of getting a message across is viable to be perceived as serving the purpose of disseminating beliefs and ideologies. The analysis of rape in the context of the Internet is not new in terms of subjects to consider (Gossett & Byrne, 2002; Kendall, 2007; Kramer, 2011; Makin & Morczek, 2015), however narrower studies on the redistribution of ideas linked to rape culture should be sought out and expanded on.

The following work aims to further demonstrate and delineate how the investigation of topic-centered comments should be thus considered contributive to what is known about the spreading of ideologies in the sphere of CMC. Digital comments will be investigated as instances of information and attitude dissemination (particularly where blame attribution (cf. Chapter 1) is concerned), and their influential ideological impact also taken into consideration. As far as any prior research on comments about rape goes, one article was found on the subject of online comments about rape, providing scientific insight into the discourse regarding one case of "female-on-male rape", and did not provide a critical discourse analysis of social actors (Levy & Adam, 2018).

In addition to discourse analysis of rape, multimodal analyses have also been carried out on the subject. Media coverage of rape cases and rape trials have seen a change along with the expansion of modalities of communication to include not only text, but also images, sound and music (Mohamed Haneef, 2019: 93). Rape has been investigated from a multimodal perspective in the case of treatment for survivors of sexual assault (Hensley, 2002), witness resistance during rape trials (Matoesian, 2008), and specific cases, such as rape in New Dehli, India (Jayachandran, 2015; Mohamed Haneef, 2019) as well as the construction of rape victims in Canada and the United States (Ehrlich, 2020). Such analyses have investigated how factors outside of discourse implicate blame on the victim of a crime.

Analyzing the pragmatics of online communication

One aspect of the analysis of digital comments will discuss the pragmatics of communication on forums and through digital comments, especially that of implicit evaluation (cf. Chapter 1). Rape, as a social problem, as well as other sexual crimes, is a subject that is often embedded within taboo discourse—creating a kind of ideological vacuum from which it becomes difficult to view rape outside of those structures—because it is considered a sensitive topic.

The democratization of the online sphere and the possibility for the public to take part in online discussions regarding important social issues has also been said to spread hate speech and generate more negative comments on various social problems or actors. KhosraviNik and Esposito (2008: 46) state that "one of the most significant and complex drawbacks of the proliferation of user-generated content, and the so-called democratization of access to symbolic resources, is the acutely increasing incidence of online hate or cyberhate." Although no one definition of hate speech has been delineated, MacAvaney et al. (2019: 3) provide several definitions, beginning with the one given by the Encyclopedia of the American Constitution. The definition states that hate speech is "speech that attacks a person or group on the basis of attributes such as race, religion, ethnic origin, national origin, sex, disability, sexual orientation, or gender identity. Hate in online discourse, with an emphasis on the genre of digital comments, has been studied more recently by scholars in linguistics, with the hope of targeting the act and uncovering a method of combating the phenomenon (Capozzi et al., 2019; Siegel, 2020; Dainas & Herring, 2021; Yin & Zubiaga, 2021).

Although the present study does not investigate hate speech as a phenomenon, the aspect of attitudes and affect are related to the subject of evaluation in digital discourse. Strong, polarizing attitudes towards the actors in rape will be investigated cross-culturally here, to determine how indirectness takes place in digital comments on rape and what the stances expressed by Internet users in their comments say about actors.

What Yus (2011) has termed *cyberpragmatics* is a burgeoning field that deals with the linguistic and discursive action of Internet users and their interaction with information in the cyberspace, because as KhosraviNik and Esposito (2018: 46) state, "the fast-emerging technologies of the participatory web have brought about an authentic socio-communicative revolution that has transformed the way we communicate, explore and connect to the world forever."

Conclusions

Because the main goal of this work is to demonstrate how existing ideologically-based notions surrounding the problem of rape are maintained through discourse via evaluation in language, it is equally important to approach the investigation of the topic in an adequate manner. I have described computer-mediated communication, and digital comments as a genre, including the aspects of register and style that differentiate them from other genres of discourse, including subgenres and registers of online discourse. It is important to bear in mind the status of digital comments as a form of new media discourse, which has more recently emerged with the popularization of written communication that also acts in a conversational (and hence interactive) way. As Biber and Egbert (2018) highlight, discourses like digital comments blur the line between spoken and written discourse, and have been described as being oral in nature, despite the fact that they are written.

This chapter was the final chapter of the theoretical ones in this work (besides Chapter 5, on the methodology) and has been presented in order to provide background on the status of digital comments and their importance in studies of computer-mediated communication. The analysis presented in Chapters 6 and 7 are an in-depth analysis of the digital comments of anonymous Internet users who discuss the subject of rape and the actors involved. The question of evaluative discourse presented in Chapter 1 is brought forward as the central framework for analyzing the presence of victim blaming in digital comment, with the question of the spreading of ideologies through such public means of communication of values constituting the viability of Critical Discourse Analysis as a framework of study of the subject.

Chapter 5: Materials and methods

This chapter precedes the two practical chapters of the work and presents the materials and methodology adopted in this study to show that victim blaming exists in both American and Polish discourses about rape, and at a high prevalence. The main tool that I will use in assessing the evaluation of actors involved in rape present in digital comments written by Internet users is that of implicit evaluation in stance-taking. By looking at the ways that evaluation takes place in the discourse of online comments about rape, I aim to show that victim blaming is ever-present in online discourses, with a focus on the indirect blaming of the victim in rape. This is not to say that victim blaming is present in every comment, but rather that there is an overwhelming proportion of victim-blaming discourse in such comments.

The way that Internet users talk about the subject of sexual crime demonstrates much more variation and its expression reflects overall social attitudes of a given culture towards rape and the actors involved. Both of the analytical chapters (Chapters 6 and 7) discuss in depth the question of how the phenomenon of victim blaming, within the context of the evaluation of social actors and rape as a crime, can be explained from a sociolinguistic and pragmatic analytical standpoint. This can be investigated via the analysis of how stance is communicated what grammatical and semantic constituents reveal regarding attitudes towards actors and events in the context of sexual crime. Directness and indirectness, as ways of evaluating actors and activities that are strictly related to a rape case, have not, to my knowledge, been analyzed, let alone in a multi-faceted discourse analysis. Thus, an investigation of implicit evaluation as indicative of the stance that Internet users have towards rape in such a context as CMC is crucial in uncovering the pervasiveness of victim blaming, a social problem that has harmful consequences on rape victims overall. The material analyzed for Chapters 6 and 7 of the presented work was two corpora, compiled manually by process of a random selection of comments,[63] one representing a total of 341 American English comments written by anonymous Internet users or those using pseudonyms (here also considered anonymous), accompanying articles which regarded the subject of rape in some respect, and a second corpus made up of 315 Polish Internet user comments on the subject of rape, following the

63 This means that they were selected on an as-they-come basis under the articles under which they were found.

same criteria. The fact that both the AEC and the PC consist of comments on the subject of rape fulfills the criteria regarding the aboutness of the corpora, which indicates that they were particularized to a specific context or topic (Scott, 2002: 44; Tabbert, 2016: 131).

Before engaging in the two-part in-depth analysis of digital comments about rape (Chapter 6 and Chapter 7), it is necessary to clearly outline the materials and methods used, as well as to highlight the effectiveness of using the program MaxQDA, a computer-assisted technology program which allows for quantitative and qualitative analyses to be carried out smoothly in various disciplines (Wodak & Krzyżanowski, 2008). Here, in addition to providing an in-depth description of the materials and methods used, I also enumerate why MaxQDA is a program that can be used for a deep analysis of discourse. This is paramount to understanding how evaluation and stance can be investigated from a critical, corpus perspective. The materials and the ways that I have calculated the statistics of the frequency at which various types of evaluation occur in the corpora are also enumerated in this chapter.

Aims of the analysis

The main goal of the analysis is to demonstrate that victim blaming is present in digital comments and that such texts are representative of evaluative discourse. Because evaluation is predominantly carried out in an indirectly, it is of paramount importance to recognize that the numerous strategies that may be employed in committing blame attribution are found through the analysis of implicit stance.

The overall goal of collecting two corpora of comments of this kind was to evaluate blame attribution levels in the discourse of Internet users in both of the cultural contexts presented (the American and Polish contexts, respectively), as well as the attitudes of common citizens towards rape through the lens of an analysis that considered linguistic representations of rape victims, perpetrators and the crime itself. It is my hypothesis that blame attribution as evaluation occurs indirectly as a result of the nature of the crime of rape, however manifesting itself differently in both cultures. Although the offender is expectedly negatively evaluated in such comments, the point of interest remains the attitudes of Internet users to the victim and the fact that negative online discourse acts as victim-blaming discourse within the context. Such discourse is seen to be the product of ideologies surrounding women's sexuality and rape myths that still present themselves in discourse about rape today (cf. Chapter 2).

The discussion of the investigated material has been divided into two practical chapters, which have further been divided into sections for the analysis of each of the two language contexts: American English and Polish, the investigation of which are discussed in turns for each section of the analysis. The discussion of the analyzed material has been divided into two main parts, with Chapter 6 presenting the structural aspects of expressing evaluation may be found and the Chapter 7 presenting the socio-semantic aspects of expressions of evaluation.

Here, I have provided a list of the research questions that I hope to answer in the analysis, highlighting the links between the theoretical threads drawn to in the first four chapters of the work and the reflections of ideologies within the actual material analyzed.

1. Are evaluative stances expressed in the structural and socio-semantic aspects of the digital comments discourse?
2. Is negative evaluation of the victim and the offender present in digital comments in the AEC and the PC?
3. Is positive evaluation of the victim and the offender present in digital comments in the AEC and the PC?
4. Do the processes of modality, negation, verbal processes in which the actors are presented as being involved in, the activation and passivation or the naming of actors present an ideological turn in the discourse about rape and its actors?
5. Do euphemization or dysphemization of rape as a crime occur in the AEC and the PC?
6. Are there cultural implications of the ways that actors are evaluated in such digital discourses as comments which accompany articles about rape?
7. Are rape myths prevalent in the AEC and the PC of digital comments?

Both structural (Chapter 6) and socio-semantic (Chapter 7) aspects are analyzed in the work, as they are both ways that the evaluation of actors can be expressed in discourse. The demarcation of both sides of discourse points to the variation in evaluative expression, both positive and negative, about the actors and events involved in rape. By looking at the structure and the socio-semantics of comments about rape, I am able to come to more robust conclusions regarding the ways in which discursive evaluation takes place.

The whole analysis aims to investigate the ways in which the main actors of a rape are represented in the discourse of Internet users, as reflective of the attitudes of Internet users as a sociolinguistic group of study. Negative attitudes towards the main actors involved in rape, as well as attitudes towards the act of rape itself, are intrinsically meshed with and influenced by overarching social constraints in both American and Polish contexts regarding sexuality, including its status as a taboo subject, and the patriarchal attitudes towards women as sexual actors in intimate and sexual settings. The chief focus, however, is on the phenomenon of victim blaming, as it presents the most negative social implications overall, constituting discourse that is harmful and which has a negative impact on those that it concerns. In the chapters that follow (cf. Chapter 6 and Chapter 7), the questions of structural constructions of stance and evaluation, like modality, negation and the analysis of the transitivity processes in which actors are involved (Chapter 6), as well as the representation of social actors through the discursive processes of nomination, identification, functionalization, appraisement, indetermination and backgrounding are investigated (Chapter 7).

Materials

In the analysis of digital comments, in both Chapters 6 and 7, the criteria were made to encompass comments which were found under any article on the subject of rape rather than a specific rape case. This included those articles which discussed rape and issues surrounding rape as a general social problem, as well as those which described specific rape cases. The time frame of the digital comments used to build the corpora was 2011 to 2020, as I have considered a 10-year time frame a long enough period to draw conclusions about the attitudes of Internet users towards such actors and events. The articles under which the comments were found (the two corpora were made up of 12 American articles and 15 Polish articles, respectively) and came from the time frame mentioned above, meaning that the research concentrates on the contemporary state of events. The criteria for selecting the comments for the corpora were as follows:

1. Comments accompanying an online article about rape (a rape case or rape as a phenomenon in general),
2. Reference to rape in which the victim or victims were female,
3. Reference to rape in which the offender or offenders were male[64]

Both the AEC and the PC were compiled so as to adhere to the aforementioned criteria.

64 The reason for such specification is due to the fact that although rape victims are usually female, and rapists usually male, this fact might be argued. The goal of the work is to bring attention to the linguistic framing that takes place around those actors who are most frequently victims (as well as offenders) of such a sex crime as rape.

Due to the fact that it was more difficult to find Polish comments than American English comments, there is a gap between the number of comments for the American English corpus and the Polish corpus. For the 341 comments which made up the American English data, 804 sentences and a total of 20,898 words were analyzed, and for the 315 comments in the Polish corpus, a total of 714 sentences and 11,200 words were analyzed. The higher comment count in the American English Corpus was the result of first collecting comments for the American data and subsequently collecting comments for the Polish data. All of the data collected for the American Corpus was seen as relevant to the study and therefore I did not want to eliminate comments for the sake of having a number equal to that in the Polish Corpus. The difference between the number of comments analyzed is not here seen as large enough to cause a significant divide in the statistical results.

The sum of all the codes,[65] including the American English and Polish corpora (placed within one coding project in MaxQDA (VERBI, 2019)), amounted to a total of 21,583 codes and were distributed between the two corpora. Not all of the codes were used for the analysis presented in the following two chapters. The breaking up of the materials into the number of comments, sentences and words was pertinent to the analysis itself, as certain aspects of the analysis could only be statistically accounted for if compared against the grouping to which they belonged.[66]

Table 1 Number of constituents analyzed in each corpus

American English Corpus (AEC)	Polish Corpus (PC)
341 comments	315 comments
804 sentences	714 sentences
20,898 words	11,200 words

The table above presents the partitioning of the data into three different countable categories of the constituents analyzed, including the number of comments in each corpus, the number of sentences, and the number of words for each corpus.

65 By which is meant the labelling technique applied in the analytical program, MaxQDA, designed to represent and code constituents of the text and for the purpose of this analysis, according to their linguistic categories (Charmaz, 2010)

66 This includes aspects, such as the investigation of speech acts and sentence structure types that had to be compared against the number of sentences analyzed in each corpus in order to achieve a viable statistical reference.

The comments which accompanied the 12 American articles chosen concerned rape cases including the Brock Turner (2015) rape case, the case of Owen Labrie (2016), cases in which Lyft and Uber drivers were accused of committing rape (2020), and the questions of bystander intervention when confronted with rape in the college setting, as well as the phenomenon of date or acquaintance rape. As far as the Polish cases were concerned, comments accompanying the 15 online articles regarded rape in the Polish context, including the rape of a female runner in Kabacki Forest (2014), the case of the rape of a translator from Elbląg (2015), a gang rape in Łódź (2016), and more broadly, the issue of women lying about rape, why women do not tell people that they were raped, as well as the problem of marital rape. Since the goal of the work is to unpack the discursive aspects of victim blaming, the reason that I have taken various types of rape into account in my analysis is to investigate how rape victims are viewed and represented overall in discourse, in juxtaposition with the ways that offenders and events are represented.

The comments chosen to represent the American media were taken from *the New York Times, ABC, the Palo Alto Weekly* and *variety.com*. The comments taken from the Polish press were chosen from sites such as *Wysokie Obcasy, Gazeta Wyborcza, Fakt24, Gazeta Krakowska, Gazeta Współczesna, Nasze Miasto, Pudelek,* and *tvn24*. The reason that there was a larger array in the sources from which the comments were taken in the PC was that many of the American sites (including Newsweek and NPR), either had no comments or the commenting option switched off for their sites.[67] It is crucial, in a work of this nature, to investigate whether there are common or differing trends where the expression of opinions (evaluative attitudes) is concerned, in comments on rape in the American and Polish contexts, via the corpora compiled. These sources were used throughout the analysis (cf. Chapters 6 and 7).[68]

67 This might be attributed to a heightened sensitivity in American culture to censoring negative commentary or the regulation of digital comments by administrators (Dekay, 2012; Stoycheff & Burgess, 2020).

68 Underneath the comments used as examples in Chapters 6 and 7, the source article has been abbreviated, the year given and the row the comment occupied.

Table 2 American English Corpus sources and codes

Date of publication	Online source	Headline	Corpus code
06.07.2011	ABC News	14 Men Accused of Texas Gang Rape of 11-year-old Girl	AEC ABC 2011
07.02.2014	New York Times	Stepping Up to Stop Sexual Assault	AEC NYT 2014a
02.04.2014	ABC News	Newly Released Documents, Tapes From Maryville Teen Alleged Rape Case Reveal New Details	AEC ABC 2014b
16.01.2015	ABC News	Vanderbilt Football Trial: Alleged Rape Details Emerge	AEC ABC 2015a
18.08.2015	ABC News	Alleged NH Prep School Rape Victim Takes the Stand	AEC ABC 2015b
18.03.2016	Palo Alto Weekly	Woman testifies in Brock Turner trial	AEC PA 2016
21.03.2016	Mercury News	Herhold: Thanking two Stanford students who subdued campus sex assault suspect	AEC MN 2016
06.06.2016	New York Times	Light Sentence for Brock Turner in Stanford Rape Case Draws Outrage	AEC NYT 2016
013.09.2017	New York Times	Campus Rape, a Survivor's Story	AEC NYT 2017
09.10.2019	Variety (variety.com)	Roman Farrow Book Alleges Matt Lauer Raped NBC News Colleague	AEC VTY 2019
5.12.2019	New York Times	Uber Says 3,045 Sexual Assaults Were Reported in U.S. Rides Last Year	AEC NYT 2019
11.02.2020	ABC News	Defense Witness Testifies Weinstein's Rape Accuser Called him a 'Spiritual Soulmate'	AEC ABC 2020

Table 3 Polish Corpus sources and codes

Date of publication	Online source	Headline	Corpus code
18.05.2012	Gazeta Współczesna	Internetowa randka skończyła się tragedią. Śledczy: Zgwałcili ją we trzech [An online date ended in a tragedy. Investigators: Three of them raped her]	PC GWsp 2012a
07.08.2012	Gazeta Współczesna	Gwałcili ją dwaj bracia. Zwabili do samochodu i wykorzystali [Two brothers raped her. They lured her to their vehicle and took advantage of her]	PC GWsp 2012b
15.12.2014	Gazeta Wyborcza	Zgwałcona w Lesie Kabackim. A policja jej nie wierzy [Raped in the Kabacki Forest and the police don't believe her]	PC GWyb 2014
24.06.2015	Wysokie Obcasy	Zgwałcono mnie na wyjeździe służbowym [I was raped on a business trip]	PC WO 2015a
27.06.2015	Pudelek	Ofiara gwałtu: „Prosili, żebym OPISAŁA CZŁONEK GWAŁCICIELA! Zrobili ze mnie zdzirę!" [Rape victim: „They asked me to describe the rapist's penis! They made a slut out of me!"	PC PUD 2015
11.07.2015	Wysokie Obcasy	Alkohol nie gwałci, gwałci gwałciciel [Alcohol doesn't rape, a rapist rapes]	PC WO 2015b
1.08.2017	Pudelek	26-latka z Łodzi przez DZIESIĘĆ DNI była przetrzymywana i gwałcona przez zwyrodnialców! [26-year-old from Łódź imprisoned and raped for ten days by degenerates!]	PC Pud 2017a

(Continued)

Table 3 *Continued*

Date of publication	Online source	Headline	Corpus code
27.08.2017	Pudelek	Polka BRUTALNIE ZGWAŁCONA NA OCZACH MĘŻA podczas wakacji we Włoszech [Polish woman brutally raped in front of her husband while on vacation in Italy]	PC Pud 2017b
26.09.2018	Gazeta Wyborcza	Horror na łódzkim Zarzewie. Monika była więziona, gwałcona, bita i przypalana przez 10 dni [Horror in Łódź's Zarzew. Monika was tied up, raped, beaten, and burned for 10 days]	PC GWyb 2018
05.02.2019	Gazeta Współczesna	W tych województwach jest najwięcej gwałtów. Sprawdź, gdzie! [The highest number of rapes happen in these voivodeships. Check where!]	PC GWsp 2019
28.03.2019	Naszemiasto.pl	Kobiety wstydzą się mówić. Te historie wstrząsnęły Polską [Women are ashamed to speak. These stories shocked Poland]	PC NM 2019
16.09.2019	Moje-gniezno.pl	Została zgwałcona—trafi do więzienia! Absurdalny wyrok gnieźnieńskiego Sądu [She was raped—now she's going to jail! An absurd sentence in a court in Gniezno]	PC MG 2019
16.09.2019	Wysokie Obcasy	Żona zgwałcona przez męża: „Mocno mnie chwyta. Jest gotowy, ja nie. Myśli, że jego brutalność mnie ożywi" [Wife raped by husband: „He grabs me tightly. He's ready and I'm not. He thinks his brutality will bring me to life]	PC WO 2019

(Continued)

Table 3 Continued

Date of publication	Online source	Headline	Corpus code
24.10.2019	Gazeta Wyborcza	Kobiety, które wymyślają gwałt. „Może ci wsadzić miotłę, co?" [Women who make up rape. „Maybe someone should shove a broom up there, huh?"]	PC GWyb 2019
12.02.2020	Naszemiasto.pl	Częstochowa: 27-letni Gruzin zgwałcił 41-letnią kobietę na Północy. Mężczyzna został tymczasowo aresztowany [Częstochowa: A 27-year-old Georgian man raped a 41-year-old woman in the north. The man has been detained]	PC NM 2020
09.03.2020	Gazeta Wyborcza	Pokazuję swoją twarz, bo już się nie wstydzę, że zostałam zgwałcona. I nie zgadzam się na piętno ofiary [I am showing my face because I am no longer ashamed that I was raped. And I will not accept the label of victim]	GWyb 2020

The discourses present in the comments made by Internet users are ones which are impacted by the overarching social attitudes towards rape and the actors that are involved, which, as was mentioned in Chapters 2 and 3, are, in part, attributed to negative and repressive social attitudes towards sexuality. Digital comments are, themselves, more revealing of attitudes in that they present lay discourses that are not constrained by the stylistic limitations that of, for example, news reporting discourses (cf. Chapter 4), thus demonstrating a wider variety of strategies of evaluation in discourse.

Digital comments as a material of study

In this work, Chapter 4 introduced the notion of digital comments and their proneness to spread information and ideologically based attitudes and opinions to the realm of public discourses, as well as to act as general gateways to understanding collective opinion and attitudes on various issues of social magnitude. As was also mentioned in that same chapter, digital comments are those comments found on forums that act as a medium for the expression of user opinions (cf. Chapter 4; Bou-Franch, 2013). This fairly novel access to such platforms, which allow for the expression of opinion, acts as a platform to share in the dissemination of information and opinion (Hughey & Daniels, 2013: 332–3). As a representation of discursive democracy through participation, "in this new public sphere, the people—rather than news media pundits or news corporations—would shape democratic discourse through direct participation" (*ibid.*; Perlmutter, 2008).

Because digital comments belong to the category of new media discourses (Thurlow & Bell, 2009; Thurlow & Mroczek, 2011), which are defined as combining components of style associated with traditional written discourse, as well as spoken or conversational discourses (*ibid.*), it was necessary to choose the proper strategy by which to conduct the investigation of evaluation. I have taken up the investigation of pragmalinguistic implicit evaluation as a strategy of expression to look at positive and negative evaluative digital comments. The length of digital comments in general has not been specified in the literature on the subject, however they may be as short as one character long (Ben-David & Soffer, 2018). By looking at the stance of Internet user comments, as expressed through discursive evaluation, both in reference to the subject at hand and using the knowledge regarding cultural attitudes towards rape and the actors involved, implicit evaluation can be used to investigate the overall nature of digital comments and how and what they express about rape.

The issue in question here is, of course, that of rape, the propensity to engage in victim blaming and that, as a social phenomenon, such negative behavior is ever-present in common discourses that represent the attitudes and collective thought of lay-people, even where offender-blaming also takes place in discourse. This is seen, in the discursive sense, as leading to a phenomenon referred to here as discursive secondary victimization.

Methods

Coding methods presented in qualitative research studies typical for a sociological analysis were applied for the linguistic analysis in this work (Gibbs, 2009; Charmaz, 2010). The material for analysis was also organized using a method common in both corpus linguistics and qualitative data analysis for linguistic research (Tabbert, 2016).

The texts were imported from an Excel file into which they had been compiled after their selection,[69] with each comment imported into a separate cell, into the

69 By which is meant that the data were not "cherry-picked" during the process of selecting the comments for the analysis. Rather, the comments found under articles were chosen

program MaxQDA (VERBI, 2019). The code system was systematically expanded throughout the process of the analysis, particularly where the semantic differentiations in representations were concerned.

The comments, sentences, and words in the corpora mentioned above underwent analysis on the basis of the categories for the analysis of the stance of Internet users, where attitudes, victim blaming, and overall evaluation of actors and events were concerned, and were coded accordingly.[70] As stated above, implicit evaluation and stancetaking are seen as adequate tools in investigating new media discourses which are both written and conversational in their style (Kiesling, 2022). This is because the comments exist within the social context of rape (and knowledge about rape) and within the context of the article to which they refer. I argue that such a strategy is seen within the sentence structure, negation, and modality, as well as transitivity processes. These linguistic constituents are viewed as representative of the attitudes they presented within the frame of blame attribution (cf. Chapter 2).

The codes were run through a frequency analysis in MaxQDA (*ibid.*) (using the code frequencies feature for the quantitative analysis of the data), and on this basis, tables, graphs, and maps were produced to present the results attained. Some of the data has been presented in tables rather than graphs due to the number of constituents or aspects expressed, making a tabular form more suitable for its presentation.[71]

MaxQDA as a tool for data analysis

Computer-Assisted Qualitative Data Analysis Software programs (CAQDAS) have grown in popularity in the social sciences, including in sociology, psychology and linguistics. These programs are software designed to assist researchers and analysts to gain insight from materials they are looking at. One such program for conducting in-depth analyses of texts is MaxQDA, which has been deemed by social scientists an adequate tool in measuring the occurrences of linguistic and semiotic phenomena in texts, written and otherwise recorded (Consoli, 2021). It is important to note that such tools do

---

on an "as they come" basis, where all or a fraction of the most recent comments were taken for the corpus material.

70 It was during these steps that the coding process was used to label all constituents taken into consideration for the analysis.

71 The presentation of the data in a graph would have overly compressed the material, rendering it unreadable.

not suggest interpretations for researchers, but rather allow them to organize their data by sorting, structuring and analyzing large amounts of text only to facilitate the way that they are managed. Through CAQDAS programs, it becomes possible for researchers to viably interrogate their material for analysis and code it according to a code book that reflects the nature of the work (VERBI, 2019).

One of the additional and perhaps more marginal goals of the analyses presented in Chapters 6 and 7 is to demonstrate that MaxQDA constitutes a tool that may also be used in carrying out a critical discourse analysis of a corpus, allowing for the statistical data to be gathered and categorized (i.e., via coding) in accordance with the methodologies chosen by the researcher. Since I have chosen to analyze transitivity processes and social actors in digital comments, the code book that I have created for the analysis subsumes all of the categories which fall under those methods of critical investigation, including those categories for significant lexical items like verbs or nominalizations in the representations of actors, and processes such as activation or passivation.

MaxQDA allows its user to highlight any segment of the text (smaller and larger) analyzed and to code it according to the category that the analyst wishes to place it in. Such segments may be coded either manually or automatically, allowing for control over how the researcher names his or her categories and what goes into each one. Above all, the program allows for the researcher to compare various coded segments against one another for their frequency or size, and to observe the percentages or raw number of occurrences within various categories. The categories for analysis that I have used in the code book created for the analysis of digital comments range from more narrow categories reflecting the linguistic processes and constituents looked at for the analysis of social actors (i.e., various types of nomination or the specific verbs in verbal process representation) to broader categories reflecting the social ideologies investigated in the discourse (i.e., rape myths).

Tables of aspects of analysis

The types of texts presented in the analysis are of importance when considering aspects of the discourse mentioned above, as these are the discursive aspects that differed most when considering the discursive associations of actors inside each cultural context. They are even more important when considering the goal of an analysis of collective and cultural (in this case American and Polish) attitudes to rape and the social actors involved.

Table 4 Aspects of analysis and the variables analyzed

Social actors/ events	**Behavioral scripts**	**Linguistic variables analyzed**
Victim	1) Rape myths about victims 2) Sexual scripts 3) Gendered linguistic behavior 4) User attitudes towards victims 5) Victim blaming	1) Evaluative speech acts (direct and indirect) 2) Modality and negation in the structure 3) Nominal and predicative representations Analysis of the representation of social actors 4) Verbal processes in which the actors are involved 5) Metaphor and metonymy
Rapist/ perpetrator	1) Rape myths about rapists 2) Sexual scripts 3) Gendered linguistic behavior 4) User attitudes towards offenders	1) Evaluative speech acts (direct and indirect) 2) Modality and negation in the structure 3) Nominal and predicative representations Analysis of the representation of social actors 4) Verbal processes in which the actors are involved 5) Metaphor and metonymy
Rape	1) Rape myths 2) Attitudes towards rape	1) Indirect naming 2) Direct naming 3) Metaphors 4) Euphemisms 5) Dysphemisms

For the analysis of overall attitudes in sentences within the comments, sentence structure has been analyzed for what it presented about the meaning behind what was written. This included investigating what grammatical form evaluative sentences take in both of the corpora (the AEC and the PC), presented in the following chapter (Chapter 6). Hence, whether or not evaluative sentences (which evaluated the actors and the rape) occur in the form of declarative sentences, interrogative sentences, imperative sentences or exclamatory sentences have been subjected to analysis. Within the investigation of structure, the questions of modality and negation have been analyzed, as well. This was done to ascertain whether or not victim blaming occurs directly or indirectly for each linguistic and cultural context (American English and Polish). As far as the socio-semantic aspects of evaluation are concerned, nominal representations of actors, as well as metaphorical ones are investigated for their appraising value, and the act of rape, as well as euphemization and dysphemization are also looked into.

Because digital comments make up a type of text associated with informal language, it should be noted that the discourse presented within them is of a more informal or colloquial register, making the evaluation of user attitudes easier to ascertain (cf. Chapter 4 of this work for the definitions of style, genre and register) (Ehret & Taboada, 2019). This also signifies, however, that the linguistic means by which such attitudes will be expressed are to be direct or indirect based on the cultural context in which they take place, as such comments are largely reflective of everyday discourses of American and Polish culture (Grainger & Mills, 2016). The indirectness in the comments may also be attributed to the fact that the antecedent (which is the knowledge that the question of rape is being discussed) is taken for granted in the case of many of the user's messages on the public forum, thus reflecting any cultural attitudes had towards the subject of sexual crime and sexuality in general. Here it is also important to note that no changes have been made to the original text written by authors of digital comments, which means that any errors in spelling, grammar, or missing diacritics (in Polish) in the examples are not oversights on my part, but part of the texts in the corpora.

Conclusions

The materials and methods described in this chapter are an intrinsic part of the novelty of the study. To my knowledge, implicit evaluation expressed in digital comments about rape has not been investigated before. The application of MaxQDA for the quantitative and in-depth, qualitative investigation of the various constituents by which positive or negative attitudes are expressed has also not yet been done before.

The chapters which follow present the in-depth analyses of digital comments, with Chapter 6 investigating the structural aspects of evaluation in digital comments, and Chapter 7 looking at the representations of social actors through the lens of a socio-semantic analytical view and how evaluation can be reflected in choice of the discursive representation of actors.

It is my aim to demonstrate that the negative and positive evaluation of actors and events in a rape are expressed through the evaluation that is expressed implicitly by Internet users who write comments in the online space that accompanies articles about rape. This comes out of the overarching social context of revictimization and secondary victimization of victims in both American and Polish cultures, contributing to what I have called discursive secondary victimization. The reason for my placing attention on the implications that such discourse has for the victim of rape is the fact that modern scholasticism about rape has made a concerted effort to combat the problem of victim blaming as a rising social phenomenon.

Chapter 6: Analysis of (implicit) evaluation in the structure of digital comments in American and Polish online discourses on rape

The following analysis of how discursive form or structure can imply evaluative attitudes about rape has been carried out in order to show that victim blaming is present in the public participatory discourses on the subject of rape and enacts a phenomenon that may be described as discursive secondary victimization in both American and Polish cultural contexts (cf. Chapter 2). It is also my goal to show that the way that the expression of victim blaming comes about is culturally conditioned and that although it is a phenomenon that widely takes place in conversations about rape, various strategies are used in distinct levels of structure, depending on the cultural context. Because the subject matter (of rape) is sensitive, indirect communication dominates and the strategies of indirectness vary between the two cultures analyzed.

This means that inference, induced by structural markers in sentences, such as the use of modality and conditional structures, negation or the active and passive voice creates meaning that is evaluative and expresses blame attribution on the part of the Internet user writing the comment. The aforementioned devices are the ones that I have chosen to analyze for their evaluation when it comes to communicating attitudes about rape and the actors involved (Chapters 5, 6, and 7). They may be investigated through looking analytically at the strategy of discursive evaluation in comments about rape. The subject of implicit evaluation, as it is relevant to the two analytical chapters, has been expanded on in Chapter 5 (the chapter which concerns the work's methodology). The examples that are provided throughout this chapter and the one that follows (Chapter 7) have been numbered subsequently and should be viewed as separate from the examples that were provided in the theoretical part of this work (Chapters 1 through 4).

It is important to note that the investigation of the analysis overall looks at representations of the victim, offender, and the rape itself and how each is juxtaposed alongside the cultural interpretations of implications of rape. This chapter, however, looks at the representations of only the offender and the victim in the light of structural expressions of evaluation. The chapter which follows (Chapter 7), then, looks at the victim, offender, and the subject of rape as well.

Structure of the chapter

Before presenting the discussion of the material analyzed, a layout of the subsequent discussion will be presented in this section. As this chapter discusses only the structural aspects of the implicit evaluation of victim or offender blaming and supporting, I have had to choose which structural aspects deserve the most focus, and have, in doing so, taken inspiration from Tabbert's (2016) investigation of modality and negativity and what such constructions mean when looking at discourse on crime.

The first part of the discussion of this chapter regards the nature of the comments themselves, namely the attitudes towards actors they present, a category of analysis that will also be used for the discussion in Chapter 7. The division of the overall attitudes of comments relates to negative attitudes towards the victim and offender, attitudes that were supportive of the victim or the offender, or comments in which it was unclear which of the main actors was targeted.[72]

After the discussion of the comments as whole constituents, the analysis of the comments on the level of a speech act analysis is presented, providing an investigative look into the structure of evaluative sentences (i.e., whether they are interrogative, declarative, exclamatory, etc.) and how they act as evaluative sentences. After this, the question of Internet users expressing alternative hypothetical scenarios in discourse is considered and investigated from a cultural comparative perspective, namely through the investigation of modality and negation as strategies of stancetaking.

Subsequently, the analysis of transitivity is included, in accordance with Halliday's (1985) Systemic Functional Linguistic Analysis (in terms of both activation—in which, the question of activation through possessivation is briefly discussed—and passivation). This has also been taken by van Leeuwen (2005) as a part of the presentation of social actors, however, because it is an aspect which is based on the formal structure of where actors are found in clauses and sentences, I have left it in this chapter.

This analysis is presented in such a way as to show the material for each subsection so that both actors (the victim and offender) and language contexts (American English and Polish) are shown in order to present a clear comparison on a given subject. Thus, in each section of discussion (i.e., that of modality,

72 This also included those comments in which an institution was targeted as being at fault for rape or rape culture, if not pinpointed for a lack of proper handling of the problem. Such comments were considered as belonging under the umbrella category of *unclear who is targeted* because the main actors were not evaluated as strongly, if at all, in such comments.

negation, activation, and passivation or transitivity) I first take those that relate to the victim for the AEC and then those that relate to the victim for the PC, and do the same with relation to the offender for each language context.

When reading the frequencies that are given in the sections which present the results of the analysis, it is important to bear in mind that comments, sentences and clauses may overlap, thus making up for the overlaps in frequencies that do not add up to the total of comments or sentences. For the analysis of comments, the percentage of occurrence out of all the comments is calculated. For the analysis of sentence types, the percentage of occurrence out of all the comments which mentioned the actors is calculated. For single-word analyses, the percentages of occurrence have been accounted for by category of analysis for each separate actor and the representation of rape, as well as the entire corpus. These analyses are presented in either graph or table form throughout the work for adequate illustration.

Attitudes to rape victims and offenders in digital comments

The first section presents an overview of the distribution of attitudes found in the comments, and has been divided into five subsequent categories reflecting positive (here referred to as supportive comments, due to the fact that the positive comments reflect support of the victim through linguistic and discursive means) and negative attitudes towards the victim and offender (i.e., those comments which either implicitly or explicitly blame the actors), as well as categories that concern posts in which it was unclear what actors were targeted.

The graphs from the AEC are presented first and, subsequently, the graphs from the PC are provided to illustrate trends.

Figure 5 Division of overall attitudes presented in comments in AEC

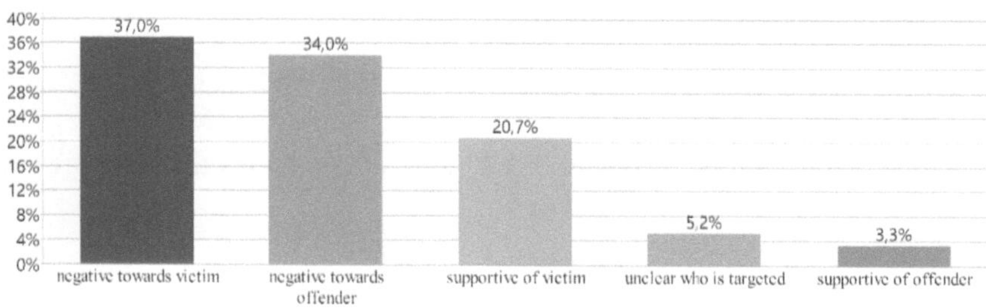

As shown in the graph above, the attitudes present in the comments that make up the American English Corpus for this chapter's analysis are predominantly those that contain negative attitudes towards the actors (both the victim and offender). 136 of the comments in the AEC presented negative attitudes towards the victim of rape (making up 37% of the comments in the AEC). This is here understood as either partitioning the blame on her or placing her as fully to blame. On the other hand, 76 of the comments (20.7% of the comments in the AEC) were purely victim supporting, not demonstrating blame for the victim. A total of 125 of the comments presented negative sentiment towards the offender (constituting 34% of the comments in the AEC), and only 12 were fully supportive of the offender (3.3% of the comments in the AEC). Additionally, there were 19 comments (5.2% of the comments in the AEC) in which it was unclear which actor was targeted.

For the following section, examples have been given in order to demonstrate the nature of negative and supportive comments,[73] as well as those in which it was unclear which actor was targeted. This is done solely for the reader's ease in navigating the notion of such comments, as well as to familiarize readers with the form in which the comments are presented. The comments are followed by the code that corresponds with those codes from Table 2 and Table 3, above. The row number enumerated indicates the comment number in the subcorpus. The first two examples (examples 1 and 2) present comments that are negative towards the victim.

> 1) In the most devastating testimony against Harvey Weinstein to date, a woman *who claims the disgraced movie mogul raped her* in *2013 painted a grotesque picture of Weinstein as* angry, controlling and manipulative, *but acknowledged* under cross examination *that she maintained* a consensual sexual relationship with him before and after the 2013 incident. And *angry controlling and manipulative does not equate to rape.*
> (AEC ABC 2020, Row: 20)

> 2) And…there are some young women, who have no money, and no self-esteem and are reading that *this woman got 7 figures in money from a powerful organization because one of the men, also powerful and wealthy, violated them. Does that send a message to power hungry women that they too can win 7 figures in money if they are raped by a man who is powerful and wealthy?* This is *a big horrible circle of no moral values.*
> (AEC NBC 2019, Row: 19)

The next two examples (examples 3 & 4) present comments that support the victim and her testimony in the AEC.

73 This being indicative of attitudes towards the main actors in a rape, the rapist(s) and/ or victim(s).

3) And if you get drunk and someone takes your wallet, watch, etc., they should not be punished b/c you got drunk and so exposed yourself to the criminal behavior of the person who took your wallet. *What you're doing is exactly blaming the victim.*
(AEC NYT 2016, Row: 17)

4) She has done *nothing wrong. Drinking and engaging in consensual sexual activity are not "wrong."* They are an expression of body autonomy and personal freedom.
(AEC ABC 2014, Row: 34)

The two examples that follow, taken from the AEC of digital comments, are examples of negative sentiment towards the offender.

5) *"Predatory offender" needs to be permanently on all his resumes for every job application.* When he gets a passport, the picture should have "predatory offender" stamped across the front. The name Brock Allen Turner is now and forever synonymous with "predatory offender." So he misses a few rib eye steaks.
(AEC NYT 2016, Row 26)

6) Agreed. *Too many times*, people *get off on the excuse that they were too drunk* to understand what they were doing. *That is a load of crap*, especially these drunk driving cases where drivers who kill, walk away from any jail time, because of the "too drunk to understand what they were doing" excuse.
(AEC NYT 2016, Row 9)

The next examples provided are comments that were supportive of the offender in the AEC. The examples of support for the offender in the AEC were only indirect (examples 7–10), including discourse that reinforced beliefs that women are responsible for dangerous encounters in which they are faced with the possibility of being assaulted.

7) Might be easier said than done, with *getting drunk and hooking up* being so much *along-standing feature of collegiate life and culture.*
(AEC NYT 2014, Row:)

8) *Women need to know they CAN defend themselves and are smart enough* to identify and avoid high risk situations. Men also need to know how to identify and avoid high risk situations. It does not get much clearer than telling young men not to touch any female who has had a sip of alcohol or ingested a drug regardless of what the female is saying. In fact, to be safest, males should get up and leave when females are becoming intoxicated.
(AEC NYT 2017, Row:)

9) Honestly, *he was 19 years old. He was drunk, she was drunk. Everyone was drunk. What is the point of ruining his life like this?* Kicking him out of a *TOP school AND* handing him a felony he'll carry for the rest of his life on his record? [Portion removed.]
(AEC PAW 2016, Row:)

10) "If you are one of those millions, you should understand that a young woman does not deserve having her body violated, her sanity threatened, and her future jeopardized because she didn't make the right decision about how much she had to drink that night." *But it's okay if a young man doesn't make the right decision about how much had to drink is labeled a rapist and tossed out of school because he had sex with an equally drunken partner?* (AEC NYT 2017)

The comment in example (9) presents what Jeffries (2010a: 55) has called *parallelism*, which is a syntactic opposition trigger that places the offender both in the same position as, as well as in opposition to the victim. Such a strategy uses structure, such as *he was drunk, she was drunk* (cf. example 9) to highlight that the victim is just as much at fault for the rape as the offender.

Examples of comments from the AEC, in which it is unclear who was targeted were as follows:

11) Amazing. "were the two intervenors bolder because they come from Sweden, a country with relatively low crime" Do not think its the reason and the Swedes living abroad would somehow be a bigger factor I would say, somehow more likely to help out (AEC MN 2016, Row: 2)

12) And this excuses....WHAT?
(AEC ABC 2015, Row: 33)

The graph presented below provides a representation of the distribution frequency of the overall attitudes presented in the comments in the PC. What is visible in this representation is that the comments negatively targeting both victim and offender are virtually statistically equal in the Polish corpus. In both the AEC and PC, investigating the representations of these actors, and how victim blaming takes place on a discursive level in American and Polish cultures will lead to the revealing of what lies at the bottom of misconceptions about offenders and victims.

Figure 6 Division of overall attitudes presented in comments in PC

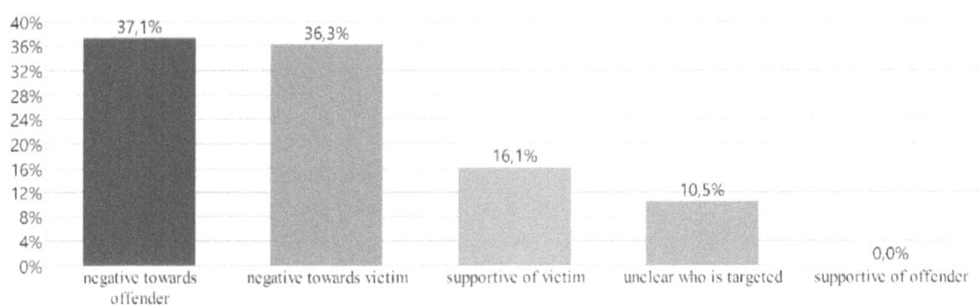

Of the Polish comments, 124 of them (36.3% of the comments in the PC) displayed negative (fully blaming or partially blaming) attitudes toward the victim and 55 comments (16.1%) were victim-supportive. In the PC, 127 comments (37.1%) displayed negative attitudes (blaming) toward the offense. In contrast, no comments (0%) were fully supportive of the offender. In 36 comments (10.5%) it was unclear who was targeted, or outside actors were targeted (such as the government or the church as an institution, which are actors that have been targeted in Poland as passive or enabling actors in the face of sexual assault (Nowicka & Regulska, 2020)).

The first two examples (examples 13 and 14) present comments that are negative towards the offender in the PC.

13)...kara winna być jedna...*uciąć narzędzie przestępstwa...*
(PC GWsp 2012, Row: 11)
[...there should only be one type of punishment...*cut off the weapon used in the crime*]

14)a tez *niech tych zboczencow ktoś zg***** i* niech cicho siedza
(PC PUD 2015, Row: 4)
[someone *should r*** those perverts* and then they should be quiet]

Comments that displayed attitudes which were negative about the victim were as follows (examples 15 and 16).

15) „Nigdy tego nie lubiłam i dalej nie lubię"—*ale to chyba podstawa małżeństwa, to dlaczego wyszłaś za faceta, z którym nie lubisz tego robić? Nie można było tego zweryfikować PRZED ślubem?*
(PC WO 2019, Row: 1)
["I never did like it and I still don't"—*but that's the basis of marriage, so why did you marry a man that you don't like to do it with? Couldn't you makesure BEFORE the wedding?*]

16) a co ona myślała że na kawkę i ciastka tam idzie??? *kobieto gdzie twój rozum*
(PC PUD 2017a, Row: 31)
[so what did she think she was going there for coffee and cake?? *woman where is your brain*]

The following examples (examples 17 and 18) illustrate attitudes that are supportive of the victim in the PC.

17) bardzo Ci *współczuję, trzymaj się*
(PC PUD 2015, Row: 31)
[I *feel so sorry for* you, *hang in there*]

18) Do komentujących. Brak seksu usprawiedliwia rozwód, ale *NIE USPRAWIEDLIWIA GWAŁTU*!
(PC WO 2019, Row: 13)
[To those writing comments. No sex is a legitimate reason for divorce, but does *NOT LEGITIMIZE RAPE*!]

There were comments which did not target either of the main actors involved in rape, but targeted an institution such as the government, the police, or the church. Example 19 targets the government (here, leaders of the EU), and examples 20 and 21 target the police. These have been categorized as not demonstrating attitudes towards the main actors, and have thus been placed into a category together (unclear who is targeted). In the PC, there were no comments that displayed attitudes supportive of the offender.

19) na tej plaży *powinni być MERKEL I MACRON.*
(PC PUD 2017b, Row: 61)
[*MERKEL AND MACRON should* be on that beach]

20) Brak słów *policja w Gnieźnie nie reaguje na zgłoszenia*. Dopiero zareaguje jak stanie się tragedia.
(PC MG 2019, Row: 7)
[No words. The *police in Gniezno do not react to reports.* They react only when a tragedy has occurred.]

21) Idę o zakład, **że** *niebieska mafia* zamiast szkoleń nt. postępowania z dziennikarzami, zasad używania siły, zasad ruchu drogowego itp. *przechodzi szkolenia z wyłudzania haraczu, perswazji—że przestępstwa nie było*, krycia siebie nawzajem i pompowania statystyk (czasami przez podrzucanie dowodów przestępstwa). W tym są naprawdę mistrzami!
(PC GWyb 2014, Row: 5)
[I bet that instead of going to training sessions regarding how to deal with journalists or about the rules of using force or the rules of the road etc., *the blue mafia* is *trained in protection rackets and persuasion—that no crime occurred*, covering each other's asses and pumping statistics (sometimes by planting the evidence of a crime). They're real masters of that!]

This focus contributes to the construction of social actors involved in rape, because it erases the victim and the offender, creating a more politicized image of the crime. Although placing the blame on another, outside party is not seen as directly lending to victim blaming, it imparts the representation of the crime to leaving out the actors, thus abstracting the act of rape even further.

The question of how exactly victim blaming as a phenomenon takes place in the discursive sense can be explored by looking at the implicit evaluation of the comments that exists within the syntactic choices made for expression, as well as the socio-semantic choices. What is of interest here is the way that evaluative comments regarding the social actors, especially where blame attribution (to the victim) is concerned, are expressed in American and Polish online discourses about rape, and how this is carried out in terms of the use of modal verbs and negativity, as well as the activation and passivation of actors (i.e., who is foregrounded), and the transitivity processes by which they are represented.

Indirectness in digital comments within the structure

It was important to find and utilize tools to describe how victim blaming occurred in the corpora. Throughout this chapter, I will describe how discursive strategies used by Internet users in digital comments are rarely directly evaluative of the actors they target.[74] It was noted that a majority of the comments (334 out of 341 comments in the AEC—97.9% of the comments, and 314 out of 315 in the PC—99.6% of the comments) that placed partial or full blame on the victim showed that such attitudes take place through indirect means.

With respect to this aspect of the analysis, for both of the corpora, the sentences that contained comments about the actors and event of the rape were taken into consideration for the analysis of such evaluation. The sentences were categorized according to their surface structure: *declarative*, *interrogative*, *imperative* and *exclamatory*, and were all assessed as carrying evaluative weight expressing opinion about the actors, either positive or negative.

There were 804 sentences analyzed as such in the AEC and 714 sentences analyzed in the PC. The tables below provide the differentiation into the various sentence types for the AEC and the PC.

The sentences selected for the analysis of their evaluative weight were those that displayed positive or negative attitudes towards actors and events. This could have been about the rapist, victim, society, the rape or a general emotionally charged comment, as all of these factors relate somehow to the issue analyzed, namely blaming. The investigation had in mind the demonstration of how victim blaming takes place indirectly in American and Polish cultures and that such a socio-pragmatic phenomenon is therefore representative of victim blaming from the position of not relating directly—discursively—to one's negative attitude to the victim.

74 Examples of direct evaluation may be found in Chapter 7, where the category of *appraisement* is discussed.

Table 5 AEC evaluative sentences for all actors

	Frequency	Percentage of AEC
declarative	616	76.6%
interrogative	125	15.6%
imperative	33	4.1%
exclamatory	30	3.7%
TOTAL	804	100%

Table 6 PC evaluative sentences for all actors

	Frequency	Percentage of PC
declarative	488	68.3%
interrogative	111	15.5%
exclamatory	68	9.5%
imperative	47	6.6%
TOTAL	714	100%

To investigate where indirect victim blaming was present in the discourse, the actual intention (illocution) conveyed by the written "utterances" of the Internet users was analyzed and the evaluative speech acts (positive and negative) were identified with the structural (this chapter) and socio-semantic aspects of the discourse (Chapter 7). This is done through the use of inference on the part of the analyst (Yus, 2016: 6–7). Such an investigation is important because "in order to become a competent speaker of a natural language it is not enough to know a number of rules for grammatical construction, semantic and phonological reference, etc., but it is also necessary to use a wide range of 'commonsense' knowledge and inferences and principles about other people's inner and intentional worlds" (Belinchón et al., 1992: 184).

The significance of indirectness and evaluation

For the purpose of analyzing speech acts and indirectness in relation to attitudes towards actors and how the phenomenon that is victim blaming takes place, in particular, the 804 sentences in the AEC were investigated for how speech acts correlate with the blame attribution on the victim, the perpetrator or outside actors or institutions (education, the church, society, etc.). In the AEC, there were 616 declarative sentences (76.6% of the evaluative sentences in the AEC) that presented an evaluative stance, 125 interrogative sentences (15.6% of the evaluative sentences in the AEC) which did the same, 68 exclamatories (9.5%) and 47 imperatives (6.6%).

In the PC, a total of 714 sentences were analyzed for their evaluative nature. There were a total of 488 declarative sentences (68.3% of the evaluative sentences in the PC) which acted as evaluatives. A total of 111 of the evaluative sentences in the PC were interrogatives (15.5% of the evaluative sentences in the PC), 68 were exclamatories (9.5% of the PC) and 47 were imperatives (6.6%). In sentences that acted as declaratives, interrogatives, exclamatories, or imperatives, the speech act type of *evaluatives* was found to be present in both the whole corpora, of the AEC and PC.

Here, the category of evaluatives is used to describe the act of blaming the victim, for it has evaluative quality and presents negative evaluation of the rape victim in particular. These sentences concerned the rape or the involvement of the victim in the rape and were indirect or direct (cf. discussion for the breakdown of the sentence structure types).

Examples of declaratives that blamed the victim in the AEC were as follows:

22) Rape is a serious issue and *we need to talk to boys and girls*, yes i said girls *because they want sex but don't understand the consequences either.*
(AEC NYT 2014, Row 1)

23) Maybe he didn't know she was 14. At 13, I looked like I was 16. *The way they dress now, is a shame and no one can tell their age.*
(AEC ABC 2014, Row: 26)

24) *She admitted she offered sexual favors for booze.... She is equally to blame in this case.*
(AEC ABC 2014, Row: 18)

Examples of *declaratives* that placed blame on the victim in the PC were as exemplified in examples 25–27.

25) *Dorosła mądra kobieta wie, że nie wszyscy ludzie są cudowni i dobrzy. Nie idzie* do mieszkania z nowo poznanym facetem jednym, a do dopiero z trzema. *Tak samo mądra kobieta nie wchodzi* w zoo do klatki z lwem bo wie jak to się może skończyć.
(PC PUD 2017a, Row: 6)
[A grown, smart woman knows that not all people are wonderful and good. She does not go to the apartment with a man she has just met, let alone with three. Just the same way a smart woman does not enter the lion's den at the zoo, because she knows how it might end.]

26)*Robi śniadanie, czule zegna ale to gwałt*, jassssne.
(PC GWyb 2020, Row: 14)
[*She makes breakfast, bids a fond farewell but it was rape*, suuuure.]

27) *Każda kobieta chce być gwałcona tylko tego nie mówi*, trzeba się samemu domyśleć a kiedy się zaczyna bronić lepiej sex smakuje niech sama rozłoży nogi wtedy będzie spokojna takich nikt nie rucha.
(PC GWsp 2019, Row: 8)
[*Every woman wants to be raped just doesn't say it.* You have to guess what she wants yourself. And when she starts to defend herself the sex tastes better. She should spread her legs by herself. Then she'll be calm. Nobody wants to have sex with those kinds [of women].]

Of course, declarative sentences are not the only means through which victim blaming are evident in the digital comments. Victim blaming also occurred in the form of questions, or *interrogatives*, meant to be insinuating partial or full blame on the victim. Several examples of interrogatives that indirectly blamed the victim in the AEC have been provided (examples 28–30).

28) *Girls, where are your mothers? Weren't you taught not to put yourself in any situations where your virtue might be questioned*
(AEC NYT 2016, Row: 17)

29) Hate to say this but I agree. I am a Democrat I am a woman *but if she cannot remember what happened, why does she assume she was violated? Did I miss a sentence or paragraph?*
(AEC NYT 2017, Row: 3)

30) *Why is she telling these salacious details in a book and not to law enforcement*? If there is a wealth of witnesses (i.e., colleagues she confided in), she should have plenty of corroboration. 3.) She continued having a sexual relationship with her alleged rapist.
(AEC NBC 2019, Row: 9)

Interrogatives were also present in the PC. Some examples of interrogatives that acted as indirect instances of victim blaming were the following, provided in examples 31–33.

31) *A co tam robiła tłumaczka?* Ta pani znana jest w środowisku z konfabulacji .
(PC PUD 2015, Row: 34)
[*What was the translator doing there?* That woman is known there for her confabulations.]

32) *Ale kto normalny idzie na imprezę z nieznajomymi?*
(PC PUD 2017a, Row: 2)
[*What kind of normal person goes to a party with strangers?*]

33) *a co ona myślała że na kawkę i ciastka tam idzie??? kobieto gdzie twój rozum*
(PC PUD 2017a, Row: 31)
[*Did she think she was going there for coffee and cake??? Woman, where is your brain*]

The structure in this case appears to be a question, thus taking on the form of an interrogative, however it acts evaluatively in its underlying meaning, making a statement about the attitude of the Internet user towards the actor. Blame is also conveyed by socio-semantic constituents, to be discussed later in the work (cf. Chapter 7).

Imperatives were also found in both of the corpora as containing evaluative weight to their meaning (cf. examples 34–36).

34) In every other area of life, we are told to be responsible: *Don't drink and drive. Don't park next to a van. Walk with a friend. Stay away from dark alleys. Walk assertively. Be aware of your surroundings. Have your keys ready.*
(AEC NYT 2017, Row: 5)

35)*Educate yourselves* on the characteristics of a sexual predator.
(AEC PAW 2016, Row: 5)

36)How about teaching your sons and daughters NOT TO DRINK UNTIL BLOTTO? Getting drunk = gateway to bad sexual activity......*stop getting drunk*!!! *Show some respect for yourself*
(AEC NYT 2014, Row: 16)

Examples of *imperatives* that indirectly blamed the victim in the PC were also present. In the PC, there were two types of imperatives, those directed at a singular actor (example 37) and those directed at a collective of actors (in this case, victims) (example 38). This can be seen on the formal level in Polish (i.e., *licz się* ('reckon with'—sg.) and *drzyjcie się* ('scream')—sg. and pl.), whereas in English it cannot (i.e., *don't drink*, stop, *show*, etc.).

37) Ale *licz się* z tym, że nie wszyscy są poczytalni, i kogoś możesz takim ubiorem „zachęcić".
(PC WO 2015, Row: 5)
[But *reckon with* the fact that not everyone is sane and that you might "encourage" someone if you're dressed like that.]

38) *Drzyjcie się* o pomoc i *uciekajcie.*[75]
(Pudelek 2015 Row 47)
[*Scream* for help and *run away.*]

---

75 Examples 34 and 35 present different qualities of evaluatives expressions through directives, namely in that example 34 evaluates the behavior of the victim by stating what she should do in a given situation more negatively, and in example 35, the surface of the comment seems to advise the victim on what to do, but does so by playing on the myth that the outcome of rape might look more favorable for the victim if she screams and runs away. The belief that a victim should use both verbal and physical resistance to escape an attacker has been acknowledged in the literature (Crawford, 1999) as not recognizing other ways in which a victim might react to sexual assault (cf. Chapter 2 of this work).

Examples of *exclamatories* that both directly and indirectly blamed the victim are exemplified in examples 39–41.
39) Agreed. How low her self-esteem must be in order to trade liquor for her body. *So sad.*
(AEC ABC 2014, Row: 50)

40) I am not a Matt Lauder fan, but come on…no one who has been raped would have an extramarital affair with the same individual. *Shame on her!*
(AEC VTY 2016, Row: 30)

41) *'spiritual soulmate'!? There's a new one!* (ABC 2020, Row 1)

Exclamatories in the PC also blamed the victim, however, were less frequent than in the AEC (cf. example 42).

42) *Brawo* dla niej za brak mozgu.
(PC PUD 2017a, Row: 3)
[*Bravo* to her for not having a brain.]

The examples presented above are simply demonstrative of the way that comments expressing attitudes towards the actors, especially negative ones presenting attitudes of victim blaming, take place mostly indirectly, however, they also take place directly. In the AEC, there were 11 sentences in 8 comments which showed direct blaming of the victim (making up 1.3% of the AEC on the basis of sentence count), and in the PC there was 1 comment and 1 sentence which demonstrated direct blaming (making up .1% of the corpus on the basis of sentence count). The direct instances of blame attribution were counted on the level of sentence structure.[76] As for the direct blame attribution to the offender, there were 7 sentences in 7 comments in the AEC blaming the offender and only 1 sentence in 1 comment doing the same in the PC (making up .9% of the AEC and .1% of the PC, respectively).

For this reason, the need for such an investigation of indirectness to use the proper tools for uncovering the structural and semantic strategies, which evaluate the actors and the event. What is most interesting for this analysis are the ways that evaluative speech acts in the form of digital comments utilize various linguistic strategies to indirectly place blame on or express support for the rapist and the victim.

76 Other more direct blaming types can be found in Chapter 7 of this work, where the issue of negative and positive appraisement is concerned (with the reference to social actors).

Modality and negation

In this analysis of structural aspects of the evaluation of actors in a rape, I have chosen to look at modality and negation as methods of indirectly expressing sentiment, for they are strategies which implicate the possibility of alternative hypothetical situations taking place. Modality is discussed first, and the question of negation in both corpora is described (Singh, 2019).

Modality concerns a speaker's opinion about, or attitude towards, a certain proposition (Simpson, 1993:47; Singh, 2019: 56–57). As a discourse strategy, modality produces hypothetical alternative situations that demonstrate what an utterer or writer believes could have happened in a situation given other, alternative, circumstances. This strategy fits into the categories of the evaluation of actors, for, given the context of the discourse, modality presents the belief that other choices made by the actor (as an example), could have been done to present a different situation. In the case of the subject discussed in this work, this is the rape or, according to interpretations, the belief that the victim has of having been raped.

I will have to remain brief about the role of forms of modality in producing hypothetical alternative scenarios in the context of rape, however, this does make for a significant difference between the AEC and the PC in the way that evaluative sentences are expressed (at varying levels of indirectness). American culture highly values politeness (Grainger & Mills, 2016), hence the tendency to utilize strategies of indirectness when making an evaluative or critical remark. Because rape is a highly polarizing subject, this strategy can be expected in discourses wherein American Internet users make comments about the role of the victim.

The tables below present the frequencies at which attitudes towards actors are shown through modal expressions in the CMC discourse discussed. For one, the use of the conditionals (or *if*-clause in the AEC and *jeżeli* and *gdyby/jakby* in the PC) are indicative of such alternative scenarios that the victim could have been part of, which in turn raises questionability of the merit of the victim's testimony. The use of the conditionals is also demonstrative of indirect strategies for victim-blaming discourses to be expressed because the "conditional structure constructs a hypothetical world" (Tabbert, 2016: 122). Such hypothetical scenarios found in discourses about rape imply that blame is placed on the actors they discuss. Any alternative scenario constructed using a conditional structure is that the rape could have been prevented had any other action been undertaken or any other circumstances been sought out or created. The modality types presented, where the act of victim blaming is concerned, are that of epistemic or deontic modality, with epistemic making headway where the assessment of truth is presented in the user comments and deontic modality showing through in examples of certainty about the actors' behavior (cf. Chapter 1).

Table 7 If-clauses (conditionals) in the AEC

	Frequency	Percentage[77]	Percentage of AEC
IF-clause victim-blaming	45	54.9%	5.6%
IF-clause offender-blaming	34	41.5%	4.2%
IF-clause doubt of offender's fault	2	2.4%	.2%
IF-clause rape preventable	1	1.2%	.1%
TOTAL	82/804	100%	10.2% of AEC

Some examples have been provided to illustrate the depth at which conditional sentences communicate an alternative that calls the victim's actions into question. Example 43 provides a window into how a conditional structure more obviously targets the victim, by creating the condition seeking out danger (the lion's den) and providing that the result is rape (or here, getting mauled). The use of the conditional structure, as provided in the examples below, implicates that the victim is at fault, considering that alternative situations or circumstances were not chosen in light of the threat that is sexual assault.

Within the categories of *if*-clause constructions, all of which are evaluative in nature, there were declarative sentences present in such form, as well as interrogatives with *if*-clauses. Examples 43–45 show the way that declarative sentences with the conditional construction demonstrate evaluative stances towards the actors. Examples 46 and 47 show the conditional in the form of a question, where the implicated blame is placed on the victim, who made the decision to drink, and where we are additionally confronted with the fact that men do rape when they are drunk, i.e., stating that rape is a natural behavior for men. There were those *if*-clauses that discussed the offender, but still targeted the victim (cf. example 45). These examples show certainty on the part of the writer, reflecting deontic modality in the sentences.

43)But *if you* (repeatedly) *jump* into a lion's den, *you're going to get mauled* (AEC NBC 2019, Row: 14)

77 These percentages present the percentage within the given category, i.e., in this case, the percentage within the category of all *if*-clauses for the actors in the AEC

44) In this case, though I confess I can't help thinking *this would not have happened if the young woman had not allowed herself to get falling-down drunk.*
(AEC NYT 2017, Row: 7)

45) *If he was drunk during the intercourse,* then *she should be charged with rape.*
(AEC ABC 2014, Row: 10)

46) And a question which nags me in these cases is *if the woman is so drunk she cannot give consent and is not responsible for her behavior, are we certain that a young man might never otherwise do what is done while drunk?*
(AEC NYT 2017, Row 20)

47) *IF she is a victim,* how do you know the accused were not drunk also?
(AEC ABC 2015, Row 18)

The use of the conditional to target actors in the AEC demonstrates how evaluation, mostly where the negative evaluation of actors is concerned, takes place indirectly and is a common way of expressing opinions in English (Tabbert, 2016: 122–123). The conditional constructions make up a particularly insidious type of structure in the context of reference to a victim of rape in American English discourse, because it provides an alternative choice that the victim had, giving her agency in the crime. Because the rape has already been discussed, providing examples of circumstances (including decision-making or undertaking actions) that may not be realized in the aftermath of rape, since the act is already in the past, such conditional constructions take on the dimension of being highly negatively evaluating of the victim, as she is the one who would have any control in actions taken out against the offender. When such discourse discusses rape victims in general (i.e., example 43), it places constraints on the decision-making of women and the expectations that society has from them even in the context of their physical persons being threatened.

Modality, of course, was also used to evaluate the offender, namely in that the offender is discussed more generally. Some examples have been provided below (cf. examples 48 and 49). The table above (cf. Table 7) demonstrates that such constructions were still more prevalent with reference to the victim

48) Remember the words "Her first" and a lot of a woman's intentions will be told to you...and *if* at any time, *you aren't 100% sure* that she wants to do it, *stop.*
(AEC NYT 2014, Row: 12)

49) *If you have sex* with someone who does not consent, *that is rape.*
(AEC NYT 2017, Row: 8)

The use of modality has also been found with reference to the offender in both the AEC and the PC. In the PC, the various forms of conditionals were expressed using *jeżeli* (or *jeśli*), as well as various forms of *gdyby/jakby*. A table of the number of *jeżeli*-clauses related to each actor in the PC has been provided.

Table 8 Jeżeli-clauses and gdyby-clauses (conditionals) in the PC

	Frequency	Percentage	Percentage of PC
JEŻELI-clause offender-blaming	4	18.1%	.5%
JEŻELI-clause victim-blaming	7	31.8%	.9%
JEŻELI-clause other-blaming	3	13.6%	.4%
GDY-clause offender-blaming	4	18.1%	.5%
GDYBY-clause victim-blaming	3	13.6%	.4%
GDYBY-clause other-blaming	1	4.5%	.1%
TOTAL	22/714	100%	3% of PC

The *jeżeli*-clauses were found in the PC as a strategy of indirectly blaming the victim or the offender, as it also presented alternative hypothetical scenarios, similarly to the AEC. The use of the conditional cast doubt on the validity of what was thought to be rape (examples 48–50). Similarly to the examples taken from the AEC, the conditionals found in the PC, although less frequent, also pointed to the existence of alternative situations and insinuation that the victim's version of events was not plausible (example 50) or that rape is only what one calls it (example 51). The question of possibility is raised in the following examples, creating a tone of possibilities expressed.

50) Wątpliwości są naturalnym elementem umysłu, *jeżeli* ogląd sytuacji kłóci się z logiką. Nie ma zatem co pluć na Policje.
(PC GWyb 2014, Row: 14)
[Doubt is a natural element of the mind *if* the view of the situation argues with logic. Therefore there is no reason to spit on the Police.]

51) *Jeśli* to był gwałt to połowa mężczyzn z powiatu jest gwałcicielami... Sąd bez powodu nie wydał takiego wyroku
(PC MG, Row: 3)
[*If* it was rape then half of the men in the district are rapists… the court didn't pass that kind of judgement without reason.]

52) *Jeśli* pani nie lubi seksu, to powinna to wyznać przed ślubem.
(PC WO 2019, Row: 17)
[*If* the woman doesn't like sex, then she should have said so before the wedding.]

There were also instances in which the use of a *jeżeli*-clause was used in sentences which referred to the offender or offenders, to blame the offender indirectly, similarly to the way the *if*-clause constructions were found to work in the AEC. In the PC, the use of the conditional was also found to place doubt or disbelief in the occurrence of the rape, embedded within a comment that was offender-blaming (example 54). Again, the question of possibility is raised in the following examples, creating a tone of possibilities expressed.

53) *Jeśli* gwałciciele nie mogą iść siedzieć, bo są przykładnymi mężami i tatusiami (żygać [sic!] mi się chce), to niech za karę przez najbliższe powiedzmy 10 lat działają na rzecz ofiar gwałtu.
(PC WO 2015, Row: 1)
[*If* rapists can't be behind bars because they are model husbands and fathers (I want to throw up), then they should have to work to increase awareness about rape victims for the next ten years or so as punishment.]

54) *Jeśli* faktycznie to jej zrobili to śmierć to za mało.
(PC GWyb 2018, Row: 5)
[*If* they did in fact do that to her then death is even too little.]

The use of *gdyby* and *jakby* to present alternative hypothetical situations (through the use of the conditional form) was found in the PC, however infrequently. There were 4 conditional clauses which were offender-blaming in the PC (making up .5% of the entire PC on the basis of sentence count) and 3 clauses which were victim blaming of the same type (.4% of the PC).

There were fewer instances of the use of the conditional in the PC (3%) than in the AEC (10.2%) because the conditional presents an air of indirectness that is not as representative in Polish culture as it is in American culture. American cultural discourses are more geared towards expressing negative stances indirectly (Grainger & Mills, 2016), and the conditional structure to express hypothetical alternative situations is one such way of doing so. The following examples show the use of *gdyby* to indirectly blame the victim.

55) właśnie poszła z obcymi facetami do mieszkania, pili ćpali, dobrze że k***y nie zabili i pomijam wszelkie podteksty, tak się nie robi, *gdyby została porwana to zupełnie inna historia*
(PC Pudelek 2017a, Row: 27)
[she went to an apartment with [male] strangers, they drank and did drugs, and it's a good thing that they didn't kill the wh*re. And I'm ignoring all innuendos. You just don't do that. *If she had been kidnapped, then it would have been a whole different story*]

56) *Gdyby* przez przypadek *policji by sie udało złapać bandziora*, to zupełnie *inaczej by postępowali wobec dziewczyny.*
(PC GWyb 2014, Row: 35)
[*If* by some chance *the police had been able to catch* the bandit, *they would have approached the girl* completely *differently*.]

57) A *jakby 3 dziewczyny zaczepily* chlopaka w autobusie i zaprosily na impreze *to co-normalne ze by poszedł* prawda, a tutaj mowicie ze brak mozgu.
(PC Pudelek 2017a, Row: 43)
[*If 3 girls were to make a move on a boy* on the bus and then invited to a party *then what? It would be normal if he went, wouldn't it,* and you're here talking about her not having a brain.]

58) skoro poszła to *jakby się zgodzila*, durne te baby oj durne.
(PC PUD 2017a, Row: 30)
[since she went, that's the same *as if she had agreed*, those women are silly, oh so silly.]

The conditional structure, as has been demonstrated in the above description and examples, shows that indirect blaming on the level of structure takes place in digital comments, in both of the cultural contexts. Other expressions of modality, however, were also present.

Other modal expressions for evaluation

Other modal expressions found in the corpora were those that discussed what should have been done by actors in order to create an alternative possible situation or a choice that could have been made in the face of rape in order to avoid it. This included expressions such as *could have* or *should have* in the AEC and *mógł/mogła* ('could have') and *powinien/powinna* ('should have') in the PC.

In the AEC, the use of *could have* expressed alternative situations only in 3 instances (.3% of the AEC) (see examples 59 and 60), with all of them relating in some way to the choices of the victim. The use of *could have,* as seen in the examples, expressed criticism towards the victim and offender, explaining that the rape might have been sex, which in turn suggests that the rape claim was false (example 59). The use of *could have* also expressed alternative choices that the victim theoretically had before her and that she could have avoided being raped altogether (example 60).

59) She concludes that, because sexual relations took place, "I had been violated." No, you may not conclude that. Both of you *could have drunkenly had sex willingly.*
(AEC NYT 2017, Row: 2)

60) She *could have protected herself better* in the first place.
(AEC ABC 2015a, Row: 6)

In the AEC, there were 6 sentences where *should have* expressed an alternative situation for the victim (.7% of the AEC on the basis of sentence count) and 2 sentences where *should have* was used to talk about the offender (.2% of the AEC). There were also 2 instances (.2% of the AEC) in the AEC where *should have* was found to describe alternative other actors and circumstances that could have prevented the rape, such as the parental guidance in example 61, and the screening for date rape drugs in the victim's system by the police in example 62.

59) If the anal sex was "excruciatingly painful," why didn't she yell, get up, or leave the hotel room? I acknowledge the power difference and how some people feel paralyzed in shock, but he penetrated her anus without lubricant. The pain from that *alone should have given her no option* but to stop him. According to her story, she just let it happen.
(AEC VTY 2019, Row: 29)

60) The excuse is *she shouldn't have taken her nasty butt out of the house*, drunk, in the first place.
(AEC ABC 2014, Row: 29)

61) Winerip critically omits the missing -in- action essential parental guidance that *should have been inculcating right* from wrong for 18 long years.
(AEC NYT 2014, Row: 14)

62) The girl *should have had a blood tox screen* for ruffees and other drugs ......cops blew the case again!
(AEC MN 2016, Row: 11)

For the AEC, the use of modals to express past alternative scenarios places the focus on the victim and her role in decision-making, giving the victim hypothetical agency in a situation where the focus should be on her victimhood, seeing as the crime has already been committed at the point of expressing such opinions by Internet users.

In the PC, this strategy was also found. The PC showed that such alternative constructions were expressed with *mogła* ('could have') a total of 4 times (.5% of the PC). The verb *powinna* ('should'/ 'should have') for the victim was present in a total of 12 clauses in the PC (1.6% of the PC on the basis of sentence count). Examples 63–66 express what could have been done, with reference to the rape itself (i.e., how to avoid being raped in examples 65 and 66), or the negative consequences of reporting rape in Poland, which reaps situations of secondary victimization at the hands of the police (example 64). The *powinna* construction for the victim was also found in presenting alternative hypothetical situations (cf. examples 65 and 66). No clauses with *powinien/powinni* or *mógł/mogli* were found in reference to the offender(s) in the PC (0% of the PC).

63) Dwóch obcych facetów na bani, *mogła pomysleć*, ze to się może dla niej źle skonczyć.
(PC Pudelek 2015, Row: 11)
[Two strangers (men) who were completely hammered, *she could have guessed* it would end badly for her.]

64) Równie dobrze *mogłam sobie podarować zgłaszanie* całej sprawy...
(PC GWyb 2014, Row: 26)
[I just as well *could have not reported* the whole thing…]

65)*Powinna* uciec i wezwać pomoc.
(PC PUD 2015, Row: 47)
[She *should have* run away and called for help.]

66) moze i była na wyjeździe i chciała się pobawić lub oderwać od domowej rzeczywistości ale jeżeli ci kolesie byli poniżej jej poziomu to *powinna* iść do swojego pokoju zadzwonić do męża lub porobić coś innego a po 2 dlaczego wpuścił pijanego kolesia do swojego pokoju ?
(PC PUD 2015, Row: 22)
[maybe she *was* on a trip and wanted to have some fun or get away from her home reality, but if those guys were below her standards then she *should have* gone to her room and called her husband or done something else. Second of all, why did she let a drunk guy into her room?]

Comparably to the AEC, such expression of modality presents an alternative situation which, according to the user making the comment could have changed or prevented the outcome of the situation, whether it be social ostracism or having been raped at all. This has a similar focus to that of the AEC and foregrounds the victim and her role.

As was stated earlier, the use of conditional structures to express alternative hypothetical situations was more frequent in the AEC than in the PC (10.5% of *if*-clauses in the AEC, for all actors and 3% of *jeżeli*-or *gdyby*-clauses in the PC). The differences in the AEC and the PC are demonstrative of the differences in cultural expression of blame attribution. The strategies of indirectness of expression are more prevalent where conditionals are used in the AEC, seeing that more often used were the conditional forms in English than in Polish, to express opinion and to evaluate the actors.

This between the AEC and the PC can be contributed to several factors, including that in American culture, giving advice is more acceptable a strategy for the expression of opinions regarding other people's behavior (van Dijk, 1997), as well as that American culture values indirect expression in the form of polite language and Polish speakers find direct expression (both positive and negative) to be more acceptable in interaction (Wierzbicka, 1985; Lubecka, 2000; Mills, 2016).

These structural aspects are of interest, for they show that, where conditional constructions are concerned, American English expressions of evaluation using such a strategy reflect a greater level of acceptance of indirectness in discourse than in Polish discourse. When confronted with a social problem, such as rape, American discourses have a higher tendency to refer to them indirectly, in this case when taking on a critical stance towards the victim, which may be reflective of a social unacceptability to blame the victim in the American cultural context.

In addition to conditionals, the use of modal constructions was found in both of the corpora, however not as frequently, with 1.2% of the AEC demonstrating *should have* or *could have* constructions to express alternative hypothetical situations for the victim only, and 2% of the entire PC expressing *powinna* or *mogła* and only with reference to the victim. The use of modal expressions was about equal in the AEC and the PC.

Negation as a strategy of indirect evaluation

Negation is another means by which, in evaluative discourse, alternative hypothetical situations are expressed as having been possible. As a discourse strategy, negation can be used as a premodifier for verbs, noun phrases, prepositional phrases or adjectives in order to communicate the possible existence of an alternative, thus expressing an evaluation of the situation discussed.

In the AEC, there were several types of negation found, including the negation of verb phrases and adjectival phrases with *not* and the negation of noun phrases with *no*. Negation with *not* was the most prevalent type of negation in the AEC, especially in clauses which blamed the victim for the rape. In the AEC, there were 22 clauses with the negation of the verb, which blamed the victim (2.7% of the AEC), 9 clauses with the negation of the verb, which supported the victim (1.1% of the AEC), 9 clauses with the negation of the verb, which blamed the offender (making up 1.1% of the AEC) and only 3 clauses with the negation of the verb, which supported the offender (.3% of the AEC).

Negation of a noun-phrase with *not* occurred a total of 16 times in the AEC (1.9% of the corpus), with 5 such clauses victim-blaming (.6% of the AEC), 5 clauses victim-supporting (.6% of the AEC), 5 clauses offender blaming (.6% of the AEC) and 1 clause offender-supporting (.1% of the AEC).

Negation of an adjective with *not* was also found in the AEC, however only with reference to the victim, in both victim-blaming and victim-supporting comments, however rarely. These instances (4 instances) made up .4% of the AEC (cf. Table 9, below).

Negation of a prepositional phrase with *not* only took place in reference to the victim in 2 cases, in sentences that presented victim-supporting attitudes (.2% of the AEC). A table has been provided to illustrate:

Table 9 Negation with not for actors in the AEC

	Frequency	Percentage	Percentage in AEC
not + verb (victim-blaming)	22	33.8%	2.7%
not + verb (victim-supporting)	9	13.8%	1.1%
not + verb (offender-blaming)	9	13.8%	1.1%
not + noun phrase (victim-supporting)	5	7.7%	.6%
not + noun phrase (victim blaming)	5	7.7%	.6%
not + noun phrase (offender-blaming)	5	7.7%	.6%
not + adjective (victim-blaming)	3	4.6%	.3%
not + verb (offender-supporting)	3	4.6%	.3%
not + prepositional phrase (victim-supporting)	2	3.1%	.2%
not + adjective (victim-supporting)	1	1.5%	.1%
not + noun phrase (offender-supporting)	1	1.5%	.1%
not + prepositional phrase (offender-blaming)	0	0.0%	0.0%
not + prepositional phrase (offender-supporting)	0	0.0%	0.0%
not + prepositional phrase (victim-blaming)	0	0.0%	0.0%
not + adjective (offender-supporting)	0	0.0%	0.0%
not + adjective (offender-blaming)	0	0.0%	0.0%
TOTAL	65/804	100%	8% of AEC

Negation mostly took place in the context of verbs, calling into question the fact that the victim was raped. The following examples are of negations which took place within the context of a conditional sentence in the AEC, suggesting that an alternative situation or alternative circumstances were possible, or that the situation of rape could have been avoided had other choices been made or had the choices that were made by the actor not been carried out. The use of the negation in such cases circumvents the act of directly stating that the victim is at fault, yet indirectly suggests, through processes of deduction, that she is at fault for the rape. The use of negation was discovered in both *if*-clause structures where the victim-blaming comments were concerned and in imperative sentences and in the negation of participles. Examples have been provided.

67) Um, yea, tell your daughter *not to go out binge* drinking with a bunch of drunk guys... (AEC ABC 2015, Row: 6)

68) Yes, if young women *didn't* sometimes *drink* to excess, they would be less likely to be assaulted in these situations.
(AEC NYT 2017, Row: 19)

69) and definitely *don't pass out.*
(AEC ABC 2015a, Row: 6)

70) By *not getting black-out drunk*, they are far less likely to be raped or accused of rape. (AEC NYT 2017, Row: 6)

The negation of noun phrases was also found in victim-blaming sentences, which indirectly stated that the victim was either lying or misinterpreted the situation. By negating nouns with *not*, doubt is raised and the reader is drawn to an alternative situation which is implied to be more true than the fact of having been raped. The following examples demonstrate how such negation negatively evaluated the victim in the AEC.

71) "I don't remember what happened after that" is *not evidence* for rape.
(AEC NYT 2017, Row: 2)

72) Looks like if all is true she whored herself out for her job. This *wasn't a one-time thing.*
(AEC VYT, Row: 5)

73) She (and her supporters) think others are blaming her when there is significant evidence that shows all she says is *not necessarily the way it was.*
(AEC VTY, Row: 12)

Negation also occurred in the victim-supporting comments, and are shown in several examples below. This type of negation presented more direct victim-supporting comments though the presentation of direct statements, with negation of words and phrases such as *at fault* and *deserve*, which are in themselves strictly related to the rape.

74) But *she's not at fault for the rape.* that is the fault of the man who thought it was ok to rape someone who couldn't defend herself. who was so drunk that he left her passed out outside in the freezing weather
(AEC ABC 2014, Row: 11)

75) "If you are one of those millions, you should understand that a young woman *does not deserve* having her body violated, her sanity threatened, and her future jeopardized because she didn't make the right decision about how much she had to drink that night."
(AEC NYT 2017, Row: 21)

In considering adjectival modification with *not*, this type of negation signifies that the alternative, which is the opposite of what has been negated is a better choice for the actor in question.

76) The bottom line is that binge drinking to the point of oblivion *is not healthy* for young men or women. This is the common denominator here.
(AEC NYT 2014, Row: 8)

77) In that same vein, women should indeed have the right to get passing-out drunk at a frat party without fear of getting violated; -- and they have that right, *but it's not smart.*
(AEC ABC 2015a, Row: 16)

Where the offender was concerned, the negation of a verb in offender-blaming clauses included such examples as those in examples 78–81. Here, conditional clauses and question forms indirectly state that the offender made a bad choice given the circumstances. In the case of conditional sentences, the fact that the verb is negated in such sentences which relate to the offender implies that had the opposite been done in the situation of rape, the outcome would have been different (i.e., the woman saved). In the case of the negation of verbs in declarative sentences which seem to present facts, the fault of the justice system or the tendency for social norms to support rapists are criticized. This occurrence makes up 1.1% of the AEC.

78) "This would not have happened" if *the rapist had not chosen* to forcibly attack someone and commit an assault on their person.
(AEC NYT 2017, Row: 9)

79) However, No means No. If she was saying no, *why didn't he stop*?
(AEC VTY 2019, Row: 19)

80) The boy, however, *has not had any consequence.*
(AEC ABC 2011, Row: 32)

81) But her piece of shit rapist *has not had to own up to* what he's done.
(AEC MN 2016, Row: 14)

Negation to excuse the offender was viewed in light of the analysis as offender-supporting comments or sentences (cf. examples 82 and 83).

82) Most men are stronger than women. Some of them, drunk or not, *don't get* that when a woman says no—or when she's too drunk to say anything—that means stop.
(AEC NYT 2017, Row: 30)

83) He is *not responsible* for decades if people that created the culture.
(AEC ABC 2015b,| Row: 46)

Negation with *no* implies a lack of something, thus calling into question in this case that a crime ever occurred. This, however, took place only 3 times in victim-blaming (.3% of the AEC), once in a sentence that was victim-supportive (.1% of the AEC), and 5 times in offender-blaming sentences (.6% of the AEC).

Table 10 Negation of actors with no in the AEC

	Frequency	Percentage	Percentage of AEC
no + noun phrase (offender-blaming)	5	50%	.6%
no + noun phrase (victimiblaming)	3	30%	.3%
no + noun phrase (both offender- and victim-blaming)	1	10%	.1%
no + adjectival phrase (victim-blaming)	1	10%	.1%
no + adjectival phrase (offender-blaming)	0	0%	0%
TOTAL	10/804	100%	1.2% of AEC

Some examples of the presentation of absence through the use of *no* are as follows, and were found in sentences that blamed the victim (example 84) and the offender (example 85) or for both the actors (examples 86–88). In the case of the negation with *no*, the subject of absence presents itself as a marker of critical evaluative stances.

84) That said, it's just amazing to me that the "victim" *takes no responsibility* for making herself vulnerable -- by getting falling-down-blacked-out-drunk. It's all the guy's fault for taking advantage of her, and if it hadn't happened, *she'd have had no remorse* for her own behavior. (AEC NYT 2016, Row: 30)

85) I see *no evidence* of a crime......two teens willingly had sex. (AEC ABC 2015b, Row: 16)

86) No one is "clean "in this story. It sounds like the kids in this town have *no boundaries*. (AEC ABC 2014, Row: 1)

87) The men that come out as predators have *no values, no will power*, & they're horrible because there is nothing they need that they can't buy. (AEC VTY 2019, Row: 19)

88) She's *no better* than he is. (AEC VTY 2019, Row: 12)

It is important to mention the use of negation in its various forms when looking at the AEC, because of the implications that it presents. The use of negation is a powerful linguistic device that can present absence, which in the case of rape leads to doubt in the fact that the victim was raped at all (cf. examples 84 and 85: *no remorse* and *no evidence*) and may even imply insidious behavior on the part of the victim (example 84). The use of the negation with *no*, modifying a noun, in the AEC represents things that the author of the comment believes are the conditions of proper behavior or evidence in a situation, as in the example of *no boundaries* (example 86). In the case of references to the offender, negation of a noun phrase with *no* included example 87, where *no values* and *no will power* were present. This use of the negation realizes an absence of something which, in the eyes of the author, would have created different circumstances had such an object been present at the time of the rape. Where victim blaming is concerned, this draws attention to the absent object, thus implying that the victim would have been able to avoid the rape had the circumstances been different and contributes to the belief that rape is a figment of one's imagination or the result of having no control over one's behavior (i.e., uncontrollable sexual desire).

Negation was also present in the PC, however, because of the different language context, negation was expressed slightly differently than in the AEC. There were a total of 62 sentences in the PC that presented negation (8.6% of the entire PC). The only type of negation that occurred in the PC was through modification by *nie* ('no' or 'not') of either a verb phrase or a noun phrase.

Table 11 Negation with nie in the PC to represent actors

	Frequency	Percentage	Percentage in the PC
nie + verb (victim-blaming)	30	48.4%	4.2%
nie + verb (offender-blaming)	11	17.7%	1.5%
nie + verb (victim-supporting)	10	16.1%	1.4%
nie + verb (society-blaming)	5	8.1%	.8%
nie + verb (offender-supporting)	3	4.8%	.4%
nie + noun phrase (offender-blaming)	2	3.2%	.2%
nie + noun phrase (victim-blaming)	1	1.6%	.1%
nie + noun phrase (victim-supporting)	0	0.0%	0%
nie + noun phrase (offender-supporting)	0	0.0%	0%
TOTAL	62/714	100%	8.6% of PC

Negation for the victim in the PC presented alternative hypothetical situations, as well as evaluations of what the victim did not do to prevent the rape. As can be seen in the examples from the PC (examples 89–91), such discourse draws attention to common stereotypical beliefs that a woman should not go out in the dark or physically resist being raped, and that because such actions were not decided on, that she is at fault for being raped.

89) A ofierze szczerze współczuję i życzę, aby *nigdy nie wybierała się po ciemku* na pustkowie.
(PC GWyb 2014, Row: 14)
[I really feel sorry for the victim and wish that she *never goes out* into the wilderness after dark.]

90) Jaki gwałt sama wsiadla, do samochodu, *nie opierala sie* a teraz, ze ja slabo wygrzmocili Pojda siedziec.
(PC GWsp 2012b, Row: 7)
[What rape? She got into the car herself and *didn't resist* and now that they didn't do her hard enough they are going to do time.]

91) *Nie zgłaszają* bo same pod wpływem alkoholu i narkotyków są chętne a potem *nic nie pamiętają* i robią z siebie ofiarę…
(PC GWsp 2019, Row: 2)
[They *don't report* because they themselves are under the influence of alcohol and drugs and they're willing (to have sex) and then they *don't remember* anything and make themselves the victim…]

Where the offender was concerned, the negation of verbs in the PC concerned criticisms of what they did to the victim (cf. examples 92 and 93). The use of the negation juxtaposes alternative behavior, which are to be attributed to a normal and good person, and that engaging in outlying behavior renders a person inhuman or places focus on the lack of an action (in this case, penetration) to negate the fact that rape occurred.

92) normalny mężczyza *tak nie robi* i przez 10 dni *nie katuje* kobiety bo weszła do niego do mieszkania. winni są tylko oni—a ona niech spoczywa w pokoju!!!!!
(PC PUD 2017a, Row: 18)
[a normal man *doesn't do* something like that and *doesn't torture* a woman just because she went into his apartment. Only they are the guilty ones—and may she rest in peace!!!!]

93) nie przesądzam ale co by zyskała ogłaszając się ofiarą gwałtu? Co prawda skoro jej *nie spenetrował* to była to napaść na tle seksualnym a nie gwałt stricte.
(PC GWyb 201, Row: 41)
[I am not pre-empting, but what would she achieve in reporting herself a victim of rape? It was in fact sexual assault if he *didn't penetrate* her, and not rape per se.]

Negation for the offender in offender-supporting sentences were explanatory of why the rapist raped the victim, as shown in the following examples (cf. examples 94 and 95). This type of negation places particular focus on the role of the victim in the rape, implying that she is to blame.

94) Pewnie nie tak to sobie wyobrażała, a chłopaki *nie potrafili zrozumieć* „nie", bo przecież z nimi poszła bez oporów, a nagle coś się jej odmieniło.
(PC PUD 2017a, Row: 39)
[She probably didn't imagine it happening like that and the boys *weren't able to understand* "no" because she went with them willingly, and then all of a sudden she changed her mind.]

95) Nikt jej tam siłą *nie ciągnął.*
(PC PUD 2017a, Row: 32)
[Nobody took her there by force.]

Negation denoting absence or opposition was present in the PC as well. This is comparable to the presence of *no* in the AEC. In the PC, this was found in impersonal negation forms, and only in 3 clauses. Such negation as *nie znaleziono* and *nie ma* impersonally refer to a lack of evidence for the rape, implying that the victim was lying.

Table 12 Impersonal negation with nie in the PC to mark absence

	Frequency	Percentage	Percentage of PC
Nie znaleziono	2	66.7%	1.1%
nie ma	1	33.3%	.1%
TOTAL	3/714	100%	1.2% of PC

96) Na jej odzieży *nie znaleziono śladów nasienia. Nie miała też obrażeń* typowych przy gwałcie. zdania kluczowe.
(PC GWyb 2014, Row: 27)
[There was *no trace* of sperm found on her clothes. She also *did not have* any injury typical in rape. Those are key sentences.]

97) Skoro *nie ma dowodów* albo dowody są skąpe to po prostu nie należało orzekać aresztu.
(PC GWyb 2019, Row: 1)
[Since there is *no evidence*, or the evidence is barely there then there shouldn't have been an arrest made, simply put.]

In the PC, there were also negations where other social actors were concerned, and evaluations of society, including doctors or the police expressed through strategies of negation (again, expressing what could have or should have been done).

98) Mnie nawet lekarz *nie obejrzał.*
(PC GWyb 2014, Row: 29)
[A doctor *didn't even examine* me.]

99) A więc *nic się nie zmienia*, policja konsekwentnie od lat traktuje ofiary gwałtu zgodnie z podejściem JKM—karzą ofiarę za to, że dała się zgwałcić,
(PC GWyb 2014, Row: 23)
[Thus *nothing has changed* and the police are still treating victims of rape just like JKM would—they punish the victim for allowing them to rape her]

As stated above, the presence of negation in the discourse in such cases, in both the AEC and the PC, suggests an absence of something or presents the possibility of an alternative situation. In the literature, it is said that negation, as a discourse strategy, has two primary functions, namely rechanneling and blocking information (Hidalgo-Downing, 2000; Nahajec, 2009; Tabbert, 2016; Nahajec, 2021).This strategy places in opposition events and non-events, hence constructing "unrealized worlds" (Tabbert, 2016: 127). In the case of the above-exemplified comments, this pertains to any kind of evidence that might prove the person accused of rape to be guilty or that might prove that the victim is telling the truth. Generally, the use of negation was about the same in the AEC (8% on the basis of sentence count) and in the PC (8.6% on the basis of sentence count).

This strategy was important to note in the context of victim blaming, as it shows the way that negation is used in the evaluation of actors, indirectly targeting certain actors in the context of rape, in both American and Polish cultures through the highlighting of absence or what did not occur in order to emphasize a believed state of events, i.e., that the victim was not in fact raped.

Analysis of the activation and passivation of actors

In the following section, the question of role allocation has been considered, and within that vein the transitivity processes in which the actors were involved, described, and later, several of the categories as given by van Leeuwen (1996, 2008; cf. Chapter 1). The activation and passivation categories are where I begin, because they relate to the sections on structure, described and analyzed above.

The activation and passivation of the victim and offender as the main actors in a rape crime have been investigated. Verbs in which the victim or offender are activated (where a given actor is the active subject in a clause or sentence) and passivized (where the actor is either the beneficiary of an action or is subjected in a sentence) are taken into consideration for this representation of inclusion in the vein of *the representation of social actors* (van Leeuwen 1996, 2008; cf. Chapter 1 and Chapter 7 of this work) within the framework of CDA (Fairclough &Wodak, 1997).[78]

Activation and passivation of the victim

The frequencies at which the victim undergoes activation and passivation in the AEC, where various verb processes are concerned were counted at activation occurring a total of 267 times (58.5% of the transitivity processes in the AEC and 33.2% of the corpus on the basis of sentence count) and passivation at 175 times (41.5% of the AEC making up 21.7% of the entire AEC on the basis of sentence count). The processes analyzed (transitivity processes and processes of passivation) relate to the actions or states of the victim, as well as the actions and states related to the victims' general involvement in the sex crime(s). This means that those actions which are seen as relevant to the act of blame attribution are analyzed with relation to their judgment value, on the basis of relation to the topic of discussion, namely that of rape.

Figure 7 Activation and passivation of the victim in the AEC

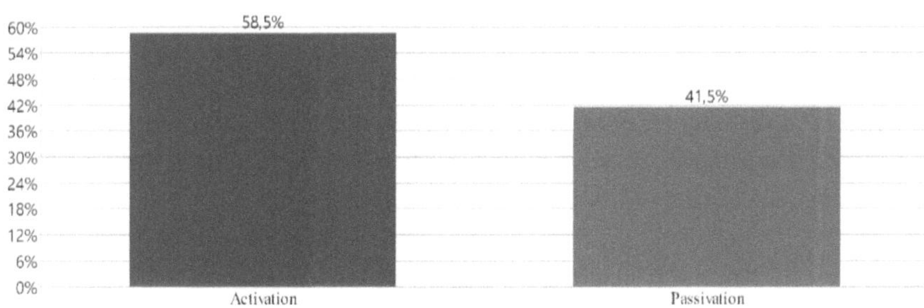

In the PC, the victim underwent activation a total of 220 times (66.1% of clauses analyzed for the victim in the PC, making up 30.8% of the PC based on sentence count) and passivation, 113 times (33.9% of clauses for the victim in the PC, 15.8% of the PC based on sentence count).

78 As far as the verbal processes that are described, and in which the actors are activated, Halliday's (1985) Systemic Functional Linguistics model has also been applied.

Figure 8 Activation and passivation of the victim in the PC

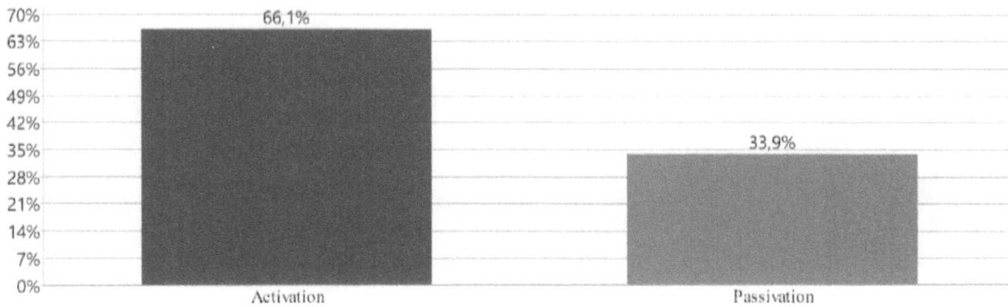

It is of significance that the victim is activated more often than she is passivized in both corpora, since the victim's activation signalizes that she took part in activities that led to, surrounded, or happened during the rape. By focusing on the actions in which the victim took an active part, her role in the rape is emphasized either alongside that of the offender or given more focus than the offender.

Activation of the victim

For this aspect of the analysis, transitivity processes were divided in accordance with Halliday's (1985) SFL typology for the activation of actors (cf. Chapter 1). In the AEC, the victim was represented in material processes (131 times—49.1% of the transitivity processes in the category of activation for the victim in the AEC, making up 16.2% of the AEC on the basis of sentence count), verbal processes (58 times—21.7% of activation processes for the victim in the AEC and 7.2% of the AEC), relational processes (51 times—9.1% and 6.3% of the AEC), mental processes (25 times—9.4%, constituting 3.1% of the AEC) and behavioral processes (2 times—0.7% of the activation processes for the victim in the AEC and .2% of the entire AEC on the basis of sentence count).

> 100) He was married and she *knew* (MENTAL) it. 2) He invites her to his room for a second visit and she *goes* (MATERIAL). Did she *think* (MENTAL) they were going to play Scrabble? 3) She says she *hated* (MENTAL) "it" but *tells* (VERBAL) him she *liked* (MENTAL) it.
> (AEC VTY 2019, Row: 12)

The breakdown of the activation processes for the victim in the AEC of digital comments has been provided below.

Figure 9 Activation of the victim in the AEC

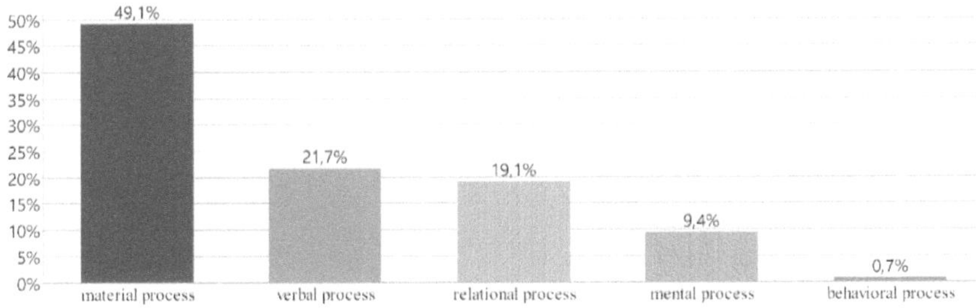

The majority of the verbs denoting material processes in which the victim was activated were found at one count each, with the highest number belonging to the verbs *drink* (16 times, making up .07% of the AEC on the basis of word count), *get drunk* (8 times, .03% of the AEC) and *put oneself in a situation* (4 times, .01% of the AEC).

101) If at 14, this girl was *sneaking out* (MATERIAL) of the house, *sending* (MATERIAL) explicit texts, and *binge drinking* (MATERIAL), her parents are failing her.
(AEC ABC 2014, Row: 46)

102) The guys can do that safely, but if girls *party* (MATERIAL), aren't they just *begging* (MATERIAL) to be raped?
(AEC ABC 2015, Row: 13)

103) Although *she put herself* (MATERIAL) in a precarious situation, and *they were both drinking* (MATERIAL), she made (MATERIAL) a bad choice.
(AEC NBC 2019, Row: 19)

The reference to the material processes through the activation of the victim in the AEC demonstrates the association of the actor with any act leading up to the rape, which inherently—via the discourse—makes room for victim blaming. Because the victim is associated with what she did in the context of the rape, her role in the rape is highlighted. Most of the material process verbs were related to the intoxication of the victim or the circumstances surrounding the rape, including verbs like *drink* or *get drunk*, and additionally, verbs associated with the process of intoxication such as *make a bad choice* and *party* were accounted for in the case of the victim. Other verbs which describe processes leading up to the rape and were directly linked to the victim were included, such as *send emails*, *maintain* and *contact* were found. Additionally, verbs through which the victim was activated included *have sex* and *hook up*.

As for the verbal processes (7.2% of the AEC based on sentence count) in which the victim is activated in the AEC, all are rather neutral, contrary to the hypothesis that reporting verbs used in evaluative comments show evaluative verbal processes as well. Verbs such as *say* and *tell* were predominant in the description of the victims' testimonies as discussed by Internet users. In the AEC, the victim was activated in a total of 58 verbal processes.

It is important to note that the verbal processes shown in the chapter bear much to say about the evaluation of actors, although the list is not as long as that belonging to the material processes. The verbal processes illustrate how the victim's testimony is represented in discourse, reflecting the degree of believability that she is granted.

Figure 10 Verbal processes for the victim in the AEC

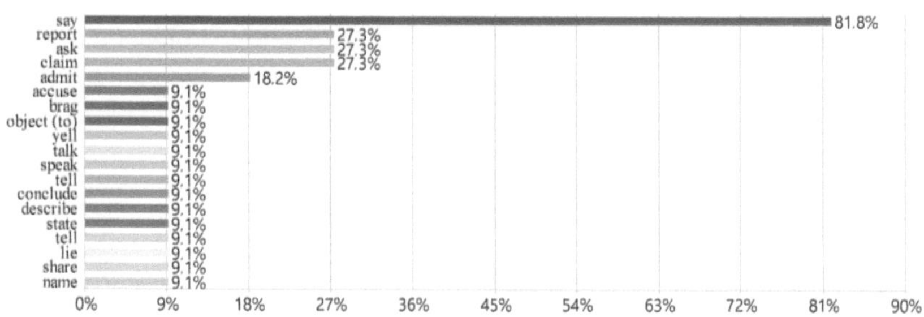

The graph above shows the verbal processes for the victim in the AEC. The most prevalent was *say* (with 23 instances in the AEC, making up 34.3% of the verbal processes for the victim and .1% of the entire AEC based on word count). The verb *claim* was also representative of a verbal process and is one which implies that the victim might be lying, and was found 8 times in the AEC (13.1% of all verbal processes for the victim in the AEC and .03% of the entire AEC). The verb *ask* was used in victim clauses 7 times (11.5% of verbal processes for the victim and .02% of the AEC), the verb *report* was found a total of 6 times (.02%), the verb *tell* 5 times and *admit* 4 times (.01% of the whole AEC).The verbs *speak, accuse, brag, describe, object to, yell, state, lie, yell, share, name* and *talk* were only found with 1 iteration each in the AEC, making up for 1.6% of the verbal processes for the victim in the AEC each and .004% of the entire AEC each). As can be seen in the examples below, verbs for verbal processes were either overtly negative or neutral, however given both the linguistic and social context, the use of such verbs also blame the victim (cf. examples 104 and 105).

104) Even if the target of the assault was *"asking for it"* (VERBAL) or "behaving unwisely" or you can find some other rationalization for the act, the fact remains: committing one rape makes you a rapist.
(AEC NYT 2017, Row: 14)

105) She's comfortable *telling* (VERBAL) the world intimate details about her sex life with a man whom she *says* (VERBAL) raped her. Ick.
(AEC VTY 2019, Row: 12)

Only 6 of the verbal processes for the victim (10.3% of all verbal processes for the victim in the AEC) were found in victim-supporting comments, whereas the remaining 52 verbal processes for the victim were found in victim-blaming comments (89.7% of the verbal processes for the victim in the AEC). This shows that the verbal processes for the victim in the AEC demonstrated a tendency to negatively evaluate the victim and either what she said or the testimony that she gave about having been raped.

Relational processes for the victim in the AEC constituted ones that made assumptions about the victim's status or described victims in general. The relational verbs for the victim in the AEC were found in sentences used to describe her status or identity (cf. examples 106 and 107).

106) IF she *is* (RELATIONAL) a victim, how do you know the accused were not drunk also?
(AEC ABC 2015a , Row: 10)

107) They are predators who target freshmen (note that 63% of victims *are* (RELATIONAL) freshmen).
(AEC NYT 2014, Row: 10)

Mental processes for the victim in the AEC included verbs such as *like*, *remember*, and *regret*. The mental processes present in instances of the activation of the victim drew on stereotypes of rape victims, including that women like to be raped (example 108), that they lie about having been raped (cf. examples 109 and 110—with the verb *remember* and *regret*).

108) She says she hated "it" but tells him she *liked* (MENTAL) it.
(AEC VTY 2019, Row: 12)

109) If she didn't *remember* (MENTAL) anything how did it turn into her worst day?
(AEC ABC 2015a, Row: 23)

110) In a college environment, a woman can get drunk, have sex then *regret* (MENTAL) it and call it rape. It's fairy comment for women to drink and have *regret* (MENTAL) sex then it is for that same woman to be raped
(AEC NYT 2014, Row: 1)

There were only two instances of behavioral processes for the victim in the AEC, both clauses with the verb *laugh* (0.01% of the corpus). The behavioral processes, however few, also demonstrate how the same verb can be used within the context of victim blaming (example 111) and victim-supporting (example 112) sentences.

> 111) The fact that she is *laughing* (BEHAVIORAL) about this in her texts should have stopped any decent DA from filing charges.
> (AEC ABC 2015b, Row: 49)

> 112) So if we follow that delusional logic anyone who attends a party, and is enjoying themselves *laughing* (BEHAVIORAL) or talking with friends having a drink is basically saying, in your opinion, "I want to have sex with anyone who wants to take advantage of me".
> (AEC PAW 2016, Row: 5)

It is important to bear in mind that what the activation of the victim does is foreground her within the context of the sexual assault. Constructions express the role of the victim as the doer of an action, thus the actor or behaver places the focus on her role in the circumstances surrounding or during the rape.

In the PC, the victim was found to be represented in a total of 267 transitivity processes presenting activation processes (thus constituting 37.3% of the PC on the basis of sentence count). Most of these processes were material processes, with a total of 141 verbs (52.8% of the activation processes in the PC, making up19.7% of the PC), 51 verbs representing mental processes (19.1%, making up 7.1% of the PC), 48 verbs representing relational processes (18%, 6.7% of the PC), 27 verbs representing verbal processes (10.1%, 3.7% of the PC) and no verbs representing behavioral processes in which the victim was involved (0%).

Figure 11 Activation of the victim in the PC

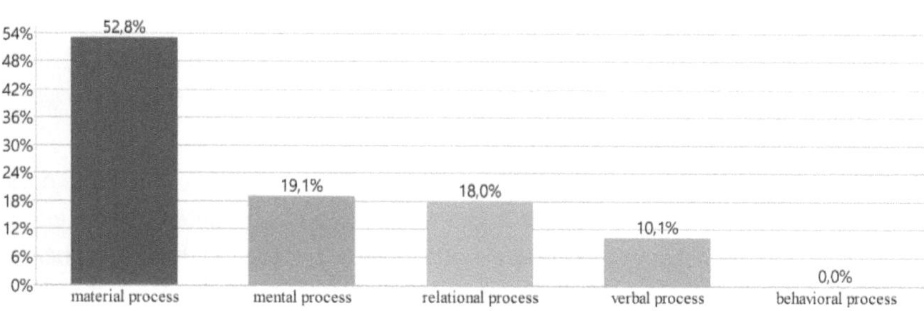

In the PC, most of the material processes for the victim have to do with the events that led up to the rape or enact some sort of active involvement in the rape. The material processes include verbs such as *wpuszczać* ('let in') (example 113), *chodzić* ('to walk' or 'to go'), *iść* ('to go'), *pić* ('to drink') (example 114), *przyczynić się do* ('cause') (example 115), *romansować* ('to have an affair'), among other verbs involved in the events that have led up to the rape or contributed to the circumstances in which the rape occurred. Comparably to the AEC, the majority of the material process verbs found to represent the actions of the victim occurred one time each.

113) nie bronię ich, ale ta kobieta *wpuszczając* (MATERIAL) ich do pokoju, nie była święta. Dwóch obcych facetów na bani, mogła pomysleć, ze to się może dla niej źle skonczyć.
(PC PUD 2015, Row: 11)
[I'm not defending them, but by *letting them into* her room, that woman was no saint. Two male strangers who were completely hammered, she could have guessed it would end badly.]

114) Kobieta *pije* (MATERIAL) alkohol z przed chwilą poznanymi mężczyznami, a potem idzie z nimi do mieszkania jednego z nich.
(PC GWsp 2019, Row: 15)
[A woman *drinks* (MATERIAL) alcohol with men she had only met moments ago and then goes with them to one of their apartments.]

115) Podejrzana sprawa być może sama *się przyczyniła* (MATERIAL) do gwałtu na swojej osobie chociażby poczęstunkiem alkoholu, zbyt dużym dekoldem, zbyt dużym biustem niektóre panie *wypychają* staniki nawet watą, dobrym pożywieniem i wtedy jeszcze bardziej *wzmagają się* podniecenia seksualne
(PC NM 2018, Row: 1)
[A suspicious case. Maybe she *caused* (MATERIAL) the rape on her person herself by drinking alcohol, showing too much cleavage, having too big of breasts. Some ladies even *stuff their bras* (MATERIAL) with cotton balls or hearty food and by that they *intensify* (MATERIAL) sexual arousal.]

116) nie twierdzę że nie, ale jest tez spory procent kobiet które tylko poprzez płacz i ściemę *rujnują komuś życie*
(PC NM 2018, Row: 10)
[I'm not saying it didn't happen, but there is also a large percentage of women who *ruin someone's life* just by crying and lying]

Here it becomes clear that victim blaming may be insinuated through the expression of transitivity processes, as seen in examples 115 and 116. Reference to actions that are associated with common rape myths both reproduce such cultural beliefs (i.e., that the victim is somehow at fault for what happened to her) and highlight her actions or place them on an equal level with those of the offender.

Mental processes for the victim included verbs like *myśleć* ('to think') (example 117), *chcieć* ('to want') (example 118), and *bać się* ('to be afraid') (example 119). There were more verbs which represented mental processes in the PC.

117) O czym ta kobieta *myślała* (MENTAL) idą na imprezę z trzema obcymi typkami ?......ja to bym uciekła najdalej
(PC PUD 2017a, Row: 35)
[what was that woman *thinking* (MENTAL), going to a party with three strangers [men]? ...I would have run away as far as I could]

118) *Chciała* (MENTAL) się zabawić to się zabawiła. Nikt jej tam siłą nie ciągnął.
(PC PUD 2017a, Row: 32)
[She *wanted* to mess around, so she did. Nobody dragged her there.]

119) czemu nie pokaże twarzy? *boi się* (MENTAL), że jeszcze ktoś znajdzie jakieś jej ogłoszenie matrymonialne w internecie?
(PC PUD 2015, Row: 38)
[Why doesn't she show her face? *Is* she *scared* (MENTAL) that someone else will find one of her marriage offers online?]

In the PC, there were a total of 36 verbal processes involved in the representation of the victim (.4% of the PC). There were more instances of verbal processes for the victim in the AEC (7.2% of the AEC) than in the PC, which demonstrates American culture's greater tendency to pay heed to the victim's account of the rape. This provides a more multi-dimensional approach to the story, given the light shone on the testimony of the victim, in American culture. The result of such discursive tendencies might be to more quickly make assumptions about the fault of the victim in Polish culture than in American culture (Alicke, 2000; Styśko, 2006, 2007).

Such verbal processes, through which the victim was activated, showed a tendency to be biased, namely in the verbal types she was involved in or associated with in the PC. The verbs that represented the verbal processes for the victim were *zgłosić* ('report') (11 times, making up .1% of the PC on the basis of word count), and the word *mówić* ('say') was found a total of 5 times for the victim in the PC (.04% of the PC). The following verbs were found at 2 counts each (making up .02% of the PC on the basis of word count): *powiedzieć* ('say'), *zgadzaćsię* ('agree'), *twierdzić* ('claim'), *zawiadomić* ('report'), as well as *krzyczeć* ('shout', 'scream', 'cry out'), *wspominać* ('mention') and *kłamać* ('lie). Verbs that represented verbal processes for the victim which took place only 1 time in the PC (making up .001% of the PC on the basis of word count) were the following: *drzeć się* ('shout'), *ściemniać* and *kłamać* ('lie'), *narzekać* ('complain'), *wspominać* ('recount'), *żegnać* ('bid farewell'), *podzielić się* ('share'), *zabierać głos* ('take the floor'), *blefować* ('bluff'), and *powiadomić* ('inform').

Only 1 verb representing a verbal process of the victim was found in a victim-supporting comment (.001% of the PC on the basis of word count in the entire corpus). The remaining 35 were found in victim-blaming sentences (.3% PC on the basis of word count).

Figure 12 Verbal processes for the victim in the PC

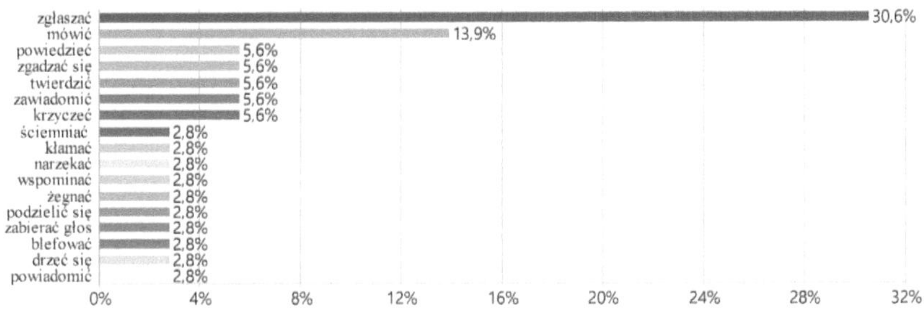

120) Na posterunek wpada kobieta i *krzyczy* (VERBAL) ze została zgwałcona w parku. Policjant pyta: Ile pani ma lat? 40... no..w takim wieku to już powinna pani sama dawać.... (PC GWyb 2014, Row: 38)
[A woman bursts into the station and *cries* (VERBAL) that she was raped in the park. The police officer asks: How old are you? 40… well… at your age you should be putting out yourself…]

121) Nie wiem jaka jest prawda ale jeśli jest tak jak *mówi* (VERBAL) ofiara gwałtu to wcale się nie dziwię że większość kobiet nie zgłasza tego krótko mówiąc że strachu i wstydu.
(PC MG 2019, Row: 1)
[I don't know what the truth is, but if it is the way the victim *says* (VERBAL) it is then I am not surprised that most women don't report it simply out of fear and embarrassment]

Just as in the AEC, processes in the PC related to the victim as having an identity, having an attribute or being similar to something else were included within the category of relational processes. These processes were found in the case of the victim in the PC a total of 50 times (0.2% of the corpus). The relational processes were found in victim-blaming comments, making less neutral usage of the relational processes for the victim than in the AEC.

122) Moze laska przeraziła sie ze wszystko wyjdzie na jaw ze *była* (RELATIONAL) chętna ze nazwą ja „k***ą" to podała kolesi o gwałt a to był moze 10dniowy melanż!!!!????
(PC PUD 2017a, Row: 45)

[Maybe the chick got scared that everything would come out about her *being* (RELATIONAL) willing, that they would call her a slut, so she reported them for rape, but maybe it was a 10-day party!!!!????]

123) W pewnym sensie sama wydała na siebie wyrok. Kobiety *bądźcie* (RELATIONAL) bardziej ostrożne, faceci maja siłe niestety i nie *bądźcie* (RELATIONAL) głupimi kozami, co to daja się zwieść
(PC PUD 2015, Row: 11)
[She sentenced herself in a way. Women, *be* (RELATIONAL) more careful, unfortunately men are strong and don't *be* (RELATIONAL) dumb goats who get duped]

The distribution of the verbs through which the victim undergoes activation, in both the AEC and the PC, shows that the transitivity processes through which she is (in a majority) described present the victim as doing something which led up to her being raped or doing something to cause the rape. This is especially true of the material processes in both the cases of the AEC and the PC. What is interesting about this particular aspect is that material processes were evaluative in their semantic, paradigmatic quality, meaning that the verbs used to describe what the victim was doing at the time of or around the time of the crime portrayed her as playing a role in the fact that she was raped.

Henley et al. (1995: 60) discovered that "news media often report violence against women […] in passive-verb format," which means that women are placed in the subject position of clauses regarding the crimes that are done to them. Hence, they are often the goal of a crime. Such processes contributing to the activation of the victim in the AEC play a role in putting the victim at the foreground of the crime, or highlighting her role. This lack of highlighting the agency of the actor committing the crime upon the victim has a significant impact on the "perceptions of violence and its effects," hiding agency of the criminal in the process (*ibid.*: 65). It is important to note that it is mostly the material processes which describe the victim as actively taking part in actions that lead up to the rape in particular. The mental processes in which the victim is involved, including verbs like *regret* and *like* in the AEC and *chcieć* ('want') or *lubić* ('like') construct the victim as not being truthful in her testimony or as having wanted to be raped in the first place. The mental processes present in digital comments in clauses about the victim additionally reveal attitudes which people have of rape victims overall, including that they have a hidden desire to be raped or that they fear social ostracism for their sexual behavior and thus claim to have been raped (cf. Chapter 7 for more on rape myths).

Activation of the victim through the possessivation of processes

Although also quite rare in the presented corpus, van Leeuwen's (1996) category of activation also includes the process through which the possessivation of process nouns occurs. This is a particularly insidious use of language, because it places at the forefront of the discourse the actor who is logically at the receiving end of an action. This type of activation occurred 24 times in the American English corpus (2.9% of the sentences in the AEC).

In the case of the victim, this type of activation takes place in the context of the rape and the assault, both erasing the offender, and placing the victim in the pre-modifying position (in the form of a possessive pronoun) (van Leeuwen 2008: 43–4).

Here it can be seen used even in reference to the first person.

124) But this shouldn't be necessary—for example, if any of the people in the house where I was hurt had intervened when I was starting to pass out from the drugs, before I was moved into the bedroom of the offender while unconscious, I think *my assault* could have been avoided.
(AEC NYT 2014, Row: 4)

125) Whereas she was, by all accounts, unconscious. I'm not sure why people struggle with what led up to this incident—*her dress, her purported flirting* (sorry, but where exactly is that on record as happening anyway?)
(AEC PAW 2016, Row:7)

126) She definitely had rough sex and was incapacitated. You can argue that *her intoxication* occurred after sex, so the boy is not guilty of rape.
(AEC ABC 2014, Row: 28)

The activation of the victim through passivation is particularly interesting because it syntactically and semantically associates the actor with an action that has been implied as in some way contributing to the crime. Here, the noun phrase *my assault* places the actor in a possessivation process as somehow owning something and therefore owing to the act of the assault brought upon her. In the second example, *her dress* (here understood as implicating "the way she dressed") and *her purported flirting* are both acts that stereotypically seat the victim into a position of blame. The victim underwent activation through possessivation of processes only 8 times in the PC (1.1% of the sentences in the PC). The possessivation of the victim pertained to processes that included consenting to sexual intercourse, the victim's behavior, and her testimony. An example of possessivation in the PC has been provided.

127) facet idzie z dziewczyna do lozka. za *jej zgoda*, zaczynaja się bzykac.
(PC, GWyb 2019, Row: 18)
[a guy goes to bed with a girl, with *her consent*, they start to have sex]

128) Z *zeznań pani* nie wynika, że została zgwałcona. Sama mówi, że coś mu nie wyszło. Chyba, że gwałt, to stan umysłu...
(PC GWyb 2014, Row: 2)
[From *her testimony* we cannot conclude that she was raped. She herself says that he wasn't able to. Unless rape is a state of mine…]

129) Zamiast tłumaczyć *każde zachowanie ofiary* winą sprawcy, należałoby napisać artykuł, jakie sytuacje i zachowania kobiet są odbierane przez mężczyzn jako mocno prowokujące.
(PC GWsp 2019, Row: 15)
[Instead of explaining away *each of the victim's behaviors* by pointing to the fault of the offender, it would be better to write an article about what types of women's behaviors are seen as provocative by men.]

In a similar way to the AEC, the activation of the victim through possessivation processes places her at the forefront of the actions strictly related to being raped in the PC. This places the focus on the role of the victim, rather than on the direct agency of the offender. The tendency to highlight the role of the victim in processes related to the rape is more prevalent in the AEC, most likely relating to the fact that modification of nouns by the possessive pronoun is more natural for English than Polish. This aspect, however, does create a chasm in the representations of victims in American discourse and Polish discourse. What can be observed is that in activating an actor through the possessivation of processes, the need to focus on the victim is highlighted, hence creating a cognitive bias which associates the act of the rape more so with the role of the victim than that of the offender.

The tendency to modify the process noun with the personal pronoun representing the actor who was on the receiving end of the act pertains to such processes that are both brought into existence by that actor (*her testimony*, *her flirting*) and processes that did not come into existence as a result of actions carried out by the victim (*my rape*, *her assault*). The fact that this occurred more often in the AEC demonstrates a higher tendency for this type of implicated victim blaming in American discourse.

Passivation of the victim

In addition to activation, passivation processes also took place in both the AEC and the PC. Passivation of the victim was observed in the AEC a total of 127 times (17.7% of the entire corpus on the basis of the sentence count), including 70 instances of beneficialization (55.1% of the passivation types for the victim in the AEC, making up 8.7% of the corpus), in which the victim was the receiver of an action and 57 instances of subjection times (43.4% of the passivation types for the victim in the AEC, making up 7.1% of the corpus on the basis of sentence count).

The victim was passivized through possessivation processes only 1 time in the AEC (0.8% of passivation processes and .1% of the AEC on the basis of sentence count). The passivation of the victim is important to note in the context of rape, because it demonstrates whether or not (or how often) the victim of the crime is placed in the structural foreground within the textual context she is mentioned (Billig, 2008). This in turn draws attention to her role.

Figure 13 Passivation of the victim in the AEC

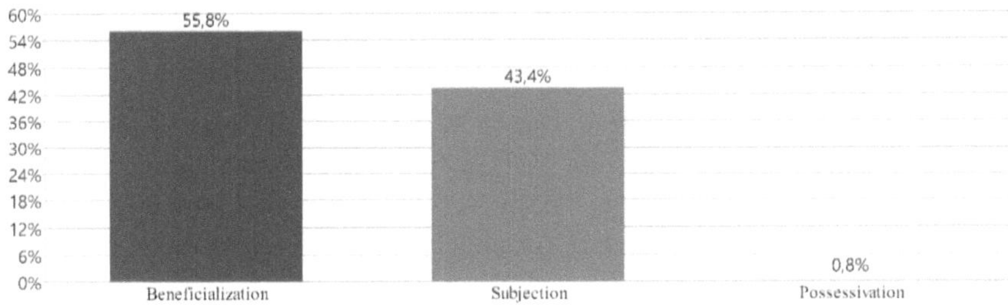

Through the process of beneficialization, the victim was presented in clauses where she was on the receiving end of rape or described in the process of providing a testimony of what occurred. Examples of the beneficialization of the victim can be found in the following examples, in bold, where the victim is the goal or the patient.

130) You can be raped by anyone no matter your relationship. A husband *can rape a wife.* (AEC ABC 2020, Row: 6)

131) Romney dismissed the 47% like these men *dismiss the rape victim* -- as obstacles to their successful futures.
(AEC NYT 2016, Row: 20)

Some examples of the subjection of the victim in the AEC are the following. This type of passivation brings the victim to the foreground, again discursively focusing attention on her and her role in the rape:

132) Given that *20% of college women are raped*, that must mean that these 3% are committing multiple rapes.
(AEC NYT 2017, Row: 10)

133) *She was found* behind a dumpster! unconscious, *being attacked* by this young man, by witnesses who held him for police.
(AEC NYT 2016, Row: 45)

134) Yes, I think *a 14 year old girl was taken advantage of* by an older teen. Just because it wasn't proven doesn't mean it didn't happen.
(AEC ABC 2014, Row: 42)

Other types of subjection completely erased any other actors, focusing solely on the role of the victim in the crime or in her testimony. Example 137 presents the only instance of the passivation of the victim through possessivation in the AEC.

135) *girls have been known* to cry rape
(AEC NYT 2014, Row: 16)

136) Still *she was encouraged* not to "ruin the young man's life."
(AEC NYT 2014, Row: 10)

137) If the accused and *his WITNESS* are correct, the sex occurred first, then she got drunk. She wanted to trade sex for alcohol. He wanted sex. They had sex; she got drunk. How are they "animals" with connections?
(AEC ABC 2014, Row: 38)[79]

The passivation of the victim either places her at the receiving end of an act (usually rape) or actions leading up to the rape, mostly in sentences in which the offender was the active actor in a material process in the AEC.

Passivation of the victim also took place in the PC of digital comments, a total of 101 times (14.1% of the PC on the basis of the sentence count). The victim underwent beneficialization processes 78 times (77.8%, making up 10.9% of the PC on the basis of the sentence count), subjection 22 times (21.2%, making up 3% of the PC) and possessivation 1 time (1.0%, making up .1% of the PC).

Figure 14 Passivation of the victim in the PC

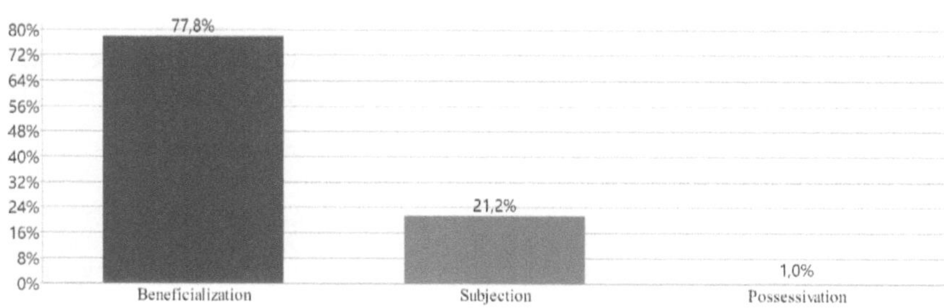

79 Although this was infrequent, it is important to highlight that such passivation (through possessivation) creates a cognitive liaison between the victim and the offender.

The passivation of the victim in the PC through the process of beneficialization has been shown in the examples below. The use of such passivation of the actor in the PC pertained to cases in which the victim's role as the patient is highlighted. This mostly took place in sentences where the victim is highlighted as the person who is on the receiving end of an attack or the recipient of sympathy. As can be seen in the examples, instances of sentences with beneficialization do not imply victim blaming, but rather support for the victim through highlighting her role as a victim.

138) Widzę dużo komentarzy w stylu „sama się o to prosiła" może i nie zachowała się rozsądnie ale te bydlaki nie miały prawa *jej krzywdzić*.
(PC PUD 2017a, Row: 36)
[I am seeing a lot of comments like "she asked for it". Maybe she didn't act the most wisely, but those animals had no right *to hurt her*.]

139) bardzo *Ci* współczuję, trzymaj się
(PC PUD 2015, Row: 31)
[I feel so sorry *for you*, hang in there]

140) Nikt tak nie potrafi *dowalić zgwałconej kobiecie* jak inna kobieta
(PC GWyb 2020, Row: 10)
[No one can *bring a raped woman down* like another woman]

141) A może *jej grozili* i nie poszla dobrowolnie?
(PC PUD 2017a, Row: 42)
[Maybe they *threatened her* and she didn't go willingly?]

Passivation of the victim through subjection occurred in the PC, as in the following examples, where doubt in the victim's testimony or victim blaming related to her behavior. This is expressed (as shown below in examples 140 and 141). Other examples of passivation were related to other processes, such as those where the act of rape was concerned, erasing the perpetrator and highlighting the victim as an actor, drawing attention to her through negative evaluation (example 142).

142) Ja rozumiem, że tą kobietę spotkała tragedia, ale *ona nie została zgwałcona*.
(PC GWyb 2014, Row: 36)
[I understand that what happened to her was tragic, but *she was not raped.*]

143) *kolejna zgwałcona*, wszystkie gwałcą, *zgwałcona, zgwałcona, zgwałcona*. teraz gwałt jest na topie.
(PC PUD 2015, Row: 50)
[*another raped*, they rape all the women, *raped, raped, raped*. Now rape is on top.]

144) dlaczego ta pani zaraz nie poszła na policję dlaczego tak długo rozmawiali [od rana do zakończenia lekcji przez syna], może *ta kobieta powinna zostać przebadana* na wykrywaczu kłamstw a może coś chciała ukryć???

(PC PUD MG 2019, Row: 15)
[Why did that woman not go to the police immediately, why did they talk for so long? (from morning until the end of her son's lessons), perhaps *that woman should be tested* using a lie detector or maybe she wanted to hide something???]

Passivation through possessivation is shown in the following example. This process only took place once in the PC (.1% of the PC), and so it was rather insignificant in the construction of the victim in the PC.

145) oby teraz panów w p*****u spotkało to samo co *ich ofiarę*
(PC PUD 2017a, Row: 28)
[let's hope that these men meet the same fate as *their victim* in jail]

What the examples from the PC demonstrate is that the victim underwent a variety of passivation processes, however the beneficialization of the actor was most prevalent. It is worth reiterating that where the beneficialization of the victim was concerned, the tendency was for the verbs to demonstrate supportive stances to the actor.

The AEC and the PC demonstrated similar tendencies where the passivation of the victim was concerned. Overall, what passivation of the victim does to the presentation of the actor is that it puts her in the position of the foregrounded actor in the context of the crime, highlighting her role in the rape. The American English corpus of digital comments has demonstrated that the victim is passivized in three main ways, and the same three types of passivation processes for the victim were also found in the PC (beneficialization, subjection, and possessivation). The subjection of the victim varied from the frequency of subjection undergone by the offender. The placement of the victim at the foreground of the discourse here too creates a cognitive link between her and the act of rape, which constructs her as having an active part in the crime, and also reflects the social attitudes that see her as having been at least partially at fault. If the rapist appears at the end of the sentence, he is highlighted only after the victim has been. The phenomenon also contributes to the backgrounding of the offender, which renders him less visible and thus less important in such discourse.

Activation and passivation of the offender

Activation and passivation of the offender also occurred in the AEC and the PC, comparable to the representations of the victim in both of the corpora. In the present analysis, when confronted with the shorter texts that are digital comments, strategies of activation and passivation take on a more significant role in expressing meaning and evaluation of actors.

There was a significant difference in the number of clauses in which the offender was activated and passivized. The offender was activated a total of 145 times (64.5% of the transitivity processes for the offender in the AEC; making up 18.03% of the corpus, on the basis of the sentence count) in the AEC, and passivized a total of 82 times (35.5% of the transitivity processes for the offender in the AEC; making up 10.1% of the corpus on the basis of sentence count). The following sections provide a more in depth look into the distributions of activation and passivation processes in the AEC, respectively, naming examples of these processes that were found to be most representative in the corpus.

Figure 15 Activation and passivation of the offender AEC

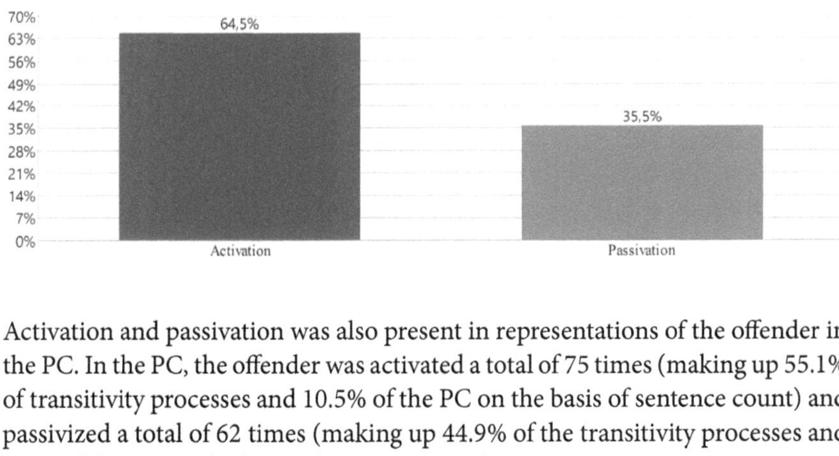

Activation and passivation was also present in representations of the offender in the PC. In the PC, the offender was activated a total of 75 times (making up 55.1% of transitivity processes and 10.5% of the PC on the basis of sentence count) and passivized a total of 62 times (making up 44.9% of the transitivity processes and 8.6% of the PC on the basis of sentence count).

Figure 16 Activation and passivation of the offender PC

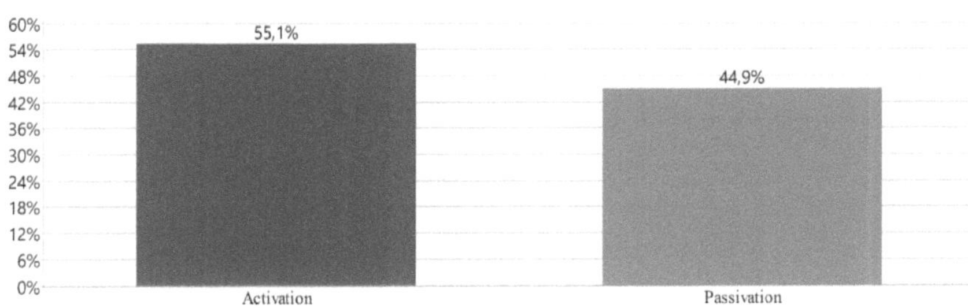

The following section breaks down the activation and passivation of the offender in both the AEC and the PC, beginning with the activation of the offender. As can be seen in the graph above, the offender is activated more often than he is passivated, highlighting his active role and the rape and contributing to offender-blaming. This grammatical strategyalso brings the actor to the foreground.

Activation of the offender

The question of the activation of the offender regards the transitivity processes (again, a total of 145 in the AEC, making up 18.03% of the AEC on the basis of sentence count) in which he or they were involved, whether they were material processes (103 times in the AEC—70.8% of activation types for the offender in the AEC; 12.8% of the AEC on the basis of sentence count), relational processes (31 times in the AEC—21.5%; 3.8% of the corpus), mental processes (7 times in the AEC—4.9% of activation types for the offender; .9% of the corpus), or verbal processes (4 times in the AEC—2.8% of the activation processes for the offender; making up .4% of the AEC). No behavioral processes were accounted for where the offender was concerned (0% for the AEC).

The graph below presents a side-by-side numerical comparison of the frequencies of transitivity processes in which the offender was actively presented in the AEC.

Figure 17 Frequencies of activation of the offender in the AEC

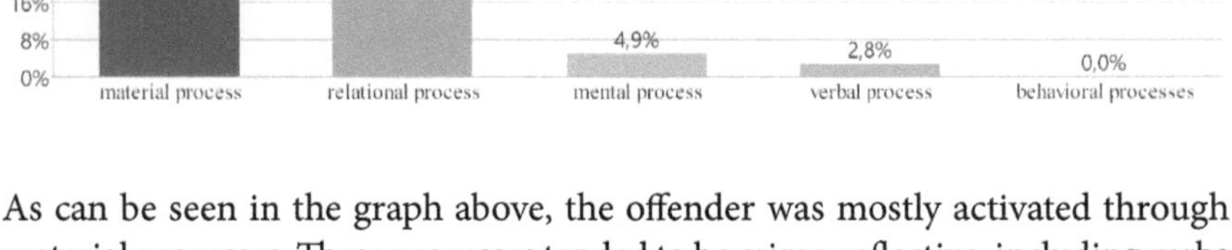

As can be seen in the graph above, the offender was mostly activated through material processes. These processes tended to be crime-reflective, including verbs such as *rape, take advantage of, commit, choose, attack*, or those verbs related in other ways to their taking part in a crime.

> 146) The article notes that 3 percent of men account for 90 to 95% of rapes.Given that 20% of college women are raped, that must mean that these 3% *are committing* (MATERIAL) multiple rapes.
> (AEC NYT 2014, Row: 10)

147) "This would not have happened" if the rapist had not *chosen* (MATERIAL) to forcibly *attack* (MATERIAL) someone and *commit* (MATERIAL) an assault on their person.
(AEC NYT 2017, Row: 9)

Relational processes for the offender included descriptions of the rapist, including appraisement or evaluation of his personality.

148)He *was* married and she knew it.
(AEC VTY 2019, Row: 12)

149) Yes, actually, it is blaming the victim. Why aren't you asking why Turner *was* (RELATIONAL) vicious enough to rape? Why aren't you blaming him for *being* (RELATIONAL) a sociopath who's trying to use drinking as an excuse for rape?
(AEC NYT 2016, Row: 18)

Mental processes for the offender in the AEC included those for processes of his cognition and feelings.

150) If she had not been drunk, he would have raped someone else. He *felt* (MENTAL) that it was acceptable to put his hands on her without consent, and therein lies the problem.
(AEC MN 2016, Row: 14)

151) Agreed. Too many times, people get off on the excuse that they were too drunk to *understand* (MENTAL) what they were doing. That is a load of crap, especially these drunk driving cases where drivers who kill, walk away from any jail time, because of the "too drunk to understand what they were doing" excuse.
(AEC NYT 2016, Row: 9)

There were five verb types that presented the verbal processes for the offender in the AEC, namely *claim* (8 times, making up 1% of the AEC on the basis of sentence count), and the remainder of the verbal processes for the offender taking place 1 time each (.1% of the AEC on the basis of sentence count), including *reply*, *say*, *lie*, *confess* and *refuse*. All of the instances of the verbal processes for the offender in the AEC were found in offender-blaming sentences.

Figure 18. Verbal processes for the offender in the AEC

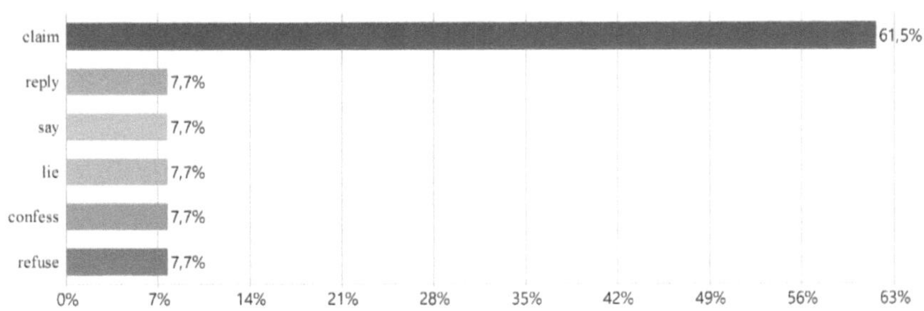

152) He still refuses to *confess* (VERBAL) and will not even face prison time.
(AEC MN, 2016, Row: 14)

153) As a woman, I just don't understand it. These young men should be embarrassed. They are basically *saying* (VERBAL) "Okay, no woman would do anything with me willingly, I have to force them or they have to be drunk or unconscious. No woman who was thinking clearly would want me".
(AEC NYT 2014, Row: 17)

What the analysis of the AEC and the representations through transitivity processes for the offender shows is that the majority of the processes in which he or they are involved highlight the criminal actions of the offender. What this means for the analysis is that in the case of the activation of the offender through various transitivity processes, his role in the crime is highlighted in the CMC discourse of Internet users. It is important to note, however, that recognizing the culpability of the offender or accused in a rape does not take away from victim blaming, which is the main question.

The offender also underwent activation with relation to various transitivity processes in the PC, however significantly less often than in the AEC (81 times, 12.1% of the PC on the basis of sentence count). As can be seen in the graph below, the offender is mostly involved in material processes in the PC, with a total of 57 counts (constituting 71.1% of the material processes in which the offender was involved in the PC), 17 instances of relational processes (20.5% of transitivity processes for the offender and 2.3% of the PC) where the offender is concerned, only 4 active mental (4.8% of transitivity processes for the offender, making up .5% of the PC) and 3 verbal processes relating to the offender (3.6% of transitivity processes for the offender, making up .4% of the PC), with no behavioral processes present (0%).

Figure 19 Frequencies of activation of the offender in the PC

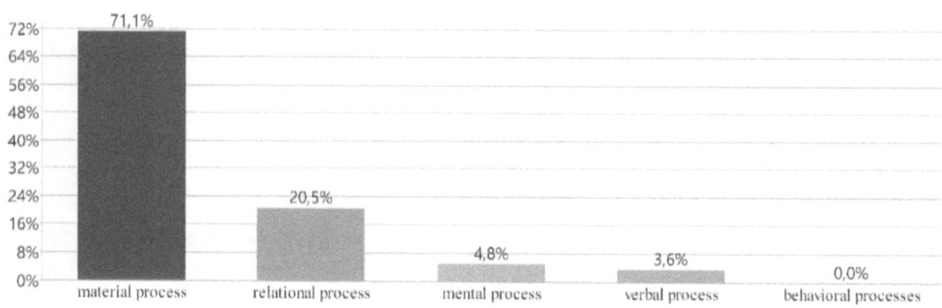

The material processes in which the offender is involved in the PC include actions such as those having to do directly with the crime, such as *gwałcić* ('rape') or *zmuszać* ('force'), i.e., only those verbs which directly placed the offender as an actor negatively viewed in the context of the crime.

154) Dopiero jak się okazało, że facet *próbował* (MATERIAL) tego wieczora *zgwałcić* (MATERIAL) w tej okolicy inną dziewczynę, potraktowali mnie poważnie.
(PC GWyb 2014, Row: 29)
[It was only when it turned out that the guy had *attempted* (MATERIAL) ***to** rape* (MATERIAL) another girl in their area that night that they took me seriously.]

155) kobieta i tak nie powinna romansowac z tym mężczyzną to jej błąd, ale nikt nie może *zmuszać* (MATERIAL) drugiej osoby bez jej woli!!
(PC MG 2019, Row: 10)
[the woman should not have been having an affair with that man in any case. That was her mistake. But no one can *force* (MATERIAL) another person against her will!!]

Relational processes in the PC, similarly to the AEC, included ones that described the offender, and the way that an offender behaves or appears.

156) bo łatwo **być** (RELATIONAL) gwałcicielem anonimowym.
(PC PUD 2015, Row: 9)
[because it's easy **to be** (RELATIONAL) an anonymous rapist]

157) Powinni opublikowac ich twarze niech wszyscy wiedza jak *wyglądają* (RELATIONAL) zwyrodnialcy a potem niech ich ktoś gwałci aż pozdychają
(PC PUD 2017a, Row: 20)
[They should publish pictures of their faces so that everyone knows what villains *look like* (RELATIONAL) and then after that someone should rape them until they die]

Mental processes include mental processes of cognition or feeling, such as *thinking*, *understanding*, and *wanting*.

158)Wtedy z pewnoscia inni amatorzy gwaltow by się *zastanowili* (MENTAL) gdzie wsadzo swoj brudny penis
(PC GWsp 2012b, Row: 9)
[Then other rape lovers would definitely *consider* (MENTAL) where they are putting their dirty penises]

159) A ona trzy razy, ojjjj miała szczęście i niech się cieszy bo za tydzień jej nie *zechcą* (MENTAL) że tak się odwdzięcza za taką przyjemność .
(PC GWsp 2012a, Row: 6)
[And she got it three times and oooh was she lucky and she should be glad because in a week they won't *want* (MENTAL) her since she's thanking them for such a nice time like that.]

There were only 4 instances of verbal processes for the offender in the PC (.5% of the PC on the basis of sentence count), the small number of which may be telling of the fact that the offender's testimonies are lacking in the Polish news reporting discourse under which the comments were found, leaving room for mostly speculation on the part of the Internet users writing comments. The verbal processes for the offender were found in offender-blaming comments, a fact which points to the likelihood that the testimony of the victim is more heavily assessed in the discourse (both the social discourses on rape and the discourses of discussion surrounding it). This is highly impacted by the fact that in Polish news reporting discourses, the offender remains anonymous and hence is not quoted in criminal cases.

Each of the verbal processes for the offender were found 1 time per word in the PC (.001% of the PC on the basis of word count), including verbs such as *przyznać się* ('admit'), *grozić* ('threaten'), *podnosić głos* ('raise one's voice') and *twierdzić* ('claim'). The lack of attention to the verbal processes of the offender is additionally highlighted in the difference between the number of verbal processes for the victim and for the offender in the PC. Where the victim's verbal processes were concerned, 35 out 36 were found in victim-blaming sentences.

Figure 20 Verbal processes for the offender in the PC

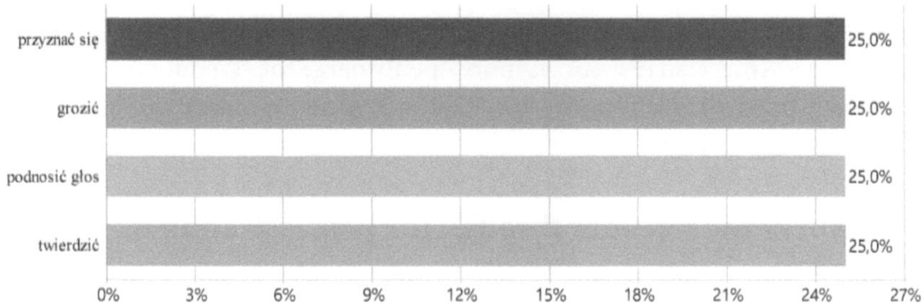

160) Ale skąd to wiesz że romansowała? On tak *twierdzi*, a ona że nie.
(PC MG 2019, Row: 2)
[How do you know that she was having an affair? He *claims* (VERBAL) that they did and she doesn't.]

161) Jeżeli miała dowód na nagraniu że *przyznał się* do tego, a organy ścigania nic z tym nie zrobiły tylko szukaly aby pogrążyć kobietę....To powiem szczerze coś tutaj śmierdzi na odległość......
(PC MG 2019, Row: 10)
[If she had proof that he *admitted to* it and those in charge of the investigation did nothing about it but still looked for evidence to bury the woman… then I'll tell you that something seems really off here…..]

In the PC, the offender's role in the crime is highlighted in the discourse through his activation in various verb processes, similarly to the AEC. In both the AEC and the PC, the offender underwent activation through verbal processes at a minimal count: 5 times in the AEC (.6% of the AEC on the basis of sentence count) and 4 times in the PC (.5% of the PC on the basis of sentence count), a fact which highlights the backgrounding of the offender where his testimony is concerned. In light of the problem of victim blaming, the fact that such minimal attention is discursively given to the offender, the lack of such representation might in fact work in favor of the victim, in that the attention is placed on her victimhood rather than on the role of the offender.

In both the AEC and the PC, the activation of the offender in transitivity processes was more prevalent in the material processes which highlighted his role in the rape. This works towards the offender-blaming discourse in the corpora. As for the material processes, which was the category of transitivity processes activating the offender in both the AEC and the PC, there was a significant difference in the representation in both corpora. Material processes for the offender were found 103 times in the AEC (12.8% of the AEC) and 57 times PC (7.9% of the PC), demonstrating that the actions of the offender were slightly more focused on in the American discourse than in the Polish discourse. This is partially due to the fact that American discourses more openly name the offenders in criminal cases, which in part leads to more speculation and commentary on the subject of such an actor's actions.

Activation of the offender through the possessivation of processes

Activation through possessivation processes was also present in the case of references to the offender. In the AEC, the offender was activated through possessivation of processes in only 2 clauses in the AEC (.2% of the AEC on the basis of sentence count).

162) *His actions*, not hers, caused a rape to occur.
(AEC MN 2016, Row: 14)

163) He is responsible for *his drunken decisions/actions* but not a woman?
(AEC NYT 2017, Row: 18)

In the PC, the offender was activated through possessivation processes a total of 2 times as well (.2% of the entire PC on the basis of sentence count). This was done in relation to the actions of the offender (cf. examples 164 and 165).

164) Żona zgwałcona przez męża: „Mocno mnie chwyta. Jest gotowy, ja nie. Myśli, że *jego brutalność* mnie ożywi"
(PC WO 2019, Row: 18)
[A wife raped by her husband: 'He grabs me hard. He is ready and I am not. He thinks *his brutality* will revive me.]

165) Wy wierzycie że to był pierwszy gwałt w *wykonaniu tych zboczeńców*? Ktoś tak okrutny gwałcił nie raz i jeszcze zgwałci
(PC PUD 2017a, Row: 41)
[Do you really believe that it was the first rape in *the rendition of those perverts*? Someone that cruel has raped before and will rape again.]

What the possessivation of the offender's actions does is activate him through the direct relation of his person with the action or actions that he carried out. This functions as offender-blaming language, however, was also scarce in the AEC. Between the AEC and the PC, this process of activation was used equally. The fact that the offender was not activated in such a way as to highlight his role in the crime is telling, however, in that the direct juxtaposition of the offender and the crime are hardly present in the corpus (see the next chapter on backgrounding for more information about the backgrounding of actors).

Passivation of the offender

In the AEC, there were 82 various processes which represented the passivation of the offender, those of beneficialization, subjection and possessivation. There were 60 instances of passivation of the offender through beneficialization (73.2%; 7.4% of the AEC on the basis of sentence count) found in the digital comments in the AEC, whereas 18 instances of passivation through subjection of the offender (22%; 2.2% of the entire AEC on the basis of sentence count). Possessivation as passivation was found only 4 times in the AEC of digital comments (4.9% of passivation types for the offender; .4% of the AEC on the basis of sentence count).

Figure 21 Frequencies of passivation of the offender in the AEC

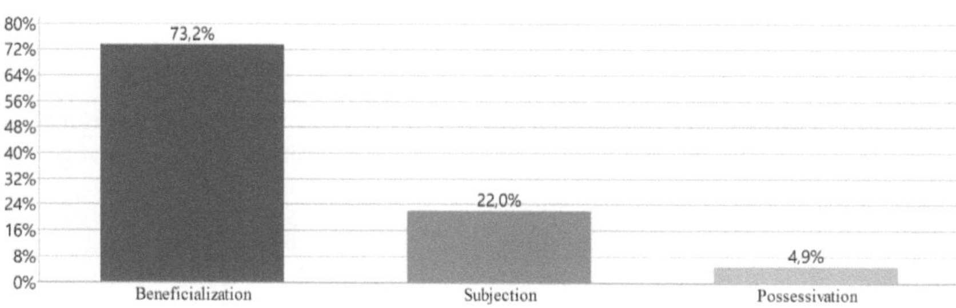

In clauses and sentences in which the punishment of the offender was concerned, or his relationship with the victim described, the actor underwent the process of beneficialization.

166) If this had been anyone else, say a brother from the hood, his "20 minutes of action," would've have gotten *him* a 20 year sentence upon conviction.
(AEC NYT 2016, Row: 22)

167) She says she hated "it" but tells *him* she liked it.
(AEC VTY 2019, Row: 12)

168) I have more worry towards men because they are at more danger of having their lives ruined by a woman falsely accusing *them* of rape because a rape victim can heal and recover but a false accusation is more common in colleges and can have affects that can last decades.
(AEC NYT 2014, Row: 1)

The passivation of the offender through beneficialization took place most often where passivation of the offender was concerned in the AEC, similarly to the passivation of the victim in the AEC.

The other category of passivation in which the offender was involved in the AEC was subjection (23.1% of all passivation types for the offender in the AEC). Such types of sentences can contribute to offender-blaming (cf. example 169 and example 170)

169) BTW, *he was also charged* with the misdemeanor consensual sexual assault, for whatever reason.
(AEC ABC 2015b, Row: 8)

170) I am appalled that *these men and young men* (who participated and witnessed this assault on this 11 year old child), *are not being held in jail* until the trial.
(AEC ABC 2011, Row: 1)

Passivation of the offender through possessivation in the AEC took place a total of 4 times (.4% of the AEC on the basis of sentence count). Two examples of *her rapist* have been given to illustrate how it is that the discourse passivizes the offender through focusing on the victim, even when calling the rapist a rapist.

171) she did NOT GIVE CONSENT; she DID NOT SAY YES. That is the ONLY fact that matters here. We should not be confusing and diluting the fact of her rape with talk about her behavior; that is just another way of excusing *her rapist.*
(NYT 2016, Row: 31)

172) In a recent case the victim did not need to name *her rapist*, the administration knew who she was talking about before she even began her story. Still she was encouraged not to "ruin the young man's life."
(NYT 2014, Row: 10)

The passivation of the offender via possessivation in the discourse shapes both the view of the offender and the victim. In light of the question of victim blaming, such constructions place hidden agency on the victim of the rape by naming her claim to the perpetrator as the main agent in bringing about the existence of the rape in the first instance. The offender is passivized in such a sentence because the victim is foregrounded via the grammaticalized foregrounding of her relationship to the offender, in that a cognitive link is made between the actors so as to highlight the fact that the perpetrator could not commit the crime without the victim having been engaged. In the PC, the offender also underwent all three passivation types.

Figure 22 Frequencies of passivation of the offender in the PC

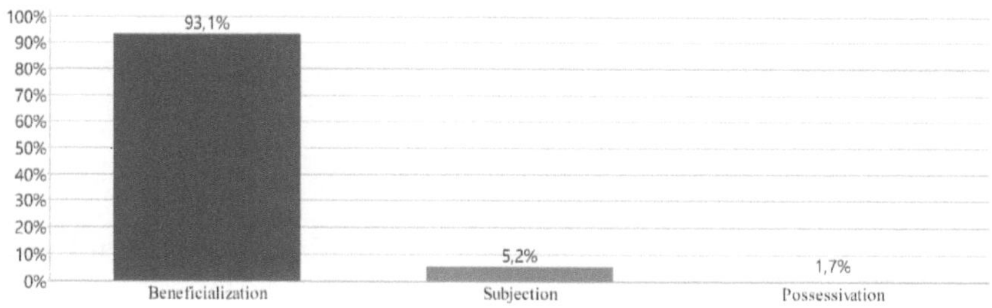

As can be seen in the graph presented above, the most frequent passivation process in which the offender is involved in the PC is that of beneficialization, with a total of 55 clauses (7.7% of the sentences in the PC) in which the offender underwent passivation and only 5 instances of subjection of the offender (.5% of the sentences in the PC) and 3 instances of possessivation in the PC (.4% of the sentences in the PC). The following examples illustrate the structure, exemplifying supporting and blaming comments.

173) Czy *komuś takiemu* można dać wyrok w zawieszeniu?
(WO 2014, Row: 2)
[Can they give *someone like that* probation?]

174) nie bronię ich, ale ta kobieta wpuszczając *ich* do pokoju, nie była święta.
(PC PUD 2015, Row: 11)
[I'm not defending them, but that woman letting *them* into her room was not a saint.]

175) *Napastnika* nie widziałam, poczułam silne uderzenie w tył głowy, upadłam jak długa.
(PC GWyb 2014, Row: 22)
[I didn't see *the attacker*, I just felt a hard blow to the back of my head and I fell like a sack of bricks]

176) Ja nie bronie *tych kolesi* ale nie dziwie się pytania które zadawali jej w sądzie bo normalna osoba która ma rodzinę nie będzie przebywała w takim towarzystwie kiedy ma swój pokój do którego może w każdej chwili wrócić.

(PC PUD 2015, Row: 22)
[I am not defending **those guys** but I am not surprised at the questions they asked her in court because a normal person with a family is not going to be spending time in that kind of company when she has a room of her own she can go back to]

Two examples of the subjection of the offender are as follows, where the accusation and sentencing of the offender come into play. Such fronting of the actor in the Polish corpus points to the offender-blaming types of evaluations that we see in the following examples, where the role and fault of the offender are put into focus. Here, the erasure of the parties that are incriminating the offender is taken away, hence the expression of negative evaluation of the offender.

177) *Został oskarzony i skazany* za gwałt.
(PC GWyb 2014, Row: 18)
[He was *accused and sentenced* for rape.]

178) *Sprawca nie był* przedwcześnie *osądzany*
(PC GWyb 2019, Row: 7)
[*The offender was not tried* prematurely]

Passivation through the possessivation of the victim's person took place in 3 cases in the PC and is demonstrative of passivation of the offender through possessivation (here, of the victim).

179) oby teraz panów w p*****u spotkało to samo co *ich ofiarę*
(PC PUD 2017a, Row: 28)
[I hope that those men get the same thing that *their victim* did]

180) Tu wszystko jest jasne jak słońce. Tak nas traktujecie i na dodatek nie wstyd wam tłumaczyć zbrodniarza i oskarżać *jego ofiarę* !!!
(PC WO 2015, Row: 5)
[Everything here is clear as day. This is the way you treat us and you're not even ashamed that you're making excuses for the criminal and accusing *his victim*!!!]

Although such passivation of the offender is very telling of attitudes, meaning that the actor is backgrounded as a participant in the crime through the discursive action taking place in such CMC communication, the question of backgrounding also presents the absence of the offender in parts of the discourse (i.e. sentences) that are associated with the act of the rape itself. As mentioned at the start of this chapter, representations of the rape are discussed in the socio-semantic analysis presented in the chapter which follows.

Discussion

The first and main goal of this chapter was to demonstrate that victim blaming can be embedded within the structure of those informal CMC discourses about rape that are digital comments. The actors involved are present in social discourses on the subject in both cultures, ranging from the social knowledge of the common actors in rape to the official media discourses on rape, and subsequently discussed within the context of more informal discourses which derive from those overarching discourses. The data analyzed support the view that victim blaming is present in American and Polish discourses on rape, however, offender-blaming takes place prevalently throughout both of the corpora as well. Because victim blaming in two cultures is the focus of this work, however, it is important to point out that although offender-blaming takes place in such discourse, victim blaming is a social problem which pervades and directs social attitudes about those who are the victims of sexual crime (Eigenberg & Garner, 2008; Randall, 2010; Łys, 2015).

Indirectness is the leading discursive strategy in the evaluation of the actors in rape on the structural level. I would like to state here that for both this chapter and the one which follows, the victim blaming that takes place in the discourse is representative of what I have called *discursive secondary victimization.* It is safe to state that the comments represent attitudes that are reflective of Internet user attitudes towards the actors in a rape, as the strategies analyzed in the presented chapter are many, and most represent either direct or indirect evaluation of actors.

Figure 23 Mapping of the discursive secondary victimization for the AEC and the PC through negative evaluation

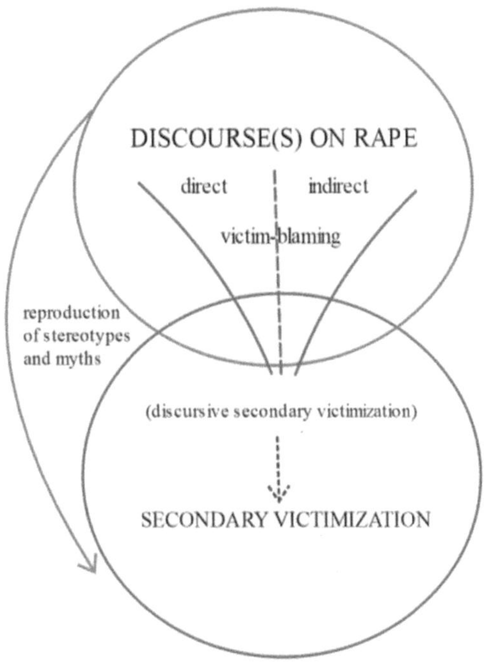

The visual presented above represents the overall discursive processes that are used to refer to and represent the main actors involved in rape when it comes to victim blaming, in both the AEC and the PC. One must bear in mind that all discourses on rape do, to extents of varying degree, draw on the role of the victim in the rape, since it is the victim who was the object of the rape. As mentioned earlier in this work, victim blaming is a cause for secondary victimization (cf. Chapter 3) and this foremost takes place discursively, where discourses of evaluative expression and common myths about rape victims are reproduced (Ehrlich, 2001; Franiuk et al., 2008; McMahon & Farmer, 2011; Ehrlich, 2020).

To expand on this, it is necessary to explain the visual provided above (Figure 19), which displays the main processes that come about in the CMC discourses of lay citizens about rape. The entirety of the presented chapter has dealt with the question of strategies undertaken by internet users in evaluating situations of crime and expressing their thoughts or opinions on public forums. Such evaluation can take place in two main ways, namely through direct or indirect means. Both of these aspects, when the negative evaluation of the victim is involved, lead to discursive secondary victimization, since the secondary victimization in question takes place through written CMC discourse. Where indirect evaluation is concerned, such processes take place via implicit evaluation, wherein the meaning must and can be inferred by the reader. Where directness is concerned, on the other hand, the processes of secondary victimization is more obvious, as the victim is explicitly blamed for the rape. Although many of the comments analyzed pertained to individuals in different cases of rape, these concluding remarks may be perceived as making generalizations about all rape victims, as cultural knowledge is reflected in the stereotyping and rape myths which are referenced in the discourses presented in the theoretical part of this work (cf. Chapter 2).

The map of discourse processes illustrated in Figure 19 demonstrates, most importantly, that secondary victimization does occur in discourse in the context of CMCs, and will also be discussed in the following chapter where representations of actors and rape myths are concerned. Such victimization was seen at the level of the structure of the victim-blaming sentences and comments, i.e., where conditional sentences made alternative hypothetical situations, and where questions suggested or implied that there was an untold truth behind the victim's testimony. This was clear in both the AEC and the PC, among other strategies used, including negation (cf. Chapter 6).

On the whole, the map presents the directions in which discursive victim blaming occurs, which was the main focus of the analysis presented in this chapter. The fact that victim blaming often takes place through indirectness, including (but not limited to) the foregrounding of the victim in the context of material processes in which she participates, through interrogative forms, or placing her in sentences giving alternative hypothetical choices she could have taken, in both of the cultural contexts, makes it clear that victim blaming physically manifests in discourse in both American and Polish cultures. In light of this, the major differences and the important points in the discourse on the actors involved in rape between the AEC and the PC should be reiterated.

Table 21 shows the preliminary division of the comments on the basis of attitudes towards actors, as shown below. The most populated category in the AEC was that of victim blaming (37% of the comments in the AEC), with an almost equal number of offender-blaming comments (34% of the comments in the AEC). In the PC, victim-blaming comments were nearly equal to offender-blaming comments (victim-blaming comments made up 36.3% of comments in the PC, and offender-blaming comments made up 37.1% of the comments in the PC and). It is also significant that the ratio of victim- and offender-blaming comments was virtually equal in both the AEC and the PC. The negative attitudes towards the actors in the comments show that there is a tendency in American and Polish cultures to blame both the offender and the victim for the rape. The remainder of the comments (not accounted for in the percentages) were those in which it was difficult to discern which actors were being targeted in particular.

The analysis has demonstrated a greater polarization of attitudes in the Polish discourse (i.e., more negativity than support of the victim of rape and more negative attitudes towards the offender of rape, as well). Polish culture is known to have strong attitudes towards sexuality, which present conservative attitudes that are especially repressive towards the sexuality of women.

Table 13 Division of overall attitudes presented in the analyzed comments

	Frequency	**Percentage of AEC**	**Frequency**	**Percentage of PC**
Victim-blaming	136	37%	124	36.3%
victim-supporting	76	20.7%	55	16.1%
offender-blaming	125	34%	127	37.1%
offender-supporting	12	3.3%	0	0%
unclear target	19	5.2%	36	10.5%
TOTAL OF TYPES	368	100%	342	100%

It is important to summarize how the conclusions about the victim blaming came about as a result of the analysis performed. As the main tool for analysis used was that of linguistic stancetaking, it was crucial to discern the sentence types in which evaluative attitudes were expressed (i.e., Internet users expressed their own thoughts about the rape and the actors involved). In both the PC and the AEC, most evaluative sentences (cf. Chapter 1 for a definition of the category of speech acts) were in the form of declarative sentences (76.6% of the AEC and 68.3% of the PC). It is important to note that even in declarative sentences, statements which were made by Internet users indicated what their attitudes were, the conclusions of which were drawn in the socio-semantic study of constituents and the cultural connotations that are attached to the paradigmatic choices made in the discourse. Declarative sentences were also found to be in conditional forms, expressions with modality and negation which presupposed hypothetical alternative situations, also suggesting the attitude of a given user as positively or negatively oriented to the actors.

In both of the corpora, interrogative sentences were second most frequent (15.6% of the AEC and 15.5% of the PC), at near-equal statistical significance in both of the corpora. This demonstrates that evaluative stances were expressed in question form in both of the corpora nearly equally, showing that such indirectness exists in both American and Polish cultures.

In the AEC, 4.1% of the sentences were imperatives and 3.7% exclamatories, whereas in the PC 9.5% of the sentences of an evaluative nature were exclamatories and 6.6% were imperatives. Here, the use of imperatives retains a stance that expresses strong attitudes of what actors should do in situations of rape. The differences in proportion between the two cultures may be explained by that fact that somewhat stronger ideologies regarding the role of the actors in the rape should be within the Polish context. The American comments, however, do not evaluate in such obvious forms that are so expressive in nature. This might be due to the predominating tendency to be indirect in American culture. Table 14 shows that the imperative form was used in sentences referring to the offender more so than to the victim.

Table 14 Evaluative sentences for all actors

	Frequency	Percentage of AEC	Frequency	Percentage of PC
declarative	616	76.6%	488	68.3%
interrogative	125	15.6%	111	15.5%
imperative	33	4.1%	47	6.6%
exclamatory	30	3.7%	68	9.5%
TOTAL	804	100%	714	100%

A table showing the stances in each of the corpora (the AEC and the PC) towards the actors and the given sentence types has been provided below, in order to show the differentiations of sentence structure in evaluations of the two main actors: the victim and the offender (cf. Table 15). There is a large discrepancy between the total sentence counts in the AEC and the PC because of the more complex nature of the sentences in the AEC, where there were multiple clauses and multiple actors mentioned in one sentence.

Table 15 Evaluative stances expressed in sentence types

	Frequency	Percentage AEC	Frequency	Percentage of PC
negative towards victim + declarative	476	26.7%	184	25.1%
negative towards offender + declarative	398	22.3%	144	19.6%
supportive of victim + declarative	319	17.9%	133	18.1%
negative towards victim + interrogative	109	6.1%	41	5.6%
negative towards offender + interrogative	87	4.9%	21	2.9%
unclear who is targeted + declarative	77	4.3%	44	6.0%
supportive of victim + interrogative	61	3.4%	21	2.9%
supportive of offender + declarative	48	2.7%	0	0%
negative towards offender + exclamatory	45	2.5%	32	4.4%
negative towards offender + imperative	37	2.1%	27	3.7%
negative towards victim + exclamatory	26	1.5%	17	2.3%
supportive of victim + exclamatory	24	1.4%	14	1.9%
negative towards victim + imperative	23	1.3%	12	1.6%

(Continued)

Table 15 Continued

	Frequency	Percentage AEC	Frequency	Percentage of PC
supportive of victim + imperative	22	1.2%	8	1.1%
supportive of offender + interrogative	14	0.8%	41	5.6%
unclear who is targeted + interrogative	10	0.6%	7	0.9%
unclear who is targeted + exclamatory	5	0.3%	4	0.5%
unclear who is targeted + imperative	2	0.1%	1	0.1%
TOTAL	1783	100%	734	100%

In the AEC, the comments that were considered to be victim-blaming ones mostly took of the form of declarative sentences and the same occurred where the offender was concerned (cf. Table 15). This, however, does not mean that the types of blaming that took place for the victim and the offender were the same, as was discussed in the presented chapter. The AEC demonstrated a greater tendency towards interrogative blaming sentences of both actors, while the PC demonstrated significantly fewer (cf. Table 15). Exclamatory sentences also contained more blaming than supporting in both of the data sets analyzed. Interestingly, imperative structures sentences were mostly blaming of the offender and the victim in the AEC and the PC, however were more common in the AEC. This being said, while analyzing the illocution or intention of evaluative sentences, it was important to look at the structures of sentences and the meanings that lay behind those structures, ranging from conditional sentences, and statements with negation to questions behind which lay attitudes suggestive of assumptions that the victim was, if not fully to blame, partially to blame for the rape.

One of the ways in which blame was indirectly framed, in the structural sense, was through the use of modality and conditional constructions of sentences. These aspects have been subsumed into the following table where the evaluative stance towards actors and events were concerned (cf. Table 16). The expression of blame as an alternative hypothetical situation in the form of a conditional clause or sentence was more prevalent in the AEC than in the PC, with conditional clauses making up 10.2% of the sentences in the AEC and only 3% in the PC.

Table 16 Comparison of the clauses expressing modality in AEC and PC

	Frequency AEC	Percentage of AEC	Frequency PC	Percentage PC
Conditional victim-blaming	45	5.6%	10	1.4%
Conditional offender-blaming	34	4.2%	8	1%
Conditional doubt of offender's fault	2	.2%	0	0%
Conditional rape preventable	1	.1%	0	0%
Conditional other-blaming	0	0%	4	.6%
TOTAL	82/804	10.2%	22/714	3%

The AEC showed more use of the conditional construction in indirect evaluation that the PC did. This demonstrates that, because victim blaming is an act that is viewed as a social impropriety, it should take place indirectly. By expressing an opinion on a subject that is considered controversial and taboo, and opinions regarding the actions of the actors, it takes more inference than in a direct sentence to uncover the blame placed on the victim. The difference between the AEC and the PC in this respect showed that such indirectness in Polish culture is not as prevalent through the presentation of alternative hypothetical situations. This has been confirmed by the discussions on directness and indirectness in culture, where it has been pointed out that Polish culture values directness (Van Dijk, 1997; Wierzbicka, 1999; Grainger & Mills, 2016) and that American culture values indirectness (Cheng & Warren, 2003; Grainger & Mills, 2016).

Modality was another structural aspect which expressed alternative hypothetical situations in both the AEC and the PC. Here, *should have* and *powinna/powinien* were investigated for such modality, as well as *could have* and *mogła/mógł* in the AEC and the PC. What is important to note here is that the modal expressions are directed at the victim and more present in the PC than in the AEC, demonstrating that the use of such modal expressions is more prevalent in Polish victim-blaming discourse than in American victim-blaming discourse.

Table 17 Modality of alternative hypothetical expression in the AEC and the PC (should have)

	Frequency	Percentage of AEC	Frequency	Percentage of PC
should have victim-blaming	6	.7%	12	1.6%
should have offender-blaming	2	.2%	0	0%
should have other	2	.2%	0	0%
TOTAL	10/804	1.1%	12/714	1.6%

Table 18 Modality of alternative hypothetical expression in the AEC and the PC (could have)

	Frequency	Percentage of AEC	Frequency	Percentage of PC
could have victim-blaming	3	.3%	4	.5%
could have offender-blaming	0	0%	0	0%
could have other	0	0%	0	0%
TOTAL	3/804	1.1%	4/714	.5%

Negation in the corpus also showed alternative hypothetical situations in the sense that the expression of what actors did not do when they could have done. Negation was used most often in the context of victim blaming, in sentences where the actions or circumstances not undertaken by or surrounding the victim might have had an impact on her rape in the first place. The category of negation is made up of all negation types that were discussed, including negation of verbs, noun phrases and adjectival phrases. The use of negation is also more present in the PC victim-blaming comments than in the AEC, demonstrating its greater prevalence as an indirect strategy in such Polish online discourses.

Table 19 Negation and attitudes

	Frequency	Percentage of AEC	Frequency	Percentage of PC
negation victim-blaming	28	3.4%	33	4.6%
negation offender-blaming	19	2.3%	11	1.5%

(Continued)

Table 19 Continued

	Frequency	Percentage of AEC	Frequency	Percentage of PC
negation victim-supporting	17	2.1%	10	1.4%
negation offender-supporting	4	.5%	3	.4%
negation offender- and victim-blaming	1	.1%	0	0%
negation society-blaming	0	0%	5	.7%
TOTAL	69/804	8.5%	62/714	8.6%

The negation used in sentences discussing the actors involved in a sexual crime evokes alternative scenarios, as well as the idea that other possibilities for decisions to be made or actions undertaken could have been presented in the situation. The use of negation is also presuppositional and produces implied meaning by constructing an alternative hypothetical situation. It is a form which indirectly expresses the stance of the person writing the comment as critical of the actors involved, hence supporting the idea that implicit evaluation takes place in the structural elements of discourse.

The activation and passivation of the actors is a significant part of the analysis of the structural aspects of evaluation, which sees the actors as "active forces" or "agentless patients" (Tranchese & Zollo, 2013: 145). The following table breaks down the frequencies at which each of the actors was activated and passivated in the AEC and the PC. The actors in the AEC were evaluated more often through the processes of activation and passivation, with more attention paid to the offender in the AEC than in the PC. In both of the corpora, the victim underwent activation processes most frequently, which foregrounded her most often in the actions which she carried out.

As mentioned above, the passivation of the actors also foregrounded them, however the victim was passivized about 6% more often in the AEC than in the PC, showing that such structural differences in role attribution were more prevalent in American online discourse than in Polish online discourse. In both the AEC and the PC the offender underwent significantly less passivation and activation than the victim did, however cultural variation also presented itself to be significant. The offender of the crime was found to undergo passivation processes about 30% more often in the AEC than in the PC, meaning that in such a cultural context the offender is highlighted by backgrounding other actors in the discourse. Overall, the attention in discourse is explicitly drawn more often to the victim than to the offender. This fact begs the question of the contribution of such factors to the social tendency in both American and Polish cultures to focus on the role of the victim in the rape, rather than that of the offender (at least to an equal extent).

Table 20 Table comparing the activation and passivation of actors in AEC and PC

	Frequency	Percentage of AEC	Frequency	Percentage of PC
Activation of victim	267	33.2%	220	30.8%
Passivation of victim	175	21.7%	113	15.8%
Activation of offender	145	18%	75	10.5%
Passivation of offender	82	35.5%	62	8.6%
TOTAL	669/804	83.2%	470/714	65.8%

Based on the literature (van Leeuwen 1995, 2005, 2008; Tabbert 2016), the transitivity processes in which the actors are presented as activated and passivized play a crucial role in their overall discursive representation. Transitivity processes for the activation of the victim and the offender showed that the actors were described as being involved in select verb processes which were expressed in the Internet user comments. The activation processes discussed in the table above were then divided into the various transitivity processes.

Two tables (Tables 21 and 22) have been provided, one for the representations of the victim in both the AEC and the PC and the other for such representations of the offender in the AEC and the PC. It is clear that the material processes were most prevalent in the activation of the victim in both the AEC and the PC. As can be seen below, in the AEC and the PC, there were more material processes presented in the activation clauses for the victim than for the offender. In the AEC, the victim was activated through 16.3% of material processes and the offender was activated through 12.7% of material processes. In the PC, the difference is more significant, with the victim's activation through material processes in 19.5% of the PC on the basis of sentence count and 8.2% for the offender.

Verbal processes and relational processes were about equal in both the AEC and the PC, taking place significantly less than the material processes (verbal processes made up 7.2% of the AEC and 7% of the PC and relational processes made up 6.3% of the AEC and 6.7% of the PC). Even less frequent were mental processes and behavioral processes in the AEC and the PC (with mental processes found in 3.1% of the AEC and 3.6% of the PC and behavioral processes found in only .2% of the AEC and .7% of the PC). The frequencies of the activation processes show that there is more such focus on the victim in the PC and more focus on the offender in the AEC.

Table 21 Comparison of the transitivity processes of victim in AEC and PC (activation)

	Frequency AEC	Percentage AEC	Frequency PC	Percentage PC
Victim material process	131	16.3%	139	19.5%
Victim verbal process	58	7.2%	50	7.0%
Victim relational process	51	6.3%	48	6.7%
Victim mental process	25	3.1%	26	3.6%
Victim behavioral process	2	0.2%	5	0.7%
TOTAL	267/804	33.2%	268/714	37.5%

Table 22 Comparison of the transitivity processes of offender in AEC and PC (activation)

	Frequency AEC	Percentage AEC	Frequency PC	Percentage PC
Offender material process	102	12.7%	59	8.2%
Offender relational process	31	3.8%	17	2.1%
Offender mental process	7	0.9%	4	0.6%
Offender verbal process	4	0.5%	3	0.4%
Offender behavioral processes	0	0%	0	0%
TOTAL	144/804	17.9%	83/714	11.6%

What is of importance is the fact that the material processes for the victim dominated where such activation was concerned, showing that the victim's role in the crime committed against her is viewed as playing a part in her rape. This focus on what the victim was doing in light of the rape indirectly assumes the blame to be on the victim where verbs that discuss the circumstances of her rape in accordance with myths that lead to the false belief that she was to blame are concerned.

In view of the fact that rape is usually a crime that is first reported and subsequently investigated, I wish to highlight the significance of the verbal processes in the analysis of such corpora. In both the AEC and the PC, there was significantly more verbal process representation for the victim than for the offender, most likely owing to the aforementioned fact. In the AEC, although there was a statistically equal occurrence of verbal process verbs for the victim as in the PC, there was a greater variation in the verbal representation (cf. Table 23).

Table 23 Victim verbal processes (activation)

	Frequency	Percentage of AEC		Frequency	Percentage of PC
say	23	.1%	zgłaszać ('report')	11	.1%
claim	8	.03%	mówić ('say')	5	.04%
ask	7	.02%	powiedzieć ('tell')	2	.02%
report	6	.02%	zgadzaćsię ('agree')	2	.02%
tell	5	.01%	twierdzić ('claim')	2	.02%
admit	4	.01%	zawiadomić ('inform')	2	.02%
conclude	1	.004%	krzyczeć ('shout')	2	.02%
tell	1	.004%	ściemniać('lie')	1	.01%
yell	1	.004%	kłamać ('lie')	1	.01%
talk	1	.004%	narzekać ('complain')	1	.01%
speak	1	.004%	wspominać ('recall')	1	.01%
object (to)	1	.004%	żegnać ('big farewell')	1	.01%
lie	1	.004%	podzielićsię ('share')	1	.01%
describe	1	.004%	zabieraćgłos ('say')	1	.01%
state	1	.004%	blefować ('bluff')	1	.01%

(Continued)

Table 23 Continued

	Frequency	Percentage of AEC		Frequency	Percentage of PC
name	1	.004%	drzećsię ('scream')	1	.01%
accuse	1	.004%	powiadomić ('inform')	1	.01%
share	1	.004%			
brag	1	.004%			
TOTAL	67/20,898	.3%	TOTAL	36/11,200	.3%

Table 24 Offender verbal processes (activation)

	Frequency	Percentage of AEC		Frequency	Percentage of PC
claim	8	.03%	przyznaćsię ('admit')	1	.008%
reply	1	.004%	grozić ('threaten')	1	.008%
say	1	.004%	podnosić głos ('raisevoice')	1	.008%
lie	1	.004%	twierdzić ('claim')	1	.008%
confess	1	.004%			
refuse	1	.004%			
TOTAL	13/20,898	.06%	TOTAL	4/11,200	.03%

The verbal processes representing the offender reflected negative attitudes towards him/them, however their number was so insignificant that the activation of the victim through the predominantly negative view of her testimony or version of the story highlights the difference between the representation of such actors. Because the version of events as given by the victim is referred to more often, this leads to an increase in victim blaming as a disadvantage in the unequal representation of the story of the assault is interpreted as working in her favor rather than as being believable.

The analysis of the transitivity processes in which the actors were involved demonstrated that activation and passivation create a divide in the ways that the actors are construed in discourses representing attitudinal expression regarding sex crimes, where the victim and offender both undergo activation and passivation. The types of verbs that are chosen to activate the victim in such discourses are also important in such an analysis. When actors were placed in the position of the active participant, this bore more importance to their construction, as they were presented as being more actively involved in their role in the crime from a lay perspective, hence reflecting the attitudes that Internet users have towards the actions in which they were involved and their relation to the crime discussed.

The role of the structure of sentences in analyzing the phenomenon of blame, and especially victim blaming, demonstrates that blame can be placed on actors (i.e., they can be evaluated) in manners that are more indirect than others, which has as many consequences in the way that rape victims are viewed and treated as in the case of blaming the victim for having been raped. This can be seen within the corpus of digital comments as made by the Internet users who partake in discussions on public fora. The use of modal verbs and conditional structures create alterative hypothetical possibilities that make a reader question whether or not a different outcome (other than rape) could have come about in the situation. Such structures do not explicitly state that . The aspect of negation does something similar, but also presupposes that the absence of an aspect of the crime points to culpability of one party or the other (i.e., the victim or the offender).

All of the above categories of the structural analysis have pointed to the fact that much of the evaluation of actors in rape (in both American and Polish analyzed corpora) depends on the use of structural markers which can spread ideologies regarding rape victims and offenders (which is to be extended in the discussion of the next chapter, including the highly-ideologically geared subject of rape myths). The analysis demonstrates that both victim blaming and offender blaming are the most prevalent attitudes in the comments and that the structure points to indirect methods of communicating doubt in the victim's testimony, presenting alternative hypothetical situations in order to provide evidence of other options that the victim might have had to get out of the situation or otherwise suggesting that a victim's account of rape is unreliable.

Conclusions

The initial assumption that victim blaming is reproduced in discourses of digital comments in American and Polish culture was shown in both of the corpora of Internet user comments analyzed. What is of interest are the strategies through which such attitudes and opinions are expressed discursively and how they differ with respect to the culture in which they occur. There were visible similarities and differences between the two corpora, demonstrating that the two cultures use common strategies when discussing a subject that is seen as socially controversial in some way, and that they also use different strategies or draw on different aspects of the subject in discussing it. In accordance with cultural communication theories, American discourse on the subject of rape is critical of both the victim and the offender, however draws on strategies of indirectness where the structure is concerned, while Polish communication on the subject of rape is more direct and hence more expressive (Van Dijk, 1997; Wierzbicka, 1999; Cheng & Warren, 2003; Grainger & Mills, 2016). Although offender-blaming is present in the American and Polish discourses, when it comes to sexual assault, the discourse which commits the act of secondary victimization and blames the victim is the most harmful, as it reinforces the idea that the victim is to blame for being assaulted, even if the offender is blamed as well.

There are limitations to the investigations carried out in this chapter, and for future research on the subject it would be advisable to look into more structural aspects of such evaluative discourses, including various adverbial forms of modality (i.e., *supposing*, *perhaps*, *maybe* etc.). What this chapter has done is introduce and examine the main structural features which encompass the strategy of evaluation in Internet user comments. At this stage of the analysis, it has been made clear through the analysis and the discussion that even on the level of structure meaning can be implied instead of explicitly stated on the subject of rape.

The chapter which follows (Chapter 7) also aims to provide evidence for the tendency to indirectly evaluate actors and negatively portray the victim of a sexual crime. The analysis of the representations of social actors is equally important in dissecting how the construction of actors can imply whether an actor is viewed as good or bad within the context of rape. In addition to this, the presence of rape myths is investigated, as they have been stated in the literature to be outdated and generally unfounded beliefs which implicate the victim in the crime committed against her.

Chapter 7: Analysis of the evaluation in socio-semantic representations of actors and events of digital comments in American and Polish online media communication

In the preceding chapter, structural aspects which highlighted attitudes in digital comments about rape were analyzed for American and Polish online discourses. This chapter continues the discussion on evaluation, however investigates the socio-semantic representations of the actors and the rape itself to further look at the ways of blaming and supporting of the victim and offender in order to make clear the cultural nature of how attitudes about sexual crime are expressed. The investigation of the representations of social actors shows how the socio-semantic constituents of discourse can construe meaning that is negative or positive, both directly and indirectly, thus further demonstrating how it is that evaluative speech acts present themselves in Internet user comments on the subject of sexual crime.

For the analysis of social actors, mainly nominal and adjectival and predicative qualifying constituents were taken into consideration (cf. Chapter 1). The category of appraisement is investigated by looking at the linguistic representation of social actors which are evaluative, including metaphorical and metonymic[80] representation (cf. Chapter 1). As far as the analysis of the representation of rape as a crime or event (Grant & Woodham, 2007), naming strategies are also investigated, including such naming which includes metaphorical expression or reference, as well as euphemism and dysphemism.

The informal and conversational nature of the discourse of digital comments (cf. Chapter 4) provides insight into social attitudes, especially through the investigation of the linguistic strategies used to evaluate sexual crime and express opinions on the subject. The importance of how social actors are represented lies in

80 Metonymic reference is considered in the analysis where PART OF A WHOLE is concerned (Lakoff & Johnson, 1980; 2003). The reference to body parts of the actors in discourse on other terms is taken into account in how they present the actors as their own body parts or referring to the actors with reference to their body parts. I consider these references, although different, to be related to one another, as they utilize the corporal sphere to refer to actors, drawing attention to or foregrounding the body, which is the main site in a sexual crime overall.

what is communicated to readers about Internet users' attitudes towards the actors that are involved in a rape, especially where victim blaming is concerned. Similarly to the previous chapter, such attitudes are viewed as representative of overall social attitudes to the actors and the event discussed. The goal of the presented chapter is to demonstrate that there are cultural differences (between American and Polish contexts) on the level of socio-semantic representation of rape in lay discourses and that victim blaming is also present at this level in both cultural contexts.

In the previous chapter, it was noted that American culture tends to be more indirect in the expression of opinions and attitudes regarding subjects such as sexual crime than Polish culture, which takes place on the level of structure of discourse. It is my goal to show that the evaluation of actors is also visible on the level of socio-semantics, where both direct and indirect expression of attitudes are concerned, but especially where negative attitudes of blaming are found. This also differs from a cultural perspective, where the Polish blaming of actors takes place more directly on the socio-semantic level than American blaming, reflecting the cultural differences in communication between the two.

Structure of the chapter

Before moving on to the discussion of the analyzed material, it is pertinent to provide a presentation of the chapter's structure. The first category for analysis of the socio-semantic representations of social actors is that of nomination. Following this, the category of the identification of the actors, which includes classification identification, relational identification, and physical identification is discussed. Within the category of identification, the tendency to present the victim and perpetrator as a pair is discussed within the context of the discursive construction of what is referred to as the "penal couple" (Zaykowski, 2015; Tabbert, 2016; Bergelson, 2020). After this, the functionalization of actors is investigated, examining how the actors are related to what they do or the actions that are carried out on their persons.

Next, the categories of analysis which are indetermination and backgrounding are discussed, focusing on the abstraction of actors in discourse. The category of appraisement, which highlights a strategy that is more explicit in revealing attitudes to actors and situations through naming strategies (van Leeuwen, 2008), including metaphor and metonymy and the reference to the body parts of the actors, is also investigated in this chapter as a socio-semantic means for expressing evaluation (cf. Chapter 1 of this work for definitions of the categories for the representations of social actors). The final aspect of the analysis of the representation of social actors is a summary illustration of the ways that each actor is named in the discourse, according to categories of social variables whereby they are presented in the comments.

In this chapter, the subject of how rape is represented in discourse is looked at, investigating the euphemization of rape analyzed in both the AEC and the PC. After this, a brief analysis of the use of analogy in comments about rape will be discussed and then the analysis of the presence of rape myths in comments is looked at to show how ideologies (cf. Chapter 2) are reproduced in discourses about rape, leading to the discursive victimization of rape victims (cf. Chapter 2). The final aspect of this analysis is an investigation and discussion of the blaming of outside actors for rape or the way that rape as a crime is handled (i.e., the law, education, the church and other institutions).

Nomination and direct address to social actors

In van Leeuwen's (1996, 2008) category of *nomination*, the ways in which actors are named based on the levels of formality are investigated and named accordingly, i.e., formal nomination, semiformal nomination, and informal nomination types (cf. Chapter 1 for a descriptive introduction to the category). I have added *direct address* to this category so as to save space, and because it is most suited to this section of the analysis. What is meant by the representation of actors through direct address is that the use of personal pronouns (in both English and Polish contexts) such as *you* or *ty/wy* ('you'), as well as the use of honorific markers in direct reference to an actor (as if speaking to him or her) (i.e., *pani* and *panowie*). The following sections begin with the analysis of references to the victim in both cultural contexts and move on to the analysis of the representations of the offender. The subsequent discussion begins by talking about the traditional categories of nomination and then reflects on the act of directly addressing the actors.

Nomination and direct address of the victim

In the AEC, there were few cases of nomination for the victim, namely 1 count of semiformal nomination (.004% of the AEC), a reference to television producer *Brooke Nevils* of NBC (involved in the case against Matt Lauer) (cf. example 176). The fact that nomination did not take place significantly in the corpus of digital comments has to do in part with the anonymity of the victims of sex crimes held by the media in American culture, as well as the fact that the discussion of rape and the actors involved did not refer to the unique identities of the actors, but rather grouped them to show more general attitudes towards victims, perhaps viewing them more collectively rather than individually.

176) SO The way this reads, I think that *Brooke Nevils* probably did initially consent to sexual contact with Matt Lauer (and she continued to have sexual contact with him after this incident).
(AEC VTY 2019, Row: 4)

A graph of the representations has been provided below.

Figure 24 Nomination and direct address of the victim in the AEC

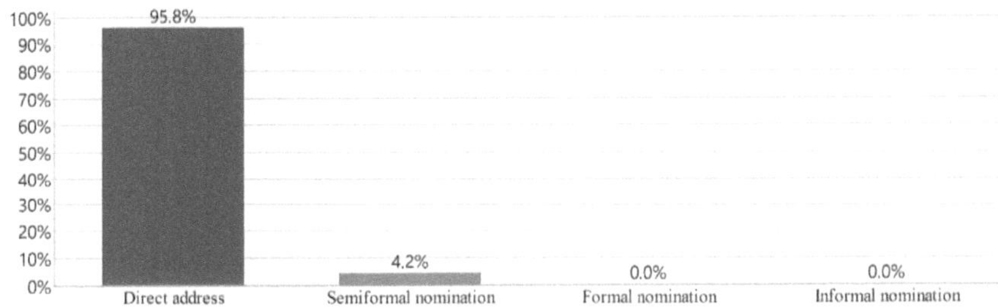

As mentioned above, although not directly belonging to the traditional categorization of nomination, it is worth stating that direct address geared towards the victim was a significant part of the analysis of reference in the AEC. This type of reference to the actor took place a total of 23 times in the AEC (.1% of the AEC) and is located within the category of *direct address* in the graph above. Yet, this fact remains rather insignificant, as most of the uses of *you* were found in two comments in the AEC. It is important to note, however, that the use of such a strategy does two things, namely that it shortens the distance between the Internet user and the subject being addressed (i.e., the victim) when directly addressing one actor and secondly indirectly targets any rape victim by using the general *you* form to refer to all rape victims. By manner of direct reference (through the second person pronoun *you*), the pronoun acts as a discursive marker of blame, because it is a powerful tool in drawing attention to the victim and her role in the crime committed against her (cf. examples 181–183).

181) She concludes that, because sexual relations took place, "I had been violated." No, *you* may not conclude that. Both of *you* could have drunkenly had sex willingly. *You* could have jumped him. *You* have NO evidence for anything. The real question is why do *you* assume rape? Why do *you* assume something awful happened? Is it because our society shames women (wrongfully) for having drunken sex? Enough with the witch hunts.
(AEC NYT 2017, Row: 2)

182) *You* can't speak well of your rapist after the "rape" and think anyone will believe your story 10 years later.
(AEC ABC 2020, Row: 10)

183) If *you* drink to excess, do not expect others to protect **you** from harm or prevent **you** from harming others. *You* must protect yourself and control yourself. Acquaintances are not to be trusted if **you** are incapacitated from alcohol. In the event that *you* drink to excess and someone takes advantage of *you* while you are in that state, or *you* take advantage of someone else in that state, whether *you* are in that state or not, *you* may seek justice, or be accused of committing a crime. If *you* are the victim, *you* are unlikely to be satisfied with the justice meted out because there won't be any witnesses. And independent of whether justice is served, *you* will have wrecked your life. Don't put yourself in this position. If your social clique drinks to excess, find a better one.
(AEC NYT 2017, Row: 16)

In the PC, nomination was also quite infrequent, however represented in more nomination types than in the AEC. This reflected its role in the assessment of social actors involved in a rape with a total of 14 instances of nomination in the PC (making up .1% of the PC on the basis of word count). The victim underwent nomination in the PC, including semiformal nomination 5 times (making up .04% of the entire PC), 5 instances of direct address (making up .04% of the entire PC), 3 instances of formal nomination (making up .03% of the PC) and 1 instance of informal nomination (making up .01% of the PC).

Figure 25 Nomination and direct address of the victim in the PC

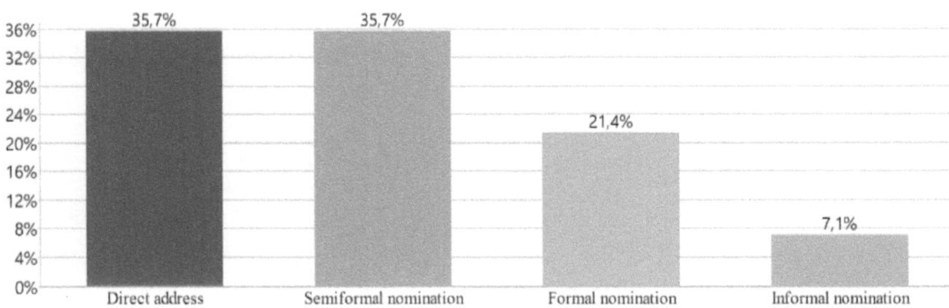

184) *Pani Aleksandro!* Prosze dziś wrócić do tej sprawy i do min. Ziobry. Wiem, że to szok i trauma ale jest szansa.
(PC PUD 2015, Row: 1)
[*Ms. Aleksandra!* Please get back to the case today and go to minister Ziobro. I know that it's a shock and also traumatic, but there is a chance]

185) *Pani Marto Pz*—proszę prędko udać się do psychiatry, może będzie potrafił pomóc. (PC NM 2019, Row: 4)
[*Ms. Marta Pz*—please go to a psychiatrist ASAP, maybe he or she can help.

186) Przecież jest *pani* mężatką, a nie jakąś żądną wrażeń dziewoją. (PC PUD 2015, Row: 10)
[But *you're (formal)* married, not some wench looking for a good time.]

Whereas the victim in the AEC hardly underwent any nomination, but for in one case, the nomination of the victim (including where she was addressed directly) was more common in the PC, however only slightly. The nomination of the victim in the PC demonstrates a tendency for the use of nomination in the case of semiformal nomination or informal nomination to denote instances of solidarity with or support for the victim. The direct address in the PC (cf. examples 184–186 above) was present in both negatively evaluating comments and supportive comments in the PC. In the AEC, it was the direct address of the victim (i.e., the reference to actors in the second person—*you*) that demonstrated more negative attitudes towards the victim, with these types of comments themselves thus being more direct in their meaning, since they are addressed to the person who was allegedly raped. This demonstrates a difference in the socio-semantic choices for the victim in the AEC and the PC, as well as the meanings that they might entail, although only visible in the few examples provided. Such representations of the victim do not overtly imply blame, but the strategy used shows that distance can either be made shorter or greater via nomination or direct reference.

Nomination and direct address of the offender

In the AEC, nomination took place for the offender 16 times (constituting .07% of the AEC), most of the instances of which fall under the category of formal nomination (with 14 counts, making up .06% of the AEC).

Figure 26 Nomination and direct address of the offender in the AEC

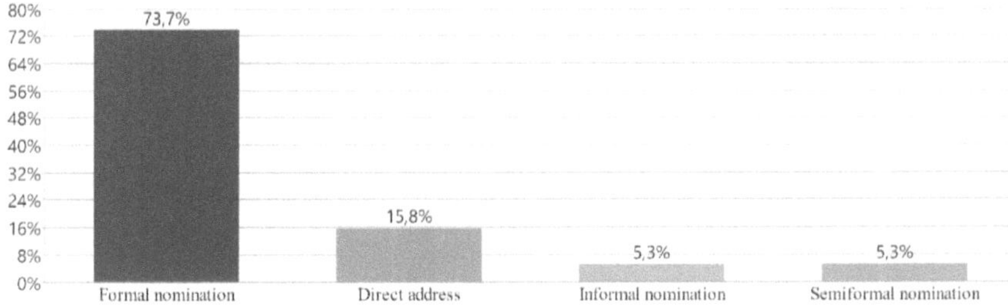

It is safe to state that in the AEC the nomination of the offender only took place with reference to high-profile cases, such as the Brock Turner case and the case of NBC's Matt Lauer (example 187) and Harvey Weinstein (example 188).

187) Of course it is possible *Lauer* is lying.
(AEC VTY 2019, Row: 31)

188) There are "multiple" women. It seems *Weinstein* meets the definition of sexual predator.
(AEC ABC 2020, Row: 18)

The one example of informal nomination occurred in the form of a direct address to the offender (Brock Turner) (example 189). The nomination of the offender in the AEC represents the acknowledgement of the offender's identity having been revealed. Direct address with *you* was also found in reference to the offender, however only 3 times (.01% of the AEC on the basis of word count).

189) Hey *@Brock*—you might have had a chance with the affluenza defense, then the state of the victim wouldn't matter. A blame-the-victim defense is going to earn you a long prison sentence, which I guarantee will not be pleasant for you.
(AEC PAW 2016, Row: 12)

190) I can consent to *you* today and say no tomorrow and you have no right to my body. I can say, "I want to have sex later" and then change my mind and say no, you have no right to my body.
(AEC ABC 2014, Row: 15)

In the PC, nomination of the offender only occurred in the vocative semiformal form of address of *panowie* ('gentlemen'/ 'guys') a total of 4 times (.04% of the PC on the basis of word count). There was one count of informal nomination in the form of *gwałciciel Mariusz* ('Mariusz the rapist').

Figure 27 Nomination and direct address of the offender in the PC

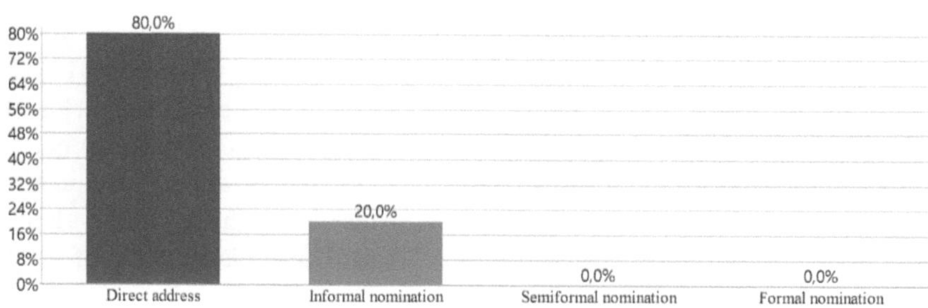

Direct address of the offender was most prevalent within the category of nomination for the offender in the PC, however in this case the honorific form of *panowie* was used, as shown in the examples below. This strategy is seen in both offender-supporting (examples 191 and 192) and offender-blaming comments (example 193).

191) stare bułgarskie przysłowie mówi: z panną ze sklepu rowerowego nie uprawiaj nigdy seksu grupowego. I tego należy się trzymać, *panowie*...
(PC GWyb 2019, Row: 6)
[An old Bulgarian proverb says: don't have group sex with the woman from the bike shop, and we should keep it that way, *gentlemen*.]

192) ...cóż *panowie*, nie chcecie babrać się w quanie nie właźcie do szamba.
(PC GWyb 2019, Row: 9)
[...there you have it *gentlemen*, if you don't want to get into shit, don't go into the septic tank.]

193) *Panowie* zacznijcie szanować kobiety, wszystkie, tak samo jak szanujecie siebie.
(PC WO 2015, Row: 5)
[*Guys*, start respecting women, all of them, the same way that you respect yourselves.]

This fact may be attributed to several factors. In the AEC, the rape cases discussed involved celebrities or the names of the offenders had been disclosed, making nomination a more readily available strategy, whereas in Polish the use of the offender's first name is not as common. The cultural differences that this presents demonstrate that in Polish culture, naming suspects in a crime in full is neither legal nor acceptable.

Such a lack of nomination also may be seen as significantly owing to the fact that various other representation strategies are put to use in the discourses about offenders in the context of sexual crime, such as the use of fiend naming, which adds to the direct negative evaluation of the perpetrator.

Categorization of actors in the AEC of digital comments

Categorization refers to the type of representation of social actors which occurs "in terms of identities and functions they share with others" (van Leeuwen, 2008: 40), characterized more narrowly as the subcategories of *identification* and *functionalization*. Identification was one of the most heavily populated categories in the analysis of social actors, and the frequency of gender reference was most common, where both the victim and the offender were concerned. The category of identification is made up of three subcategories: *classification identification*, *relational identification* and *physical identification*, whereas functionalization names the actors in reference to what they do. Functionalization occurred most commonly with reference to the roles of the actors in the crime in both the AEC and the PC, for the victim and offender.

Identification of the victim

The identification of the victim was accounted for by gender or age references to the victim, as well as those which represented the victims relations to other people (family or marital). Physical identification was considered any reference to the way that the victim looked or might have looked at the time of the crime.

In the American English corpus, the victim is represented through means of identification processes a total of 471 times (2.2% of the AEC). The leading identification category was, of course, that of *classification identification*, where gendered pronouns were considered, as well as reference to the age of the victim. Pronouns *she* and *her* were most frequent in the case of classifying features, and the age of the victim referred to a total of 37 times in the AEC (.1% of the AEC). A graph presenting a numerical comparison between the three different identification types has been presented below.

Figure 28 Identification of the victim in the AEC

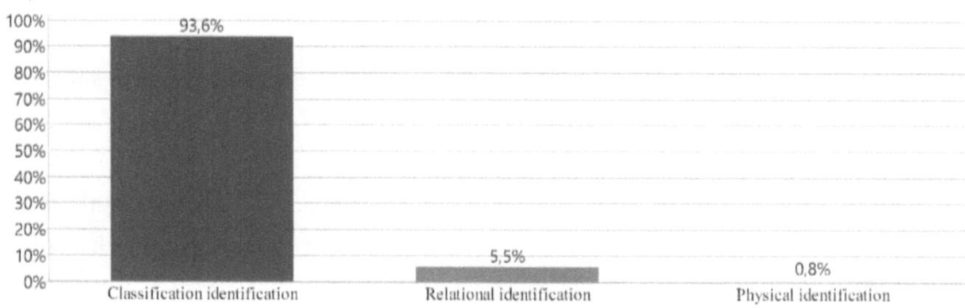

Due to the fact that gender falls into the category of classification identification, it is not surprising that the number is so high. The presence of gendered pronouns only reinforces the obvious nature of rape as a gendered crime, however there is nothing outstanding about this fact.

Figure 29 Classification identification of victim in the AEC

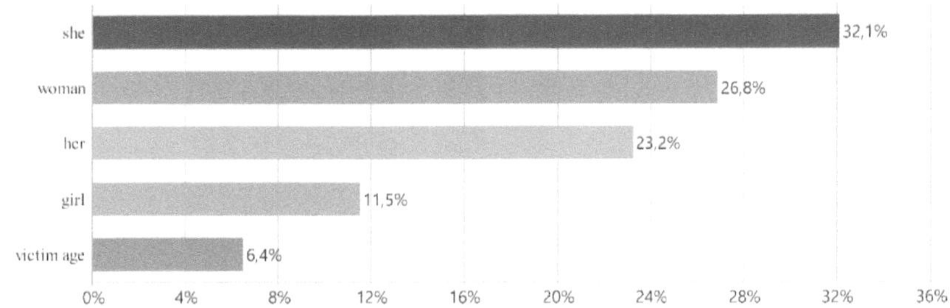

Several examples of classification identification have been provided. Examples 194 and 195 demonstrate how classification identification concerned just gender (i.e., through pronouns), and examples 191–193 show age identification for the victim.

194) *She* was unconscious, unconscious, unconscious.
(AEC PAW 2016, Row: 7)

195) The excuse is she shouldn't have taken her nasty butt out of the house, drunk, in the first place. Any *girl* or *woman* that puts themselves in that position, I don't feel sorry for them. Her own brother told her to stop texting him.
(AEC ABC 2014,| Row: 29)

196) *15 year old girls* are generally more mentally mature than 18 year old boys.....................I'd think she would have the upper hand.
(AEC ABC 2015b, Row: 42)

197) If someone almost 18 years old doesn't know its wrong to have sex with *a 14-year old*, get her hopelessly intoxicated and leave her out in 22 degree weather, more supervision isn't going to help.
(AEC ABC 2014, Row: 17)

Relational identification was also present in the AEC, with a total of 26 instances (5.5% of identification types for the victim—.1% of the whole AEC). The relational identification of the victim constructs her as a person who is a dependent in relation to other people (such as siblings or parents) and by way of discussing their role in the rape, or her role in juxtaposition to them as outside actors, the victim is foregrounded in the discourse. She may also be seen as a weak and vulnerable person in the position of family relationships (cf. examples 198–200).

198) A friend of mine was dating a girl in his teenage years and got her pregnant... he turned 18 before she did, and *her parents* immediately filed stat rape charges on him.
(AEC ABC 2015b, Row: 11)

199) *Her own brother* told her to stop texting him.
(AEC ABC 2014, Row: 29)

200) If at 14, this girl was sneaking out of the house, sending explicit texts, and binge drinking, her parents are failing her. And now because of *her parents*, the whole world knows who she is and what she's been up to.
(AEC ABC 2014, Row: 46)

Physical identification was quite rare in the AEC, as there were only 4 instances, with the majority indirectly referring to the appearance of the victim. Reference to the physical identification of the victim in the AEC usually had to do with the victim's appearance, adhering to common rape myths (cf. Chapter 2). This kind of reference draws on the common knowledge of rape myths (cf. examples 201 and 202 that girls dress older than they are, hence in a way that presents a kind of sex-appeal) or cultural knowledge about appearance (i.e., example 203 that a beauty queen presents a certain standard of beauty, thus focusing on her appearance in reference to her within the context of sexual crime).

201) Maybe he didn't know she was 14. At 13, I looked like I was 16. *The way they dress now, is a shame* and no one can tell their age.
(AEC ABC 2014, Row: 26)

202) The girl had been gone for 3 days. I couldn't see her face, but *he[r] body looked like she could have been 20.*
(AEC ABC 2014, Row: 26)

203) When Tyson raped that *beauty Queen,* and let's face it he lured her to his room under the guise of having a party, he got 6 years, he was 25 and had priors, Dershowitz got him a three year bid at Danburry Correctional. So, privilege and money can buy a light sentence. This kid had no priors and was a good student athlete...
(AEC NYT 2016, Row: 23)

The category of identification of the victim shows very little overt negative appraisement (with only 4 counts of negative evaluation of the victim with reference to physical appearance) (cf. examples 201 and 202),[81] yet it is worth noting

---

81 The reference to the appearance of the victim is automatically associated with the rape myths that claim that a woman who dresses a certain way (i.e., more provocatively) is asking to be raped.

that where identification was concerned with the victim, gender played the most significant role, which is to be expected in such an analysis on sex crimes. It should be stated, however, that the comments only reinforce the knowledge that we already have about rape, that women are the most common victims of sexual crime, and thus, generalizations are more easily made about the role that women play in whether or not they are subjected to rape or secondary victimization (discursive and otherwise). The gendered aspect of sexual crime, which is reflected in the rape myths that show gendered stereotypes of female and male sexuality, is discussed in later sections (cf. Chapter 2).

The victim also underwent identification processes in the PC. It comes as no surprise that classification identification was most prevalent in the corpus, with a count of 136 (84.5% of identification types for the victim in the PC, and 1.2% of the entire PC), relational identification at 22 counts (13.7% of identification processes for the victim in the PC, .1% of the entire PC), and physical identification at 2 counts (1.9%, and .01% of the PC) in the Polish corpus.

Similarly to the AEC, relational identification was any reference to the victim as having a relationship with someone else, be that a familial, amicable or matrimonial one. In the case of physical identification, which was found to be expressed the least number of times in the PC, reference to the appearance of the victim was present, either in the nominal position or as a predicative. It is worth noting that there is a much greater tendency in the AEC for classification identification (about 10%) than in the PC.

Figure 30 Identification of the victim in the PC

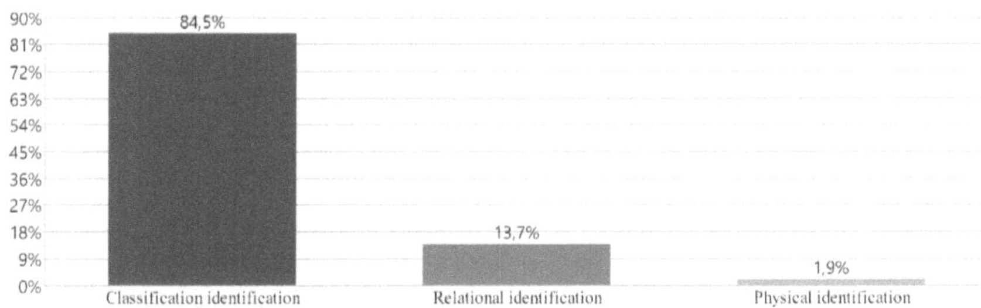

In the PC, gendered classification identification was included in all of the classification identification types,[82] making up 1.6% of the entire PC, with a total of

82 This is due to the fact that Polish inflects for gender (hence it was included in all classification identification categories in the PC).

181 instances, numerically. This means that all classification identification for the victim in the PC referred to her gender. This included words such as *kobieta* ('woman') (62 times—33.5% of the classification for the victim in the PC, .5% of the PC), gendered pronouns (*ona, jej, niej,* etc.) (54 times—29.2% of the classification identification for the victim in the PC, .5% of the PC), *pani* ('miss' or 'Mrs.') (34 times—18.4% of the classification identification for the victim in the PC, .3% of the PC), *dziewczyna* ('girl') (24 times—13%, .2% of the PC), *laska* ('chick') (5 times—2.7%, .04% of the PC), *panna* ('young single woman') (3 times—1.6% of classification identification of the victim in the PC and making up .03% of the PC), *panienka* ('young lady') (1 instance 0 .5%, making up .01% of the PC), *dziewoja* ('lassie'/'wench') (1 instance 0 .5%, .01% of the PC), *dziewczynka* ('little girl') (1 instance 0 .5%, .01% of the PC). The terms *panienka, dziewoja* and *dziewczynka* are all derogatory terms when used to refer to an adult woman, which, in reference to the rape victim, create a negative image of her, and act as victim-blaming strategies that do not directly state that she is at fault for the rape, but imply that she is. It is worth noting here that such instances were not found in the AEC, which highlights the fact that such derogatory naming was used as a means to negatively evaluate the victim implicitly of the Internet user making the comment in the PC. Cultural knowledge of the meanings of such forms is required to identify the indirect negative value of such an expression.

Other types of classification identification for the victim in the PC were not present, contrarily to the AEC, which contained reference to the age of the victim.

Figure 31 Classification identification of victim in the PC

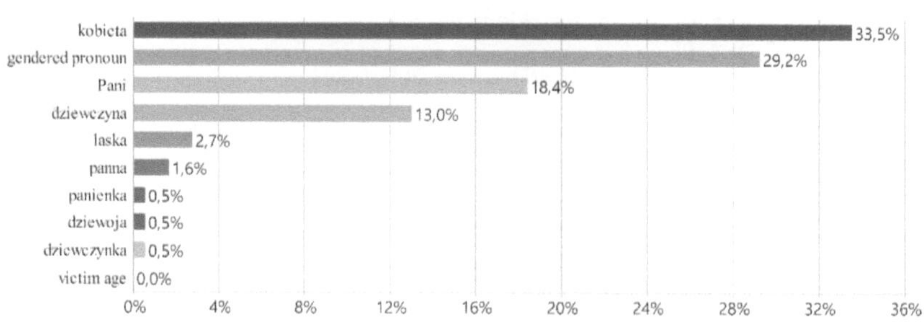

What can be seen in the classification identification of the victim in the PC are various biases based on the gender of the actor. The first three examples provided below exemplify the use of gender reference to the victim in the PC without the negative connotations.

204) A przeciez ta *pani* zna nazwiska tych zboczeńców i wie gdzie pracują, niech poda ich adresy bo oni pewnie gwałcą *kobiety* w karetce, powinna to zrobić dla innych *kobiet*, jestem zdziwiona ze do teraz tego nie zrobiła, powinna zrobić to już dawno.
(PC PUD 2015, Row 34)
[But that *lady* knows the last names of those perverts and she knows where they work. She should give out their addresses because they probably rape *women* in their ambulance. She should do it for other *women*. I'm surprised that she hasn't done that yet. She should have done it long ago.]

205) W Zambrowie chyba jakieś naiwne *dziewczyny*, czy CO.
(PC GWsp 2012b, Row: 1)
[Are there some naïve *girls* in Zambrów, or WHAT?]

206) no..w takim wieku to już powinna *pani* sama dawać....
(PC GWyb 2014, Row: 38)
[at that age, you should be putting out *yourself*]

There were 15 instances in which gender was used to negatively evaluate the victim, through the use of gendered nominalizations which are derogatory, given the context (.1% of the PC). Analyzing indirectness can help readers to discern that such evaluation is in fact negative, especially given that cultural knowledge allows one to discern that in the context of sexual crime, these terms carry negative and blaming meaning, which is why I have given examples separately from what was demonstrated above. Some of the examples have been provided above, and others have been given below to illustrate the issue more succinctly. Here it is clear that the use of the gendered nominalization for the victim may carry with it negative connotations, where in other cases the context itself lends to the negative nature of using a term (cf. examples 207–209).

207) O co tu walczyć, ta *dziewczynka* i tak ma wygrane.
(PC Wsp 2012a, Row: 6)
[What is there to fight for, that *little girl* has won either way.]

208) alkohol, zdemoralizowanie a finalem sa gwalty po pijaku!!!! a jak się wytrzezwieje, *panienka* poczula się zgwalcona!!!!
(PC GWsp 2019, Row: 3)
[alcohol, demoralization and the grand finale which is drunken rapes!!!! And when she sobers up, *the young lady* feels like she was raped!!!!]

209) Jakaś dziwna historia, nie wpuszcza się do pokoju obcego faceta. Przecież jest pani mężatką, a nie jakąś żądną wrażeń *dziewoją*.
(PC PUD 2015, Row: 10)
[This is a strange story. You don't let a stranger (man) into your room. I mean, you are a married woman and not a *wench* looking for thrills.]

210) Chyba *laska* lubi się zabawic.
(PC PUD 2017a, Row: 4)
[It seems like the *chick* likes to have fun.]

211) Na kilka sekund przed wytryskiem, *panna* mowi, żeby przestal.
(PC GWyb 2014, Row: 18)
[A few seconds before he ejaculates, the *lady* tells him to stop.]

The way that girls and women are referred to in Polish is culturally conditioned, with references bearing negative or positive connotations, some having evolved over time (Piechnik 2019). Where the victim is concerned, in the PC, this specific phenomenon is very relevant to the hypothesis, as it shows the way that socio-semiotic linguistic representations can take on evaluative meaning given the context in which they occur, both textual and social. Examples 207–211 demonstrate nouns which denote the victim, but carry negative semantic weight in the given context, drawing on negative connotations which surround the actor, whether in a sense of encumbering the actor with sexual association (example 209 and 210) or undermining her maturity (examples 207–209). By referring in such ways to the victim of a rape, she is placed in a position of being to blame for either her promiscuity, stupidity or immaturity, which has led to the rape, or her lying about the rape or getting away with dishonest behavior.

Relational identification occurred in the case of the victim especially where marital status was present, and reference to the woman as *żona* ('wife') occurred. Explicitly naming the victim *żona* occurred in discussions or mentions of marital rape, where the rights and responsibilities of married women were concerned (example 212) or in victim-supporting comments (1 instance—making up .004% of the PC; cf. example 213), as well as in the discussion of the role of a woman who was raped (cf. example 214).

212) niech ktoś zbada problem odmawiania seksu mężom przez *żony* z punktu widzenia mężów. Co ma zrobić żonaty facet któremu żona odmawia bo „nie lubi", „głowa boli" lub po prostu „nie bo nie" ?
(PC WO 2019, Row: 6)
[someone should research the problem of *wives* refusing to have sex with their husbands from the perspective of the husbands. What is a married man supposed to do when his wife refuses to have sex with him because "she doesn't like it", "her head aches" or simply because "no"?]

213) Średni polski policjant ma takie doświadczenia, że ojciec bił matkę, dziadek babkę, ksiądz go molestował, sąsiedzi i rodzina znęcali się nad zwierzętami, on sam wymusza seks na *żonie*, więc o co chodzi.
(PC GWyb 2014, Row: 24)
[The average Polish police officer has had the experience of having a wife-beating father, his grandfather beating his grandma, being molested by a priest, the neighbors and family torturing animals and he himself forces his *wife* to have sex with him, and so?]

214) matka, *żona* wdaje się w długoletni romans i to nie randkowy i nie patrzy na swoje dzieci, męża, a teraz cnotkę odgrywa, może to zgłoszenie które nastąpiło po x czasie od gwałtu to zemsta.
(PC MG 2019, Row: 14)
[a mother and *wife* gets into a long-standing affair and it isn't just dating, and she doesn't even look at her kids or husband. Now she's playing the virtuous one. Perhaps the claim of rape that she made after x (amount of) time was really just revenge.]

Through the analysis of implicit meanings, it can also be stated that relational identification of the victim was also more notably present in comments that were more supportive of the victim, in the Rimini case in Italy, where the victim was paired in the discourse with her husband, who according to many users, suffered equally at the hands of the rapists. This identification is more indirect, for its reference to the marital status of the 'woman' (*kobieta*) takes place through the reference to her husband, as juxtaposed in the same sentence with classification identification related to the victim's gender (example 215). This contributes to why there is a significantly greater share of such referential identification in the PC than in the AEC.

215) Trauma na całe życie. Współczuję *kobiecie*.... Chociaż *mąż* też pewnie nie jest w dobrym stanie skoro na to patrzył i będzie żył z myślą, że nie mógł jej pomóc... Niech znajdą tych s*******i i zrobią im to samo... Karma wraca
(PC PUD 2017a, Row: 94)
[Trauma for the rest of her life. I feel sorry for the *woman*.... Although *her husband* probably isn't in the best state either since he saw it and will have to live knowing that he couldn't help her... I hope they find the m*********rs and do the same to them...karma comes back.]

Physical identification only took place in more descriptive, and therefore predicative, discursive reference to the victim (in 2 instances in the PC—making up .01% of the PC on the basis of word count). This type of representation, due to its evaluative quality, was considered to be an example of physical identification, as it reflects well-known rape myths regarding the role of the appearance of the victim in a rape.

216) dobrze, że zapamiętała jego imię spośród tylu innych mężczyzn... kobieta zgwałcona- *pomalowane pazurki, krótka mini* ... Celebrytka
(PC PUD 2015, Row: 36)
[It's a good thing she remembered his name among all those other men... a woman raped—*painted nails, mini skirt* ... a celebrity]

217) Oczywiście, że możesz chodzić *w krótkiej kiecce*, a choćby *nago*. Ale licz się z tym, że nie wszyscy są poczytalni, i kogoś możesz *takim ubiorem* „zachęcić".
(PC WO 2015, Row: 3)
[Of course you can walk around *in a short dress*, or even *naked*. But reckon with the fact that not everyone is sane and you could "encourage" someone *dressed like that*.]

The reference to the victim's make-up and style of dress is an indirect allusion to the rape myth involving the role a of a woman's appearance in contributing to her rape. Such identification types also contribute to the analysis of the presence of rape myths in discourse on the subject of sexual crime expressed through means of implicit evaluation. The fact of focusing on the appearance of the rape victim belongs to the most common rape myths in American and Polish culture, demonstrating one such was in which rape victims are reproduced. This was infrequent in the PC, however.

Overall, in the AEC, there was less negative bias toward the victim within the category of identification than in the PC, where negative evaluation of the victim was seen on the level of the implication of the noun representations for the victim, where gender was concerned. The difference between the AEC and the PC demonstrates that the identification of the victim plays a role as a discourse strategy which expresses negative evaluation of the victim.

Identification of the offender

In the AEC, the offender(s) underwent identification processes a total of 387 times (1.8% of the AEC on the basis of word count), and similarly to the case of the victim(s), *classification identification* was most prevalent, especially where gendered pronouns are concerned (261 instances—88.7% of identification types for the offender in the AEC; making up 1.3% of the AEC).

Figure 32 Identification of the offender in the AEC

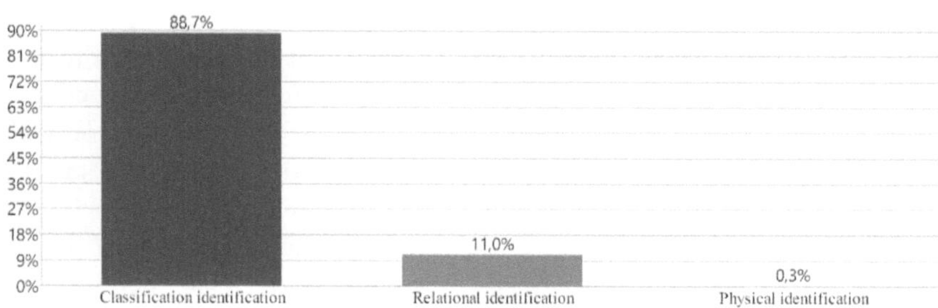

Classification identification of the offender in the AEC included most prevalently references to the gender of the offender, but also the classification category of age.

Figure 33 Classification identification of the offender in the AEC

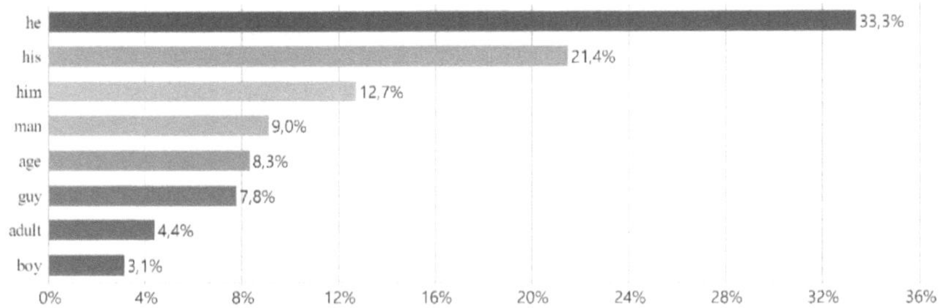

The word *man* in reference to the offender in the AEC was found 35 times (.2% of the AEC), the word *guy* was found 30 times in the AEC (.1% of the AEC), and *boy* 12 times (.06% of the AEC). Other classification types for the offender included those which also included age, such as *adult* (17 times in the AEC—.08% of the AEC) and reference to the age of the offender (32 times in the AEC—.1% of the AEC). The informality of the term *guy* in the AEC draws from the severity of the rape and additionally abstracts the actor even further from the crime, as such a reference to a person renders him more abstract (Sacks & Schegloff, 2007: 24).

Relational identification in the AEC was present in the case of Brock Turner, who was discursively constructed in the context of his father and known for having testified in defense of his son, who raped Chanel Miller in the formally known *The People of the State of California v. Brock Allen Turner* case of 2015. This kind of identification was expressed in the possessivation of the person of relation (i.e., *his father*) or in noun form (i.e., *son*). It is important to note here that such references are also considered relational identification throughout the analysis because of what the possessivation of the person in relation with the actor (here, the offender) represents on a cognitive level. The cognitive link made between the offender represented and the relationship had with the family member in question presents the actor as being in a close relationship with the person mention, hence the categorization of relational identification in such cases.

For example, associating the offender with his father (cf. example 218) creates the association of close familial ties, making the actor more sympathetic to the reader.

218) Clearly, *this young man and his father* are of the mindset that I've encountered a number of times in my life: a drunken woman is to blame for allowing herself to be vulnerable.
(AEC NYT 2016, Row: 5)

219) That's what bothers him after his *son* raped a woman like a piece of meat?
(AEC NYT 2016, Row: 20)

Although physical identification was also non-existent in the AEC (0%), the fact that there is a difference in such representation between the victim and the offender is indicative of the fact that in rape cases, the victim's appearance is viewed as more relevant to the subject than that of the offender, thus leading to its presentation as a cause for rape. Such discourse, although only several examples were found, leads to victim blaming, in that it abides by the rape myth that a woman's way of dressing can entice a man to rape her as a result of men's uncontrollable sexual urges.

In the PC, the offender underwent identification processes a total of 89 times, with classification identification for the offender in the PC taking place 81 times (.7% of the PC on the basis of word count), relational identification present 8 times for the offender in the PC (.09% of the PC) and physical identification present in only one instance in the PC.

Figure 34 Identification of the offender in the PC

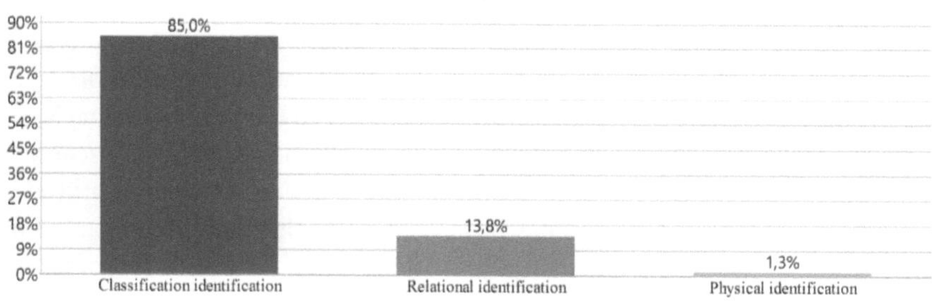

The classification identification of the offender in the PC was mostly made up of gendered representations, as can be seen in the graph presented below. In both the AEC and the PC, this is only significant in reiterating the gendered nature of the crime, however it does little to contribute to the victim blaming investigated in this study.

Figure 35 Classification identification of the offender in the PC

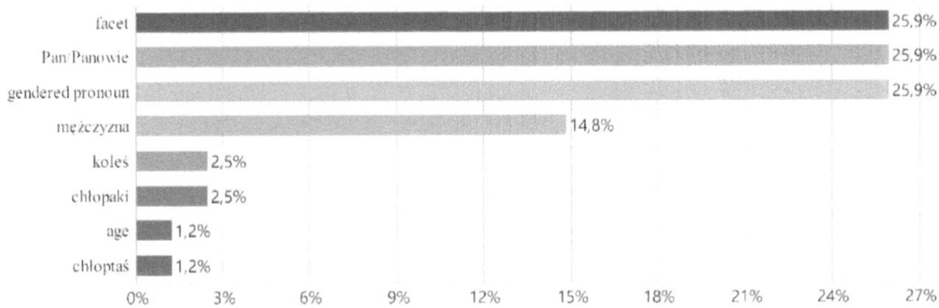

Here, only the semantic representations that referred strictly to the gender or age of the offender were considered, not those expressions additionally referring to the relational identification of the actor (i.e., *syn* 'son' or *ojciec* 'father'). The word *facet* ('guy') was present in the corpus 21 times (.2% of the PC on the basis of word count), *pan* or *panowie* ('Mr.' or 'Sir/Sirs') occurred 21 times (.2% of the PC), the gendered pronoun (*on, jego, jemu,* etc.) also occurred 21 times in the PC (.2% of the PC). The term *mężczyzna* ('man') was found in both the singular and plural forms 12 times (.1% of the PC). Both *koleś* ('guy') and *chłopaki* ('boys') occurred 2 times each and the diminutive form *chłoptaś* ('little boy'), as well as the age of the offender, occurred 1 time each (.01% of the PC). This is no surprise, since the gender of the actor is used to refer to him and his role in the crime discussed.

The use of the terms *facet, koleś* and *chłoptaś*, within the context of rape, bear more negative evaluative qualities of all of the classification identification types for the offender in the PC. This also bears similarity to the differences in classification identification of the victim between the AEC and the PC, as those terms that denote gender are used in the context of rape to denote negative attitudes towards the offender. On the whole, however, the classification identification of the offender in the PC presented nominalizations which did not, in and of themselves, place the actor in a negative light.

There were 8 instances of relational identification for the offender in the PC, as shown in the graph below (making up .09% of the PC on the basis of word count). What the relational identification of the offender does is place him in a position that allows him to be seen as an actor, with whom one can sympathize, making him seem less criminal and therefore abstracts him from the crime, as well as criminal status.

Figure 36 Relational identification of the offender in the PC

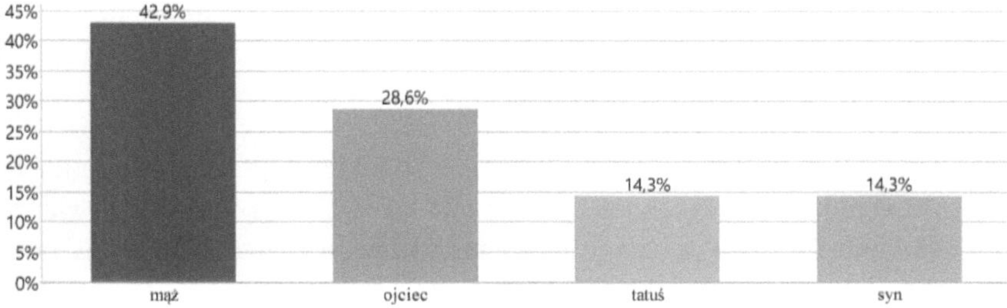

220) Co z tego, ze poszła z nimi do mieszkania, powinno się uczyć **swoich synów**, że kobiet się NIE GWAŁCI, a nie kobiety, że nie mogą nikomu zaufać.
(PC PUD 2017a, Row: 5)
[So what if she went to their apartment with them, people should teach **their sons** that you DON'T RAPE women and not women that they can't trust anybody.]

221) Jeśli gwałciciele nie mogą iść siedzieć, bo są przykładnymi **mężami** i **tatusiami** (żygać mi się chce), to niech za karę przez najbliższe powiedzmy 10 lat działają na rzecz ofiar gwałtu.
(PC WO 2015, Row: 1)
[If rapists can't be put behind bars because they're exemplary **husbands** and **daddies** (I want to barf), then they should at least have to work for the benefit of rape victims for the next ten years as punishment.]

The one instance of physical identification for the offender accounts for examples of both metonymy and metaphor in the references to the offender, to be explored later in this chapter.

222) przecież wiedziała w jakim celu idzie—oby kolesie w autobusie nie zmuszali ją siłą sama poszła coś ją zachęciło chyba *ICH NABRZMIAŁE ROZPORKI*, ale chyba mieli *k***ski za małe* i jednak zgłosiła to na policje bo straciła niepotrzebnie aż 10 dni
(PC PUD 2017a, Row: 50)
[she knew why she was going there—the guys on the bus didn't force her, she went herself and there was probably something that enticed her, probably *their bulging crotches*. But they probably ended up having *di**s that were too small* and she decided to report them to the police because she unnecessarily wasted 10 days]

All three types of identification were present in both the AEC and the PC for the offender, however they were not as prevalent as for the victim. Where the identification types were concerned, the PC references to the victim demonstrated the greatest tendencies towards victim blaming (.1% of the PC) via such strategies, whereas in the case of the offender, such strategies denoted negative sentiment through implication only 3 times (.02% of the PC).

Identification and the penal couple

The precipitation of victim blaming also comes about through the presumption of a dyadic relationship between the offender and the victim. In equating the victim and offender with a pair or couple, hence prescribing them a certain status, both the status of the crime and their mutual or equal roles in the rape's taking place are undermined,

The idea of the penal couple (Mendelsohn, 1963) has transformed into a construction of the male as an innocent victim of women's behavioral transgressions (Kitzinger, 2009; Stanko & Williams, 2009; Tabbert, 2016). Here, the penal couple is considered the paralleling of actors in a discursive sense, by placing them on the same level of retention of responsibility for the rape. This took place more frequently in the AEC than the PC, with differences in their form. The representation of the victim and offender as a pair was expressed through nominalization in the AEC, whereas in the PC representation was on a formal level (expressed grammatically through tense). The actors represented as the penal couple have been analyzed on the basis of sentence count, as the representations took place in some cases as phrases.

Table 25 Types of identification of the victim and offender together in the AEC

	Frequency	Percentage	Percentage in AEC
both	24	51.1%	2.9%
adults	8	17.0%	1%
teens	5	10.6%	.6%
men and women	4	8.5%	.5%
boys and girls	2	4.3%	.2%
folks	1	2.1%	.1%
sons and daughters	1	2.1%	.1%
both parties	1	2.1%	.1%
kids	1	2.1%	.1%
TOTAL	47	100%	5.8%

The penal couple relationship was expressed in the AEC through strategies of parallelism (i.e., placing the victim and the offender in the same clause, conjoined by *and*), as well as through plural nouns and pronouns denoting their existence as a pair.

223) She concludes that, because sexual relations took place, "I had been violated." No, you may not conclude that. *Both of you* could have drunkenly had sex willingly.
(AEC NYT 2017, Row 2)

224) How about teaching your *sons and daughters* NOT TO DRINK UNTIL BLOTTO? Getting drunk = gateway to bad sexual activity......stop getting drunk!!! Show some respect for yourself
(AEC NYT 2014, Row: 9)
225) I see no evidence of a crime......*two teens* willingly had sex
(AEC ABC 2015b, Row: 16)

In the PC, the penal couple was only present as a representation of the actors in 2 instances (.3% on the basis of sentence count). This was in reference to the rape as sexual intercourse in verb form, as well as in the pronominal indeterminate form *jedni i drudzy* ('one and the other'). In the PC, the representation of the actors as the penal couple also took place grammatically, where the subjects were not overtly mentioned.

226) facet idzie z dziewczyna do lozka. za jej zgoda, *zaczynaja się bzykac*. Na kilka sekund przed wytryskiem, panna mowi, żeby przestal.
(PC GWyb 2014, Row: 18)
[A guy goes to bed with a girl with her consent, *they start to fuck*. A few seconds before he's supposed to cum, the girl tells him to stop.]

227) Niestety czasem należy korzystać z głowy—*zarówno jedni i drudzy*.
(PC PUD 2017a, Row: 39)
[Unfortunately sometimes you have to use your head—*one and the other*.]

Such juxtaposition of the victim and offender as taking part in a criminal act together places the victim on a similar level to that of the person who raped her. This strategy demonstrates the tendency to, because rape is a sexual crime, obfuscate the severity of the crime, and make it so that the victim plays just as important a role in the crime as the person who perpetrated it.

The fact that the recognition of actors together, as the penal couple, took place significantly more often in the AEC than in the PC is also significant. This points towards a tendency for people in American culture rather than Polish culture to believe that the offender and victim function together in the context of sexual crime, rather than to acknowledge that they are individuals. This counts as victim blaming, because not only is the offender's agency in the crime highlighted, but also the victim's, associating her with the act of having been raped.

Functionalization of actors

In both the AEC and the PC, the victims and offenders underwent functionalization processes, whereby their actions or things they did were what they were named by, making for such representations that associated them with their actions. This category is important in analyzing the subject of crime and the discourses which concern the subject because it reveals the social mechanisms at work in constructing the significance of the actions that the actors are involved in, relative to the crime itself, as well as the social roles reflected in what they do.

Figure 37 Functionalization of actors AEC

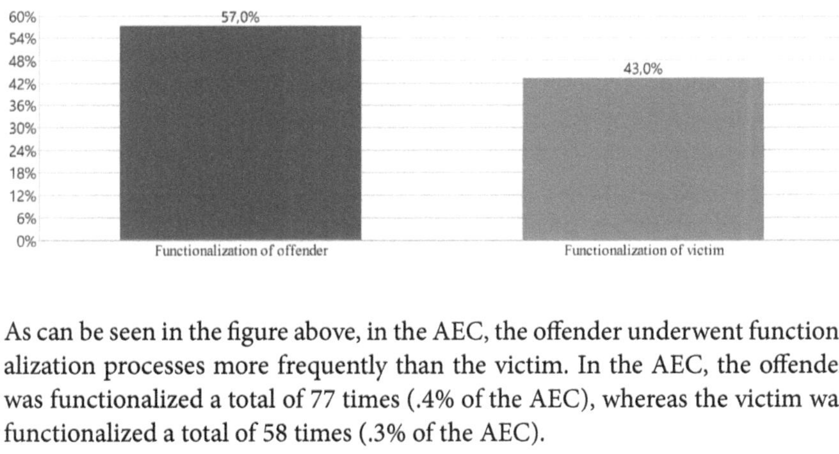

As can be seen in the figure above, in the AEC, the offender underwent functionalization processes more frequently than the victim. In the AEC, the offender was functionalized a total of 77 times (.4% of the AEC), whereas the victim was functionalized a total of 58 times (.3% of the AEC).

Figure 38 Functionalization of actors in the PC

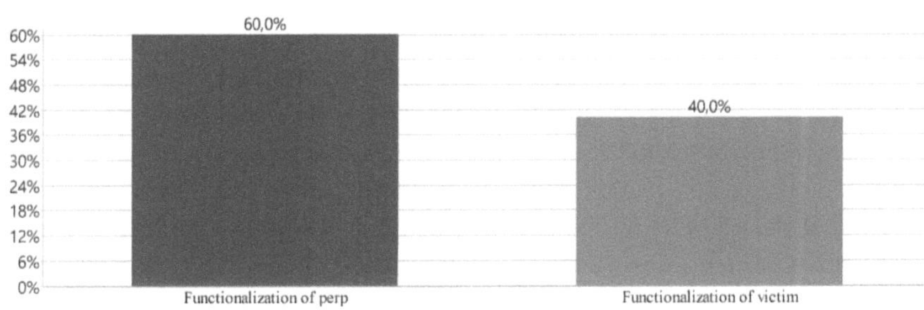

As can be seen in the figure above, in the PC, the offender also underwent functionalization processes more frequently than the victim. In the PC, the offender was functionalized a total of 72 times (.6% of the PC), whereas the victim was functionalized a total of 48 times (.4% of the PC). The functionalization of the victim in the PC focused on her role in the crime (i.e.,*ofiara*- 'victim', *pokrzywdzona*- 'harmed'), whereas there was more variation for the functionalization of the offender. The category of functionalization has been broken down and discussed even more in depth below.

Functionalization and the victim

The category of functionalization presented a large variety of types of representation of the victim. The graph presenting the functionalization types for the victim in the AEC shows that the term *victim* (50 times—89.3% of functionalization for the victim in the AEC, making up .2% of the entire AEC on the basis of word count) was used most often where functionalization is concerned. Other types of functionalization of the victim included her role in the educational system—*freshman* (2 times in the AEC—.01% of the AEC) or *student* (1 time in the AEC—.004% of the AEC). The terms *participant*, *survivor* and *beauty queen* were also found in the AEC (1 time each in the AEC—.004% of the AEC).

Figure 39 **F***unctionalization of the victim in the AEC*

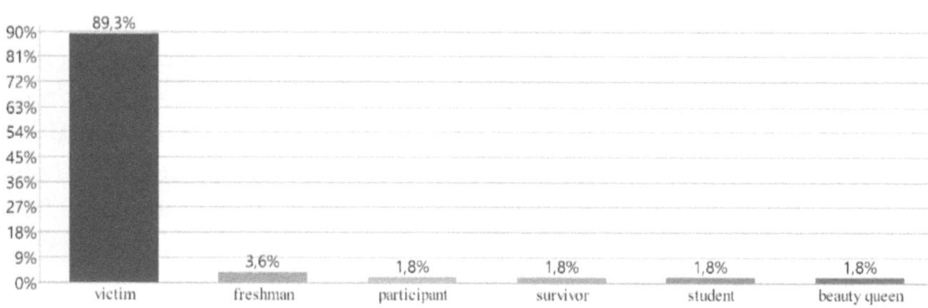

Some examples of functionalization of the victim in the AEC have been provided below.

228) In a recent case the *victim* did not need to name her rapist, the administration knew who she was talking about before she even began her story.
(AEC NYT 2014, Row: 10)

229) That doesn't sound like an *unwilling participant.*
(AEC ABC 2015b, Row: 44)

230) When Tyson raped that *beauty Queen*, and let's face it he lured her to his room under the guise of having a party, he got 6 years, he was 25 and had priors, Dershowitz got him a three year bid at Danburry Correctional. So, privilege and money can buy a light sentence. This kid had no priors and was a good student athlete...
(NYT 2016, Row 23)

Although such language may be thought to uphold the discourse of secondary victimization, one may also see it as reflective of the actual state of affairs in the case of rape. The term *victim* maintains a lower evaluative stance, and may demonstrate higher levels of solidarity with the victim of rape. Although there has been a drive to use the term *survivor* within feminist discourses, Brenner claims that "both terms are problematic in that each frames that role according to implicit assumptions about agency and harm" (2013: 505). What is visible from the tendencies in the corpus is that the term *victim* is still used more often than survivor in lay discourses about rape.

In the PC, functionalization of the victim took place almost as often as in the AEC, with a total of 42 counts altogether (making up .3% of the entire PC). The most common functionalization representation of the victim was that of *ofiara* ('victim'), similarly to the AEC. The word *ofiara* ('victim') was present total of 37 times in the PC (.2% of the PC), close to the frequency of the word *victim* in the AEC (.2%).The use of the term *ofiara* in Polish is the most frequent way of referring to a victim of a crime, including sexual crime. There is no equivalent in Polish to the term *survivor*, which has taken off in English discourses on sexual crime (Kościańska, 2019).

In the PC, other types of functionalization included the victimization of the actor, including *zgwałcona* ('raped'), *pijana* ('drunk') and *pokrzywdzona* ('harmed'), however all occurred at 1 counts each in the PC. There were also 2 instances of the occupation of the victim, only where the rape of the Elbląg translator was concerned, *tłumaczka* ('translator') (making up .02% of the entire PC).

Figure 40 Functionalization of the victim in the PC

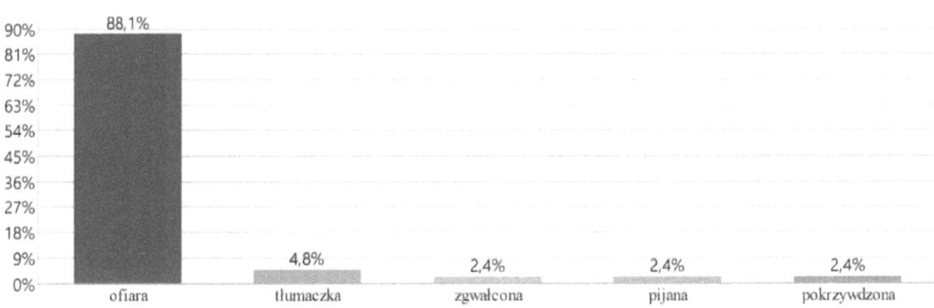

Some examples of the functionalization of the victim have been provided below.

231) *Ofiara* nie była posądzana o to że gwałt sprowokowała
(PC GWyb 2019, Row: 7)
[*The victim* was not accused of provoking the rape]

232) A ratownicy medyczni którzy podczas służbowego wyjazdu zgwałcili *tłumaczkę* dalej cieszą się nieposzlakowana opinia, co artykuł to teza.
(PC GWyb 2019, Row: 5)
[And the paramedics who raped *the translator* during their work trip still have a good reputation, every article has its own hypothesis.]

233) ***uderzać w interes *pokrzywdzonej*, ale i oskarżonych***
(PC GWyb 2018, Row: 4)
[***strike at the interest of the *victim*, but also the accused***]

The functionalization of the victim in both the AEC and the PC demonstrates a high tendency to name the actor *victim* or *ofiara* ('victim'). Such naming reflects the role of the actor in the crime and also recognizes her status as a victim. Such naming does not reflect victim blaming, but when drawn against the naming of the offender, differences can be noted. Other types of functionalization of the victim also showed little bias. This is of interest, because the high number of victim-blaming comments in the entire corpus (37% of comments in the AEC and 37.3% of comments in the PC) demonstrate that victim blaming took place through other strategies, including other ways of referring to the actors (i.e., through naming or backgrounding), the rape itself or through certain structural processes (cf. Chapter 6).

Functionalization and the offender

The functionalization of the offender in the AEC occurred equally as frequently as the victim in both of the corpora, highlighting a difference in the focal points for the victim and offender in a rape. In the PC, functionalization for the offender took place more often.

In the case of the offender in the AEC, functionalization was present a total of 73 times (.3% of the AEC). The most frequent occurrence of functionalization representation type for the offender was the term *rapist* (34 counts, making up .2% of the AEC), with the second leading category being that of the occupation of the offender, however occurring significantly less (16 times in the AEC, making up .07% of the AEC). Other functionalization types were reflective of the criminal status of the offender, including nominal representations such as *predator* (12 times, making up .05% of the AEC on the basis of word count), *accused* (10 times, making up .04% of the AEC), *offender* (8 times, making up .03% of the AEC), and *criminal* (3 times, making up .01% of the AEC).

Figure 41 Functionalization of the offender in the AEC

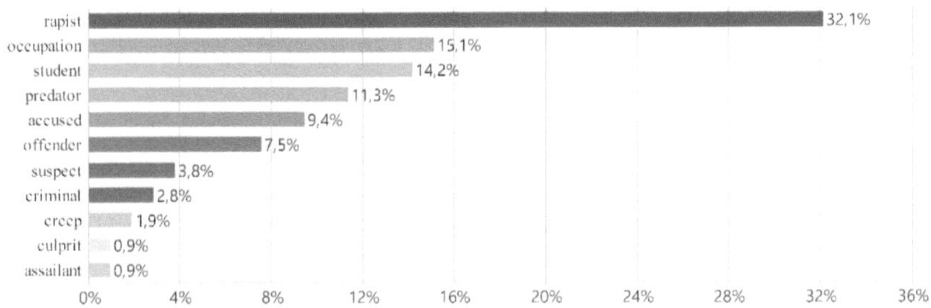

What is significant here is that most of the functionalization representations for the offender are reflective of participation in a criminal act, reflecting attitudes that do not support or positively assess the actor. A crime-reflective semantic state of the expressions does little to alleviate the blame from the victim, however, as seen in the examples below.

> 234) "This would not have happened" if *the rapist* had not chosen to forcibly attack someone and commit an assault on their person.
> (AEC NYT 2017, Row: 9)

> 235) There are "multiple: women. It seems Weinstein meets the definition of *sexual predator*.
> (AEC ABC 2020, Row: 18)

> 236) "Predatory *offender*" needs to be permanently on all his resumes for every job application. When he gets a passport, the picture should have "predatory *offender*" stamped across the front. The name Brock Allen Turner is now and forever synonymous with "predatory *offender*".
> (AEC NYT 2016, Row: 21)

Although such language reinforces the status of the offender as a criminal, one can observe that, as in example 235, the crime-reflective naming is used in juxtaposition with sarcastic language about the victim.

There were other functionalization types for the offender, which were also representative of negative evaluation.

> 237) Women who want to be with these *creeps* to enhance their career are just as bad.
> (AEC VTY 2019, Row: 19)

The fact that functionalization of the offender indicates for the most part his (or their) role in the crime presents attitudes that acknowledge the criminal nature of the sex crime. This representation, as opposed to the way that the functionalization of the victim is shown in the corpus, demonstrates negative evaluation of the actor in the AEC. The PC showed similar results where the offender was concerned.

In the PC, functionalization for the offender took place a total of 78 times (.7% of the PC). The most frequent occurrence of functionalization of the offender was the term *gwałciciel* ('rapist') (29 counts, making up .2% of the PC). Other functionalization types were, equally to the AEC, reflective of the criminal status of the offender, including *sprawca* ('offender') (10 times, making up .09% of the PC on the basis of word count), *oskarżony* ('accused') (5 times, making up .04% of the PC), *oprawca* ('criminal'), *przestępca* ('criminal') and *napastnik* ('attacker') (found 4 times each, making up .03% of the PC each), *zbrodniarz* ('criminal') (3 times, making up .03% of the PC), *zwyrodnialec* ('villain') (2 times, making up .02% of the PC), *winny* ('guilty') and *recydywista* ('recidivist') were each found in the PC at 1 count (making up .008% of the PC). Other functionalization types included the occupation of the offender (7 times in the PC, making up .06% of the PC).

Figure 42 Functionalization of the offender in the PC

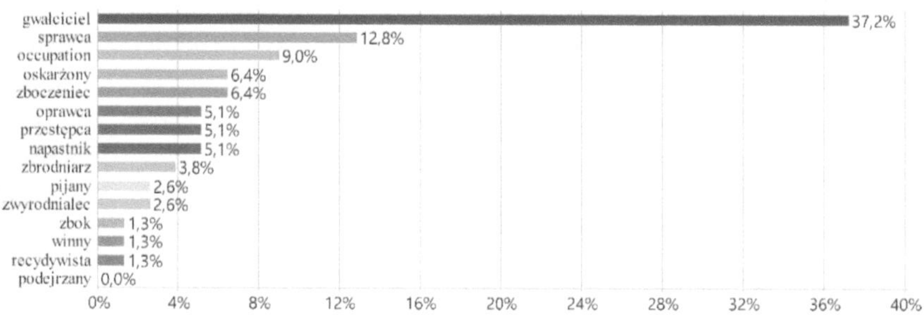

238) Oburzające jest nie tylko to co zrobił *ten gwałciciel*, ale też brak mądrej reakcji otoczenia, a w końcu wyrok sądu dający do zrozumienia, że tak naprawdę to nie ma sprawy. (PC PUD 2015, Row: 2)
[Not only what *that rapist* did is appalling, but also the lack of a smart reaction on the part of the community, and finally the court's sentence which has us all know that nothing really happened.]

239) ***uderzać w interes pokrzywdzonej, ale i *oskarżonych****
(PC GWyb 2018, 4)
[***target the victim, but also *the accused****]

240) Znam *ratowników*. Prawie wszyscy ćpają!
(Pudelek 2015, Row 32)
[I know *paramedics*. Almost all of them do drugs!]

There were other functionalization types for the offender, which were also representative of negative evaluation. In the following example, the juxtaposition of a thief, which culturally carries negative connotations, is placed alongside a rapist. This example, interestingly, negates the negative status of the rape and inversely places blame on the victim, although the lexical clues refer to the criminal status of the act. On the other hand, what arises from this comment is that apparently perverted people—likely, men—who commit the most atrocious kinds of rape.

241) mówi się że okazja czyni *złodzieja* moim zdaniem tak samo jest z gwałtem—okazja czyni gwałciciela, nie mówię tu o *zbokach* którzy i bez okazji potrafią napaść i zgwałcić
(PC PUD 2015, Row: 16)
[They say that the opportunity makes someone a *thief* and in my opinion it's the same with rape—opportunity makes the rapist. I'm not talking about *perverts* who can attack and rape without pretense.]

Overall, both the AEC and the PC showed that the functionalization of the offender reflected the criminal status of the offender, however functionalization of the offender was more prevalent in the PC than in the AEC. This demonstrates a greater tendency in Polish online discourse to associate the offender of a rape with what he does. This type of naming in itself is reflective of negative appraisement, as it represents an overt recognition of the criminal nature of the act carried out by the actor(s). This difference shows that in the functionalization of actors involved in sexual crime, less negative appraisement is geared towards the victim of the crime than the offender.

Backgrounding and indetermination of actors

Although the actors are never completely excluded in the presented corpus, the sub-category to that of exclusion in van Leeuwen's (1995: 39–40) categorization, that of *backgrounding*, in which the actor is known by the reader or hearer to be present because he or she was mentioned elsewhere in the discursive context (here, in headline or article) has been found in sentences which discuss the rape and none of the actors or only one of them.[83] Within the category of background-

83 Here it is important to reiterate that in the case of rape, the backgrounding of actors may occur when the presence of an actor, as well as his or her (active) role in the crime, is partially erased by not explicitly mentioning him. This may occur through

ing, indetermination has been placed first in the analysis of the exclusion of social actors, because by using indeterminate language to signify an actor, the actor is backgrounded to the extent that he or she becomes less concrete and less visible in the discourse. The actor is still mentioned, albeit in vague terms, whereas in backgrounding, the presence of the actor is only known through inference, based on the context or knowledge of the subject (i.e., which actors are usually involved in a rape). The backgrounding of actors may take place for one of the actors (i.e., the victim or offender is backgrounded and one actor is explicitly mentioned in the context) or for both of the actors (where none of the actors are mentioned, but just the act itself).

Indetermination of actors

Although indetermination of the actors did not occur as often as the other categories of inclusion (presented in the analysis above), there were enough examples for the process to be considered significant to the work. The indetermination of actors is an example of how indirect evaluation can take place on a socio-semantic level as a result of the symbolic associations made when confronted with such discourses.

Indetermination is a discursive process or strategy by which an actor or actors are somewhat erased from the discourse, or at least their identity muddled to the extent that they are made very vague. In his classification, van Leeuwen (2008: 39) states that indetermination is "typically realized by indefinite pronouns ('somebody,' 'someone,' 'some,' 'some people') used in nominal function." Because the strategy of indetermination "*anonymizes* a social actor" (*ibid.*: 40), I have also added some aspects, such as representations of actors through the use of percentages or other quantifying expressions, to the category of indetermination for the actors. This is because in the corpus presented, such representations refer to generalizations of statistics rather than acute estimates that would accurately represent the actors or specify them.[84]

---

the presence of process nouns in a sentence where the person "doing" that action is not mentioned anywhere in the immediate context of the act.

84 In his classification of indetermination, van Leeuwen (*ibid.*) considers percentages and numbers to be aspects which specify the actors in question, however due to the nature of the digital comments as belonging to informal (lay-person) discourses, I consider them to be indeterminate in what they do for the representations because they make reference to broad statistics and sweeping generalizations.

In the AEC of digital comments, indetermination was present in the representations of both the victim and the offender. The victim underwent indetermination 20 times (50% of indetermination of actors in the AEC—.09% of the entire AEC), and the offender also underwent indetermination processes 20 times (50% of the indetermination of actors in the AEC—.09% of the AEC). Although in relation to the entire corpus, the number is seemingly insignificant, the subject of the indetermination of actors within the context of victim blaming anonymizes both the victim and the offender, however with different consequences for each. Although such representations do not directly relate to victim blaming, they do have the effect of watering down the victim in the discourse to indeterminate actors, taking away any specific reference which might help to place more concrete focus on the social problem on the whole.

Figure 43 Indetermination of victim and offender in the AEC

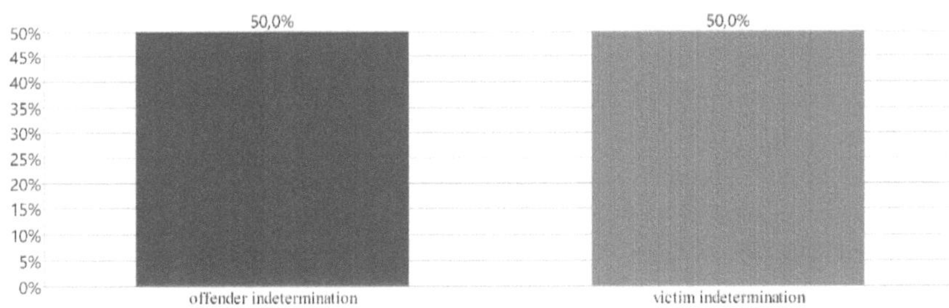

The examples below (examples 242 and 243) show that the victim is abstracted when referred to via indetermination. As mentioned above, this type of reference to the victim detracts from the gendered nature of sexual crime, further muddling the gravity of rape as a social problem which mostly affects women (cf. Introduction).

242) "This would not have happened" if the rapist had not chosen to forcibly attack *someone* and commit an assault on their person.
(AEC NYT 2017, Row: 9)

243) If she had not been drunk, he would have raped *someone else*.
(AEC MN 2016, Row: 14)

The offender was also referred to indeterminately in the AEC. Some examples have been provided. In example 240, the use of *someone* as an indeterminate noun and the use of *they* as an indeterminate pronoun render the offender more abstract, taking away from the gendered nature of sexual crime and also creating an air of anonymity for the actor (here, the offender). This example is also a good demonstration of how analogies are used in discourse about rape to indirectly blame an actor (in this case, the offender). Examples have been provided below of indetermination types for the offender where the actor is discursively abstracted.

244) And if you get drunk and *someone* takes your wallet, watch, etc., *they* should not be punished b/c you got drunk and so exposed yourself to the criminal behavior of the person who took your wallet.
(AEC NYT 2016, Row: 17)

245) It isn't good for **anyone** to drink to excess. Hello! As in, tell your sons to not go out binge drinking with a girl. And tell them especially to keep it in their pants.
(AEC ABC 2015a, Row: 11)

246) Yeah, maybe if you ran into *that person* again (while trying your best to avoid him) and you felt that you needed to put on a good face and smile because you're in fear, maybe I can believe that. But willingly contacting *the person* again for any reason is suspect.
(AEC ABC 2020, Row 7)

247) A child endears [sic] rape and incest for years because they have nowhere to turn, they usually live with **the person** and are scared to tell, this was not the case here.
(AEC VTY 2019, Row 5)

Other kinds of indetermination of the offender were quantifying expressions, which may be either concrete or abstract, in this case as a *percentage* or as a *minority*. See the examples below.

248) Given that 20% of college women are raped, that must mean that *these 3%* are committing multiple rapes.
(AEC NYT 2014, row 10)

249) I applaud the effort to teach young men to police their behavior and that of their friends. The real change that must occur is to punish rapists severely. This will identify and eliminate the predators, and prevent them from being shuttled off to some other school where they are once again free to target and rape innocent young women. If 3% of men are committing 95% of rapes, targeting this *small vicious minority* would dramatically reduce the incidence of rape.
(AEC NYT 2014, Row 10)

The indetermination of actors, although not majorly significant in the corpus as far as frequency is concerned, does demonstrate how generalizations are made in the discursive sense and how such generalizations can make a crime like rape seem suppositional. The question of this strategy is meaningful in discourses on sexual crime, because it gives sweeping and imprecise generalizations of actors, creating logical fallacies that take place on a cognitive level. The examples given above show that an indeterminate pronoun of *someone* or the use of the indeterminate noun *person*, which in turn abstracts the offender both in terms of who an offender could be, as well as his relation to the crime. In the AEC, one can observe that when this is done with reference to the offender, he is not specified or referred to as an individual, but dehumanized through abstracting him or using vague language to refer to him.

Indetermination manifested differently in the PC than it did in the AEC.

Figure 44 Indetermination of victim and offender in the PC

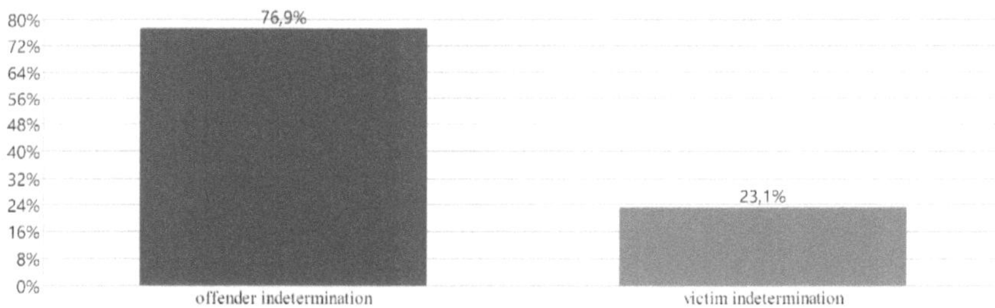

Indetermination in the PC took place in the form of the impersonal pronoun *kto* ('who'), and percentile representation. Indetermination as a representation of the victim took place in the Polish corpus a total of 3 times (0.02%). Indetermination of the offender took place a total of 10 times (0.08%) in the PC. The following examples refer to the victim in the PC (examples 250 and 251). The mechanism of reference is similar to that of the AEC, however takes place less frequently in the PC overall and significantly less where the victim was concerned.

250) nie twierdzę że nie, ale jest tez *spory procent kobiet* które tylko poprzez płacz i sciemę rujnują komuś życie
(PC NM 2018, Row: 10)
[I'm not saying it didn't happen, but there is also *a large percentage* of women who ruin someone's life just by crying and lying]

251) Ale *kto normalny* idzie na imprezę z nieznajomymi.
(PC PUD 2017a, Row: 2)
[But *what kind of a normal person* goes to a party with strangers.]

In the PC, the indetermination for the offender was presented by means of pronominal reference. What the indetermination of the offender in the PC shows is that the offender is abstracted through such discursive representation. Although the form of *ktoś* ('someone') is formally masculine in Polish, the meaning erases the gender of the rapist, abstracting the actor even further from the gendered nature of sexual crime.

252) *Ktoś* tak okrutny gwałcił nie raz i jeszcze zgwałci.
(PC PUD 2015, Row: 41)
[*Someone* that cruel has raped more than once and will rape again]

253) też kiedyś zostałam skrzywdzona, pojechałam na policję (milicję) złożyłam zeznanie, powiedziałam *kto* to zrobił, a oni zadzwonili do mojej pracy (to był *ktos* z tej samej firmy) do kadr żeby porozmawiali o tym
(PC NM 2018, Row: 9)
[I was also hurt once and I went to the police (the militia) to file a report, I told them *who* had done it and they called my workplace (it had been *someone* from the same company) in order to talk to the staff about it]

The reference to offenders in the PC was an example of direct offender blaming evaluation in the comments, which pointed to the inhumanity of committing a crime such as rape.

254) Bestie a *nie ludzie*, zapici, niedouczeni, prymitywni aż do bólu
(PC GWyb 2018, Row: 6)
[Beasts, *not humans*, drunk, uneducated, primitive to the bone]

These processes of indetermination also contribute to the backgrounding of actors, in that they do not specify any particular perpetrator and do not focus on the gender of the actor, which is of great import in the case of sexual crime (cf. Introduction and Chapter 2).

Backgrounding of actors

Backgrounding may also take place in the partial erasure of the actors, where one infers from the context the role or presence of the actor, thus making it another indirect strategy of evaluation. The question of the antecedent[85] is of importance in considering the backgrounding of actors, especially concerning the context in which the discourse is found (the physical context of digital comments accompanying an article on rape and the social context of larger discourses on rape as a social issue). Having this in mind, users already have some idea of the actors

85 The knowledge that the problem of rape is being discussed and all of the knowledge surrounding rape that is collected by individuals through socialization processes, including the representations of rape in the media and in discussions on the subject, as well as the social taboo that has been discussed in Chapters 2 and 3.

involved in a rape and may deliberately or non-deliberately exclude the actors from the clause referring to the act (of rape) itself.

Both the backgrounding of the victim and the backgrounding of the perpetrator have been investigated where the rape is concerned. The offender is backgrounded about twice as many times (126—66.7% of the backgrounding of actors; 15.6% of the AEC on the basis of sentence count) as the victim (63 times—33.3% of backgrounding; 7.8% of the corpus) in the AEC. It is important to bear in mind that the backgrounding of actors leaves out the actors in discourse by not specifically naming them or referring to them. In this case, any comments or sentences in which the rape was referred to as an act were considered, where either one or both of the actors were excluded from the sentence context of rape.

The victim was not backgrounded as often as the offender, meaning that she was mentioned overtly in the context of the rape more often than the offender was. This makes for a significant difference between such representations of the victim and the offender, as the backgrounding of the offender draws away from his role in the crime, since it is not stated in juxtaposition to it (i.e., in the same sentence context).

Figure 45 Backgrounding of the victim and offender in the AEC

Backgrounding was considered in the analysis where clauses in which nominalization of the rape as a crime occurred. The victim was backgrounded only in those sentences which excluded both of the actors (cf. examples 255–7).

The following examples show how the foregrounding of the crime backgrounds both the victim and the offender in the first sentence and backgrounds the offender in the next sentence, where the victim is mentioned (*women*). The comments in which both of the actors were backgrounded and the knowledge of their presence in the crime could be drawn from the surrounding social knowledge about rape as a crime. This strategy in discourse is particularly powerful in that it does not mention either of the actors involved in the crime, thus veering the focus towards those actors who are mentioned in such a context or abstracting both actors by not referring to either of them.

255) I dont think *the rape* was false. Just not enough evidence to prosecute. *There was a video of it*, which was destroyed.
(AEC ABC 2014, Row: 42)

256) Yes. Because *duration of the assault* is such an important criterion?
(AEC NYT 2016, Row: 26)

257) Many of *these attacks* happen in dorms.
(AEC NYT 2017, Row: 18)

The next two examples show comments that abstract the offender (example 258 and example 259) or both of the actors (example 260) from the crime. This demonstrates the way that the offender can evade any type of mention in lay discourses on rape, thus reinforcing that the attention is brought only to the victim's role in the crime.

258) "*20 minutes of action*" fueled by alcohol & promiscuity? *Rape* is not about promiscuity, but about *violence towards women.*
(AEC NYT 2016, Row: 44)

259) *What sexual assault??* Two teens choosing to have sex is perfectly natural. And I am *woman* who survived and got away from *an actual rape attack.*
(AEC ABC 2015b, Row: 25)

260) The real question is why do you assume *rape*? Why do you assume *something awful happened*? Is it because our society shames women (wrongfully) for having drunken **sex**? Enough with *the witch hunts.*
(AEC NYT 2017, Row: 2)

It is significant that wherever backgrounding occurs in the AEC, the perpetrator is absent from the sentence or clause discussing the crime in which he is involved.

The backgrounding of the actors was also present in the PC. Similarly to the AEC, the offender was backgrounded more often than the victim. The offender underwent backgrounding 74 times (59.7% of backgrounding processes for the actors in the PC and 10.3% of the PC on the basis of sentence count in the PC), whereas the victim underwent backgrounding 50 times (40.3% of backgrounding processes for the actors in the PC and 7% of the PC on the basis of sentence count) where both of the actors were backgrounded.

Figure 46 Backgrounding of the victim and offender in the PC

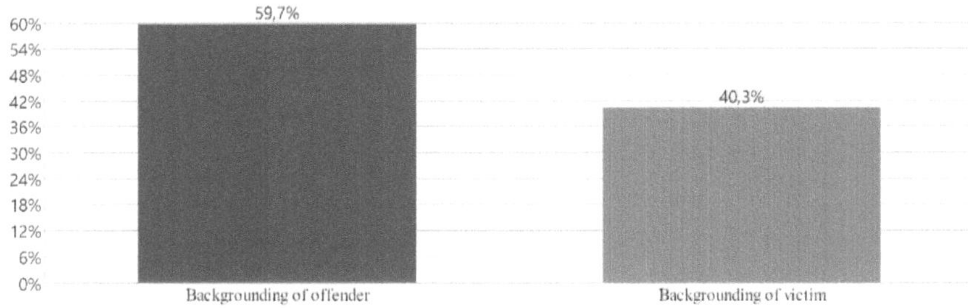

261) Cały budynek ludzi, kobieta wybiegła z pokoju krzycząc o pomoc a i tak *doszło do kolejnego gwałtu*
(PC WO 2015, Row: 4)
[A whole building full of people, the woman ran out of the room screaming for help but it led to *rape* anyway]

262) No i właśnie stąd są *te gwałty*, przemoc w rodzinie, czyny kazirodcze, rozwody i procesy o alimenty, napady na tle seksualnym, odrażające czyny pedofilskie, fetyszyzm, ocieractwo w środkach publicznego transportu, czy dość częste przypadki ekshibicjonizmu lub onanizmu na przystankach autobusowych w naszych miastach.
(PC GWsp 2019, Row: 24)
[And that's where *those rapes* come from, and the violence in the family, incestuous acts, divorce and the trials for child support, sexual assault, disgusting pedophilic acts, fetishism, rubbing people up on public transport or the all too often cases of exhibitionism or public masturbation at bus stops in our cities.]

263) Oj tam oj tam zaraz tam *gwałt*.
(PC PUD 2015, Row: 30)
[Yeah yeah and it's gonna be called *rape* right away]

In cases where the offender was backgrounded, the victim was also present in the context, comparably to the AEC. Just as was stated in the analysis of the American discourse, the backgrounding in the Polish discourse draws attention to the role of the victim in the rape, erasing the offender from the discursive context. This is especially visible in examples 264 and 265, where the victim herself is actively focused on and portrayed as the main actor in the rape.

264) Słyszałam że *gwałtu* nie było, sama *wlazła mu do łóżka*, ale był tam kuzyn który mógł wszystko mężowi wygadać więc wymyśliła *gwałt*
(PC PUD 2015, Row: 26)

[I heard that there was no *rape* and that *she climbed into his bed*, but a cousin was there and he could have told her husband everything and so she came up with *rape*]

265) alkohol, zdemoralizowanie a finalem sa *gwalty* po pijaku!!!! a jak sie wytrzezwieje, panienka poczula sie zgwalcona!!!
(PC GWsp 2019, Row: 3)
[alcohol and demoralization and the finale is *rape* while drunk!!!! And when she gets sober the young lady feels as if she was raped]

266) Ej ale dlaczego *ta kobieta* nie uciekła gdzieś na recepcję tego hotelu czy na ulice nawet. *Powinna uciec* i wezwać pomoc. Skoro to b****o *jej nie pomogło*, to uciekac stamtąd gdziekolwiek i dzwonić po pomoc. *Kobiety* nie dajcie się.
(PC PUD 2015, Row: 47)
[Hey, why did *that woman* not run to the hotel reception or onto the street. *She should have run* and call for help. Since the *** *didn't help her, she should* run away from there to anywhere and call for help. *Ladies*, don't give up.]

The backgrounding of the actors involved in rape in the PC is similar to that of the AEC, abstracting the offender, if not both the victim and the offender, from the event. This type of discourse in the PC leads to victim blaming because its exclusion of actors encompasses a tone of irony not as visible in the American discourse.

The backgrounding of actors is important to consider in the analysis of the representation of rape, for it does not foreground the actors, but highlights the criminal act itself. Additionally, the agency that an actor has in relation to a given activity is left out of those sentences and clauses which exclusively refer to the crime (van Leeuwen, 1996: 39). By omitting actors from the sentences which related directly to the act of rape itself (or a man raping a woman), the responsibility of the offender is depersonalized and obfuscated, and the surrounding context is diluted and hence made more abstract.

Appraisement of social actors

The category of the appraisement of the social actors makes up another major aspect of the analysis of the representation of social actors used to describe actors "when they are referred to in terms which evaluate them, as good or bad, loved or hated, admired or pitied" (van Leeuwen, 2004: 58). As van Leeuwen (*ibid.*: 59) states in his explanation of the categorization, the appraisement of actors is a broader category which can encompass nominal, adjectival or predicative representations, including those that are metaphorical, or *symbolic* in his terms. Some examples of nominal appraisement as taken from van Leeuwen (ibid) include "'the darling', 'the bastard', 'the wretch'—or 'thugs'".

Within the category of the appraisement of social actors, namely where symbolic representations are concerned (cf. Chapter 1), I have chosen to focus specifically on the subjects of *metaphor* and *metonymy* for the reason that they present a type of implication important to the subject of the evaluation of actors through the ways they are represented in discourse. As Lakoff and Johnson (2003: 36) state, "metaphor and metonymy are different kinds of processes." Metaphor, the analysis of which has garnered much more interest in the field than its poor sister, metonymy, is a way of conceiving of one thing in terms of another. Its primary function is that of aiding human comprehension through comparison. Metonymy, however, has primarily a referential function, that is, it allows us to use one entity to stand for another. The type analyzed in this work is the case of the metonymy THE PART FOR THE WHOLE (more specifically, synecdoche), in which there are parts of an entity which can stand for the whole and what part is picked by the language user determines which aspect of the whole is given focus, making it an important part of the investigation.

Appraisement of the victim

In the AEC, the victim underwent negative representation processes in the form of negative description, reference or naming a total of 30 times (making up 94.3% of all direct appraisement of the victim in the AEC; making up 4.1% of the AEC on the basis of sentence count), and positive appraisement only 2 times (5.7% of all direct appraisement of the victim in the AEC, making up .2% of the AEC on the basis of sentence count).

Figure 47 Appraisement of the victim in the AEC

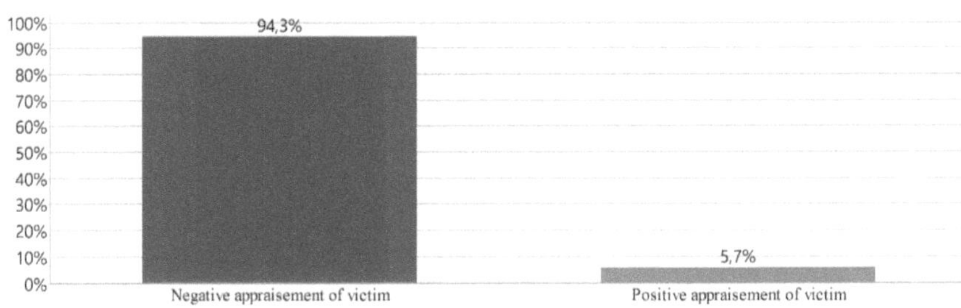

Reference to or description of the victim as being *irresponsible*, *careless*, or her unconsciousness leading to her being raped were found at 4 instances of each (.5%

of the AEC on the basis of sentence count). The victim was referred to as *naïve*, *stupid* or a *liar* in 2 sentences each (.2% of the AEC) and as *a whore, slimy, crazy, a call girl, a drunken woman, a piece of ass, a piece of meat, a predator, "victim", a grossly underage minor* and *weak* at one count per negative appraisement type in the AEC (.1% of the AEC on the basis of sentence count). The remainder of the negative representation types were descriptive.

Figure 48 Negative appraisement of the victim in the AEC

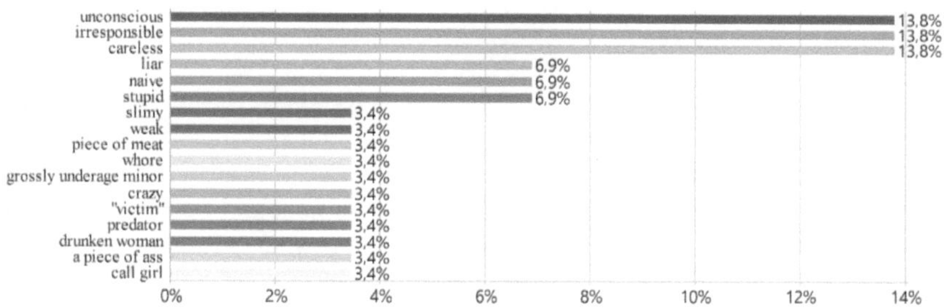

The negative appraisement of the victim in the AEC shows the strategies of name-calling of the victim, drawing on negative cultural stereotypes of the woman as whore or attribution of negative qualities to a woman's being sexually available. In examples 267–269, it can be observed how a woman's abused sexuality turns her into a product to be consumed, thus making for her even further objectification. It can be seen here as well that negative appraisement for the victim in the AEC occurs in the forms of negative verbs which, through the strategy of using metaphors (i.e., *whored herself out*) takes place, creating a strong negative image based on the stereotyping of women's role in rape, as well as reducing the actor to an objectified being. This contributes to victim blaming in that, by creating a link to negative social images of women and the subject of rape, the association drifts away from a criminal act, focusing rather on the sexual and taboo subject that is prostitution or women as a sexually desired object.

267) Looks like if all is true she *whored herself out* for her job.
(AEC VTY 2019, Row: 5)

268) Shes *a call girl* plain and simple.
(AEC VTY 2019, Row: 5)

269) That's what bothers him after his son raped a woman like *a piece of meat*?
(AEC NYT 2016, Row: 20)

The only 2 instances of positive appraisement of the victim in the AEC occurred in the modification of positively evaluative nouns by adjectival modification (example 91—*brave*) and possessive pronouns (example 271, as in *her courage and thoughtfulness*) (.2% of the AEC).The type of appraisement expresses admiration for an actor who has been subjected to rape and come out to talk about it in the eye of the public.

270) Her impact statement was one of the most chilling, eye-opening, and *brave* things I have ever read.
(AEC NYT 2016, Row: 1)

271) first thank you to the woman who shared, for her *courage* and *thoughtfulness*.
(AEC NYT 2017, Row: 18)

One might speculate as to the subject of the courage of the victim, here perhaps drawing on common public knowledge of the fact that victim blaming is a pervasive phenomenon, discursively and otherwise.

The difference in the amount of negative appraisement and positive appraisement in the AEC is a direct consequence of victim blaming in rape which occurs in society. These appraisements through the strategies of naming or modifying through adjectives constitute the more direct ways in which victim blaming takes place. Hardly any positive qualities were discursively given to the victim, whereas providing nominal and adjectival representations of the victim which either presented her in a negative light or blatantly equated her with negatively connotating representations (i.e., *a liar*, *whore* or *call girl*) were present in the corpus.

In the PC, both positive and negative appraisement were present in the discourses about the victim, as well. There were 44 instances of negative appraisement (84.6% of all direct appraisement of the victim and 6.1% of the PC based on sentence count) and 8 instances of positive appraisement in the PC (1.1% of the PC based on sentence count), for the victim.

Figure 49 Appraisement of the victim in the PC

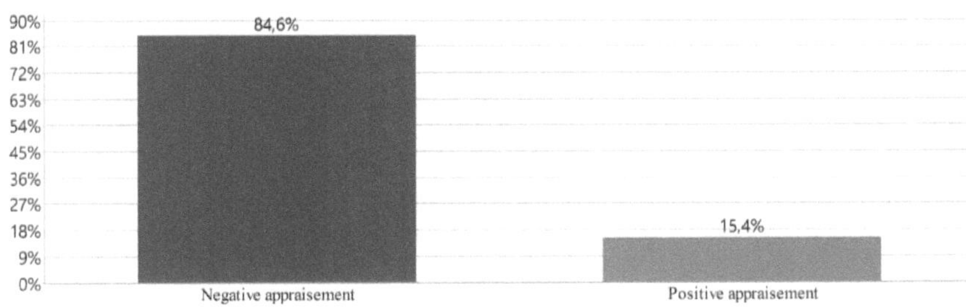

The negative appraisement of the victim in the PC also drew on various cultural stereotypes about rape victims, including that a rape victim is usually lying about being raped.

There are only two instances in which metaphorical representation is used for the victim and this is where female victims are referred to as animals, namely as *głupie kozy* ('stupid goats') in example 272 and *wymalowana su**a* ('painted bitch') in example 273. Other such references presented the common rape myths which regard women as whores (example 274). No graph has been provided here due to the fact that there is much less variation in metaphor for the victim in the PC than in the AEC.

272) W pewnym sensie sama wydała na siebie wyrok. Kobiety bądźcie bardziej ostrożne, faceci maja siłe niestety i nie bądźcie *głupimi kozami*, co to daja się zwieść
(PC PUD 2015, Row: 11)
[In a way, she brought it upon herself. Women, be more careful, men are unfortunately strong and don't be *stupid goats* that get duped]

273) wymalowana *s**a*
(PC PUD 2015, Row: 12)
[painted *b***h*]

274) właśnie poszła z obcymi facetami do mieszkania, pili ćpali, dobrze że *k***y* nie zabili i pomijam wszelkie podteksty
(PC PUD 2017a, Row: 27)
[she went with strangers (men) to their apartment, they drank and did drugs. It's a good thing that they didn't kill the *wh*re* and I'm not talking about undertones here]

However rare in the corpus, it is important to note that by overtly referring to the victim through negative name-calling, she is blamed for the criminal act of rape committed against her. The fact that negative name-calling of the victim takes place more often in the PC than in the AEC is indicative of the function of directness as a strategy of victim blaming in Polish discourse (cf. Chapter 6), rather than in American discourse.[86]

The positive appraisement of the victim mostly took place in the case of adjectival post-modification or pre-modification, or in predicative reference to the victim. Here, positive appraisement was also considered to take place where empathetic comments (considered victim-supporting comments) were presented. Positive appraisement of the victim, which was seen as also being of a supportive quality, was found a total of 8 times in the PC (1.1% of the sentences in the PC).

86 This was concluded on the basis of instances in the entire corpus, based on sentence count, where it was 6.1% in the PC and 4.1% in the AEC.

275) Dziewczyny, jesteście *wspaniałe, silne, wartościowe.* Traumę każdego dnia przekuwacie w sukces.
(PC GWyb 2020, Row: 5)
[Girls, you are *great, strong and valuable.* You are turning your trauma into success every day.]

276) *Dzielne Kobiety*!!! Trzymajcie się!!!
(PC GWyb 2020, Row: 6)
[*Strong women*!!! Hang in there!!!]

The difference in the number of times negative and positive appraisement was present for the victim in the PC is indicative of the tendency to blame the victim of a rape, even in ways that are more direct. The first part of the analytical part of this work (Chapter 6), however, demonstrated that there is a greater tendency for the victim to be subjected to victim blaming more indirectly, however. The PC also demonstrated more victim-supporting comments in the form of positive appraisement, whereas it was only found in two instances in the AEC. This was a slight difference in the corpora that was worth noting.

Appraisement of the offender

In both the AEC and the PC, the offender underwent negative appraisement. In the AEC, this took place a total of 31 times in the AEC (making up 3.8% of the AEC on the basis of sentence count). It was only in the AEC that the offender underwent positive appraisement (albeit only in 2 sentences, through adjectival modification—making up .2% of the AEC on the basis of sentence count), whereas the majority of appraisement types for the offender were negative, similarly to the victim.

Figure 50 Appraisement of the offender in the AEC

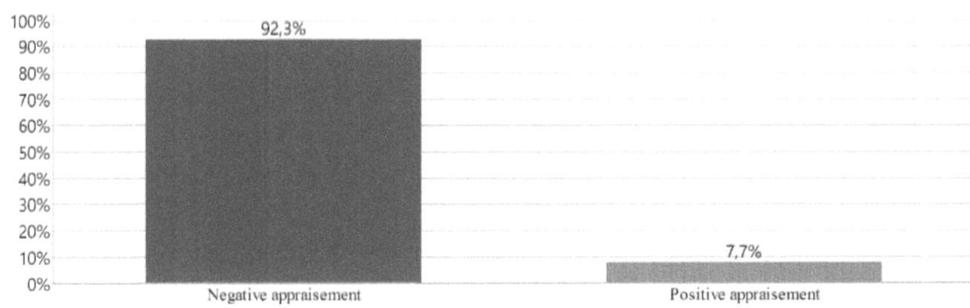

The types of negative appraisement on the offender included *fiend-naming* 9 times (1.9% of the AEC on the basis of sentence count), metaphorical reference to the offender such as *animal* a total of 8 times (1% of the AEC), *garbage* a total of 5 times or reference to weeds or plants a total of 2 times (.2% of the AEC). The offender was referred to as *dirty* (in 2 instances—.2% of the AEC), as a *paraiah* (1 time—.1% of the AEC), as *deserving of the death penalty*, as a *child*, as a *dangerous sexual deviant*, as *evil* and as *crazy*, one time per token (.1% of the AEC each). A graph of negative appraisement of the offender has been provided as a visual in Figure 28, including metaphorical categories of fiend-naming, animal-naming, plants naming and garbage naming.

Figure 51 Negative appraisement of the offender in the AEC

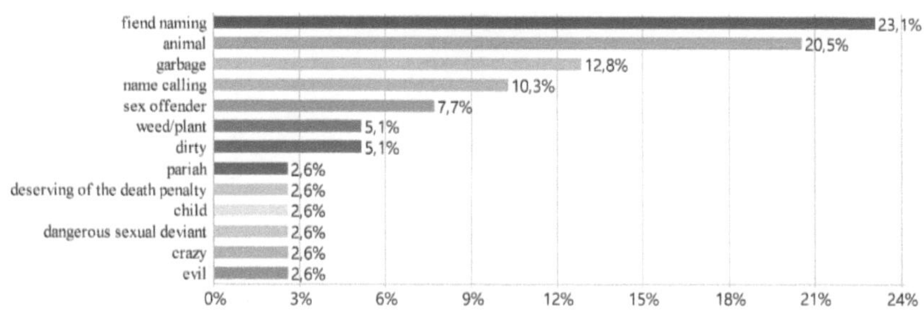

There were more metaphors found in the case of the offender (24 counts in the AEC, .05% of the AEC) than in the case of the representation of the victim (3 counts in the AEC, .01% of the AEC), all of which denoted negative appraisement types. Such data in the corpus suggests that direct appraisement for the offender takes place through naming strategies which culturally associate with negative qualities (i.e., metaphors which carry negative meaning).

Table 26 Categorization of metaphors for the offender in the AEC

	Frequency	Percentage	Percentage of the AEC
fiend metaphor	9	37.5%	1.1%
animal metaphor	8	33.3%	.9%
garbage metaphor	5	20.8%	.6%
plant metaphor	2	8.3%	.2%
TOTAL	24/804	100%	3.0%

Metaphorical categories of representation of the offender belong to the category of negative appraisement. Such representations as the ones shown in the above metaphorical categories, via cognitive bias to associate negatively with certain elements of culture (such as with certain animals or plants), act behind the negative representations of the actor that lie behind the negative evaluation in a sentence. Several examples of expressing negative attitudes to the offender via negative metaphors have been provided below.

277) Looks like if all is true she whored herself out for her job. This wasnt a onetime thing. She went back of her own accord on multiple occasions to this "*monster*".
(AEC VTY 2019, Row: 5)

278) I don't care if she snuck out of her home she didn't deserve the treatment she got from that *animal.*
(AEC ABC 2014, Row: 47)

279) Guilty. Throw this *piece of filth* in prison where he belongs.
(AEC ABC 2020, Row: 5)

280) I put my hand in a *shark tank* and got bit. It's all the *sharks* fault.
(AEC ABC 2015a, Row: 8)

281) Ladies, take a good look at him. This is what a sexual predator looks like. The *fruit of a rotten tree* hasn't fallen far given his father's remarks.
(AEC NYT 2016, Row: 6)

282) Women are nothing but receptacles to some men, and this *horny drunken dog* and his incredibly insensitive and disgusting old man are two men with that mindset.
(AEC NYT 2016, Row: 5)

Additionally, two of the direct appraisement types for the offender were positive, where the rapist's role as a student and an athlete is made explicit. The adjectival modification in the pre-modifying position defines the actor in positive terms, as can be read in the examples below. Here, Brock Turner is called a good athlete and a star athlete, adjectives which place the actor in a superlative position. The fact that there were only two examples, however, leads to the conclusion that no clear analysis can be made on the basis of such weak evidence.

283) This kid had no priors and was *a good student athlete...*
(AEC NYT 2016, Row: 23)

284) The judge who sentenced Brock Turner was himself *a star athlete at Stanford.*
(AEC NYT 2016, Row: 15)

In the PC, there were 142 instances of negative appraisement of the offender in the PC (making up 19.9% of the entire PC based on sentence count), and no instances of positive appraisement in the PC. This made up a major difference as compared to the AEC (which presented 1.9% of negative appraisement), demonstrating the higher tendency in Polish discourse to directly negatively evaluate the offender.

The lack of positive appraisement of the offender showed that the direct evaluation of the actor, a very pervasive element of the entire PC, reflected on the negative evaluation of the offender as an actor in the rape, which in turn counted as offender-blaming.

Figure 52 Appraisement of the offender in the PC

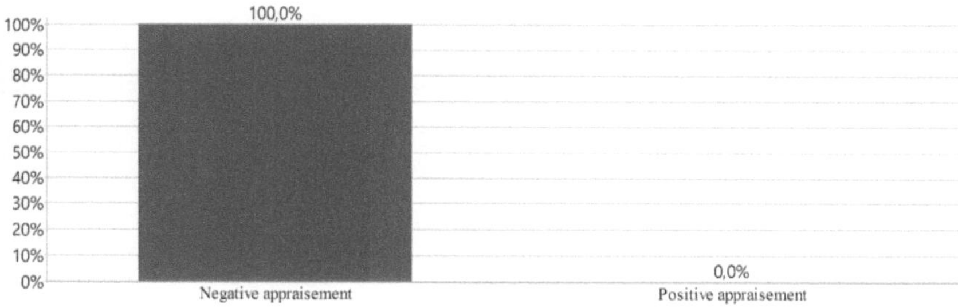

In the analysis of social actors, the negative appraisement of the offender took place through strategies such as name-calling, including the use of vulgar expression and racial slurs, and metaphorical attribution, including metonymy in fewer cases. A graph of the negative appraisement types for the offender is presented below, namely showing racial bias in the comments and expression of fiend naming (Clark, 1992).

Fiend naming (i.e., reference to the offender as a monster) took place a total of 35 times in the PC for the offender (constituting 4.9% of the PC on the basis of sentence count), *name calling*, a total of 24 times in the PC (3.3% of the PC), *racial bias* and *deserving of castration* (18 times each—2.5% of the PC each), metaphorically equating the offender to an animal, such as *bestia*, *bydlak*, *dzicz* ('beast', 'cattle', 'savage') (17 times—2.3% of the PC), *zwyrodnialstwo* ('villainousness')—8 times (1.1% of the PC), calling the offender vulgar names (profanity), pedophiles, weeds or plants or stating that the offender deserved life in prison took place 2 times each in the PC (.3% of the PC). There was 1 count each of reference to the offender as *ohydny* ('disgusting') and *zbir* ('thug') (making up .1% of the PC).

Figure 53 Negative appraisement of the offender in the PC

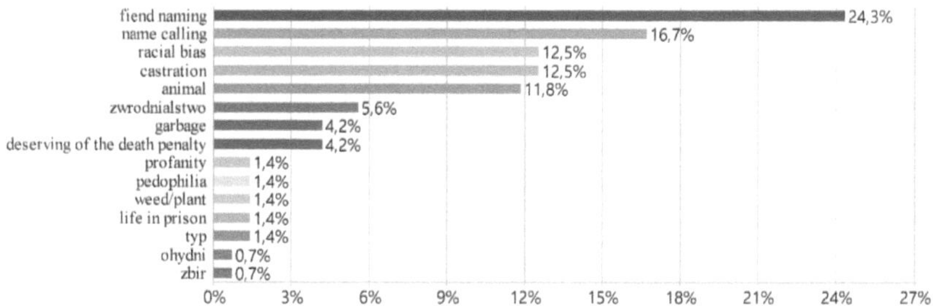

In such categorizations, similarly to the AEC, metaphorical representation of the offender was also present. These metaphors belonged to the same categories that were present in the AEC, namely that of comparing offenders to monsters (i.e., fiends), animals, garbage or plants and weeds, which has been found to exist in both cultures.

Table 27 Metaphors for the offender in the PC

	Frequency	Percentage	Percentage in PC
fiend metaphor	35	58.3%	4.9%
animal metaphor	17	28.4%	2.3%
garbage metaphor	6	10.0%	.8%
plant metaphor	2	3.3%	.3%
TOTAL	60/714	100%	8.3%

285) *Bydlaki* i *dzicz* nad kim tu się litować jak nie maja szacunku do innych ludzi precz z nimi z Europy.
(PC PUD 2017b, Row: 89)
[Beasts and *savages*. Who should we have mercy for if they don't have respect for people, kick them out of Europe.]

286) Ci ratownicy to jakieś *potwory* ! To tak *bestialskie*, że aż trudne do uwierzenia.
(PC PUD 2015, Row: 2)
[Those paramedics are *monsters*! It's so *monstrous* that it's hard to believe.]

287) Wyrwać *chwasty* ze społeczeństwa.
(PC GWyb 2018, Row: 8)
[We should pull *the weeds* out of society.]

In the PC, the reference to the metaphor as an animal (or a beast, making for a crossover between the fiend-naming and animal metaphor categories) was most populated (making up 2.3% of the entire PC). This demonstrates how such a category is more cognitively available when referring to a cruel act, but at the same time de-humanizes the offender, further abstracting the problem of rape from its being a problem of gendered violence that takes place on massive scales (cf. Introduction).

In both the AEC and the PC, negative appraisement was more prevalent than positive appraisement, however, the PC decidedly demonstrated a more overt negative representation of the offender (in other words, negatively evaluating the actor). This demonstrates a greater tendency in Polish culture to negatively evaluate the actor openly. The types of negative appraisement of the offender utilize dysphemistic reference to the offender, fiend-naming, negative name calling, and the application of negative metaphorical reference which either dehumanizes or makes a monstrous social outlier of the actor.

Reference to body parts and metonymy as appraisement

Reference to the body parts of actors is a particularly relevant strategy in discourses about rape. Here, I have only considered the type of metonymy that is PART OF A WHOLE metonymy (Lakoff & Johnson, 1980, 2008).[87] Such references to actors consisted of vulgar expressions for genitals and body parts (cf. Chapter 3).

In this section, I focus on the actor to whose body reference is made and the implication of blame behind such discursive representations. This includes references to the victim's body, which were found in comments that were typed as victim-blaming, victim-supporting, and offender-blaming, and references to the offender's body, which was found in comments that were either victim-blaming or offender-blaming. The reason for making this a separate section is to draw attention to how reference to the bodily sphere as metaphor is tied to the evaluation which communicates attitudes towards actors in a rape.

In the AEC, the victim's body was referred to in 3 instances of victim-supporting comments (.4% of the AEC), 2 instances of victim blaming comments (.2% of

87 Here I include van Leeuwen's (1996, 2004) category of *somatization*, as well as any other reference to the body parts of the actors because the site of rape is inherently the body, thus making it an integral part of the analysis of evaluation of actors. This means that investigating whether or not the body of actors is used in order to negatively or positively evaluate the victim and the offender must be done in order to carry out a proper and comprehensive cultural comparison of the various representations of rape in discourse.

the AEC), and in 1 sentence that was offender-blaming (.1% of the AEC). Not all of the instances presented are strictly metonymic references, however considering that the subject of the comments analyzed is rape, I have taken all references to body parts and placed them within the same section of analysis in this chapter, as well as into the same graph (cf. figure 54).

Figure 54 Reference to the victim's body in the AEC

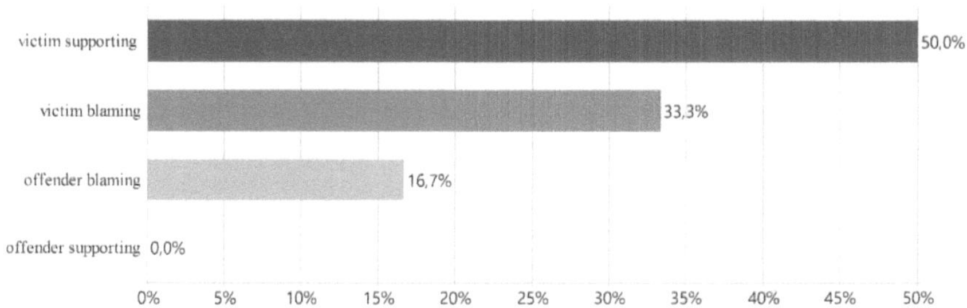

As regards the victim-blaming comments, the body of the victim was referenced. The representation of a woman as *a piece of ass* is not only done through the strategy of using a part of her body to refer to her as a person but also plays on the stereotype and myth that objectifies women as sex objects, as well as objects of sexual desire (Berger, 1972; Brownmiller, 1976, 1984). This is an example of the negative appraisement that takes place within the corpus, however here is presented through the lens of the sexist language discussed in Chapter 3 of this work. This is also indicative of metonymy, by which the victim is represented as either her whole body (example 288) or a part of her body (example 289).

> 288) Agreed. How low her self-esteem must be in order to trade liquor for *her body*. So sad. (AEC ABC 2014, Row: 50)

> 289) He grenaded his career and personal life over *a piece of ass (literally)* how much of a payoff did this high paid call girl receive all said and done.
> (AEC VTY 2019, Row: 5)

Other types of corporeal reference that did not count as metonymic reference placed emphasis on the physical appearance of the actor.

> 290) I couldn't see *her face*, but *her body* looked like she could have been 20.
> (AEC ABC 2014, Row: 26)

Victim supporting comments also contained reference to the victim's body in the AEC.

291) Putting *the face of a teenage rape victim* on your front page probably isn't a good practice.
(AEC ABC 2014, Row: 40)

292) If you are one of those millions, you should understand that a young woman does not deserve *having her body violated*, her sanity threatened, and her future jeopardized because she didn't make the right decision about how much she had to drink that night.
(AEC NYT 2017, Row: 19)

There were no offender-supporting comments that referred to the victim's body (0% of the corpus).

As demonstrated, although not very prevalent, in the AEC (a total of 6 times in the comments, making up .7% of the AEC on the basis of sentence count), reference to the victim's body is an important factor for consideration in such an analysis, since the corporal sphere is where the act of rape takes place. The reference to the victim's body in discourse about rape maintains focus on the sexualization of the appearance of the actor, as well as places more focus on the appearance of the victim than that of the offender, making it understood that the appearance of the victim is an important factor in rape.

In the PC, metonymic or bodily reference for the victim only occurred in 1 instance (making up .01% of the PC):

293) sama tego chciała!!! Szukała h.ja do *d.py*, to znalazła, aż trzy!!
(PC GWsp 2012a)
[She wanted it!!! She was looking for a dick for *her ass* and she found three of them!!]

This type of metonymy of *dupa* ('ass') as a reference to a woman and her sexuality is an example of the objectification and negative sexualization of women in Polish, hence its victim-blaming status (cf. Figure 55). However, the lack of more such examples cannot lead to many more conclusive claims with regard to how such references in Polish discourse act in evaluating actors.

Figure 55 Reference to the victim's body in the PC

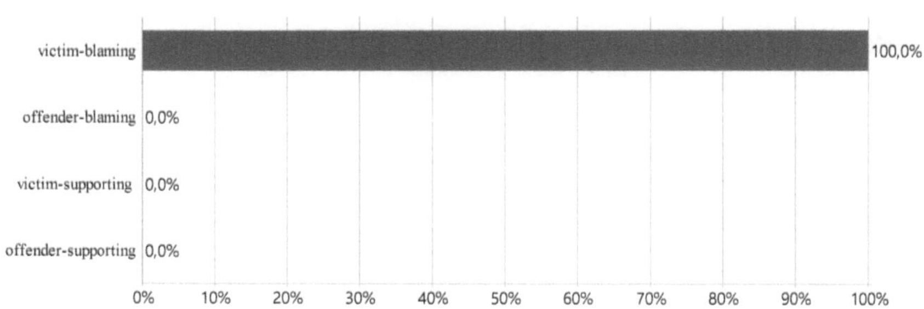

Overall, there was more reference to the body of the victim in the AEC than in the PC, presenting a cultural difference in the way that the body relates to descriptions of rape. It is impossible to ascertain to what extent the body functions as a reference to the victim in the case of Polish culture, since there was no significant evidence of this occurring in the PC.

There were 2 sentences in which the reference to the offender's body was used to express negative attitudes to the offender in the AEC (.3% of the PC), and 1 sentence (.1% of the PC, in which reference to the offender's body was made in victim-supporting comments and victim-blaming comments each (.4% of the AEC altogether), which rendered this type of reference rather insignificant to the entire corpus overall.

Figure 56 Reference to the offender's body in the AEC

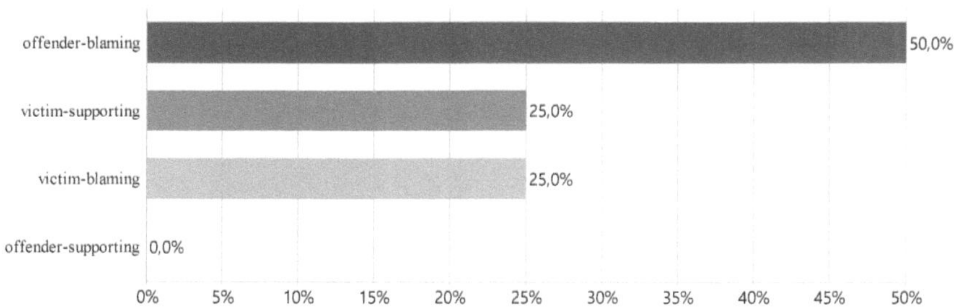

It is worth mentioning such reference to the offender for the sake of comparison with metonymic reference in the case of the victim. Example 294 demonstrates reference to the offender's body to express negative attitudes to the victim as well as to the offender, i.e., *his ass.* Examples 295 and 296 show negative attitudes to the offender through reference to his body, as in *his face* and *his ass* to represent the actor as a whole.

294) Unless she's done it many times before or Lauer has *a pecker* the size of cocktail weenie (a quite likely scenario I believe) This being said Lauer is a moron for using his power to even attempt to coerce these young career driven women into relationships with *his ass*.
(AEC VTY 2019, Row: 5)

295) If NBC had heard even a rumor that their million dollar anchor—*the face of NBC News* was being accused of raping another employee even before the me too era they would have responded immediately.
(AEC VTY 2019, Row: 16)

296) This being said Lauer is a moron for using his power to even attempt to coerce these young career driven women into relationships with *his ass*.
(AEC VTY 2019, Row: 5)

In the PC, the offender's body was referred to a total of 11 times (making up 1.5 % of the PC on the basis of sentence count). Such references were only found in comments that blamed either the victim or the offender, and not in actor-supporting comments. In 8 of the instances, the victim was blamed in a sentence where the metonymic reference to the offender was found and in 3 such sentences the offender was blamed.

Figure 57 Reference to the offender's body in the PC

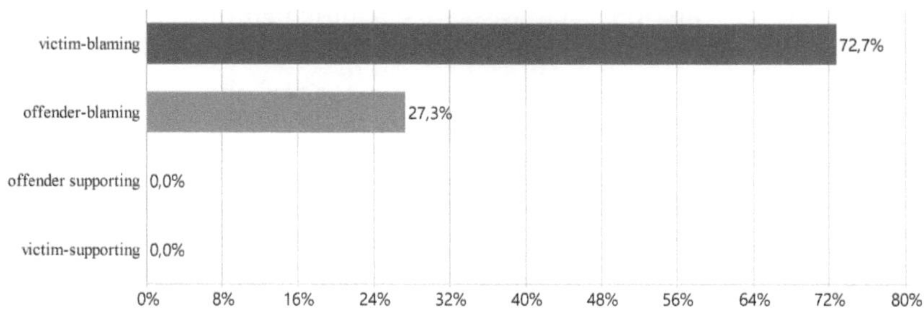

297) *Cztery czarne knagi*, teraz na męża nawet nie spojrzy.
(PC PUD 2017b, Row: 65)
[*Four black knobs* (male genitalia), and now she won't even look at her husband.]

298) szukała *h.ja* do d.py, to znalazła, aż *trzy*!!
(PC GWsp 2012a, Row: 9)
[she was looking for a dick for her *ass*, and she found *three*!!]

This kind of focusing on the genitalia of the offender in evaluating the victim brings forth the negative perceptions of female sexuality, thus negatively evaluating the victim as wishing to feed into her forbidden sexual desires. This additionally implies that the woman is lying about having been raped, as the need to frame her sexual needs behind a claim of rape is indirectly stated as deriving from the cultural tabooization of female sexuality.

Although these instances were quite infrequent for the entirety of both the AEC and the PC, the significance of such references as a strategy of evaluation in the context of rape is quite important. In both the AEC and the PC, the bodily references to the victim outweighed those types of references to the offender. The graphs show that in both language contexts, such metonymic reference is usually used in victim blaming, as both references to the victim's and offender's bodies in both the AEC and the PC were linked to victim blaming as a phenomenon. Additionally, the reference to the actors' sexual desire or sexuality is put in a negative light, hence drawing on the stereotypes regarding women's sexuality and the tendency to negatively admonish its existence.

Mapping of the naming of the victim

In the American English corpus, the victim underwent positive and negative types of representation as far as socio-semantic naming representation was concerned. Where negative naming was concerned, through which overt negative appraisement was found, metaphor was observable through both verbal process and nominal representation, including metaphorical representation.

Representations of the victim took place in instances where the victim was represented through the category of identification (especially via the discursive strategies of classification and relational identification). Gender was an important factor in victim representation, as well as age as a modifier of gender (*young woman*, *young girl*). This included expressions which suggested or revealed the age of the victim, as in *child*, xyz-*year-old* or *teen* and also in expressions which belonged to the category of functionalization, such as *student* or *freshman*, which put a focus on the youth of the actor. The representation of the victim through functionalization also focused on her role in the crime (through discursive representation of her as a *victim* or *survivor*). Although other types of functionalization occurred, they were much fewer in frequency than reference to the calling of the actor a *victim*.

The maps which are presented in this section of the analysis solely serve the purpose of providing a visual and qualitative illustration of the representations of social actors, for the ease of visualizing the variation in their discursive representation. The first map (figure 35) describes the naming of the victim in the AEC from a qualitative perspective, whereas the second map (figure 36) presents a qualitative overview of the naming of the victim in the PC. The third and fourth maps (figures 37 and 38) do the same, respectively, however for the offender.

Figure 58 Qualitative overview of the representations of the victim in the AEC

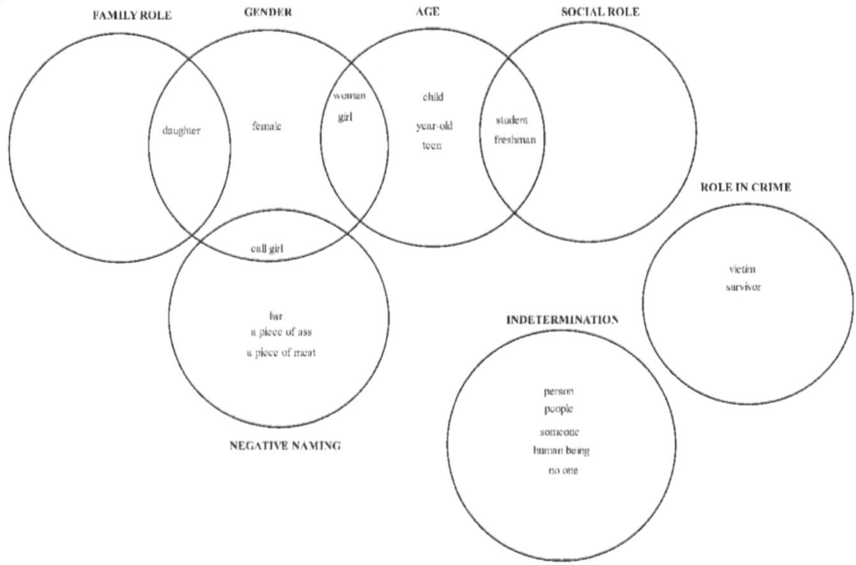

The figure above has been provided to put the naming strategies into a visual map, which expresses the data from a qualitative perspective. The map presents the overlaps between the various ways that the victim is named in the AEC. The representations of the victim in the AEC vary in the discourse of digital comments from highlighting the social role of the victim, to her role in the crime itself. As can be seen above, the categories for naming the victim in the AEC (excluding nomination) were related to gender, age and family role.

Negative naming also constituted a category of naming the victim in the AEC and overlapped with gender in the case of *call girl*. The negative naming of the victim in the AEC reflected rape myths and the objectification of women as sexual objects.

The category of indetermination, which had four separate semantic representations shows that in the generalization of the victim and a lack of gender-marked language is present—including reference to the victim as: *person*, *people*, *no one*, etc. It can be argued here that, while this category was not highly populated in terms of the entire corpus, it presents an erasure of the fact that women and girls are the social group most likely to be the victim of a sexual crime.

The following map provides a qualitative overview of the categories of naming of the victim in the PC. Similarly to the one made for the AEC, the overlaps for how the victim is named throughout the PC demonstrates the ways that she is majorly categorized. The trends that are pointed to in this visual of the PC victim naming, are that the gender of the victim is tied to her age, family role, occupation and much of the negative nominalizations used to present her as an actor, however this pertains to the structural characteristics of the Polish language, and is unavoidable. The focus on the victim in the PC tends to be on her role as a woman, as well as her role as a victim in the crime. Some instances of indetermination representation also occurred for the victim in the PC, taking away from discourse that focuses on her gender and abstracting from the fact that rape is a sexual—and thus gendered crime.

Figure 59 Qualitative overview of the representations of the victim in the PC

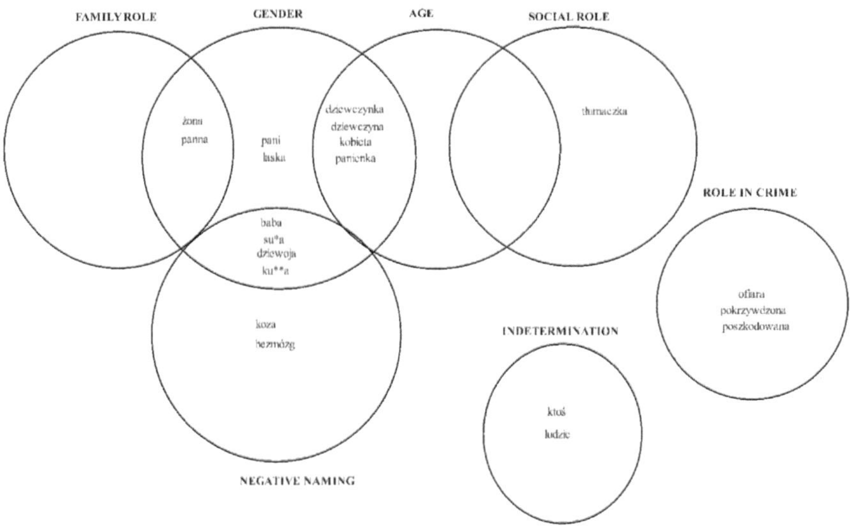

In the PC, the negative naming of the victim drew on stereotypes of women as whores, and as possessing the quality of being unintelligent. This is seen above to co-configure with the category of gender, as the Polish language inflects for gender, making room for more negative cognitive bias towards women as victims of sexual crime. Additionally, the gendered naming of the victim overlaps with family roles and age in the PC. The gendered and age categories also present negatively connotative items, such as *panienka*, which, when used in an evaluative context, such as in comments regarding sexual crime, symbolize careless behavior or lackadaisical natures.

Also, contrary to the AEC, there was less variation in the types of indeterminate reference to the victim in the PC, with only 2 items found in the corpus. What such representations of the naming of the victim in the AEC and the PC show us is that the categories of naming to represent the victim were similar in both corpora. Overall, for both of the corpora, in the case of the victim, the focus was placed on the actor's role in the crime, her gender, family role, age and social role.

Mapping of the naming of the offender

The offender underwent both positive and negative types of representation where actor naming was concerned in the AEC. In terms of identification, gender also played an important role in the representation of the offender, as well as age (*17 year old male*). Identification types were found to be quite neutral; however, the question of negative naming was very important in the representation of the offender. Where negative naming was concerned, through which overt negative appraisement was observed, the *offender as animal, offender as garbage, offender as weed or plant* metaphor were observable through both nominal and adjectival representation.

The representation of the offender also took place through the functionalization of his role in the crime (through discursive representation of his being associated with the crime through various types of naming, including *attacker, rapist, offender* and more). Other types of functionalization that occurred, included the offender's occupation, however, there were fewer instances of such representation than reference to the aforementioned naming types.

As stated earlier, the maps shown below aim to show a general model of the naming categories for the offender overall, simply to provide an overview for each of the language contexts.

The figure above provides an illustration of the overview of the social categories and naming types used to represent the offender in the AEC. It must be noted that racial representations were hardly present (with only 1 count) in the AEC. The diversity in the naming of the offender in the AEC is demonstrative of various attitudes, where the categories that were most diversified were those that reflected negative naming and the actor's role in the crime.

Figure 60 Qualitative overview of the representations of the offender in the AEC

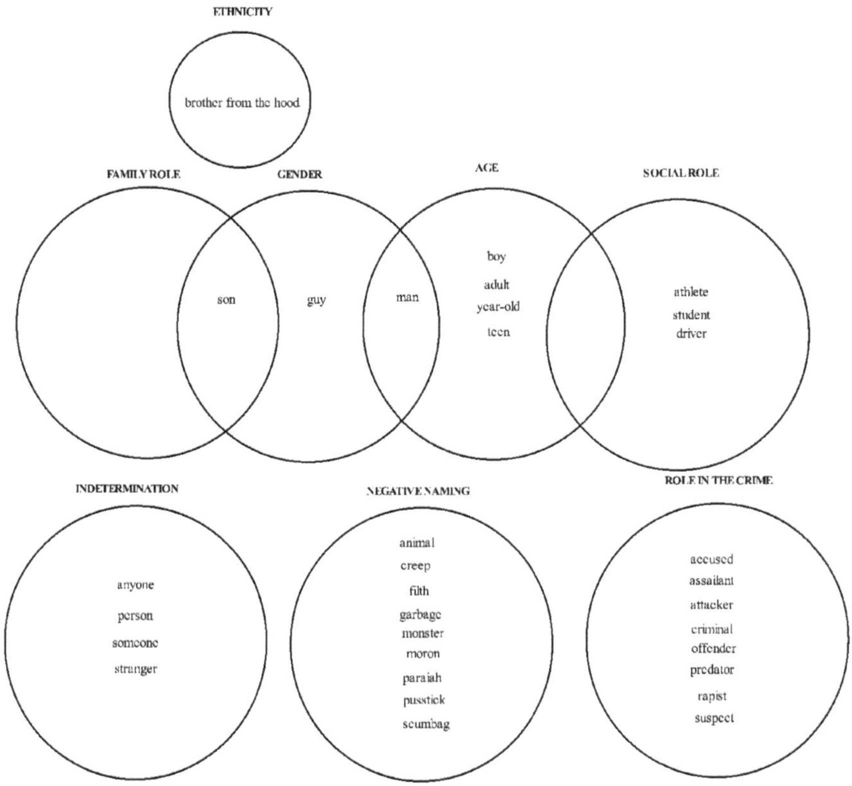

From what is shown above, as well as in the preceding quantitative analyses of representations, the references to offenders can be divided into categories, including those that relate to age, gender, family role, social role, or role in the crime. This is similar to the categories by which the victim is represented, but for the offender, the process of naming references sees more variation.

Other ways that the offender is named in the AEC is by addressing the actor through indetermination or negative naming, which contributes to the negative appraisement of the actor. As can be seen in the map, there is a larger variation in referents to the offender in the categories of his role in the crime and negative naming, whereas in the ones simply representing social variables (including *age*, *gender*, *social role*) there is less variation.

The fact that the indetermination, negative naming of the offender, and the role in the crime are categories that are most popular in the AEC naming of the offender is indicative of the fact that American culture views offenders (overall) in a negative light, thus contributing to negative social evaluation of rapists. This makes the question of victim blaming all the more an interesting one, since it is not through the naming of social actors that victim blaming necessarily takes place.

Figure 61 Qualitative overview of the representations of the offender in the PC

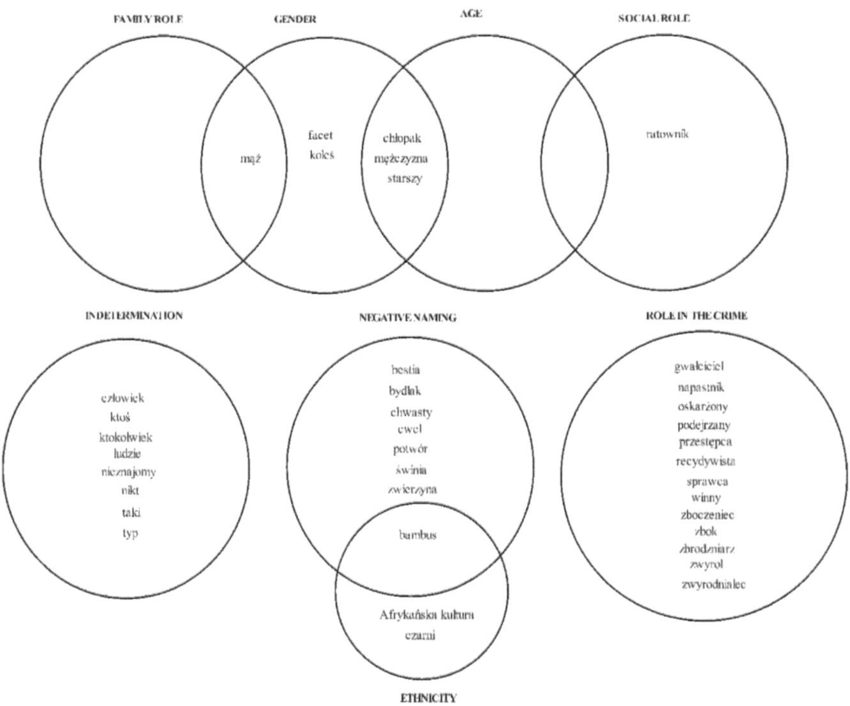

As can be seen in the map which represents the various ways that the offender is named in the PC, there are various tendencies for naming, however, the most varied and populated groups are those which present indetermination of the actor, negative naming (overt evaluation) and those types of naming which represent the actor's role in the crime. Hence, it can be seen that the negative and criminal nature of the actor is highlighted in the Polish Internet user discourse. Other categories of representation did not see much variation in the corpus and rarely was the social role referred to in the corpus. This is indicative of overall overt negative evaluation of the offender. The negative naming that is seen in the visualization above shows that connotations of animal symbolism or reference to plants dehumanizes the offender, for one.

Where the naming of actors is concerned, the two sets of data analyzed (American and Polish) show varying tendencies. When it came to the victim, in the AEC and PC, there was less variety in naming overall, as opposed to the offender. The areas of concentration in the naming of the offender showed different tendencies, which can also be observed in the outlay of the map. Where the offender was concerned, in both the AEC and the PC, the most populated categories in terms of variation of naming were that of indetermination, negative naming (which are here considered instances of overt evaluation of the actor) and the offender's role in the crime.

The main difference between the representations in the naming of the offender in the AEC and the PC were the negative expressions for the offender, which were stronger in the PC than in the AEC. This demonstrates that discourse on rape and evaluative comments about actors tend to be more expressive in Polish. Interestingly, in both of the cultural contexts, the naming of the offender focused on his/their role in the crime, rarely describing the actor(s) in terms of positive attributes, a fact which indicates that offender blaming takes place more explicitly through the naming of the actor.

Representations of rape

The representation of the rape itself is equally important to the analysis of the attitudes that Internet users have regarding rape and the actors involved. By investigating the way that such users name the crime itself, it becomes clearer what trends in beliefs about rape and its status as a serious crime exist. From the AEC, it is clear that *rape* (122 times, making up .5% of the AEC on the basis of word count) and *sex* (78 times, constituting .3% of the AEC on the basis of word count) are often equated with one another, as they are the two naming types with the highest frequencies. This has been demonstrated in the differentiation between types of naming, namely crime-reflective naming and euphemization.

299) If the accused and his WITNESS are correct, the **sex** occurred first, then she got drunk. She wanted to trade **sex** for alcohol. He wanted **sex**. They had **sex**; she got drunk. How are they "animals" with connections?
(AEC ABC 2014, Row: 38)

300) He asked her if she liked **the anal sex** and she said yes.
(AEC VTY 2019, Row: 29)

There were 159 instances of euphemization of rape in the AEC (making up .7% of the AEC overall), which makes quite a significant impact on the way that rape is viewed in the social sense. As stated above, there were 122 counts of the word *rape* used to represent the crime (.5% of the AEC). The fact that euphemization was more prevalent in the corpus than actual rape naming contributes to heightened victim blaming, in that it distances from the severity of the crime.

Figure 62 Euphemization and direct naming of rape in the AEC

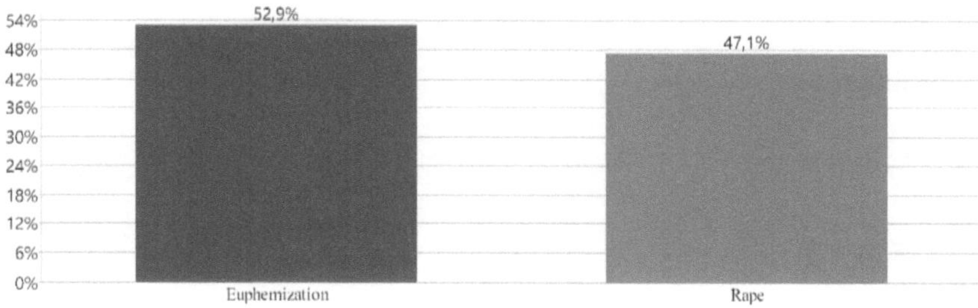

The reason that the word *rape* has been pinpointed out of all the crime-reflecting naming types as not being of a euphemistic nature is because it is the one which reflects the actual act of raping. Other crime-reflecting nominal representations of rape have been deemed slightly dysphemistic, as they can denote other crimes (such as the word *assault*, which might also refer to battery, a crime that is not necessarily of a sexual nature).

Crime-reflecting naming of rape

The majority of the references to rape in the AEC were crime-reflective, occurring a total of 213 times, making up 1% of the entire corpus. The categories of naming types for the crime that I have chosen to use are those that reflect the crime, those that euphemize and those that show dysphemism. Among the crime-naming representations of rape in the AEC were *rape* (122 times—constituting .5% of the AEC), *assault* (47 times- constituting .2% of the AEC), *crime* (31 times—constituting .1% of the AEC), *criminal behavior* (7 times- constituting.03% of the AEC), and *attack* (6 times- constituting .02% of the AEC).

Table 28 Crime-reflecting naming of rape in the AEC

	Frequency	Percentage	Percentage of AEC
rape	122	57.3%	.5%
assault	47	22.1%	.2%
crime	31	14.6%	.1%
criminal behavior	7	3.3%	.03%
attack	6	2.8%	.03%
TOTAL	213/20,898	100%	1.0%

A graph has also been provided in a visual form for facilitating the visualization of the differences.

Figure 63 Crime-reflecting naming of rape in AEC

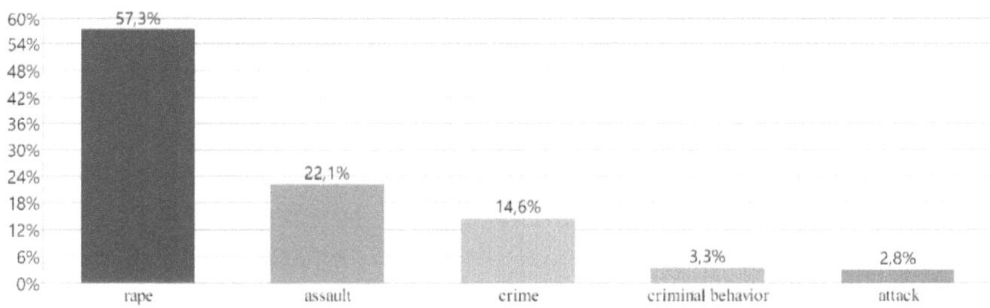

Some examples of the crime-reflective naming of the rape in the context of the AEC are as follows.

301) If you have sex with someone who does not consent, that is *rape*. A person drunk to the point of blacking out is not capable of giving consent.
(AEC NYT 2017, Row: 4)

302) *Sexual assault* is a *crime*, and should be handled by the criminal justice system.
(AEC NYT 2017, Row: 13)

303) It's not blaming the victim to say that she acted in an irresponsible manner, and in doing so left herself open to the *criminal behavior* of the man who victimized her.
(AEC NYT 2017, Row: 16)

304) Universities have abdicated policing because they don't want to be rated online as "no fun" places. Many of these *attacks* happen in dorms.
(AEC NYT 2017, Row: 18)

305) But was it *Rape-Rape*!!
(AEC ABC 2015b, Row: 39)

The use of crime-reflecting language in the AEC acknowledges the status of the rape as a crime in the Internet user discourse. Although this strategy contributes to the backgrounding of the actors in many cases, especially that of the offender, the naming of the rape as a crime places it in a position that is reflective of its being a negative act.

In the PC, direct naming of *gwałt* ('rape') took place a total of 76 times (.6% of the PC). This was the most frequently repeated type of direct rape-naming that occurred in the Polish corpus. Of course, there were other types of crime-reflective linguistic representations present in the corpus, with a total of 90 instances altogether (.8% of the PC)

Table 29 Crime-reflecting naming of rape in the PC

	Frequency	Percentage	Percentage of PC
gwałt	76	84.4%	.6%
przemoc	7	7.8%	.06%
przestępstwo	5	5.6%	.04%
atak	1	1.1%	.01%
zbrodnia	1	1.1%	.01%
TOTAL	90/11,200	100%	.8%

A graph has been provided in addition to the table above in order to facilitate the visualization of the differences.

Figure 64 Crime-reflecting naming of rape in PC

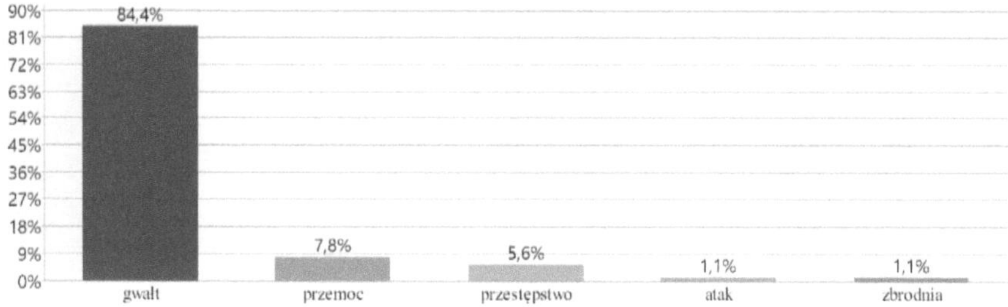

Other crime-reflective naming types were much less numerous and included fewer alternatives than in the AEC. These types include *przemoc* ('violence'/'aggression') (7 times—.06% of the PC on the basis of word count), *przestępstwo* ('crime') (5 times—.04% of the PC), *zbrodnia* ('crime') (1 time—.009% of the PC on the basis of word count) and *atak* ('attack') (1 time—.009% on the basis of word count). Such equation of the rape within the category of a crime places the rape as a subject in a discursive position which reflects the true nature of it (as a crime). Other types of naming of rape that were present in the PC belonged to the category of euphemization.

Euphemization and rape

Euphemizing references to rape were an important aspect of the analysis, and was present in the AEC. Here, what was taken into consideration were any expressions which took away from the severity of the crime, equated it with sexual intercourse or abstracted it through making it seem an indeterminate act (Crespo-Fernandez, 2008: 104–105). Euphemism is grounded on minimizing a negative property of a word or expression, or on switching the means or names by which it is referred to, hence creating a more disguised, but desirable connotative meaning (Lutz, 1989). This could be exchanging an expression with an overtly negative or taboo meaning with one that either has positive connotations or is abstracted in its meaning, muddling the negative or taboo nature of which it speaks. In the case of reference to rape, this is also seen.

It is important to note that in the AEC, rape was described as *sex* a total of 79 times (.4% of the AEC on the basis of word count), which does pose a difference when juxtaposed against the 122 times that the crime was called *rape* (.5% of the AEC on the basis of word count).

Figure 65 Various references to rape as sex *in the AEC*

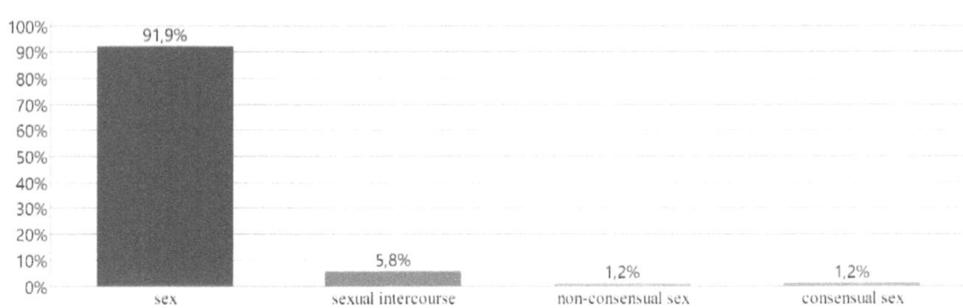

This linguistic strategy of calling rape *sex* demonstrates the negative appraisement of the victim, and hence by making a correlation between a sex crime and consensual sexual interaction doubt is placed in the victim's testimony.

The euphemization of rape, as described in the discourse of Internet users, is important, as it reflects attitudes of the treatment of rape as either a taboo subject, or comparing it to sex, which is understood as a consensual act (cf. Chapter 2). It may also be said that euphemization, especially with reference to *rape* as *sex* is reflective of the rape myth that "women desire to be raped" (Burt, 1980, 1998).

306) Sexual bullying by having sex with someone who wants to *have sex* with you? BTW some girls are mentally unstable and some are greedy who abuse the court systems to try to extort some money.
(AEC ABC 2015b, Row: 32)

307) If the accused and his WITNESS are correct, the *sex* occurred first, then she got drunk. She wanted to trade sex for alcohol. He wanted *sex*. They had *sex*; she got drunk. How are they "animals" with connections?
(AEC ABC 2014,| Row: 38)

308) If one *has sex* with an incapacitated 14-year old girl, they have committed a rape.
(AEC ABC 2014, Row: 28)

This was one type of euphemization of the rape. Others have been provided within the table below because a graph of such size would have been illegible in this work. The reference to rape as a type of *behavior*, *thing*, *this/that* or *what happened* detracts from the severity of the crime, adding a dimension of non-concreteness in the discourse, which can lead to victim blaming in that rape is not perceived as a crime serious enough to sympathize with the victim.

Table 30 Other types of euphemization of rape in the AEC

	Frequency	Percentage	Percentage of AEC
behavior	28	17.6%	.1%
what happened/going on	25	15.7%	.1%
this/that	20	12.6%	.09%
situation	12	7.5%	.05%
incident	9	5.7%	.04%
issue	8	5.0%	.04%
affair	7	4.4%	.03%
hookup	7	4.4%	.03%
it	6	3.8%	.02%

(Continued)

Table 30 Continued

	Frequency	Percentage	Percentage of AEC
intercourse	5	3.1%	.02%
he said she said	4	2.5%	.02%
thing	4	2.5%	.02%
thing/things	4	2.5%	.02%
what he did	3	1.9%	.01%
event	3	1.9%	.01%
high-risk situation	2	1.3%	.009%
sexual bullying	2	1.3%	.009%
encounter	2	1.3%	.009%
potential danger	1	0.7%	.004%
urge	1	0.7%	.004%
mistake	1	0.7%	.004%
not the right decision	1	0.7%	.004%
actions	1	0.7%	.004%
sexual relations	1	0.7%	.004%
controversy	1	0.7%	.004%
a little something something	1	0.7%	.004%
TOTAL	159/20,898	100%	.7% of AEC

In the AEC, the reference to the rape as a *behavior* undertaken by the offender was most prevalent when it came to different euphemization types, with 28 counts (making up .1% of the AEC), abstract references to the rape included calling the rape *what happened* or *what was going on* or *this/that* (making up about .2% of the AEC together; cf. Table 30). Other references included the euphemization of the rape by calling it a *situation*, *incident*, or *affair*, which again drew from the criminal status of the rape.

In the PC, the rape was referred to as *seks* ('sex') a total of 9 times (making up .08% of the PC on the basis of word count), which differed greatly from the references to rape as sex in the AEC (79 times, making up .4% of the AEC). This direct making of sex and rape equivalent to each other additionally diminishes the severity of rape as a crime, thus creating a cognitive link between sexual intercourse and the violent act of rape. Such backgrounding is more prevalent in the AEC than in the PC.

There were more various types of euphemization for rape in the PC that did not include the reference to rape as *seks* ('sex'), which equated rape to sex. The euphemization has been presented in a table (cf. Table 31).

Table 31 Other types of euphemization of rape in the PC

	Frequency	Percentage	Percentage of PC
to/tego ('that')	26	23.8%	.2%
sprawa ('affair')	22	20.2%	.2%
sytuacja ('situation')	15	13.8%	.1%
gwałt ('rape') censored*	8	7.3%	.07%
złe zachowania ('bad behavior')	6	5.5%	.05%
takie rzeczy ('those things')	6	5.5%	.05%
czyn ('act')	5	4.6%	.04%
zdarzenie ('event')	4	3.7%	.04%
historia ('story')	3	2.7%	.03%
co się stało ('what happened')	3	2.7%	.03%
zaliczenie ('third base')	2	1.8%	.01%
paranoja ('paranoia')	1	0.9%	.01%
sprzedanie sie ('selling oneself')	1	0.9%	.01%
randka ('date')	1	0.9%	.01%
skutki ucieczki żydowskich bandytów z Niemiec i Francji ('the effect of the fleeing of Jewish bandits from Germany and France')	1	0.9%	.03%
traktowanie ('treatment')	1	0.9%	.01%
zaspokojenie potrzeb ('satisfying needs')	1	0.9%	.01%
rzecz ('thing')	1	0.9%	.01%
przeżycie ('experience')	1	0.9%	.01%
przyjemność ('pleasure')	1	0.9%	.01%
TOTAL	109/11,200	100%	.9% of PC

The fact that the euphemization for rape occurred in greater numbers than the word *gwałt* ('rape') itself in the PC is indicative of the taboo of the term *rape* in Polish culture. Even though *gwałt* was present in the corpus, it was juxtaposed with euphemistic expressions in the same comments or followed by responses using such covering expressions—i.e., covering the criminal aspect of rape and clouding it with abstracting notions or ones which reflected a sexual facet. Such euphemization as the one discussed illustrates the taboo nature of rape, as a crime which is of a sexual nature, rather than a violent act as obvious as murder. This, mixed with the tabooization of sexuality in Polish culture is illustrated in the variety of euphemisms to discuss rape, as well as their frequency. This is made even more visible in user censoring of the word *rape* (examples 310–312).

309) po prostu *Skandal*!
(PC MG 2019, Row: 12)
[it's a complete *scandal*!]

310) Komentarze jakby to były Indie. Tam po *g****ie* po którym ofiara zmarła też skupiono uwagę na nię przyzwoitym zachowaniu kobiety.
(PC PUD 2017b, Row: 9)
[The comments are acting as if this was India. When a woman died after *r**** there, they also focused on the inappropriate behavior of the woman.]

311) Wprowadzic karę śmierci! Pozamykać granice, wyjazdy tylko turystyczne pod ścisła kontrola !! Tragedie, *g****ty*, morderstwa i co jeszcze ...,, a świat patrzy i słucha a podatnicy utrzymują tych zeurodnialcow w więzieniach !
(PC PUD 2017b, Row: 91)
[Implement the death penalty! Close the borders and allow for only tourists to cross and under strict control!! Tragedies, *r***es*, murders and what else... and the world is watching and listening and taxpayers are keeping those villains in jail!]

312) wszedzie za *g***** powinna byc kara smierci albo kastracja i chemiczna i ciach fizycznie.
(PC PUD 2017b, Row: 79)
[the death penalty should exist everywhere for *r**** or castration, both chemical and physical—chop.]

An important aspect of investigating taboo in language is noting where and in what cases taboo subjects undergo some kind of censorship. Conversely to the AEC, there were instances of the censorship of the word for rape with asterisks. There were eight counts of censorship for the term for rape in the Polish corpus (.07% of the corpus), whereas this did not occur at all in the American English corpus. When set against the PC, there was more diversity in the euphemistic expressions in the AEC.

Using analogies to talk about rape as a situation

As a linguistic strategy to make different experiences understood, analogy has been described in the literature as a type of metaphor which allows for "an explanation of an unfamiliar concept by directly likening it to a familiar one (i.e., a bird' s nest is like a person' s house)" (Gurney, 1999: 1709). In the discourse on rape, analogy is also used to indirectly evaluate the actions that social actors undertake or which they are involved in by way of comparison to unrelated situations. This strategy also demonstrates that speaker or writer implicit evaluation is used to express attitudes about the positions of actors in a rape. This is because such situations are seen as mirroring the events involved in sexual crime and can be used as a victim or offender-blaming strategy or as a victim or offender-supporting strategy.

The analogous statements utilize the structures which were discussed in Chapter 6 of this work, namely in the conditional (*if*-clause) structure to show a relationship between a situation which might be more familiar or accessible to a reader and the one of rape.

In the AEC, analogy was found in a total of 3 comments (.9% of the comments in the AEC). A total of 2 comments in the AEC that used analogy as an indirect discourse strategy were victim-blaming (making up .6% of the AEC) and 1 victim-supporting comment in the form of an analogy (.3% of the AEC on the basis of comment count). It is important to remember that, like metaphor in the case of the representations of actors, analogy acts to compare the situation of rape with a situation that might be more familiar, and thus uses familiar domains—such as stealing—to discuss the criminality of rape (cf. examples 313 and 315).

Figure 66 Analogies of evaluative quality in the AEC

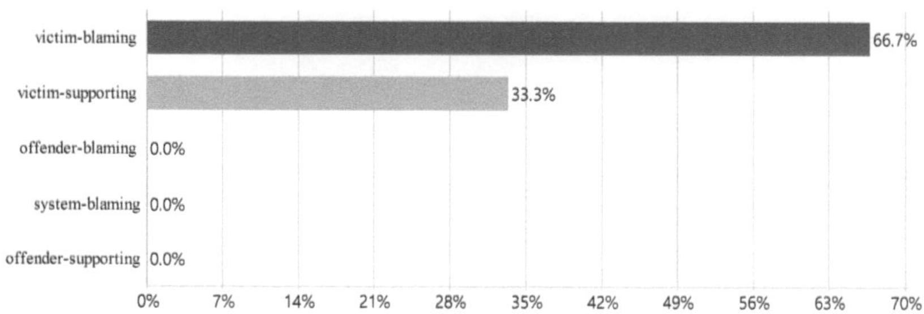

313) And *if you get drunk and someone takes your wallet, watch, etc., they should not be punished b/c you got drunk and so exposed yourself to the criminal behavior of the person who took your wallet.*
(AEC NYT 2016, Row: 17)

314) If she didn't remember it, then how does she know she didn't consent. *I did several shots of tequila once and don't remember anything, until my friend showed me video of me singing karaoke. I seriously have no recollection of it, but I'm sure no one made me do it.*
(AEC ABC 2015a, Row: 24)

315) *If you give me consent to drive your car and then pass out does that mean you didn't give me consent? If I drive your car and you wake up and don't remember loaning it to me, does that mean I stole it?*
(AEC ABC 2015a, Row: 25)

The above examples show that situational analogies can be used in victim-supporting comments (as in example 313) and in victim-blaming comments (as in examples 314 and 315). By comparing rape to situations such as singing karaoke or lending one's car, the criminal nature of rape is taken out of the discourse. In excluding the fact rape hinges on the fact of having one's body violated, the representation of rape loses in severity involved, additionally taking away the gendered aspect. This strategy is here viewed as having a reductive quality when looking at crime (Kort, 2017), as it reduces the act of rape to an event with which more people (i.e., the readers) may be able to identify, since the situation of theft may be more imaginable or singing while drunk might be more conceivable to those on the receiving end of such discourse.

Figure 67 Analogies of evaluative quality in the PC

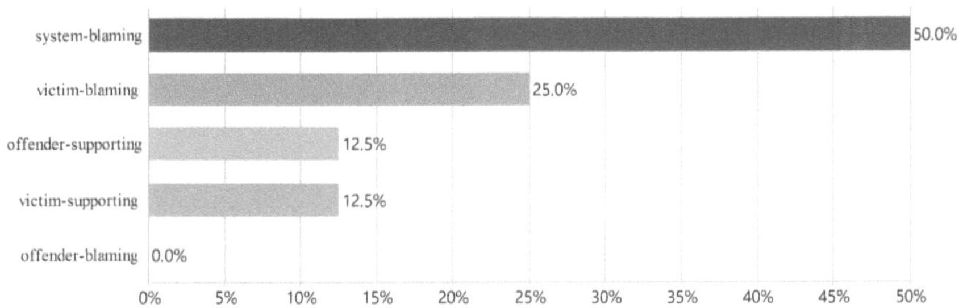

There were more instances of analogy in the PC than in the AEC. In the PC, this device was found to be present in 7 comments (making up 2.2% of the entire PC on the basis of comments). There were 4 comments which were system blaming, namely blaming the lack of action taken on the part of the police (1.2% of the PC on the basis of comment count), 2 victim-blaming analogous comments (.6% of the PC on the basis of comment count), and 1 offender-supporting comment and one victim-supporting comment of this kind (making up .3% of the corpus each on the basis of comment count). There were no offender-blaming comments in the form of analogies in the PC (0%).

The examples of analogous discourse strategies differed from those in the AEC, where there is more inference made to conclude that a comparison is being made. When it comes to the police dealing with rape or evaluating women and the stereotype of women as liars, stories are used as analogies to evaluate the situation and those actors dealing with the case (examples 316 and 317). Where marital rape is concerned (example 318), the supposed contract made between a husband and wife that are the marriage vows are compared to a contract with a telephone service and the denoting of sarcasm can be found within the whole context as it is not related to rape or sexual interaction.

316) Taa, ostatnio samochód rodziców porysował inny bus. Życzliwy zostawił numer rejestracyjny który po moich własnych poszukiwaniach potwierdził wersję, że to żółty VW. Do tego nagranie z monitoringu (przed biurowcem). *Policja pana nadal szuka....Od 3 tygodni.*
(PC GWyb 2014, Row: 3)
[Yeah, yeah, and recently my parents' car was scratched by another bus. A kind person left the license plate number, which, after my own search, confirmed the version that it was a yellow VW after my own research. In addition to the recording from the CCTV cameras (in front of the building). *The police are still looking for the man... for three weeks now.*]

317) Miałem kiedyś sytuację w butiku. Laska schowała do torby szpilki za 3500pln. Gdy złapałem ją przy wyjściu ze sklepu, to twierdziła, że to przez roztargnienie. *Tylko tak dalej, traktujcie kobiety taryfą ulgową.*
(PC PUD 2017a, Row: 13)
[I had a situation in a boutique once. A chick put a pair of 3500zł high heels into her bag. When I caught her exiting then store, she said that it had been because she was distracted. *Just keep giving women special treatment.*]

318) *Szanowny Abonencie: w nawiązaniu do zawartej przez nas umowy o świadczenie usług telekomunikacyjnych pragniemy poinformować, że ze względu na spadek atrakcyjności Pana jako abonenta oraz zmiany zainteresowań naszych telefonistek usługi telekomunikacyjne będziemy Panu świadczyć tylko wtedy, gdy sami będziemy chcieli. Proszę zwrócić uwagę, że nasza umowa pozostaje nadal w mocy i jest Pan w dalszym ciągu objęty obowiązkami wynikającymi z programu lojalnościowego, obowiązkiem regularnego uiszczania abonamentu oraz dbania o stację odbiorczą.*
(PC WO 2019, Row: 10)
[*Dear subscriber: with reference to the contract we have made for the provision of telecommunication services, we would like to inform you that as a result of your decrease in attractiveness as a client, as well as the changes of interest of our female phone operators, we will only be providing you telecommunication services when we want to. Please be mindful of the fact that our contract still stands and that you are still required to hold all responsibilities related that come with being part of our loyalty program and you will be required to pay the subscription and maintain the reception station.*]

Although the use of analogy is not a common strategy used in either the AEC or the PC, it is an important one because it creates a link between the structural and socio-semantic aspects of discussions on rape. This particular strategy shows how analogy can, through implication of a stance, communicate the evaluation of actors and events about rape in either negative or positive ways.

Rape myths present in the corpora

Another aspect that was described in the theoretical part of the work was the presence of rape myths about victims in discourses on sex crimes since it is such myths that tend to lead to victim blaming (Franiuk et al., 2008; cf. Chapter 2). Rape myths function on stereotypical ideas about the roles of the victim or offender in rape, usually emphasizing the circumstances surrounding the crime. Rape myths were counted in terms of the number of comments in each corpus and judged based on whether the language reflected a belief in or reference to a rape myth as being the reason why the victim was assaulted.

The AEC demonstrates that in American culture, the most prevalent rape myth is that of alcohol playing a role and being the reason for maintaining the blame of the victim. These types of comments represent a major part of the comments that place blame on the victim in the AEC.

Table 32 Rape myth maintaining comments about the victim in the American English corpus

	Frequency	**Percentage**	**Percentage in AEC**
victim was intoxicated, so she is to blame	128	81.5%	37.5%
victim is lying	13	8.1%	3.8%
victim wanted fame	5	3.2%	1.4%
victim consented to one thing, so she also consented to rape	5	3.2%	1.4%
victim deserved to be raped	2	1.3%	.5%
victim's revealing clothing caused her to be raped	2	1.3%	.5%
victim wanted to be raped	2	1.3%	.5%
victim did not resist, so she was not raped	0	0%	0%
TOTAL	157/341	100%	46% of AEC

In the American English corpus, the most common rape myth found in the comments represented beliefs that the victim's intoxication played a role in her being raped. A total of 128 comments (37.5% of the comments in the AEC) contained rape myth maintaining negative stances that associated intoxication with the rape of a woman. The reference to rape myths was either directly or indirectly presented in the corpus, similarly to the appraisement in the evaluative speech acts which showed victim-blaming attitudes.

319) Um, yea, tell your daughter not to *go out binge drinking* with a bunch of drunk guys... and definitely don't pass out. It's not right what they did at all, and I hope they get convicted to the highest degree, but come on. She willingly got drunk.
(AEC ABC 2015a, Row: 6)

320) These young inexperienced women are identified, *encouraged to drink to excess* (or sometimes drugged), purposefully isolated from their friends and then raped. It is not a casual hook up gone awry, it is a premeditated crime.
(AEC NYT 2014, Row: 10)

13 of the comments (3.8% of the comments) in the AEC abided by the common rape myth that victims lie about having been raped.
321) Hun......*if he actually raped her, do you think they would be passing friendly joking emails about having sex afterwords?*
(AEC ABC 2015b, Row: 35)

322) I think *she is a liar*. She's having regrets about what she chose to do and *now wants to claim rape*.
(AEC VTY 2019, Row: 34)

There were 5 comments (1.4% of the comments in the AEC) which abided by the rape myth that a woman is looking for attention or fame in saying that she has been raped.

323) Also, why 2 years later and you want to drag his name through the mud...*how much are you getting paid for this one*?
(AEC VTY 2019, Row: 30)

324) Well, there is a difference between having your actual job on the line and "*wanting that big break into show business*".
(AEC ABC 2020, Row: 22)

There were 5 comments that expressed the myth that if a woman consented to one thing (i.e., on a date), she also consented to sexual intercourse.

325) These are not the middle ages when you accuse the King of a crime and you were hanged. People now have a true sense of justice, but in this case *it looks like Nevils had a consensual sexual relationship with Lauer*. She was attracted to power and wanted to advance her career.
(AEC VTY 2019, Row: 32)

326) tho im on the victims side, it's a bit odd *she continued to have sex with Lauer*....on later occasions.
(AEC VTY 2019, Row: 33)

There were 2 comments reflecting the myths that women deserve to be raped (example 327), and 2 comments which reflected the idea that a woman's revealing clothing caused a man to rape her (example 328) and that victims want to be raped (example 329) (.5% of the comments in the AEC each).

327) That said, it's just amazing to me that the "victim" takes no responsibility for *making herself vulnerable -- by getting falling-down-blacked-out-drunk.*
(AEC NYT 2016, Row: 30)

328) Why aren't parents telling their daughters they should be able to get drunk and sashay down a dark alley *in a miniskirt*, or hang out in a parking garage, and not expect anyone to touch them?
(AEC NYT 2017, Row: 23)

329) These young girls *want* to be selected. They *vie for it.*
(AEC ABC 2015b, Row: 48)

The reference to rape myths that blamed the victim made up 46% of the corpus on the basis of comments, which is a very significant factor in creating representations of the rape victim.

It must be kept in mind that, similarly to the AEC, rape myths were not present in all of the digital comments analyzed in the Polish corpus, and therefore only those comments which reflected common rape myths concerning the victim (cf. Chapter 2 for rape myths defined) were accounted for in the analysis.

The following table shows the number of times the most common rape myths regarding the victim were present in the Polish corpus (in 102 of the comments in the PC—making up 32.3% of the entire PC). There were fewer instances of victim blaming on the basis of reference to rape myths in the PC, as shown below, and the rape myths which were most frequent in the PC also differed from those that were most frequent in the AEC (i.e., the intoxication of the victim).

Table 33 Rape myths present in comments in the PC

	Frequency	Percentage	Percentage of PC
victim is lying	37	36.6%	11.8%
victim consented to one thing, so she also consented to sex	24	22.7%	7.6%
victim wanted to be raped	17	16.8%	5.5%
victim was intoxicated, so she is to blame	10	9.0%	3.2%
victim deserved to be raped	5	4.9%	1.5%
victim did not resist, so she was not raped	4	3.9%	1.2%

(Continued)

Table 33 Continued

	Frequency	Percentage	Percentage of PC
victim's revealing clothing caused her to be raped	3	3.0%	.9%
victim wanted fame	2	2%	.6%
TOTAL	102/315	100%	32.3%of PC

In the Polish corpus, the most common rape myth found in the comments represented beliefs that the victim was lying (36 comments—11.4% of the comments). Some of the comments used rape myths in defending the victim by mentioning the social norms which link stereotypical behaviors of women with their victimization (cf. example 331).

330) A co tam robiła tłumaczka ? *Ta pani znana jest w środowisku z konfabulacji.*
(PC PUD 2015, Row: 24)
[What was the translator doing there? *That woman is known in that environment for her confabulations.*]

331) Co tu dyskutować, *pogubiła się w zeznaniach*, pewnie jakiś przygodny seks na boku, przybrał nieoczekiwny obrót i *trzeba było wymyśleć historyjkę dla męża*!
(PC GWyb 2014, Row: 25)
[What is there to discuss here. She *got lost in her testimony*, there was probably some casual sex on the side, it all took a wrong turn and *she had to think up a story for her husband*!]

332) Gdyby przez przypadek policji by sie udało złapać bandziora, to zupełnie inaczej by postępowali wobec dziewczyny. Ale że jak ze śledztwa nici *to robię z dziewczyny kłamczuchę.*
(PC GWyb 2014, Row: 35)
[If by some miracle the police manage to catch the bandit, they would approach the girl differently. But if the investigation comes to nothing, *I'm going to say the girl is a liar.*]

The other rape myth that was most prevalent in the PC was, for one, the rape myth which spreads the belief that if a victim consents to one thing (such as going to a party), she also consents to sexual contact, hence she consents to being raped. This rape myth occurred 24 times in the PC, making up 7.6% of the PC on the basis of comment count.

333) Ale kto normalny *idzie na imprezę z nieznajomymi.*
(PC PUD 2017a Row: 2)
[What kind of normal person *goes to a party with strangers*..]

334) *a co ona myślała że na kawkę i ciastka tam idzie*??? kobieto gdzie twój rozum
(PC PUD 2017a, Row: 31)
[What? *Did she think she was going there for coffee and cookies*??? Woman, where is your common sense]

Rape myths of the victim being at fault for the rape because she had been drinking were present in 11.8% of the corpus on the basis of comment count.

335) Znane przyslowiemowi—*kobieta pijana*, d***a sprzedana
(PC PUD 2015, Row: 15)
[A well-known proverb says—*a woman drunk* means an a**sold]

336) *alkohol*, zdemoralizowanie a finalem sa gwalty po pijaku!!!! a jak się wytrzezwieje, panienka poczula się zgwalcona!!!!
(PC GWsp 2019, Row: 3)
[*alcohol* and demoralizing oneself—and in the end there's rape under intoxication!!!! And when she gets sober, the young lady feels like she was raped]

The rape myth of the victim wanting fame was present twice in the PC (making up .6% of the corpus on the basis of comment count), as shown in the example below.

337) *Tak to jest jak szuka się wrażeń* w towarzystwie nieznajomych mężczyzn. No ale ,'dzieki temu" *stała się celebrytką*.
(PC PUD 2017a, Row: 40)
[*That's what happens when you look for adventure* among strangers (men). But she did *become a celebrity* "thanks to what happened".]

The myth that women secretly desire to be raped was also present in 17 of the comments (making up 5.3% of the comments in the PC).

338) *Każda kobieta chce być gwałcona* tylko tego nie mówi, trzeba się samemu domyśleć a kiedy się zaczyna bronić lepiej sex smakuje niech sama rozłoży nogi wtedy będzie spokojna takich nikt nie rucha
(PC GWsp 2019, Row: 19)
[*Every woman wants to be raped;* they just don't say so. You just have to guess. When she starts to defend herself, the sex is only better. She should spread her legs herself and then she'll be calm because no one fucks those kinds.]

339) *Chciała się zabawić* to się zabawiła. Nikt jej tam siłą nie ciągnął.
(PC PUD 2017a, Row: 32)
[*She wanted to have some fun* and so she did. No one took her there by force.]

The rape myth which reflects the belief that a woman is at fault for being raped because she was wearing revealing clothes was also present in the corpus, a total of 3 times (making up .9% of the PC, based on the number of comments).

340) dobrze, że zapamiętała jego imię spośród tylu innych mężczyzn... kobieta zgwałcona—*pomalowane pazurki, krótka mini* ... Celebrytka
(PC PUD 2015, Row: 36)
[It's a good thing that she remembered his name among all those other men… woman raped—*painted nails, mini skirt*… a celebrity]

There were more rape myths surrounding the victim in the AEC (46% of the comments) than in the PC (32.3% of the comments), which shows a greater tendency to draw on rape myths in victim blaming in American culture than in Polish culture. This says much about the nature of stereotyping in American culture, as rape myths can be considered the negative stereotyping of actors. The fact that this was done in over ten percent more comments than in the PC is significant in the way that stereotypes shape beliefs about rape in American culture.

Expressing blame for rape on outside actors

It is worth noting that not only were the main actors in the rape cases placed in the position of blame in either corpus, but there were also comments that targeted outside parties and institutions as being responsible for the rape discussed or rape culture in general.

In the AEC, this was found in comments that concerned Uber, the rape of teenagers or the rapes that took place in the college campus setting. Placing the blame for the rape or criticizing the way that the rape is dealt with on other parties took place in a total of 24 sentences in the AEC (making up 2.9% of the entire AEC on the basis of sentence count). Uber, as a company, was blamed in 6 sentences, making up .7% of the AEC (on the basis of sentence count). The police, the court system, and the education system were either blamed for not preventing the rape or not dealing with the rape adequately 4 times each (.5% of the AEC each). The government was blamed in 2 sentences (.2% of the AEC on the basis of sentence count) and the blame was placed on pornography, the school, a lack of conversation between parents and children, and the internet at 1 count each (.1% of the AEC each on the basis of sentence count).

341) So is Stanford going to expel him now? Since his sentencing is a joke, *the school should take action and expel him*. Revoking his scholarship means nothing.
(AEC NYT 2016, Row: 46)

342) Surely *college orientations need to include education about behaviors that can lead to harmful consequences* including drinking.
(AEC NYT 2017, Row: 17)

343) she was drugged and after Brock was arrested they should have got a warrant to search his car and home for the drugs. The girl should have had a blood tox screen for ruffees and other drugs ......*cops blew the case again* !
(AEC MN 2016, Row: 4)

Below, a graph presenting the various frequencies of blame on other parties for rape has been provided. As can be seen below, where the blaming of another party is expressed, in the AEC, there is a total of nine categories of blame that were not associated with the victim or the offender.

Figure 68 Frequencies of blame attributed to other party AEC

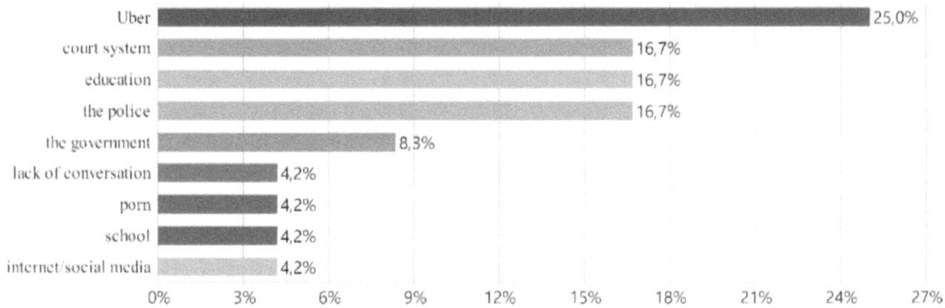

In the PC, the blame was placed on other parties in a total of 49 sentences (6.8% of the PC). The police took the most blame in sentences (as well as comments) in the PC, at 17 counts (making up 2.3% of the PC on the basis of sentence count). The government was blamed in a total of 14 sentences 1.9% of the PC) and the court system was blamed in 9 instances (1.2% of the PC). The church was blamed 6 times (.8% of the PC) and the country was blamed in two instances (.3% of the PC). The education system was blamed 1 time in the PC (.2% of the PC).

Figure 69 Frequencies of blame attributed to other party PC

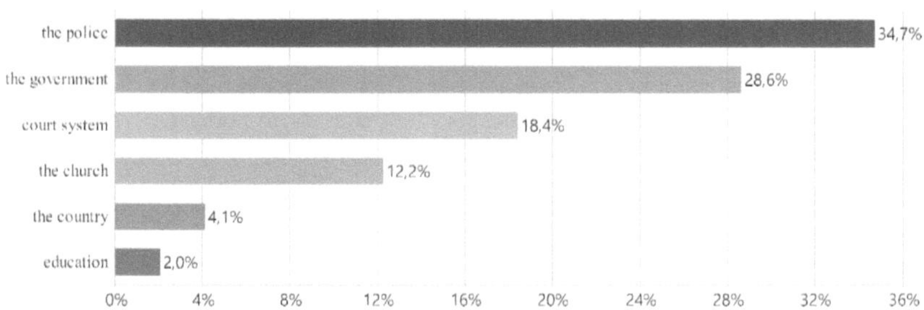

Here, rape is presented as a social problem on a grander scale than simply the problem of men hurting women, but also one that lacks the proper attention from the criminal justice system or politicians. As can be seen in the examples given below (examples 344–346), various institutionalized systems and parties are presented as having an impactful hand in bringing about or maintaining rape culture.

344) Szanowna *policjo* to tylko świadczy o was jak patrolujecie miasta takie rzeczy nie powinny mieć w ogóle miejsca.
(PC GWsp 2019, Row: 17)
[Dear *police*, this only goes to show how you patrol the city. Things like that should not even be taking place.]

345) Najwięcej gwałtów pedofilii w Banana Republik mają **księża** na koncie.
(PC GWsp 2019, Row: 4)
[*Priests* are the ones who have the most pedophilic rapes in their history in Banana Republic.]

346) Straszne. I *prokuratorzy* umarzający 60 procent spraw. I wyroki w zawieszeniu.
(PC GWyb 2020, Row: 4)
[Horrible. And *prosecutors* dismiss 60% of the cases. And then they [the rapists] go on probation.]

There was a significant difference between the AEC and the PC in the blame given to other parties who were not the two main actors discussed throughout the presented chapter. Only 2.4% in the AEC and 6.8% of the PC. This difference might demonstrate the way that rape is not viewed as a problem caused by parties that were not the offender or the victim in the American context, but rather as an event that is the fault of the offender or the victim. This was not as clear in the Polish context, where the police and the church are targeted as blameful in the Polish cultural context.

Discussion

Selected aspects of the analysis have been taken into consideration for the discussion of the investigation presented in this chapter, those being the aspects that impinge most on and show the evaluation of actors in rape most clearly. It is important to note here that in the representations of social actors in digital comments about rape, there was a relative lack of nomination for the actors in both the AEC and the PC. Other socio-semantic strategies of the construction of actors find themselves to be more prevalent than those belonging to the category of nomination, including identification, functionalization, indetermination, the backgrounding of actors, and their appraisement, all of which have an impact on the way that the actors are viewed.

Of the various types of socio-semantic representation of the actors, I have chosen to discuss the functionalization of the actors first, because it is in this category that roles, including the role of actors in the crime, are discussed, which impacts the way that actors are seen on the basis of the actions that they are involved in. This is presented in the table below for the cases of the victim in the AEC and the PC (cf. Table 34).

Table 34 Functionalization of the victim

	Frequency	Percentage of AEC		Frequency	Percentage of PC
victim	50	.2%	ofiara	37	.3%
freshman	2	.01%	tłumaczka	2	.02%
student	1	.004%	pijana	1	.01%
participant	1	.004%	pokrzywdzona	1	.01%
survivor	1	.004%	zgwałcona	1	.01%
beauty queen	1	.004%			
TOTAL	56/20,898	.3% of AEC		41/11,200	.4% of PC

As can be seen when comparing the two tables on functionalization (Tables 34 and 34), there was significantly less variation in the functionalization of the victim than of the offender in both the AEC and the PC. The functionalization was almost equal for the actors in both the AEC and the PC, which is important to note, as the naming of the criminal in relation to the crime committed belonged to such a categorization (cf. Table 35).

Table 35 Functionalization of the offender

	Frequency	Percentage of AEC		Frequency	Percentage of PC
rapist	34	.2%	**gwałciciel ('rapist')**	29	.3%
occupation	16	.08%	**sprawca ('offender')**	10	.09%
student	15	.07%	**occupation**	7	.06%
predator	12	.05%	**oskarżony ('accused')**	5	.02%
accused	10	.04%	**zboczeniec ('pervert')**	5	.02%
suspect	4	.01%	**oprawca ('torturer')**	4	.02%

(Continued)

Table 35 Continued

	Frequency	Percentage of AEC		Frequency	Percentage of PC
criminal	3	.01%	**przestępca ('criminal')**	4	.02%
creep	2	.01%	**napastnik ('attacker')**	4	.02%
athlete	1	.005%	**zbrodniarz ('criminal')**	3	.01%
culprit	1	.005%	**zwyrod-nialec ('villain')**	2	.009%
assailant	1	.005%	**pijany ('drunk')**	2	.009%
			zbok ('pervert')	1	.008%
			winny ('guilty')	1	.008%
			recydywista ('recidivist')	1	.008%
TOTAL	99/20,898	.5% of AEC		78/11,200	.7% of PC

One reason for such a difference in representation of the victim and the offender in the AEC and the PC might be because the role of the offender in the crime (i.e., *rapist*) is the one given the most attention in discourse on rape. Other functionalization types for the offender were also primarily found to focus on the role of the actor in the crime, indicating more offender-blaming attitudes in the case of the naming of the offender. There were also more offensive terms in the PC than in the AEC, leading to the same conclusion as stated in the preceding sentence. The fact that functionalization of actors in the CMC discourse of digital comments places a focus on the role in the crime is indicative of the tendency to view those actors in a binary way.

Such categorization of actors might lead to victim blaming when considering that it is the victim who is activated through what she does in the given circumstances and thus the state of being a victim might become associated with negatively connotating actions.

Other significant categories were the indetermination and backgrounding of actors, both of which abstracted the actors from the rape in some way. The indetermination of actors used generalizing nominal constituents (i.e., a percentage) or pronouns (i.e., *someone* or *ktoś*), which took away from the specificity of the rape crime and also abstracted the actors from the gendered nature of sexual crime. This was carried out by not explicitly referring to the gender of the actors but by using non-specific representations in discourse which imply that too little is known about perpetrators to properly categorize them (i.e., as men).

There was a slightly higher frequency of the process of the indetermination of actors in the AEC than in the PC, and the victim in the AEC underwent indetermination processes more often than the victim in the PC, most likely due to the fact that the offender is seen as more anonymous and because rape as a taboo subject engenders greater abstraction of those involved. Such abstraction can both express and lead to victim blaming, because the non-concreteness of reference to offenders makes them seem unreal and thus mystified in a way (cf. Table 36).

Table 36 Indetermination of actors in sentences

	Frequency AEC	Percentage AEC	Frequency PC	Percentage PC
Indetermination offender	20	.09%	10	.08%
Indetermination victim	20	.09%	3	.02%
TOTAL	40/20,898	.2%	13/11,200	.1%

The backgrounding of actors in which the rape as an act was highlighted and one or both of the main actors were excluded from a sentence, which thus muddled their involvement, abstracting them even further from the context of the rape. It is important to note that in both of the corpora, the offender was more frequently backgrounded than the victim, however there was an even greater difference in this in the AEC (cf. Table 37).

Table 37 Backgrounding of actors in sentences

	Frequency AEC	Percentage AEC	Frequency PC	Percentage PC
offender backgrounded	126	15.6%	74	10.3%
victim backgrounded	63	7.8%	50	7%
TOTAL	189/804	23.4%	124/714	17.3%

What such a discourse strategy does is hide the actor from thought or view, minimizing the association of his or her role in the processes that are described in the discourse (in this case, those processes involved in rape). This strategy is particularly powerful, as it creates victim blaming discourse and brings about secondary victimization, because it partially erases the responsibility of the offender in discourse. The fact that this takes place more often in the AEC is significant, for it presents an issue of talking about rape as including an active doer.

Another aspect considered for the investigation of the evaluation of actors was that of appraisement, where direct evaluation of the actors through adjectival modifiers, nominalizations and predicatives that overtly expressed negative or positive attitudes to the actors was investigated. Where such discourse was concerned, in both of the corpora analyzed, negative appraisement was more prevalent for both the victim and the offender than supportive attitudes and evaluation. In the AEC, negative appraisement of the victim (3.7%) was less frequent than in the PC (6.1%).

As stated in Chapter 1, evaluation may take place either implicitly or explicitly. Explicit appraisement is here described as being more direct than indirect. The offender underwent more direct negative appraisement in the PC than the victim in the PC, however (19.9% on the basis of sentence count). In the AEC, on the other hand, the victim and offender underwent an equal number of direct appraisement counts (3.9% for the victim and 4% for the offender). This fact is particularly interesting to the analysis of victim blaming, for it shows that explicit victim blaming through appraisement is more prevalent in Polish discourse than American discourse, which can be said to be reflective of the cultural differences in expression of opinion in American and Polish interaction and talk (Lubecka, 2000; Grainger & Mills, 2016). This relates to a conclusion in that when it comes to negative naming, knowledge of cultural representations of negative and positive ideas is necessary in order to discern that negative or positive evaluation is taking place. The use of appraising linguistic representations in discourse about rape still comes from writers and readers that a common socio-cultural knowledge is acknowledged, thus making implicit evaluation all the more common a strategy in use when discussing rape. Tables 38 and 39 below show the frequencies for positive and negative appraisement of actors in the AEC and the PC, respectively.

Table 38 Appraisement of victim

	Frequency AEC	Percentage AEC	Frequency PC	Percentage PC
Negative appraisement	30	3.7%	44	6.1%
Positive appraisement	2	0.2%	8	1.1%
TOTAL	32/804	3.9%	83/714	7.2%

Table 39 Appraisement of offender

	Frequency AEC	Percentage AEC	Frequency PC	Percentage PC
Negative appraisement	31	3.8%	142	19.9%
Positive appraisement	2	0.2%	0	1.1%
TOTAL	33/804	4%	142/714	19.9%

Such an aspect is important in the interpretation of blame for a rape, as it demonstrates that more direct, explicit and strong attitudes towards the actors are expressed. The negative appraisement of the victim always correlated with the victim blaming in both of the corpora. This category of analysis was seen as encompassing both direct and indirect evaluation of actors because it presented naming that made overt comparisons to symbols that have negative connotations in both American and Polish societies (i.e., metaphorical categories) or indirectly referred to them in adjectival or predicative form.

In addition to naming actors, the representation of the rape itself is considered just as pertinent to such an analysis. Crime-reflective language provides objectivity to the discourse, which means that by describing a sexual crime as rape, it acquires the value of communicating that rape is a social problem and not associative with the other euphemistic expressions that might be seen as having a relationship to sexuality in discourse (cf. Table 40).

Table 40 Crime-reflective naming of rape in AEC and PC

	Frequency	Percentage of AEC		Frequency	Percentage of PC
rape	122	.5%	**gwałt**	76	.6%
assault	47	.2%	**przemoc**	7	.06%
crime	31	.1%	**przestępstwo**	5	.04%

(Continued)

Table 40 Continued

	Frequency	Percentage of AEC		Frequency	Percentage of PC
criminal behavior	7	.03%	**atak**	1	.01%
attack	6	.03%	**zbrodnia**	1	.01%
TOTAL	213/20,898	1.0%		90/11,200	.8%

Crime-reflecting naming, present in both of the corpora, was counted at similar frequencies in both the AEC and the PC. *Rape* was most common in this category in the AEC, whereas *gwałt* ('rape') was most common in this category in the PC. This aspect is important in comparing how often crime-reflective naming of the event presented itself in each of the corpora, in comparison to how often the euphemization of the event takes place, a strategy in the discourse on rape which detracts from the criminal nature of the crime.

Table 41 Euphemization of rape in AEC and PC

	Frequency	Percentage AEC		Frequency	Percentage PC
behavior	28	.1%	**to/tego ('that')**	26	.2%
what happened/ going on	25	.1%	**sprawa ('affair')**	22	.2%
this/that	20	.09%	**sytuacja ('situation')**	15	.1%
situation	12	.05%	**gwałt ('rape') censored***	8	.07%
incident	9	.04%	**złe zachowania ('bad behavior')**	6	.05%
issue	8	.04%	**takie rzeczy ('those things')**	6	.05%
affair	7	.03%	**czyn ('act')**	5	.04%
hookup	7	.03%	**zdarzenie ('event')**	4	.04%

(Continued)

Table 41 Continued

	Frequency	Percentage AEC		Frequency	Percentage PC
it	6	.02%	**historia ('story')**	3	**.03%**
intercourse	5	.02%	**co się stało ('what happened')**	3	.03%
he said she said	4	.02%	**zaliczenie ('third base')**	2	.01%
thing	4	.02%	**paranoja ('paranoia')**	1	.01%
thing/ things	4	.02%	**Sprzedanie-sie ('selling oneself')**	1	.01%
what he did	3	.01%	**randka ('date')**	1	.01%
event	3	.01%	**Skutki ucieczki żydowskich bandytów z Niemiec i Francji ('the effect of the fleeing of Jewish bandits from Germany and France')**	1	.03%
high-risk situation	2	.009%	**traktowanie ('treatment')**	1	.01%
sexual bullying	2	.009%	**Zaspokojenie potrzeb ('satisfying needs')**	1	.01%
encounter	2	.009%	**rzecz ('thing')**	1	.01%
potential danger	1	.004%	**przeżycie ('experience')**	1	.01%
urge	1	.004%	**przyjemność ('pleasure')**	1	.01%
mistake	1	.004%			

(Continued)

Table 41 Continued

	Frequency	Percentage AEC		Frequency	Percentage PC
not the right decision	1	.004%			
actions	1	.004%			
sexual relations	1	.004%			
controversy	1	.004%			
a little something something	1	.004%			
TOTAL	159/20,898	.7% of AEC		109/11,200	.9% of PC

Another difference between the AEC and the PC regarded the more overt discursive tabooization of rape. For one, where there was no censoring of the word *rape* in the AEC, the word *gwałt* ('rape') was censored in the PC. In both of the linguistic contexts (as representative and reflective of cultural contexts), rape is treated as a taboo subject. This can be seen in the equal occurrence of euphemistic expressions in both the AEC and the PC to represent crime of a sexual nature.

One very important consideration for the presented project was to investigate if rape myths function in current discourses about rape (Franiuk et al., 2008; Suarez & Gadala, 2010; Ryan, 2011). Both of the corpora present significant percentages of rape myths in the comments (counted within whole comments), however the types of rape myths differ in the AEC and the PC. In the AEC, victim blaming that related to the intoxication of the victim was significantly more prevalent than in the PC (37.5% in the AEC and 3.2% in the PC). This phenomenon in the discourse contributed to the overall discursive secondary victimization and was reflective of social associations of rape with college life and so-called campus party culture.

The most prevalent rape myth in the PC was the belief that the victim was lying, which coincides with negative stereotypes about women having a tendency to lie (Stabile et al., 2019). The second most common rape myth presented was that which presented the claim that if a victim had consented to one act (i.e., going to a party) then she automatically consented to sexual intercourse (7.6% in the PC and 1.4% in the AEC).

Table 42 Rape myths comparison and summary of the AEC and the PC

	Frequency AEC	Percentage in AEC	Frequency PC	Percentage in PC
victim was intoxicated, so she is to blame	128	37.5%	10	3.2%%
victim is lying	13	3.8%	37	11.8%
victim wanted fame	5	1.4%	2	.6%
victim consented to one, so she also consented to rape	5	1.4%	24	7.6%
victim deserved to be raped	2	.5%	5	1.5%
victim's revealing clothing caused her to be raped	2	.5%	3	.9%
victim wanted to be raped	2	.5%	17	5.5%
victim did not resist, so she was not raped	0	0%	4	1.2%
TOTAL	157/341	46% of AEC	102/315	32.3% of PC

In general, the fact that such a large percentage of both of the corpora included the expression of common rape myths is telling of the phenomenon of victim blaming in both cases. In the AEC, there were more rape myths present than in the PC, which again iterates the fact that in American culture, victim blaming has a more multi-dimensional discursive manifestation than in Polish culture. It can be stated here that Polish victim blaming is more direct, whereas American victim blaming is more implicational.

Another aspect that was interesting to the study was the blame placed on other parties in the aftermath of the rape. This included sentences where the blaming of society for not investigating rape properly, creating a rape culture, etc. were expressed. Although this is an aspect not as statistically significant as other categories, it is one that shows where cultural differences between American thought and Polish thought may be found, in that there is a tendency in the Polish discourse to shed responsibility from the offender and search for blame in others.

Table 43 Blame of an outside party for the rape in the AEC and the PC

	Frequency AEC	Percentage of AEC	Frequency PC	Percentage of the PC
the police	4	.5%	17	2.3%
the government	2	.2%	14	1.9%
court system	4	.5%	9	1.3%
the church	0	0%	6	.8%
the country	0	0%	2	.3%
education	4	.5%	1	.2%
Uber	6	.7%	0	0%
pornography	1	.1%	0	0%
school	1	.1%	0	0%
lack of conversation	1	.1%	0	0%
internet	1	.1%	0	0%
TOTAL	24/20,898	**2.9% of the AEC**	49/11,200	**7% of the PC**

The aspects of the blame that are placed on outside parties are also important, and when comparing the AEC and the PC, differences are visible between the two corpora. Such outside blame for the rape and for dealing with the aftermath of a rape took place more prevalently in the PC (making up 7% of the PC on the basis of sentence count).

It is important to note that the reactions presented in the comments, when comparing the two language contexts, were more expressive in the PC than in the AEC. What can be given attention, with respect to this aspect of the analysis, is the prevalence of more expressive semantic constituents in the PC on the subject of rape and the actors, including those which demonstrate strong negative feelings. Here, such comments more often had to do with the evaluation of the offender than of the victim.

Conclusions

When set against the investigation of the structure of comments about rape and the actors involved, the analysis of the representations of social actors shows that the evaluation of actors and events may be expressed within the structural context, as well as in relation to the cultural knowledge that is carried within the socio-semantic references to actors and/or events. Therefore, it is necessary to account for the fact that the socio-semantic representations investigated make more sense when looked from the social and physical contexts of the texts (i.e., the fact that they are found online in a comments section under an article about rape). On the level of their meaning, however, socio-semantic aspects of discourse do carry with them both direct and indirect reference to actors which may or may not carry connotative or symbolic meaning for the evaluation of the actors involved in a rape.

Considering the comments presented above, the question of implicit evaluation is important in discerning and interpreting the meaning of comments from a socio-semantic standpoint, for it is in such contexts that they gain their evaluative meaning. It is the knowledge of the socio-semantic weight and the connotations which such lexical choices have in the face of the social issue that is rape. The American online discourse about rape made by Internet users demonstrated less of a tendency that the PC to explicitly evaluate the actors involved. In the Polish discourse on rape, the directness of blaming was found through the use of lexical choices that clearly connotate negatively within the given socio-cultural context of writing such comments.

The presented chapter looked at the representations of the victim, offender and the rape itself to investigate whether or not cultural differences were visible between the two. The victim was more overtly blamed in the Polish corpus than in the American English corpus on the level of socio-semantics and also seen as lying about the rape, confabulating stories and in that way contributing as a catalyst for the rape itself. Thus, it becomes clear that Polish discourses on rape can be unforgiving of the victim of a sex crime, namely rape. Female rape victims are at times viewed stereotypically and negatively pinpointed through discursive strategies that work against them. Additionally, the role of the rapist is, in the American English discourse as well as the Polish discourse, seen as being outlandish, boorish and animalistic, taking away human qualities from the rapists, and pushing the testimonies of rape victims into compartments that are even less likely to see them as being in the position of a person deserving empathy or their stories viewed as reliable versions of events.

The present analysis has shed light on the aspects which need more focus in conducting such a critical discourse analysis. The lack of clear evidence for whether or not the type of rape—as a variable impacting the study—draws attention to the fact that more research in this area should be carried out in order to ascertain how certain victims of different rape (date rape, stranger rape, marital rape, etc.) are represented in the discourses that concern them. Overall, however, it can be seen that the discourse practices that lead to secondary victimization are visible on a socio-semantic, as well as structural level in discourse

Chapter 8: Conclusions

In this book, I have explored the ways that the subject of rape and the actors involved are represented in digital comments written by Internet users in response to articles about rape. As a genre, digital comments have been demonstrated to be discursive sites that oscillate between written and spoken communication, inasmuch that they represent informal discourse, communicating both with the subject discussed and with other comments written on fora.

The presented study has sought to examine the prominence of blame attribution to victims by indirect means and the results show that victim blaming is, by all means, present in social fora that discuss rape (Franiuk et al., 2008). In this final chapter, I draw on the results of the analyses which were presented in the two analytical chapters (Chapters 6 and 7), highlighting those aspects which were most significant in showing how the evaluation of the actors involved in a rape takes place at both structural and socio-semantic levels of American and Polish CMC discourses indirectly.

The gravity of the problem of rape makes for the reason behind my having chosen such a topic for analysis. It has been my goal throughout this book to demonstrate that the social and cultural contexts in which discourses come about do, in fact, impinge greatly on the way that such discourses about subjects like rape are expressed, including those which express opinion or provide a stance regarding the rape and the actors involved. When such stances are expressed discursively, opinions about who is to blame for the rape are also expressed, both explicitly and implicitly. This has been observed in both the discourses of American and Polish Internet users on the basis of the two compiled corpora of digital comments found in the online context which accompanied articles about rape cases.

As has been noted in the literature on the subject (cf. Chapter 1 for an expansion of the topics), evaluation (or appraisal) does not have a specific form, but is expressed in various ways (Hunston, 2011). Evaluation in discourse is related to the expression of appraisement in van Leeuwen's (2005) classification for the analysis of social actors, including communicating the ways that feelings, affect, judgements or reflections of ideologies surrounding actors are expressed (Martin & White, 2005: 42). Thus, evaluation makes up a fairly large category for analysis itself and may be investigated as rising through various strategies and mechanisms (cf. Chapter 1; Martin & White, 2005; Hunston, 2011).

When looking at evaluation that is found in digital comments on subjects that incite strong feelings as a result of the nature of such discourses and which are more informal in their register and conversational in their style, analyzing implicit evaluation becomes crucial in uncovering the range of modes of its expression. Digital comments are embedded in various contexts, including the surrounding social context, the cultural context and the physical context[88] also attribute to the ways in which attitudes, opinions or judgements are expressed. The subject of rape is, no doubt, surrounded by an overarching social context of taboo-enforcing and taboo-reproducing discourse, which is one that additionally infringes upon the way that it is both received and perceived as a subject, as well as the reactions that it may bring about. Investigating that type of genre of discourse at the level of structure and the level of semantic choice reveals how American and Polish cultures—as in, how they compare to one another—partake in the practice of victim blaming, as well as in the appraisal of the offender of a rape and the act of rape itself.

The original assumptions of the presented project were confirmed in the study, including that the analysis showed, overall, that victim blaming does present itself in online discourses made by anonymous Internet users who write digital comments in both American and Polish discourses, and very prevalently at that. It is clear that in such informal and public discourses, the evaluation of the victim and the offender may be expressed either directly or indirectly. Not only is the negative evaluation of victims found in digital comments about rape, but negative comments about the offender in a sexual crime are also found. The representation of the offender was seen as equally important to the investigation of how the victim is presented in the same discourses, since, when set side by side, a comparison of the two leads to results about which actors are viewed as culpable in the context of the crime.

Combining the two aspects of analysis in reaching final conclusions about victim blaming in online discourse is important to the entirety of the study, as well as to gaining insight on a broader overview of how the social actors involved in rape are evaluated in digital comments. The cultural differences in the expression of evaluation in digital comments may also be seen at the level of indirect evaluation, which can be gathered on the basis of knowledge of the context in which such discourses occur (i.e., as emerging from other discussions on rape), the cultural tendency to see the victim as being to blame. This is also related to the embedding of rape myths in discussions about rape, which is an intertextual

88 By this I mean where they are located in the online space, i.e., comments on fora accompanying articles about rape.

aspect of discourse on rape. There are several aspects of the analysis of structure and socio-semantics that I would like to highlight in this chapter, so that they may be juxtaposed against one another and the differences in what each aspect presents brought to light.

The two types of comments that are significant here are the blaming and supportive comments for the offender and the victim. In the AEC and the PC, blaming comments about the victim and the offender dominated, with 37% of comments victim-blaming in the AEC and 36.3% of comments victim blaming in the PC. There was a larger discrepancy between the percentages of victim-supporting comments, with 20.7% of comments in the AEC and 16.1% in the PC, showing a lower tendency in the Polish online comments for victim support to take place.

As far as the offender was concerned, 34% of comments were of offender-blaming nature in the AEC and the percentage was slightly higher in the PC, at 37.1%. Offender-supporting comments were either sparse (3.3% in the AEC) or non-existent (0% in the PC), which may be attributed to the lack of attention given to the perpetrators of crime in Polish media and a greater focus on the role of the victim which thoroughly outweighs the attention given to the offender in that culture. The remainder of attitudes represented in the corpora were comments in which it was difficult to ascertain who or what exactly was being evaluated. The fact that most evaluation in the comments was negative demonstrates that there is an about equal distribution of blame overall for the victim and the offender in a sexual crime. This fact alone shows that in both the American and Polish contexts, victim blaming has a similar standing to offender-blaming when it comes to sexual crime. This phenomenon can be attributed to complicated societal relationships with ideas about sexuality, negative stereotyping, and interpretation of behavior as complex and unclear (cf. Crawford [1995] for the application of miscommunication theory to rape culture).

Within the structures of evaluation in online discourses, there were differences seen in how such blaming and supportive attitudes are expressed about the victim and the offender, This is also visible from a cultural perspective. The analysis presented in Chapter 6 has shown variation in the how evaluation takes place on the level of structure in digital comments, in both American and Polish online discourses. This part of the analysis looked at the overall structure of evaluative comments and their indirect reading (including that of declarative, interrogative, exclamatory, and imperative sentence types) and various processes that also took place within those evaluative sentences, such as the grammatical formation of alternative hypothetical situations, through both negation and use of modal expressions, as well as the aspect of activation and passivation of actors. The activation and passivation of actors presented a larger amount of data relevant to the topic studied, making it more significant in the investigation of blame attribution in the context of comments.

When looking at the sentence structure of the evaluative comments, there was variation between the AEC and the PC in the distribution of sentence structure types that represented evaluative attitudes. There were more evaluative sentences in the AEC overall, since the AEC was larger than the PC. In the AEC, there were about 8% more declarative sentences, showing that in American discourse, evaluative attitudes are expressed more often than in Polish discourse as information, facts or the knowledge of the Internet user. Interestingly, interrogative sentences were equally visible in the AEC and the PC (about 15.5%). The PC showed about 2.5% more imperative sentences than the AEC and 6% more exclamatory sentences than in the AEC, demonstrating more expressive attitudes towards rape (exclamatory sentences were observed at 3.7% in the AEC and 9.5% in the PC). This aspect is interesting on a cultural level, as declarative sentences and interrogative sentences more indirectly express attitudes towards rape, as they are less emotional, and imperative and exclamatory sentences are more expressive in their indirect communicative value. This upholds the hypothesis that on the level of structure, Polish online discourse does in fact have a tendency to be more direct than American online discourse.

One of the most significant aspects of the analysis of structure was the analysis of transitivity processes in which the actors were involved. This showed that representation through activation and passivation provided various implied representations of the actors and also depended on the cultural context. It is important to reiterate that by activating or passivizing a specific actor (either the victim or the offender) in a clause of a sentence, she or he is foregrounded in discourse. The AEC demonstrated more processes of this kind overall (at 83.2%) and the PC presented significantly lower frequencies of activation and passivation (65.8%). Although in light of the representations of both actors, the frequencies of activation and passivation of the victim did not differ as greatly between the AEC and the PC, the representations of the offender in this respect were very large. In the AEC, the victim was activated about 2% more often than in the PC and passivized 6% more often than in the PC. In the AEC, the offender was activated 8% more often than in the PC and passivized about 30% more often in the AEC than in the PC.

In both the AEC and the PC, more attention was drawn to the victim than to the offender through such foregrounding structures, which means that the focus on the victim also brings more attention to her role or her potential fault in the rape. The implications of such structures are significant, as well as the differences between the corpora which are shown, with the activation and passivation of the victim either placing focus on her role in the crime or the passivation of the victim foregrounding her while backgrounding the offender. What is significant, however, is the discrepancy between the distribution in the passivation of the offender in the AEC and the PC (a 30% difference). This demonstrates a cultural tendency for Polish Internet users to place more focus on the role of the victim than the offender through passivation processes, which may in turn lead to victim-blaming sentiment.

The presentation of alternative hypothetical situations in the comments was not entirely statistically significant, but it was worth noting that cultural differences were visible with regard to this discursive strategy. Both modality and negation were investigated in the American and Polish corpora for the use of evaluation of actors that they might present. The corpus showed more use of the conditional structures (with *if*-clauses) in the AEC (1.1%) than in the PC (.5%), demonstrating that in this respect, American Internet users expressed victim blaming in structurally indirect ways more often than in the case of Polish discourse.

Another strategy that presented alternative hypothetical situations was negation in both corpora. Negation, in total, was present in both the AEC and the PC equally (at 8.5% and 8.6%). Both corpora showed that negation is one strategy that can be used to express indirect evaluation of actors, and in both corpora was found most often regarding the fault of the victim. Had a greater corpus been compiled, the significance of both of the discussed strategies of evaluation may have presented greater value of merit and statistic viability in the corpus overall.

The second part of the analysis, the socio-semantic analysis of American and Polish online discourses about rape showed that evaluation was present in the corpora on such level, as well. Here, the representations of social actors were analyzed in both of the corpora and cultural differences also accounted for (cf. Chapter 7). The analysis of the functionalization, indetermination, backgrounding and appraisement of actors showed overall that evaluation of actors may be expressed implicitly on the level of semantics, as well as more directly in the same respect, however with regard to specific semantic categories.

Among the most significant categories of the analysis was that of the backgrounding of actors, and the appraisement of actors, through which actors were directly blamed or supported through adjectival modifiers, nominalization or predicatives. The socio-semantic aspects demonstrated that the more overt blaming of actors could be found in the category that subsumed the negative naming of actors through the use of metaphorical reference or name calling (including the use of vulgar expressions). Such overt negative naming was more visible in the Polish corpus than in the American corpus, pointing to the greater tendency in Polish discourse for direct communication, even on the subject of sexual assault, a topic which has been deemed taboo in Polish culture.

As backgrounding demonstrated a difference between the two analyzed cultures, it is an important aspect of socio-semantic representation to relate. Backgrounding meant that in the sentences about the act of rape and the processes involved, certain actors were discursively made invisible or less visible in the sentences. This aspect is important because it either focuses on the only actor who is mentioned or completely abstracts the act of rape, without any reference to those who are involved, thus mystifying it and drawing attention from the agency of the offender. There was a 6% difference between the AEC and the PC with respect to the backgrounding of actors, with more backgrounding demonstrated in the AEC than in the PC. Significantly, the offender was backgrounded more often than the victim in both of the corpora, but approximately 5% more often in the AEC than in the PC. This shows a significant difference between the American and Polish evaluative discourses on rape where the actors are backgrounded far more frequently in the American online discourse, pointing to the fact that attention is drawn away from the offender more often in the American discourse, hence leading to further abstraction in that context.

Additionally within the category of socio-semantic aspects, the presence and prevalence of rape myths was analyzed in the number of comments in which they were found. As the rape myths listed in this work have been stated in the literature to be virtually universal, there were no differences taken into account when looking at their categorization. Both the AEC and the PC showed that rape myths are present in digital comments about rape, with about 14% of a higher frequency of rape myth reference in the AEC than in the PC, however the types of rape myths that were found to be most common varied according to the cultural context.

The most frequent rape myth in the AEC was the one which presented the belief that the victim was to blame for the rape because she was intoxicated. This made up 37.5% of the AEC on the basis of comment count. The belief that the victim was lying about having been raped was presented as the most frequent rape myth in the Polish corpus (however at approximately 12% of the comment count in the PC) and the second most prevalent rape myth in the PC came to 7.6% of the PC on the basis of sentence count and reflected the idea that if the victim had consented to one thing (such as drinking), then she has also consented to rape (presented most often as sexual intercourse). The fact that there was a greater frequency of rape myth prevalence in the AEC also shows that victim blaming occurs more indirectly than in the PC on the socio-semantic level in the American online discourse.

With regard to the socio-semantic aspects of the representations of rape, another important category was the analysis of the representation of the rape itself and whether or not such expressions were crime-reflective or euphemistic. The investigation of euphemization and dysphemization of rape in the AEC and the PC presented nearly similar results in both of the cultural discourse contexts. As was originally postulated, euphemistic strategies were present in both the AEC and the PC, which is one that tends to distance from the severity of the crime. Approximately .7% of the AEC was made up of euphemistic expressions for rape and .9% in the PC. The fact that rape is more taboo in Poland is a possible indicator of why such expressions were slightly more prevalent in the PC than in the AEC. The crime-reflective naming was about the same in both corpora (1% in the AEC and .8% in the PC—only .2% higher in the AEC than in the PC). This is also significant in juxtaposition with the results concerning euphemization in the PC, as more euphemization and less crime-reflection is indicative of lesser cultural perception of rape's criminal status.

Both the structural and socio-semantic analyses have demonstrated that there are cultural differences in the way that attitudes are implied in CMC about the subject of sexual crime, namely that, in line with the literature on cultural differences in communication, Polish discourses tend to be more direct than American discourses, more specifically where the aspect of socio-semantic representation of actors as expressive of attitudes was concerned. It is also worth noting here that the evaluation of the offender was more direct than the evaluation of the victim, especially in the case of the Polish online discourse. Negative evaluation of the victim was more present in comments that indirectly referred to her involvement in the rape, through negation, modality, activation and passivation, as well as by juxtaposing her with actions that reflected common rape myths, including those actions in which the victim was activated.

Despite the findings that have been presented in the preceding pages, it is important to also note that there were several limitations to the work. The fact that a metanalysis could not be done prior to conducting the full analysis of the corpus itself leaves much to be desired in terms of the influence that social variables, such as gender or age, might have on the way that evaluation is expressed (if it is at all present). This, however, does not mean that there is little value in studying anonymous comments in the online sphere, since (as was expressed in Chapter 4), the fact of anonymity is one that allows for an Internet user to express his or her opinions on seemingly controversial subjects more baldly than in a non-anonymous setting.

Another limitation to the study was the generalized view on rape as a crime overall, rather than looking at discourses on rape according to the various types of rape to which they refer and then analyzing the potential differences in attitudes with regard to the rape context. It would be recommendable to investigate how such public discourses as digital comments vary with the type of rape that is being discussed in order to discern if there is a difference between levels of implied blame in comments about stranger rape or acquaintance rape, for example. Bringing such a dimension to the discussion would provide valuable insight into the cultural valuation of rape and rape victims, as well as information regarding whether and in which cases opinions and attitudes towards the actors involved are expressed more strongly.

Looking more deeply into how the type of rape more specifically affects the type of evaluation expressed in discourse would also provide valuable insight into whether or not rape typology as a variable affects negative and positive evaluation of actors, as well as the way in which such discursive evaluation is expressed. Additionally, the size of the corpora may not have fully demonstrated the phenomenon. It should also be stated that research should still be conducted on the subject in order to investigate whether or not the conclusions reached in this work uphold over time or if there is a trend following the #metoo movement for victim blaming to wane.

Other recommendations for future work on the subject could be highlighted in the value that a comparative study of various genres of discourse on the subject of rape would bring to the discipline. There were also limitations to the analysis conducted and presented in this chapter. The limitations of this study are such that the comments collected were taken from various types of rape cases. Had there been a division in the types of rape cases, with more data included in both of the corpora, more conclusions as to the types of victim blaming that take place, with regard to the type of rape victim, could have been accounted for. This would have provided insight into how the type of rape might impact a scale of variation in the type of blame attribution that takes place, as well as to what extent indirectness might be dependent on the type of rape that occurs. Such a differentiation should be investigated in future studies on the topic, taking full account of the social variables that the actors represent, as well as rape type (Armstrong et al., 2006; cf. Chapter 2 for more information on rape typology).

The novel aspects of the project lay in the fact that digital discourses about rape have not been investigated from the angle that was done in this analysis. To my knowledge, such an investigation on online discourses about rape has not been carried out before, let alone within the context of a socio-pragmatic analysis of evaluation. By investigating anonymous digital comments through such a lens, and in a culturally comparative light, I have shown that culturally-dominant ideas about sexual violence against women both penetrate and work their way through online discussions of sexual assault. This work also adds to the growing body of work covering topics in language, sexuality and culture, thus providing additional insight into the ways that gender and sexuality (including sexual crime) are constructed in discourse.

The idea of secondary victimization is not new within the realm of study on sexual crime and the discourses surrounding it, but within the more specific sphere of discourse, it is something that has not been given a name until this point. I have found it important to differentiate between other types of secondary victimization and the phenomenon of *discursive secondary victimization*, which is expressed in discourses as a way of bringing the victim of rape back into the context of assault and implying questions of her role in acting as a catalyst for the sexual assault. Moreover, this work has demonstrated that MaxQDA is an appropriate tool for conducting a corpus analysis of discourse, as it provides the key elements necessary to properly code and create visualizations necessary to consolidate linguistic data within a CDA analysis (Yu, 2006; Sobyanina & Khokhlova, 2018; Kuckartz, 2019).

It is difficult to escape the intricacies of the language surrounding rape, especially when one aims to critically analyze it from a feminist standpoint. A linguist, it seems, must engage in the very practices that she is denouncing, and, as such, entangles herself in the same ideological discursive constructs that she wishes to unpack and deconstruct. Even so, it is my hope that this work has demonstrated the various ways in which secondary victimization is expressed, and that in addition to other genres of discourse on rape, the discourse of Internet users also contributes to the circle which reproduces beliefs that female rape victims are to blame for the crime committed against them. The reproduction of the stereotypical beliefs surrounding the idea that a victim is in some part if not fully, to blame for being raped is one that presents itself quite evidently in various discursive settings (Ehrlich, 2001; Cameron & Kulick, 2003).

Online discourses, the category to which digital comments belong, are demonstrative of a genre that introduces space for users to spread ideologies about women and their role in sexual crime that work against any system attempting to help them in their victimization. To recognize that beliefs about rape that bring about secondary victimization or revictimization of the person harmed do not only belong to the institutional settings that deal with it (e.g., the police as an institution or the legal system), and that they are also intimated within various settings, including those that are readily available and made interactive to the public, is a crucial factor in making visible the prevalence of the problem of victim blaming in both American and Polish cultures. On the level of cultural analysis, it is surprising that the differences between American and Polish modes of expressing evaluation are not as defined as the literature would have us believe (Mills, 1995, 2008). For both the American and Polish discourses, where victim blaming is concerned, the cultural differences in the discourses also hinge on negative stereotypes regarding the role of the victim. This points to the fact that such a problem as the reproduction of secondary victimization through discursive means is a product of both American and Polish cultural contexts, demonstrating that the issue is problematic from various cultural perspectives.

References

Abidi, M. (2015). "Euphemism in Tony Blair's political discourse in the Iraqi war 2003: A Socio-cognitive CDA Account." *International Journal of Humanities and Cultural Studies*, 2(1), 8–28.

Abidi, H. (2021). "The 'vehicle' of deixis in Trump's tweets: Does it hold the load?." *Global Journal of Arts, Humanities and Social Sciences*, 9(6), 19–33.

Abraham, S. K. (2002). *Attitudes of Second-Generation Asian-Indians toward Dating and Arranged Marriage: An Exploratory Study*. Thesis. San Diego: Alliant International University.

Acker, J. (2000). "Hierarchies, jobs, bodies: A theory of gendered organizations." In: M.S. Kimmel, A. Aronson (eds.) *The Gendered Society Reader*. Oxford: Oxford University Press, 105–117.

Ahmadvand, M. (2011). "Critical discourse analysis an introduction to major approaches." *Dinamika Bahasa Dan Budaya*, 5(1), 82–90.

Aijmer, K. (2015). "'Will you fuck off please'. The use of *please* by London teenagers." *Pragmática Sociocultural/Sociocultural Pragmatics*, 3(2), 127–149.

Aijmer, K., Rühlemann, C. (2015). *Corpus Pragmatics*. Cambridge: Cambridge University Press.

Alaggia, R., Wang, S. (2020). " 'I never told anyone until the #metoo movement': What can we learn from sexual abuse and sexual assault disclosures made through social media?" *Child Abuse & Neglect*, 103, 104–312.

Alba-Juez, L., Thompson, G. (2014). "The many faces and phases of evaluation." In: L. Alba-Juez, G. Thompson (eds). *Evaluation in Context*, 3–23.

Alberti, B., Back Danielsson, I. M. (2014). "Gender, feminist, and queer archaeologies: USA perspective." *Encyclopedia of Global Archaeology*. New York: Springer-Verlag, 2988–2997

Alicke, M. D. (2000). "Culpable control and the psychology of blame." *Psychological Bulletin*, 126, 556–574.

Allan, K., Burridge, K. (2006). *Forbidden Words: Taboo and the Censoring of Language*. Cambridge: Cambridge University Press.

Allen, S., Thorsen, E. (2009). *Citizen Journalism. Global Perspectives*. Bern & New York: Peter Lang.

Allmer, T. (2015). *Critical Theory and Social Media: Between Emancipation and Commodification*. London: Routledge.

Allport, D. A. (1979). "Conscious and unconscious cognition: A computational metaphor for the mechanism of attention and integration." In: L.G. Nilsson (ed.). *Perspectives on Memory Research.* New York: Psychology Press, 61–89.

Anderson, A. (2014). *Media, Environment and the Network Society.* London: Palgrave Macmillan.

Anderson, I., Doherty, K. (2008). *Accounting for Rape: Psychology, Feminism and Discourse Analysis in the Study of Sexual Violence.* London: Routledge.

Andrews, E. (1990). *Markedness Theory.* Duke University Press.

Androutsopoulos, J. (2006). "Introduction: Sociolinguistics and computer-mediated communication." *Journal of Sociolinguistics*, 10(4), 419–438.

Andrucki, M. J., Elder, G. S. (2007). "Locating the state in queer space: GLBT non-profit organizations in Vermont, USA." *Social & Cultural Geography*, 8(1), 89–104.

Antheunis, M. L., Schouten, A. P., & Walther, J. B. (2020). "The hyperpersonal effect in online dating: Effects of text-based CMC vs. videoconferencing before meeting face-to-face." *Media Psychology*, *23*(6), 820–89.

Anusiewicz, J., Handke, K. (1994). *Płeć w języku i kulturze.* Wrocław: Wydawnictwo Uniwersytetu Wroclawskiego

Ardener, S. (1975). *Perceiving Women.* London: Malaby Press.

Ardener, S. (2005). "Muted group theory excerpts." *Women and Language*, 28(2), 50–72.

Armstrong, E. A., Hamilton L. H., Sweeney, B. (2006). "Sexual assault on campus: A multilevel, integrative approach to party rape." *Social Problems* 53(4), 483–499.

Arrighi, G. (2005). "Hegemony unravelling-II." *New Left Review*, *32*(33), 23–80.

Atton, C. (2006). "Far-right media on the internet: Culture, discourse and power." *New Media & Society*, *8*(4), 573–587.

Austin, J. (1962/1975). *How to Do Things with Words.* Cambridge: Harvard University Press.

Bache, C. (2013). "Grammatical choice and communicative motivation: a radical systemic approach." *Systemic Functional Linguistics: Exploring Choice.* Cambridge: Cambridge University Press, 72–94.

Bailey, K. (2007). "Akogare, ideology, and 'Charisma Man'mythology: Reflections on ethnographic research in English language schools in Japan." *Gender, Place and Culture*, 14(5), 585–608.

Baker, R. (1974) "'Pricks' and 'chicks': A plea for 'persons.'" In: M. Vetterling-Braggin (ed.) *Sexist Language: A Modern Philosophical Analysis.* Totowa: Littlefield, Adams and Co. 161–182.

Baker, P. (2010). *Sociolinguistics and Corpus Linguistics*. Edinburgh: Edinburgh University Press.

Bakhtin, M. M. (1981). *The Dialogic Imagination*. Austin: University of Texas Press.

Bale, A., Gagnon, M., Khanjian, H. (2011). "On the relationship between morphological and semantic markedness." *Morphology*, 21(2), 197–221.

Barlow, D. H. (1986). "Causes of sexual dysfunction: The role of anxiety and cognitive interference." *Journal of Consulting and Clinical Psychology*, 54(2), 140.

Barnes, R. (2015). "Understanding the affective investment produced through commenting on Australian alternative journalism website New Matilda." *New Media & Society*, *17*(5), 810–826.

Baron, N. S. (2004). "See you online: Gender issues in college student use of instant messaging." *Journal of Language and Social Psychology*, 23(4), 397–423.

Baron, N. (2008a). *Always On: Language in an Online and Mobile World*. New York: Oxford University Press.

Baron, N. (2008b). "Adjusting the volume: Technology and multitasking in discourse control." In. J.E. Latz (ed). *Handbook of Mobile Communication Studies*, 177–193.

Barrett, R. (1998). "Markedness and styleswitching in performances by African American drag queens." In: C. Meyers-Scotton (ed). *Codes and Consequences: Choosing Linguistic Varieties*, 139–161.

Barthes, R. (1973). *Mythologies*. London: Paladin.

Barthes, R. (1977). *Image, Music. Text*. London: Paladin.

Bartky, S.L. (1988/1997). "Foucault, femininity, and the modernization of patriarchal power." In: I. Diamon, L. Quinby (eds), *Feminism and Foucault: Reflections on Resistance*. Boston: Northeastern University Press, 63–82.

Bartlett, C. P., Vowels, C. L., Saucier, D. A. (2008). "Meta-analyses of the effects of media images on men's body-image concerns." *Journal of Social and Clinical Psychology*, 27(3), 279–310.

Bassiouney, R. (2015). "Stance-taking." In: K. Tracy (ed), *The International Encyclopedia of Language and Social Interaction*, 1–11.

Bates, J. N., Pastuszak, A. W., Khera, M. (2019). "Effect of body weight on sexual function in men and women." *Current Sexual Health Reports*, 11(1), 52–59.

Beauvoir, S. (1949). *The Second Sex*. New York: Random House.

Beaver, D. I. (1996). "Presupposition." In *Handbook of Logic and Language*. North-Holland, 939–1008.

Bell, A., Gibson, A. (2011). "Staging language: An introduction to the sociolinguistics of performance." *Journal of Sociolinguistics*, *15*(5), 555–572.

Bem, S. L. (1974). "The measurement of psychological androgyny." *Journal of Consulting and Clinical Psychology*, 42(2), 155.

Bem, S. L. (1981). "Gender schema theory: A cognitive account of sex typing." *Psychological Review*, 88(4), 354.

Bem, S.L. (2008). *The Lenses of Gender*. New Haven: Yale University Press.

Bennice, J .A., Resick P. (2003). "Marital rape: History, research and practice." *Trauma, Violence & Abuse* 4(3), 228–246.

Benson, R. (2009). "Shaping the public sphere: Habermas and beyond." *The American Sociologist*, 40(3), 175–197.

Berger, B. (1972). *Ways of Seeing*. London: Penguin Books.

Berger, P., Luckmann, T. (1966). *The Social Construction of Reality: A Treatise in the Sociology of Knowledge*. New York: Doubleday.

Benedito, F. S. (2000). "The treatment of sex phraseology in the second edition of the OED." *Revista Española de Lingüística Aplicada* (14), 381–400.

Beres, M. A. (2007). "'Spontaneous' sexual consent: An analysis of sexual consent literature." *Feminism & Psychology*, 17(1), 93–108.

Bergelson, V. (2020). "Sex and sensibility: The meaning of sexual consent." *Sex and Sensibility: The Meaning of Sexual Consent" in Sexual Assault and Rape–What Can We Learn From and For Law Reform*, 1–17.

Besnier, N. (2005). "Gender and language in society." *American Ethnologist*, 29, 534–566.

Beukeboom, C. J., Finkenauer, C., Wigboldus, D. H. (2010). "The negation bias: when negations signal stereotypic expectancies." *Journal of Personality and Social Psychology*, 99(6), 978.

Biber, D. (1999). "A register perspective on grammar and discourse: variability in the form and use of English complement clauses." *Discourse Studies*, 1(2), 131–150.

Biber, D., Johansson, S., Leech, G., Conrad, S., Finegan, E. (1999). *The Longman Grammar of Spoken and Written English*. London: Longman.

Biber, D., Conrad, S. (2009). *Register, Genre, and Style*. Cambridge: Cambridge University Press.

Biber, D., & Egbert, J. (2015). "Using grammatical features for automatic register identification in an unrestricted corpus of documents from the open web." *Journal of Research Design and Statistics in Linguistics and Communication Science*, *2*(1), 3–36.

Biber, D., Egbert, J. (2018). *Register Variation Online*. Cambridge: Cambridge University Press.

Biber, D., Finnegan, E. (1989). "Drift and the evolution of English style: A history of three genres." *Language* 65, 487–517.

Birner, B. J. (2013). *Introduction to Pragmatics*. Hoboken: John Wiley & Sons.

Black, M., Coward, R. (1981). "Linguistic, social and sexual relations: A review of Dale Spender's man made language." *Society for Education in Film and Television*, 69–85.

Bloch, K. R., Taylor, T., Martinez, K. (2020). "Playing the race card: White injury, White victimhood and the paradox of colour-blind ideology in anti-immigrant discourse." *Ethnic and Racial Studies*, 43(7), 1130–1148.

Blommaert, J. (2018). *Durkheim and the Internet: On Sociolinguistics and the Sociological Imagination*. London: Bloomsbury Publishing.

Blommaert, J., Bulcaen, C. (2000). "Critical discourse analysis." *Annual Review of Anthropology*, 29(1), 447–466.

Bloor M., Bloor T. (2007). *The Practice of CDA: An Introduction*. Great Britain: Hodder Education.

Bodine, A. (1975). "Androcentrism in prescriptive grammar: singular 'they', sex-indefinite 'he', and 'he or she'." *Language in Society*, 4(2), 129–146.

Bohner, G. (2001). "Writing about rape: Use of the passive voice and other distancing text features as an expression of perceived responsibility of the victim." *British Journal of Social Psychology*, 40(4), 515–529.

Bohner, G., Danner, U. N., Siebler, F., Samson, G. B. (2002). "Rape myth acceptance and judgments of vulnerability to sexual assault: An Internet experiment." *Experimental psychology*, 49(4), 257.

Boreus, K., Bergstrom G. (2017). *Analyzing Text and Discourse: Eight Approaches for the Social Sciences*. Newberry Park: Sage.

Borkowska O., Płatek M. (2011). "Skala przestępstwa zgwałcenia w Polsce." In: Piotrowska, J., Synkiewicz, A. (eds.) *Dość Milczenia. Przemoc Seksualna Wobec Kobiet i Problem Gwałtu w Polsce*. Warsaw: Fundacja Feminoteka, 10–22.

Botta, R. A. (1999). "Television images and adolescent girls' body image disturbance." *Journal of Communication*, 49(2), 22–41.

Bou-Franch, P. (2013). "Domestic violence and public participation in the media: The case of citizen journalism." *Gender and Language*, 7(3): 275–302.

Bou-Franch, P. (2016). "'Did he really rape these bitches?' Aggression, Women, Language." In: P. Bou-Franch (ed). *Exploring Language Aggression against Women*. Amsterdam: John Benjamins Publishing Company, 1–14.

Bou-Franch, P., Blitvich, P. G. C. (2019). *Analyzing Digital Discourse: New Insights and Future Directions*. New York: Springer.

Bourdieu, P. (1986/2011). "The forms of capital." In: I. Szeman, T. Kaposy (eds). *Cultural Theory: An Anthology* 1, 81–93.

Bourdieu, P. (1990). *The Logic of Practice*. Stanford: Stanford University Press.

Bourdieu, P. (1991). *Language and Symbolic Power*. Harvard: Harvard University Press.

Brannon, L. (2004). *Gender: Psychological Perspectives* (4th ed.). Boston: Allyn & Bacon

Brannon, L. (2016). "Gender stereotypes: Masculinity and femininity." In *Gender*. London Routledge, 68–98.

Braun, V., Kitzinger, C. (2001). "The perfectible vagina: Size matters." *Culture, Health & Sexuality*, 3(3), 263–277.

Braun, V., & Wilkinson, S. (2001). "Socio-cultural representations of the vagina." *Journal of Reproductive and Infant Psychology*, 19(1), 17–32.

Brenner, A. (2013). "Resisting simple dichotomies: critiquing narratives of victims, perpetrators, and harm in feminist theories of rape." *Harvard Journal of Law & Gender*, 36, 503.

Brison, S. J. (2005). "'The price we pay'? Pornography and harm." In: A. Cohen, C. Heath Wellman. *Contemporary Debates in Applied Ethics*. Oxford: Blackwell Publishing, 236–250.

Brison, S. J. (2006). "Justice and gender-based violence." *Revue Internationale de Philosophie*, (1), 259–275.

Brodsky, A. (2017). "'Rape-adjacent': Imagining legal responses to non-consensual condom removal." *Columbia Journal of Gender and Law*, 183–210.

Broszko, M. (2017). "Jak dzyndzyk z nici w kłębek ułożonych stał się nazwą męskiego członka—analiza historycznojęzykowa wybranych nazw narządów płciowych w polszczyźnie." *Studia Filologiczne Uniwersytetu Jana Kochanowskiego*, 30, 37–49.

Brown, K. M. (2012). *Good Wives, Nasty Wenches, and Anxious Patriarchs: Gender, Race, and Power in Colonial Virginia*. UNC Press Books.

Brown, R. M. (2009). "Spinning without touching the wheel: Anticolonialism, Indian nationalism, and the deployment of symbol." *Comparative Studies of South Asia, Africa and the Middle East*, 29(2), 230–245.

Brownmiller, S. (1976). *Against our Will: Men, Women and Rape*. New York: Bantam Books.

Brownmiller, S. (1984). *Femininity*. New York: Ballantine Books.

Bucholtz, M. (1999). " 'Why be normal?': Language and identity practices in a community of nerd girls." *Language in Society*, 28(2), 203–223.

Bucholtz, M. (2002). “Youth and cultural practice.” *Annual Review of Anthropology*, 31(1), 525–552.

Bucholtz, M. (2004). “Language, gender, and sexuality.” *Language in the USA: Themes for the Twenty-First Century*, 410–429.

Bucholtz, M., Hall, K. (2004). “Theorizing identity in language and sexuality research.” *Language and Society*, 33, 469–515.

Bulawka, H. M. (2013). *Gender Representations in the Polish Press: A Feminist Critical Discourse Study.* Warsaw: Warszawska Firma Wydawnicza.

Burt, M. R. (1980). “Cultural myths and supports for rape.” *Journal of Personality and Social Psychology*, 38(2), 217.

Burt, M. R. (1998). “Rape myths.” *Confronting rape and sexual assault*, *3*, 129–144.

Burt, M. R., Albin, R. S. (1981). “Rape myths, rape definitions, and probability of conviction.” *Journal of Applied Social Psychology*, 11(3), 212–230.

Butler, J. (1988). “Performative acts and gender constitution: An essay in phenomenology and feminist theory.” *Theatre Journal*, 40(4), 519–531.

Butler, J. (1990). *Gender Trouble. Feminism and the Subversion of Identity.* New York: Routledge.

Butler, J. (1993/2011). *Bodies that Matter. On the Discursive Limits of Sex.* London: Routledge.

Butler, J. (2004). *Undoing Gender.* London: Routledge.

Butler, J. (2024). *Who's Afraid of Gender?* Bristol: Allen Lane.

Caborn, J. (2007). “On the methodology of dispositive analysis.” *Critical Approaches to Discourse Analysis Across Disciplines*, 1(1), 115–123.

Caldwell, J. C. (2006). “Demographic theory: A long view.” *Demographic Transition Theory*, 301–320

Caldwell, D. (2009). “‘Working your words’: Appraisal in the AFL post-match interview.” *Australian Review of Applied Linguistics*, 32(2), 13–1.

Calhoun, C. (Ed.). (1993). *Habermas and the Public Sphere*. Cambridge: MIT Press.

Callot, M., & Belmore, N. (1996). “Electronic language.” In: S. Herring (ed.). *Computer-Mediated Communication: Linguistic, Social and Cross-Cultural Perspectives.* Philadelphia: John Benjamins Publishing Company, 13–28.

Camaj, L., Santana, A. D. (2015). “Political deliberation on Facebook during electoral campaigns: Exploring the relevance of moderator's technical role and political ideology.” *Journal of Information Technology & Politics*, 12(4), 325–341.

Cameron, D. (1985). “What has gender got to do with sex?” *Language & Communication*, 5(1), 19–27.

Cameron, D. (1998). "Is there any ketchup, Vera?": Gender, power and pragmatics. *Discourse and Society,* 9(4), 437–455.

Cameron, D. (2003). "Gender Issues in Language Change." *Annual Review of Applied Linguistics*, 23, 187–201.

Cameron, D. (2005). "Language, gender, and sexuality: Current issues and new directions." *Applied Linguistics*, *26*(4), 482–502.

Cameron, D., Kulick D. (2003). *Language and Sexuality.* New York: Cambridge University Press.

Campbell, S. W. (2020). "Cutting the cord: Social and scholarly revolutions as CMC goes mobile." *Journal of Computer-Mediated Communication*, 25(1), 101–110.

Carpenter, S. (2010). "A study of content diversity in online citizen journalism and online newspaper articles." *New Media & Society*, 12(7), 1064–1084.

Carr, J. L., Van Deusen, K. M. (2004). "Risk factors for male sexual aggression on college campuses." *Journal of Family Violence*, 19(5), 279–289.

Carter, R. (2004). *Language and Creativity.* London: Routledge.

Castells, M. (2004). *The Network Society: A Cross-Cultural Perspective.* Cheltenham and Camberley: Edward Elgar Publishing.

Castells, M. (2011). *The Rise of the Network Society*. Hoboken: John Wiley &Sons.

Charteris-Black, J. (2004). *Corpus Approaches to Critical Metaphor Analysis.* New York: Macmillan.

Chen, L. (2005). "Transitivity in media texts: Negative verbal process sub-functions and narrator bias." *IRAL* 43, 33–51.

Cheng, W., Warren, M. (2003). "Indirectness, inexplicitness and vagueness made clearer." *Pragmatics*, 13(3), 381–400.

Chetaille, A. (2016). "Poland: Sovereignty and sexuality in post-socialist times." In: D. Paternotte, M. Tremblay (ed.). *The Lesbian and Gay Movement and the State*. London: Routledge, 119–133.

Chilton, M. (1996). *Security Metaphors: Cold War Discourse from Containment to Common European Home.* Bern & New York: Peter Lang.

Chilton, P. (1985). *Language and the Nuclear Arms Debate: Nukespeak Today.* London and Dover: F. Pinter.

Chilton, P. (2005). "Missing links in mainstream CDA." *A New Agenda in (Critical) Discourse Analysis* (1), 19–51.

Chmura-Rutkowska, I. (2012). "Przemoc rówieśnicza a płeć w gimnazjum. Kontekst społeczno-kulturowy." *Forum Oświatowe* 1(46), 41–73.

Chmura-Rutkowska, I. (2016). "Milczenie owiec: Dziewczęca perspektywa doświadczania przemocy ze względu na płeć w polskich gimnazjach." In:

A. Matysiak-Błaszczyk, B. Jankowiak (eds). *Kontrowersje Wokół Socjalizacja Dziewcząt i Kobiet.* Poznań: Wydawnictwo Naukowe UAM, 157–174.

Chouliaraki, L., Fairclough, N. (1999) *Discourse in Late Modernity.* Edinburgh: Edinburgh University Press.

Christ, C. P. (2016). "A new definition of patriarchy: Control of women's sexuality, private property, and war." *Feminist Theology*, 24(3), 214–225.

Chun, E. W. (2004). "Ideologies of legitimate mockery: Margaret Cho's revoicings of Mock Asian." *Pragmatics*, 14(2–3), 263–289.

Chun, E. W. (2009). "Speaking like Asian immigrants: Intersections of accommodation and mocking at a US high school." *Pragmatics*, 19(1), 17–38.

Clarke, M. A., Losoff, A., McCracken, M. D., Rood, D. S. (1984). "Linguistic relativity and sex/gender studies: Epistemological and methodological considerations." *Language Learning*, 34(2), 47–64.

Coates, J. (2004). *Women, Men and Language: A Sociolinguistic Account of Gender Differences in Language*. Routledge.

Coates, J., Pichler, P. (2005/2011). *Language and Gender. A Reader*. Hoboken: John Wiley & Sons.

Coduto, K. D. (2020). *Understanding Receiver Effects of the Hyperpersonal Model Using the Imagined Interactions Framework*. Columbus: Ohio State University.

Conrad S., Biber D. (2000). "Adverbial marking of stance in speech and writing." In: S. Hunston, G. Thompson (eds). *Evaluation in Text: Authorial Stance and Construction in Discourse*, Oxford: Oxford University Press, 57–73.

Connell, R. W. (1982). "Class, patriarchy, and Sartre's theory of practice." *Theory and Society*, 11(3), 305–320.

Connell, R. W., Connell, R. (2000). *The Men and the Boys*. Oakland: University of California Press.

Connell, R. W. (2003). "Masculinities, change, and conflict in global society: Thinking about the future of men's studies." *The Journal of Men's Studies*, 11(3), 249–266.

Connell, R. (2009). *Gender*. Cambridge: Polity.

Connell, R. W., & Messerschmidt, J. W. (2005). "Hegemonic masculinity: Rethinking the concept." *Gender & Society*, 19(6), 829–859.

Constant, N., Davis, C., Potts, C., Schwarz, F. (2009). "The pragmatics of expressive content: Evidence from large corpora." *Sprache und Datenverarbeitung*, 33(1–2), 5–21.

Cook, H. (2005). "The English sexual revolution: technology and social change." *History Workshop Journal* 59(1), Oxford: Oxford University Press, 109–128.

Cotterill, J. (2007). *The Language of Sexual Crime*. London: Palgrave Macmillan.

Cottle, S. (2000). "Rethinking News access." *Journalism Studies, 1*(3), 427–448.

Coupland, N. (2007). *Style: Language variation and identity*. Cambridge: Cambridge University Press.

Cowan, G. (2000). "Women's hostility toward women and rape and sexual harassment myths." *Violence Against Women*, 6(3), 238–246.

Cowan, R. (2007). "Muted group theory: Providing answers and raising questions concerning workplace bullying." *Conference Papers–National Communication Association*. Paper Presented in a Conference Organized by the National Communication Association. Chicago, IL. May 2007

Cowburn, M., Dominelli, L. (2001). "Masking hegemonic masculinity: reconstructing the paedophile as the dangerous stranger." *British Journal of Social Work*, 31 (3), 399–414.

Crawford, M. (1995). *Talking Difference: On Gender and Language. Gender and Psychology Series*. Newbury Park: Sage.

Crawford, M. (2001). "Gender and language." In: Unger, R.K. (ed). *Handbook of the Psychology of Women and Gender*, 228–244.

Crenshaw, K. (1989). "Demarginalizing the intersection of race and sex: A Black feminist Critique of antidiscrimination doctrine, feminist theory and antiracist politics." *University of Chicago Legal Forum*, 1989(1), 139–167.

Crenshaw, K. (1991). "Mapping the margins: Intersectionality, identity, politics and violence against women of color." *Stanford Law Review*. 43(6), 139–167.

Crespo-Fernandez, E. (2008). "Sex-related euphemism and dysphemism: An analysis in terms of conceptual metaphor theory." *Atlantis*, 95–110.

Crystal, D. (2001) *Language and the Internet*. Cambridge: Cambridge University Press.

Crystal, D. (2008). "Two thousand million?." *English Today, 24*(1), 3–6.

Crystal, D. (2011). *Internet Linguistics: A Student Guide*. London: Routledge.

Cuddy, A.J.C., Fiske, S. T., Glick, P. (2008). "Warmth and competence as universal dimensions of social perception: the stereotype content model and the BIAS map.". *Social Psychology*, 40, 61–149.

Cuddy, A.J.C., Crotty, S., Chong, J., Norton, M. (2010). "Men as cultural ideals: How culture shapes gender stereotypes." *Harvard Business School*. Harvard, 622–635.

Culpeper, J. (2010). "Conventionalised impoliteness formulae." *Journal of Pragmatics*, 42(12), 3232–3245.

Curzan, A. (2003). *Gender Shifts in the History of English*. Cambridge: Cambridge University Press.

Cutting, J. (2008). *Pragmatics and Discourse: A Resource Book for Students.* London: Routledge.

Czapska, J., Klosa, M., Lesińska, E., Okrasa, A. (2012). *Gender-Based Violence, Stalking and Fear of Crime: Country Report for Poland—EU Project 2009–2011.* Wydawnictwo Verlag Ferdinand Kamp Bochum.

Dahlerup, D., Dahlerup, D. (2015). *The Development of Women's Studies/Gender Studies in the Social Sciences in the Scandinavian Countries.* Stockholm: Stockholm University.

Dainas, A., & Herring, S. C. (2021). "Interpreting emoji pragmatics." In: C. Xie, F. Yus, & H. Haberland (eds.), *Internet Pragmatics: Theory and Practice.* Amsterdam: John Benjamins Publishing Company, 107–144.

Danesi M. (2016). *Language, Society and New Media: Sociolinguistics Today.* London: Routledge.

Davari, S., Moini, M. R. (2016). "The representation of social actors in top notch textbook series: A critical discourse analysis perspective." *International Journal of Foreign Language Teaching and Research*, 4(13), 69–82.

David, D. S., & Brannon, R. (Eds.). (1976). *The Forty-Nine Percent Majority: The Male Sex Role.* Manhattan: Random House.

Davis, S. N., Greenstein, T. N. (2009). "Gender ideology: Components, predictors, and consequences." *Annual Review of Sociology*, 35, 87–105.

Davison, P. (2012). "The language of internet memes." In: M. Mandiberg (ed). *The Social Media Reader*, New York: NYU Press, 120–134.

Dąbrowska, A. (1998). *Słownik Eufemizmów Polskich: Czyli w rzeczy mocno, w sposobie łagodnie.* Warsaw: Wydawnictwo PWN.

Dąbrowska, A. (2008). 'Zmiany obszarów podlegających tabu we współczesnej kulturze' in *Język a kultura*, 20: 173–196.

Dąbrowska, M. (2008). 'Rodzaj gramatyczny a seksizm', in *Studia Linguistica Universitatis Iagellonicae Cracoviensis*, 125, 67–78.

Dąbrowska, M. (2014). "Communicating emotions online. The function of anonymity and gender." *Rhetoric and Communications* 14(1), 1–22.

Dąbrowska, Z. (2001). "Małżeństwa w Polsce. Studium empiryczne." *Rodzina w Czasach Szybkich Przemian* XIII, 29–43.

Dean, M. L., Tate, C. C. (2017). "Extending the legacy of Sandra Bem: Psychological androgyny as a touchstone conceptual advance for the study of gender in psychological science." *Sex Roles*, 76(11), 643–654.

Dec-Pietrowska, J., Paprzycka, E. (2016). "Społeczne konstruowanie cielesności i seksualności. Analiza wybranego kontekstu edukacji seksualnej." *Dyskursy młodych andragogów*, 17: 325–339.

Dembowska, Z. (2013). "Postrzeganie płci w polskich i macedońskich związkach frazeologicznych." *Slavica Iuvenum XIV*, 47–51.

Deumert, A. (2014). *Sociolinguistics and Mobile Communication*. Edinburgh: Edinburgh University Press.

Deuze, M. (2003). "The web and its journalisms: considering the consequences of different types of newsmedia online." *New Media and Society*, 5(2), 203–230.

Dias Oliva, T. (2020). "Content moderation technologies: Applying human rights standards to protect freedom of expression." *Human Rights Law Review*, 20(4), 607–640.

Doroszewicz, K., Forbes, G. B. (2008). "Experiences with dating aggression and sexual coercion among Polish students." *Journal of Interpersonal Violence* 23(1): 58–73.

Douglas, K. M., McGarty, C. (2001). "Identifiability and self-presentation: Computer-mediated communication and intergroup interaction." *British Journal of Social Psychology*, 40(3), 399–416.

Doyle, B. (1995). *Disability Discrimination and Equal Opportunities*. Chicago: Mansell.

Drapalska-Grochowicz, M. (2018). "Zjawisko prostytucji–pomiędzy koniecznością a tabu?." *Acta Universitatis Lodziensis. Folia Iuridica*, (85), 33–45.

Du Bois, J.W. (2007). "The stance triangle." In: Englebretson, R (ed). *Stancetaking in Discourse: Subjectivity, Evaluation, Interaction*. Amsterdam: John Benjamins Publishing Company, 139–181.

Duguay, L. (2011). "Sexuality: Still a taboo subject?." *Exceptional Parent*, 41(2), 16–17.

Duncan, M. C. (1994). "The politics of women's body images and practices: Foucault, the panopticon, and *Shape* magazine." *Journal of Sport and Social Issues*, 18(1), 48–65.

Dutka, J. (2014). "Przemoc wobec kobiet i kobieca agresja w kontekście ról płciowych i mylnego uznania ('misrecognition')." *Filozofia Publiczna i Edukacja Demokratyczna* 3(2), 139–160.

Dworkin, A. (1987). "Pornography is a civil rights issue for women." *University of Michigan. JL Reform*, 21, 55–65.

Dworkin, S. L., & O'Sullivan, L. (2005). "Actual versus desired initiation patterns among a sample of college men: Tapping disjunctures within traditional male sexual scripts." *Journal of Sex Research*, 42(2), 150–158.

Dziewanowska, M. (2015). "Zachowania seksualne młodzieży w kontekście wyzwań współczesności." *Kultura i Wartości* (6), 59–75.

Eagleton, Terry. (1949/1976/1991). *Ideology: An Introduction*. New York: Verso.

Eagly, A. H., Steffen, V. J. (1984). "Gender stereotypes stem from the distribution of women and men into social roles." *Journal of Personality and Social Psychology*, 46(4), 735–747.

Eckert, P. (1989). "The whole woman: Sex and gender differences in variation." *Language, Variation and Change*, 245–267.

Eckert, P. (1996). "Vowels and nail polish: The emergence of linguistic style in the preadolescent heterosexual marketplace." In: D. Cameron, D. Kulick (ed). *The Language and Sexuality Reader*, London: Routledge, 189–195.

Eggins, S. (2004). *Introduction to Systemic Functional Linguistics*. London: A&C Black.

Eggins, S., & Slade, D. (1997). *Analysing Casual Conversation*. London: Cassell.

Ehret, K., Taboada, M. (2020). "Are online news comments like face-to-face conversation?: A multi-dimensional analysis of an emerging register." *Register Studies*, 2(1), 1–36.

Ehrlich, S. (2001). *Representing Rape: Language and Sexual Consent*. New York: Routledge.

Ehrlich, S. (2004). "Linguistic discrimination against women: Discursive practices and material effects." *Language and Woman's Place: Text and Commentaries*, 3, 223–236.

Ehrlich, S. (2020). "Rape victims." In: A. Johnson (ed.) *The Routledge Handbook of Forensic Linguistics*. London: Routledge, 265–280.

Ehrlich, S., King, R. (1994). "Feminist meanings and the (de) politicization of the lexicon." *Language in Society*, 23(1), 59–76.

Ehrlich, S., Meyerhoff, M., Holmes, J. (2014). *The Handbook of Language, Gender, and Sexuality*. Oxford: Wiley-Blackwell.

Eichenlaub, J. E. (1961). *The Marriage Art*. London: Mayflower.

Eisend, M. (2019). "Gender roles." *Journal of Advertising*, *48*(1), 72–80.

Ellemers, N. (2018). "Gender stereotypes." *Annual Review of Psychology*, 69, 275–298.

European Union Agency for Fundamental Human Rights. (2014). *Przemoc wobec kobiet: Badania przeprowadzone w skali UE*. FRA. Accessed: July 1 2019. https://fra.europa.eu/sites/default/files/fra-2014-vaw-survey-factsheet_pl.pdf

Eveline, J. (2005). "Woman in the ivory tower: Gendering feminised and masculinised identities." *Journal of Organizational Change Management* 18(6), 641–658.

Ezzina, R. (2015). "Transitivity analysis of 'The Crying lot of 49' by Thomas Pynchon." *International Journal of Humanities and Cultural Studies*, 2(3), 283–292.

Fairclough, N. (1992). "Discourse and text: Linguistic and intertextual analysis within discourse analysis." *Discourse & Society*, 3(2), 193–217.

Fairclough, N. (1995). *Critical Discourse Analysis: The Critical Study of Language.* London: Longman.

Fairclough, N. (2001). *Language and Power.* London: Longman.

Fairclough, N. (2003). *Analyzing Discourse: Textual Analysis for Social Research.* New York: Routledge.

Fairclough, N. (2017). "CDA as dialectical reasoning." In: J. Flowerdew, J.E. Richardson (eds). *The Routledge Handbook of Critical Discourse Studies.* London: Routledge, 13–25.

Fairclough, N., Fairclough, I. (2018). "A procedural approach to ethical critique in CDA." *Critical Discourse Studies*, 15(2), 169–185.

Fairclough, N., Wodak, R. (1997). "Critical Discourse Analysis." In T.A. van Dijk (ed.) *Discourse as Social Interaction*, London: Sage, 258–84.

Fano, R. M. (1984). "Computer-mediated communication." *Electro-Culture: International Society for Optics and Photonics* (474), 34–38.

Fergus, K. D., Gray, R. E., Fitch, M. I. (2002). "Sexual dysfunction and the preservation of manhood: Experiences of men with prostate cancer." *Journal of Health Psychology*, 7(3), 303–316.

Fernández, E. C. (2008). "Sex-related euphemism and dysphemism: An analysis in terms of conceptual metaphor theory." *Atlantis*, 95–110.

Fernandez-Martin, C. (2010). "Comparing sexist expressions in English and Spanish: (De)-constructing sexism through language." *Revista de Filología Inglesa*, 32, 67–90.

Fiske, S. (1998). "Stereotyping, prejudice and discrimination." In: D. T. Gilbert, S. T. Fiske, & G. Lindzey (Eds.), *The Handbook of Social Psychology*. McGraw-Hill, 357–411.

Fiske, S. T. (2010). "Venus and Mars or down to Earth: Stereotypes and realities of gender differences." *Perspectives on Psychological Science*, 5(6), 688–692.

Fontaine, L., Bartlett, T., O'Grady, G. (2013). *Systemic Functional Linguistics: Exploring Choice*. Cambridge: Cambridge University Press.

Foucault M. (1972). *The Archaeology of Knowledge and The Discourse on Language*. New York: Pantheon Books.

Foucault, M. (1975). "Surveiller et punir." *Paris*, *1*, 192–211.

Foucault, M. (1980). *Herculine Barbin* . New York: Vintage

Foucault, M. (1971). "Orders of discourse." *Social Science Information*, 10(2), 7–30.

Foucault, M. (1990a). *The History of Sexuality: Volume I: An Introduction*. Trans. Robert Hurley. New York: Vintage.

Foucault, M. (1990b). *The History of Sexuality, Volume II: The Use of Pleasure*. New York: Vintage.

Foucault, M. (1990c). *The History of Sexuality, Volume III: The Care of the Self*. Trans. Robert Hurley. New York: Vintage.

Fought, C. (2004). *Sociolinguistic Variation: Critical reflections*. Oxford: Oxford University Press.

Fought, C. (2006). *Language and Ethnicity*. Cambridge: Cambridge University Press.

Fowler, R., Hodge, B., Kress, G., Trew, T. (2018). *Language and Control*. London: Routledge.

Fowler, R. Marshall, T. (1985) "The war against peacemongering: language and ideology." In: P. Chilton (ed.), *Language and the Nuclear Arms Debate: Nukespeak Today*, London: Frances Pinter, 3–22.

Francis, D. (2012). *The Imaginary Indian: The Image of the Indian in Canadian Culture*. Vancouver: Arsenal Pulp Press.

Franiuk, R., Seefelt J. L., Vandello J. A. (2008). "Prevalence of rape myths in headlines and their effects on attitudes toward rape." *Sex Roles* 58(11–12), 790–801.

Freedman, E. B. (2012). "Women's long battle to define rape." *Washington Post Opinions*. Accessed April 3 2020. https://www.washingtonpost.com/opinions/womens-long-battle-to-define-rape/2012/08/24/aa960280-ed34-11e1-a80b-9f898562d010_story.html>

Freelon, D. (2015). "Discourse architecture, ideology, and democratic norms in online political discussion." *New Media & Society*, 17(5), 772–791.

Frese, B., Moya, M., Megías, J. L. (2004). "Social perception of rape: How rape myth acceptance modulates the influence of situational factors." *Journal of Interpersonal Violence*, 19(2), 143–161.

Freud, S. (1927). "Fetischismus." *Internationale Zeitschrift für Psychoanalyse*, 13(4), 373–378.

Friedman, J., Valenti J. (2008). *Yes Means yes! Visions of Sexual Power & A World without Rape*. Berkley California: Seal Press.

Frith, H. (1997). *Young Women Refusing Sex: The Epistemological Adventures of a Feminist*. Doctoral dissertation. Loughborough: Loughborough University.

Frith, H., Kitzinger, C. (2001). "Reformulating sexual script theory: Developing a discursive psychology of sexual negotiation." *Theory & Psychology*, 11(2), 209–232.

Furnham, A., Mak, T., Tanidjojo, L. (2000). "An Asian perspective on the portrayal of men and women in television advertisements: Studies from Hong Kong and Indonesian television." *Journal of Applied Social Psychology*, 30(11), 2341–2364.

Fuszara, M. (2011). "Kobiety i polityka." *Znak*, (676), 31–35.

Gagnon, J. H. (1973). "Scripts and the coordination of sexual conduct." In: J. K. Cole & R. Deinstbier (eds.), *1972 Nebraska Symposium on Motivation*, 23. Lincoln: University of Nebraska Press, 27–59.

Gagnon, J. H., Simon, W. (1973/2017). *Sexual* Conduct: *The Social Sources of Human Sexuality*. London: Routledge.

Gamson, J. (1997). "Messages of exclusion: Gender, movements, and symbolic boundaries." *Gender & Society*, 11(2), 178–199.

Gamson, J., Moon, D. (2004). "The sociology of sexualities: Queer and beyond." *Annual Review of Sociology* (30), 47–64.

Gao, C. (2013). "A sociolinguistic study of English taboo language." *Theory and Practice in Language Studies*, 3(12), 2310–2313.

Garton, S. (2014). *Histories of Sexuality: Antiquity to Sexual Revolution*. London: Routledge.

Gass, W. (1978). *On Being Blue*. Boston: David R. Godine

Gastil, J. (1990). "Generic pronouns and sexist language: The oxymoronic character of masculine generics." *Sex Roles*, 23(11), 629–643.

Gavey, N., McPhillips, K. (1999). "Subject to romance: Heterosexual passivity as an obstacle to women initiating condom use." *Psychology of Women Quarterly*, 23(2), 349–367.

Gavey, N. (2005). *Just Sex?: The Cultural Scaffolding of Rape*. Hoven: Psychology Press.

Gearhart, S. (1982). "The Future—if there is one—is Female." In: P. McAllister. *Re- weaving the Web of Life: Feminism and Nonviolence*. Philadelphia: New Society Publishers, 271–290.

Gee, J. P. (1999/2014). *An Introduction to Discourse Analysis Theory and Method*. London and New York: Routledge.

Gee, J. P. (2015). "Discourse, small d, big D." *The International Encyclopedia of Language and Social Interaction*, 3(1), 1–5.

Genova, A. C. (1971). "Assertion and Evaluation In Searle's Theory of Speech Acts." *The Southwestern Journal of Philosophy*, 2(1/2), 65–72.

Giddens, A. (1992). *The Transformation of Intimacy: Sexuality, Love and Eroticism in Modern Societies*. Hoboken: John Wiley & Sons.

Girnth, Heiko (1996): "Texte im politischen Diskurs. Ein Vorschlag zur diskursorientierten Beschreibung von Textsorten." *Muttersprache* 1, 66–80.

Goddard, A., Patterson, L. M. (2000). *Language and Gender.* Hove: Psychology Press.

Goffman, E. (1976). "Gender display." *Studies in Visual Communication*, 3(2), 69–77.

Goldstein, T. (2011). *Two Languages at Work*. Berlin: De Gruyter Mouton.

Golka, M. (2008). *Bariery w komunikowaniu i społeczeństwo (dez)informacyjne.* Warsaw: PWN.

Good, G. E., Sherrod, N. B. (2001). "The psychology of men and masculinity: Research status and future directions." In: R. K. Unger (ed.), *Handbook of the Psychology of Women and Gender*. John Wiley & Sons, Inc., 201–214.

Gorely, T., Holroyd, R., Kirk, D. (2003). "Muscularity, the habitus and the social construction of gender: Towards a gender-relevant physical education." *British Journal of Sociology of Education*, 24(4), 429–448.

Gossett, J. L., Byrne, S. (2002). "'Click Here': A content analysis of internet rape sites." *Gender & Society*, 16(5), 689–709.

Gottlieb, S. C. (2010). *The Constitution of Partnering: A Foucauldian Analysis of Dispositives, Space and Order in Danish Construction*. Doctoral Dissertation. Lyngby: Technical University of Denmark.

Goźdź-Roszkowski, S., Hunston, S. (2016). "Corpora and beyond–investigating evaluation in discourse: Introduction to the special issue on corpus approaches to evaluation." *Corpora*, 11(2), 131–141.

Grabe, S., Ward, L. M., Hyde, J. S. (2008). "The role of the media in body image concerns among women: a meta-analysis of experimental and correlational studies." *Psychological Bulletin*, 134(3), 460.

Graff, A. (2006). "We are (not all) homophobes: A report from Poland." *Feminist Studies, 32*(2), 434–449.

Graff, A. (2014). "Report from the gender trenches: War against 'genderism' in Poland." *European Journal of Women's Studies*, 21(4), 431–435.

Graff, A., Korolczuk, E. (2017). "Towards an illiberal future: Anti-genderism and anti-globalization." *Global Dialogue*, 7(1), 27–30.

Grajek, M. (2003). "Gender pay gap in Poland." *Economics of Planning*, 36(1), 23–44.

Gramsci, A. (1971). *Selections from the Prison Notebooks.* London: Lawrence & Wishart.

Grant, T. J. Woodhams. (2006). "Rape as social activity: an application of investigative linguistics." In: J. Cotterill (ed). *The Language of Sexual Crime.* London: Palgrave MacMillan, 1–15.

Greer, J., Mensing, D. (2006). "The evolution of online newspapers: A longitudinal content analysis, 1997–2003." *Internet Newspapers: The Making of a Mainstream Medium*, 13–32.

Grice, H. P. (1975). "Logic and conversation." In: P. Cole, J.L. Morgan (eds). *Speech acts* (3), 41–58.

Grice, H. P. (1989). *Studies in the Way of Words*. Cambridge: Harvard University Press.

Groes-Green, C. (2009). "Hegemonic and subordinated masculinities: Class, violence and sexual performance among young Mozambican men." *Nordic Journal of African Studies*, 18(4), 19–19.

Grubb, A., Turner, E. (2012). "Attribution of blame in rape cases: A review of the impact of rape myth acceptance, gender role conformity and substance use on victim blaming." *Aggression and Violent Behavior*, 17(5), 443–452.

Gruszczyńska, B. (2007). *Przemoc wobec Kobiet w Polsce. Aspekty Prawnokryminologiczne*. Warszawa: Wolters Kluwer.

Grzenia, J. (2006). *Komunikacja Językowa w Internecie*. Warsaw: Wydawnictwo Naukowe PWN.

Guha, P. (2020). "Facebook, WhatsApp and selective outrage: The impact of digital activism on the intersectional Identities of anti-rape feminist activists in India." *From Sit-Ins to# revolutions: Media and the Changing Nature of Protests*, 159–171.

Gumperz, J.J. (1982/1997). *Language and Social Identity*. Cambridge: Cambridge University Press.

Habermas, J. (1989). *The Structural Transformation of the Public Sphere. An Inquiry into a Category of Bourgeois Society*. Cambridge: Polity.

Halliday, M.A.K. (1976). *System and Function in Language*. Oxford: Oxford University Press.

Halliday, M. (1978). *Language as Social Semiotic: The Social Interpretation of Language and Meaning*. London: Edward Arnold.

Halliday, M.A.K. (1985/1994). *An Introduction to Functional Grammar*. London: Edward Arnold.

Halliday, M.A.K. (1998). "On the grammar of pain." *Functions of Language* 5, 1–32.

Halliday, M.A.K., Hasan, R. (1985). *Language, Context and Text: Aspects of Language in a Social Semiotic Perspective*. Geelong: Deacon University Press.

Handke, K. (1992). „Status rodzinny i zawodowy a językowe zachowania kobiet i mężczyzn." *Rocznik Naukowo-Dydaktyczny* 7, 151–160.

Handke, K. (1994). "Język a determinanty płci." *Język a Kultura*, 9, 15–29.

Handke, K. (1995). *Polski język familijny: Opis zjawiska*. Warsaw: Slawistyczny Ośrodek Wydawniczy

Handke, K. (2006). "The language of Polish women." *Studia z Filologii Polskiej i Słowiańskiej*, (41), 83–94.

Handke, K. (2008). *Socjologia języka*. Warsaw: Wydawnictwo Naukowe PWN.

Hanna, C. (1999). "Sometimes sex matters: Reflections on biology, sexual aggression, and its implications for the law." *Jurimetrics*, 261–269.

Hardaker, C., McGlashan, M. (2016). " 'Real men don't hate women': Twitter rape threats and group identity." *Journal of Pragmatics*, 91, 80–93.

Hardin, M. et al. (2009). "'Have you got game?' Hegemonic masculinity and neo-homophobia in U.S. newspaper sports columns." *Communication, Culture and Critique*, 2, 182–200.

Harding, S. (1991). *Whose Science? Whose Knowledge? Thinking from Women's Lives*. New York: Cornell University Press.

Hayward, C. R. (1998). *De-facing Power*. Cambridge: Polity.

Hazenberg, E. (2020). "Gender, Sexuality, and the English Language" In: B. Aarts, A. McMahon, L. Hinrichs (eds). *The Handbook of English Linguistics*. Hoboken: Wiley-Blackwell, 585–600.

Heise, L. L. (1995/2007). "Violence, sexuality, and women's lives." In: R. Parker, P. Aggleton (eds). *Culture, Society and Sexuality*. London: Routledge, 291–313.

Hekma, G., Giami, A. (2014). *Sexual Revolutions*. London: Palgrave Macmillan.

Heller, M., Pietikäinen, S., Pujolar, J. (2017). *Critical Sociolinguistic Research Methods: Studying Language Issues that Matter*. London: Routledge.

Hendler, J. (2011). "The semantic web 10th year update." *Proceedings of the International Conference on Web Intelligence, Mining and Semantics*, 1–3.

Hensley, L. G. (2002). "Treatment for survivors of rape: Issues and interventions." *Journal of Mental Health Counseling*, 24(4), 331–347.

Herbig, A., Herrmann, A. F., Tyma, A. W. (2015). *Beyond New Media: Discourse and Critique about Contemporary Media*. Lanham: Lexington Books.

Herring, S. C. (1994). "Politeness in computer culture: Why women thank and men flame."In: M. Nucholtz, A.C. Liang (eds). *Cultural Performances: Proceedings of the Third Berkeley Women and Language Conference*. Berkeley: Women and Language Group, 278–294.

Herring, S. C. (1996). *Computer-Mediated Communication: Linguistic, Social and Cross-Cultural Perspectives. Pragmatics and Beyond*. Amsterdam: John Benjamins.

Herring, S. C. (2000). "Gender differences in CMC: Findings and implications." *Computer Professionals for Social Responsibility*, 18 (1).

Herring, S.C. (2001). "Computer-mediated discourse." In: D. Schiffrin, D. Tannen, H. Hamilton (eds.), *The Handbook of Discourse Analysis*. Oxford: Blackwell Publishing: 612–634.

Herring, S.C. (2002). "Cyber violence: Recognizing and resisting abuse in online environments." *Asian Women*, 14 (Summer), 187–212.

Herring, S.C. (2003). "Gender and power in on-line communication." In: J. Holmes, M. Meyerhoff (eds.). *The Handbook of Language and Gender*. Oxford: Blackwell Publishing, 202–228.

Herring, S.C. (2004). "Computer-mediated discourse analysis: an approach to researching online communities." *Designing for Virtual Communities in the Service of Learning* 1, 316–338.

Herring, S. C. (2005). "Computer-mediated discourse." In: D. Schiffrin, D. Tannen, H. E. Hamilton (eds). *The Handbook of Discourse Analysis*. Blackwell Publishers, 612–634.

Herring, S.C. (2008). "Computer-mediated discourse." In: D. Tannen, H. E. Hamilton, D. Schiffrin. *The Handbook of Discourse Analysis*. Oxford: Blackwell Publishing, 127–151.

Herring, S. C. (2010). "Digital media." In: P. Hogan (Ed.), *The Cambridge Encyclopedia of the Language Sciences*. Cambridge: Cambridge University Press.

Herring, S.C. (2013). "Discourse in Web 2.0: Familiar, reconfigured, and emergent." In: D. Tannen, A.M. Tester (eds). *Georgetown University Round Table on Languages and Linguistics 2011. Discourse 2.0: Language and New Media.* Washington D.C.: Georgetown University Press, 1–26.

Herring, S. C. (2016). "Epilogue." In: C. Lee, *Multilingualism Online,* London: Routledge, 37–146.

Herring, S. C. (2017). "Introduction to Pragmatics and the law: Speech act theory confronts the First Amendment." In: L. Sutton (ed.). *Context Counts: Papers on Language, Gender, and Power*. New York: Oxford University Press. 309–313.

Herring, S. C. (2018). "The co-evolution of computer-mediated communication and computer-mediated discourse analysis." In: P. Bou-Franch, P. Garcias-Conejos Blitvich (eds.), *Analysing Digital Discourse: New Insights and Future Directions*. London: Palgrave Macmillan, 25–67.

Herring, S. C. (2019). "The coevolution of computer-mediated communication and computer-mediated discourse analysis." In: Bou-Franch, P., Blitvich, P. G. C. (eds). *Analyzing Digital Discourse*. London: Palgrave Macmillan, 25–67.

Herring, S. C., Johnson, D. A., DiBenedetto, T. (1995). "'This discussion is going too far!' Male resistance to female participation on the Internet." In:

M. Bucholtz, K. Hall (Eds.), *Gender Articulated: Language and the Socially Constructed Self.* New York: Routledge, 67–96.

Herring, S. C., Kutz, D. O., Paolillo, J. C., Zelenkauskaite, A. (2009). "Fast talking, fast shooting: Text chat in an online first-person game." *Proceedings of the Forty-Second Hawai'i International Conference on System Sciences (HICSS-42).* Los Alamitos: IEEE Press, 1–10.

Herring, S. C., Marken, J. (2008). "Implications of gender consciousness for students in information technology." *Women's Studies,* 37(3), 229–256.

Herring, S. C., Paolillo, J. C. (2006). "Gender and genre variation in weblogs." *Journal of Sociolinguistics,* 10(4), 439–459.

Herring, S. C., & Zelenkauskaite, A. (2009). "Symbolic capital in a virtual heterosexual market: Abbreviation and insertion in Italian iTV SMS." *Written Communication,* 26(1), 5–31.

Hidalgo-Downing, L. (2000). *Negation, Text Worlds, and Discourse: The Pragmatics of Fiction* (66). Greenwood Publishing Group.

Hill, J. (1999) "Language, race, and white public space." *American Anthropologist,* 100 (3), 680–689.

Hill, J., Irvine, J. (1993). *Responsibility and Evidence in Oral Discourse.* Cambridge: Cambridge University Press.

Hobbs, P. (2013). "*Fuck* as a metaphor for male sexual aggression." *Gender and Language* 7(2), 149–176.

Hodge, R., Kress, G.R. (1988). *Social Semiotics.* Ithaca: Cornell University Press.

Hofstadter, D. (1985). "Metamagical themas: Questing for the essence of mind and pattern. A person paper on purity." *Language.* New York: Basic Books, 159–172.

Holland, J., Ramazanoglu, C., Sharpe, S., Thomson, R. (1998/2004). *The Male in the Head: Young People, Heterosexuality and Power.* The Tufnell Press.

Holmes, J. (1984). "Hedging your bets and sitting on the fence: some evidence for hedges as support structures." *Te Reo,* 27, 47–62.

Holmes, J. (1991). "Language and gender." *Language Teaching,* 24(4), 207–220.

Holmes, J. (1995). *Women, Men and Politeness.* London: Routledge.

Holmes, J. (1997). "Women, language and identity." *Journal of Sociolinguistics,* 1(2), 195–223.

Holmes, J. (2007). "Social constructionism, postmodernism and feminist sociolinguistics." *Gender & Language,* 1(1), 51–65.

Holmes, J., King, B. W. (2017). "Gender and sociopragmatics." In A. Barron, Y. Gu, G. Steen, *The Routledge Handbook of Pragmatics.* London: Routledge, 121–138.

Holmes, J., Meyerhoff, M. (2008). *The Handbook of Language and Gender*. Hoboken: John Wiley & Sons.

Holt, C. L., Ellis, J. (1998). "Assessing the current validity of the Bem Sex-Role Inventory." *Sex Roles*, 39(11), 929–941.

Honneth, A. (2014). *Disrespect: The Normative Foundations of Critical Theory*. Hoboken, New Jersey: John Wiley & Sons.

Hosseinmardi, H., Ghasemianlangroodi, A., Han, R., Lv, Q., & Mishra, S. (2014). Towards understanding cyberbullying behavior in a semi-anonymous social network. *IEEE/ACM International Conference on Advances in Social Networks Analysis and Mining 2014*. Los Alamitos: IEEE, 44–252.

Hughes, D. M. (2000). "'Welcome to the rape camp': Sexual exploitation and the internet in Cambodia." *Journal of Sexual Aggression*, 6(1–2), 29–51.

Humphreys, T.P. (2004). "Understanding sexual consent: An empirical investigation of the normative script for young heterosexual adults." In: M. Cowling (ed). *Making Sense of Sexual Consent*. London: Routledge, 209–225.

Humphreys, T. (2007). "Perceptions of sexual consent: The impact of relationship history and gender." *Journal of Sex Research*, 44(4), 307–315.

Hunston, S. (2011). *Corpus Approaches to Evaluation: Phraseology and Evaluative language*. London: Routledge.

Hunston, S., Sinclair, J. (2000). "Towards a local grammar of evaluation." In: S. Hunston, G. Thompson. *Evaluation in Text: Authorial Stance and the Construction of Discourse*. Oxford: Oxford University Press, 74–101.

Hunston S., Thompson G. (2000). *Evaluation in Text: Authorial Stance and the Construction of Discourse*. Oxford: Oxford University Press.

Hurrell, A. C. (2005). "Civility in online discussion: The case of the foreign policy dialogue." *Canadian Journal of Communication*, 30(4), 633–648.

Iantaffi, A., Bockting W.O. (2011). 'Views from both sides of the bridge? Gender, sexual legitimacy, and transgender people's experiences of relationships' in *Culture, Health and Sexuality* 13(3), 355–370.

Irvine, J. M. (2005). *Disorders of Desire: Sexuality and Gender in Modern American Sexology*. Philadelphia: Temple University Press.

Irvine, J. T., Gal, S., Kroskrity, P. V. (2009). "Language ideology and linguistic differentiation." *Linguistic Anthropology: A Reader* (1), 402–434.

Izdebska, A., Zielona-Jenek, M. (2016). "Wykorzystanie seksualne w dzieciństwie a seksualność kobiet w cyklu życia." In: A. Matysiak-Błaszczyk, B. Jankowiak (eds). *Kontrowersje wokół Socjalizacji Dziewcząt i Kobiet*. Poznań: Wydawnictwo Naukowe UAM, 253–276.

Izdebski, Z. (2012). “Zdrowie seksualne mężczyzn. Wybrane zagadnienia.” *Seksuologia Polska*, 10(1), 1–8.

Izdebski, Z., Ostrowska, A. (2003). *Seks po polsku: Zachowania seksualne jako element stylu życia polaków.* Warsaw: Muza S.A.

Jäger, S. (2001a). “Dispositive.” In: M.S. Kleiner (ed), *Michel Foucault: Eine Einfuhrung in sein Denken.* Frankfurt am Main: Campus, 72–89.

Jäger, S. (2001b). “Discourse and knowledge: Theoretical and methodological aspects of a critical discourse analysis.” In: R. Wodak, M. Meyer (eds), *Methods of Critical Discourse Analysis*. London: Sage, 32–62.

Jäger, S., Maier, F. (2009). “Theoretical and methodological aspects of Foucauldian critical discourse analysis and dispositive analysis.” In: R. Wodak, M. Meyer (eds.). *Methods of Critical Discourse Analysis* 2, 34–61.

Jakubowska, H. (2012). “Kobiety i kobiecość w dyskursie o Euro 2012.” *Czas Kultury*, 176(01), 34–46.

Jaworski, A. (1989). “On gender and sex in Polish.” *International Journal of the Sociology of* Language, 78, 83–92.

Jeffreys, S. (2005). *Beauty and Misogyny: Harmful Cultural Practices in the West.* New York: Routledge.

Jeffries, L. (2010a). *Critical Stylistics. The Power of English.* London: Palgrave Macmillan.

Jeffries, L. (2010b). *Opposition in Discourse: The Construction of Oppositional Meaning.* London: Bloomsbury Publishing.

Jespersen, O. (1922). *Language: Its Nature, Origin and Development.* New York: Holt.

Jespersen, O. (1924). “The teaching of grammar.” *The English Journal*, 13(3), 161–176.

Jewkes, R., Morrell, R., Hearn, J., Lundqvist, E. (2015). “Hegemonic masculinity: combining theory and practice in gender interventions.” *Culture in Health and Sexuality*, 17, 96–111.

Johansson, T. and N. Hammarén. (2007). “Hegemonic masculinity and pornography: Young people’s attitudes toward and relations to pornography.” *The Journal of Men’s Studies.* 15 (1), 57–70.

Johnson, A. J. (2018). “ ‘How came you not to cry out?’: Pragmatic effects of negative questioning in child rape trials in the Old Bailey Proceedings 1730–1798.” In: D. Kurzon, B. Kryk-Kastovsky (eds). *Legal Pragmatics.* Amsterdam: John Benjamins, 41–46.

Johnson, G. M. (2006). “Synchronous and asynchronous text-based CMC in educational contexts: A review of recent research.” *Tech Trends 50(4), 46–53.*

Joos, M. (1976). *The Five Clocks.* New York: Harcourt Brace And World. Inc.

Jozkowski, K. N., Peterson, Z. D. (2013). "College students and sexual consent: Unique insights." *Journal of Sex Research*, 50(6), 517–523.

Jullian, P. M. (2009). *An Exploration of Strategies to Convey Evaluation in the "Notebook" Texts.* Doctoral dissertation. Birmingham: University of Birmingham.

Kahlor, L., Morrison, D. (2007). "Television viewing and rape myth acceptance among college women." *Sex Roles*, 56(11), 729–739.

Kaim, A. (2004). "Polskie media wobec przemocy seksualnej." *Health*, (14), 227–230.

Kambarami, M. (2006). "Femininity, sexuality and culture: Patriarchy and female subordination in Zimbabwe." *South Africa: ARSRC*, 1–10.

Kang, M. (2010). *The Managed Hand.* Oakland: University of California Press.

Karwatowska, M. (2010). "Ostra jazda bez trzymanki, czyli seks w werbalizacjach licealistów." *Białostockie Archiwum Językowe*, 10, 133–146.

Karwatowska, M., Szpyra-Kozlowska, J. (2006). „Stereotyp blondynki w dowcipach internetowych." *Etnolingwistyka. Problemy Języka i Kultury*, 18, 311–328.

Karwatowska, M., Szpyra-Kozłowska J. (2010). *Lingwistyka płci: Ona i on w języku polskim.* Lublin: Wydawnictwo UMSC

Katz, J. (2006). *The Macho Paradox: Why some Men Hurt Women and how All Men can Help.* Naperville: Sourcebooks Inc.

Katz, M. H. (2015). "Politeness theory and the classification of speech acts." *Working Papers of the Linguistics Circle*, 25(2), 45–55.

Kelsey, D. (2014). "The myth of the city trickster: Storytelling, bankers and ideology in the Mail Online." *Journal of Political Ideologies*, 19(3), 307–330.

Kendall, T. (2007). "Pornography, rape, and the internet." *Law and Economics Seminar Paper.* Stanford University, accessed 2 February 2019, <http://idei.fr/sites/default/files/medias/doc/conf/sic/papers_2007/kendall.pdf>

Kennedy, E. (1979). " 'Ideology' from Destutt De Tracy to Marx." *Journal of the History of Ideas*, 40(3), 353–368.

Kępińska, A. (2006). *Kształtowanie się polskiej kategorii męsko- i niemęskoosobowości. Język wobec płci.* Warsaw: Wydział Polonistyki Uniwersytetu Warszawskiego.

Kerr, E. B., Hiltz, S. R. (2013). *Computer-Mediated Communication Systems: Status and Evaluation.* Cambridge, MA.: Academic Press.

KhosraviNik, M., & Esposito, E. (2018). "Online hate, digital discourse and critique: Exploring digitally-mediated discursive practices of gender-based hostility." *Lodz Papers in Pragmatics*, 14(1), 45–68.

Kiełkiewicz-Janowiak, A. (1992). *A Socio-Historical Study in Address: Polish and English*. Frankfurt am Main: Lang.

Kiełkiewicz-Janowiak, A. (2019). "Gender specification of Polish nouns naming people: language system and public debate arguments." *Slovenščina 2.0*, 7(2), 141–171.

Kiełkiewicz-Janowiak, A., Pawelczyk J. (2006). "Gender stereotypes in language use: Polish and English." In: K. Dziubalska-Kolaczyk (ed). *IFAtuation. A Life in IFA. A Festschrift for Professor Jacek Fisiak on the Occasion of His 70th Birthday*. Poznań: Wydawnictwo Naukowe UAM, 349–383.

Kiełtyka, R. (2005). "Zoosemic terms denoting FEMALE HUMAN BEINGS: Semantic derogation of women revisited." *Studia Anglica Poznaniensia* 41, 167–186.

Kiesling, S. F. (2011). "The interactional construction of desire as gender." *Gender and Language*, 5(2), 213–239.

Kiesling, S. F. (2019). *Language, Gender, and Sexuality: An Introduction*. London: Routledge.

Kiesling, S. F. (2022). "Stance and stancetaking." *The Annual Review of Linguistics*. 21(1), 1–18.

Kiklewicz, A. (2011). "Tęcza nad potokiem...: kategorie lingwistyki komunikacyjnej, socjolingwistyki i hermeneutyki lingwistycznej w ujęciu systemowym." *Biuletyn Polskiego Towarzystwa Językoznawczego, Bulletin de la Société Polonaise de Linguistique*, 67, 361–364.

Kilmartin, C. T. (1994). *The Masculine Self*. New York: Macmillan.

Kimmel, M. S. (2000). *The Gendered Society Reader*. Oxford: Oxford University Press.

Kimmel, M. S. (2007). *The Sexual Self: The Construction of Sexual Scripts*. Vanderbilt University Press.

Kissine, M. (2013). *From Utterances to Speech Acts*. Cambridge: Cambridge University Press.

Kite, M. E., Whitley Jr, B. E. (2016). *Psychology of Prejudice and Discrimination*. London: Routledge.

Kitzinger, C. (2005). " 'Speaking as a heterosexual':(How) does sexuality matter for talk-in-Interaction?." *Research on Language and Social Interaction*, 38(3), 221–265.

Kitzinger, C. (2009). "Doing gender: A conversation analytic perspective." *Gender & Society*, 23(1), 94–98.

Kitzinger, J. (2009). "Rape in the media." In: M. Horvath, J. Brown (eds). *Rape: Challenging Contemporary Thinking*. Collumpton: Willan Publishing.

Kitzinger, C., Frith H. (1999). "Just say no? The use of conversation analysis in developing a feminist perspective on sexual refusal." *Discourse and Society*, 10(3), 293–316.

Kluczyńska, U., Wojnicka, K. (2015). „Wymiary męskości." *InterAlia: Pismo Poświęcone Studiom Queer*, (10), 1–6.

Kochman-Haładyj, B. (2007). "Low wenches and slatternly queans: On derogation of WOMEN TERMS." *Studia Anglica Resoviensia*, 4, 206–229.

Kochman-Haładyj, B. (2020). "The vexing problem of gender stereotyping in world proverbs." *SKASE Journal of Theoretical Linguistics* (1), 73–86.

Kohlberg, L. A. (1966). "A cognitive-developmental analysis of children's sex role concepts and attitudes." *The Development of Sex Differences* (1), 82–173.

Koller, V. (2008). "Identity, image, impression: Corporate self-presentation and public reactions." In: R. Wodak, V. Koller (eds). *Handbook of Communication in the Public Sphere*, Berlin: de Gruyter, 155–180.

Koller, V. (2011). "Analyzing metaphor and gender in discourse." *Unité et Diversité de la linguistique. Cahiers du Centre d'Etudes Linguistique*, 1–17.

Koniuszaniec, G., Błaszkowska, H. (2003). "Language and gender in Polish." *Gender Across Languages*, 3, 259–285.

Kondowe, W. (2014). "Presidents and ideologies: A transitivity analysis of Bingu wa Mutharika's inaugural address." *International Journal of Language and Linguistics*, 2(3), 174–180.

Korenman, J., Wyatt, N. (1996). "Group dynamics in an e-mail forum." In: S. Herring (ed), *Computer-mediated Communication. Pragmatics and Beyond New Series*, 225–242.

Korolczuk, E., Graff, A. (2017). *"Worse than communism and nazism put together": War on Gender in Poland.* London: Rowman & Littlefield.

Korolczuk, E., Kubisa, J., Szelewa, D. (2017). "Ruch feministyczny w Polsce a kwestia socjalna." *Warszawskie debaty o polityce społecznej.* Warszawa: Fundacja im. Friedricha Eberta, 4–26.

Koss, M. P. (1988). "Stranger and acquaintance rape: Are there differences in the victim's experience?" *Psychology of Women*, 12(1), 1–24

Koss, M. P. (1990). "The women's mental health research agenda: Violence against women." *American Psychologist*, 45(3), 374.

Kościańska, A. (2014). *Płeć, przyjemność, Przemoc. Kształtowanie wiedzy eksperckiej o seksualności w Polsce.* Warsaw: Wydawnictwo Etno.

Kościańska, A. (2016). "Sex on equal terms? Polish sexology on women's emancipation and 'good sex' from the 1970s to the present." *Sexualities*, 19(1–2), 236–256.

Kościańska, A. (2019). "'Z racji swoich upodobań godny napiętnowania'–homofobia i seksizm w kryminologicznym dyskursie gwałtu." *InterAlia: Pismo Poświęcone Studiom Queer*, (14), 73–85.

Kościańska, A. (2021). "Transpłciowość w Polsce. Wytwarzanie kategorii." *LUD. Organ Polskiego Towarzystwa Ludoznawczego i Komitetu Nauk Etnologicznych PAN*, 105, 316–320.

Kowalczyk, I. (2003). „Kobiety-wojowniczki—pytania o wzorcy i sposoby identyfikacji." In: M. Radkiewicz (ed.) *Gender w Kulturze Popularnej*. Kraków: Rabid, 81–102.

Kowalski, B. M., Scheitle, C. P. (2020). "Sexual identity and attitudes about gender roles." *Sexuality & Culture*, 24(3), 671–691.

Krahé, B., Tomaszewska-Jedrysiak P. (2011). "Sexual scripts and the acceptance of sexual aggression in Polish adolescents." *European Journal of Developmental Psychology* 8(6), 697–712.

Krahe, B. (2014). "Sexual aggression in adolescence: risky sexual scripts and sexual behaviors." *Rocznik Lubuski*, 40(1), 75–90.

Kramarae, C. (1981). *Women and Men Speaking: Frameworks for Analysis*. Rowley: Newbury House Publishers.

Kramarae, C. (2001). *The Third Shift: Women Learning Online*. Washington: AAUW Educational Foundation.

Kramer, E. (2011). "The playful is political: The metapragmatics of internet rape-joke arguments." *Language in Society*, 40(2), 137–168.

Krawczyk-Tyrpa, A. (1999). "Atrybuty mężczyzn i kobiet utrwalone w polszczyźnie." In: J. Adamowski, S. Niebrzegowska, *Kobieta w Zwierciadle Języka i Kultury*. Lublin: Wydawnictwo Uniwersytetu Szczecińskiego, 427–433.

Krawczyk-Tyrpa A. (2001). *Tabu w dialektach polskich*. Bydgoszcz: Akademia Bydgoska im. Kazimierza Wielkiego.

Kress, G.R. (1985). "Ideological structures in discourse." In: T.A. van Dijk (ed.), *Handbook of Discourse Analysis*, London: Academic Press, 27–42.

Kress, G. R., van Leeuwen T. (1996). *Reading Images: The Grammar of Visual Design*. London: Routledge.

Kress, G.R., van Leeuwen, T. (2001). *Multimodal Discourse: The Modes and Media of Contemporary Communication*. London: Hodder Arnold.

Krige, J., Oostendorp, M. (2015). "'Too late for tears, dear sister': Constructing victims and perpetrators of rape in the advice column Dear Dolly from 1984 to 2004." *Stellenbosch Papers in Linguistics Plus*, *46*, 7–23.

Kroska, A. (2007). *Gender Ideology and Gender Role Ideology*. Oxford: Wiley.

Krótki Z., (2014). "Eufemistyczne nazwy stosunku seksualnego w historii języka polskiego." In: J. Przyklenk (ed.) *Bogactwo polszczyzny w świetle jej historii*, 5, Katowice: PWN, 140–153.

Krysiak, P. (2020). „Dyskursywny obraz feminizmu w polskim tygodniku opinii „Uważam Rze." Studium Przypadku." 111–125.

Krysiak, P., & Małocha-Krupa, A. (2020). "Feminatywum, feminatyw, nazwa żeńska, żeńska końcówka-problemy terminologiczne." *Oblicza Komunikacji*, 12, 229–238.

Krzaklewska, E., Slany, K., Warat, M. (2016). "Równość płci w przebiegu życia. Wskazania dla polityki społecznej." *Przegląd Socjologiczny*, 65(2), 11–32.

Krzyżanowski, M. (2016). "Recontextualisation of neoliberalism and the increasingly conceptual nature of discourse: Challenges for critical discourse studies." *Discourse & Society*, 27(3), 308–321.

Krzyżanowski, M., Forchtner, B. (2016). "Theories and concepts in critical discourse studies: Facing challenges, moving beyond foundations." *Discourse & Society*, 27(3), 253–261.

Krzyżanowska, N. (2012a). *Kobiety w (Polskiej) sferze publicznej*. Toruń: Wydawnictwo Adam Marszałek.

Krzyżanowska, N. (2014). "Konstruowanie macierzyństwa jako kwestii społecznej na przykładzie dyskursów polskiej sfery publicznej." *Kultura i Edukacja*, 4(104), 142–165.

Krzyżanowska, N. (2012b). "Wokół koncepcji demokracji. Parytet płci w świetle polskiego dyskursu prasowego." *Studia socjologiczne*, 204(1), 199–223.

Ksiazek, T. B., Springer, N. (2018). "User comments in digital journalism: Current research and future directions' in *The Routledge Handbook of Developments in Digital Journalism Studies*. London: Routledge, 475–486.

Kulick, D. (2000). "Gay and lesbian language." *Annual Review of Anthropology*, 29(1), 243–285.

Kulick, D. (2003). "No." *Language and Communication*. 23: 139–155.

Kuckartz, U. (2019). "Qualitative text analysis: A systematic approach." In: G. Kaiser (ed), *Compendium For Early Career Researchers in Mathematics Education*. New York City: Springer, 181–197.

Kumari, N. (2018). "Deconstructing Stereotypes: Re-presentations of Hijra Identity." *Glocal Colloquies*, 4, 102–109.

Kwiatkowska, A. (1998). "Gender stereotypes and beliefs about family violence in Poland." In: R. Klein (ed). *Multidisciplinary Perspectives on Family Violence*, London: Routledge, 129–152.

Kwiatkowska, A. (2013). "Talking about violence: How people convey stereotypical messages about perpetrator and victim through the use of biased language." *Framing Sexual and Domestic Violence through Language*. New York: Macmillan, 87–109.

Kwiatkowska, G.E. (2013). "Społeczne spostrzeganie kobiet aktywnych zawodowo." In: M. Karwatowska, R. Litwiński, A. Siwiec (eds.). *O płci, ciele, i seksualności w kulturze i historii* Małgorzata Karwatowska. Lublin: Wydawnictwo Uniwersytetu Marii Curie-Skłodowskiej, 87–93.

Labov, W. (1972). *Sociolinguistic Patterns* (4th Ed.). Philadelphia: University of Pennsylvania Press.

Lackie, L., & Anton, F. de Man. 1997."Correlates of Sexual Aggression Among Male University Students." *Sex Roles*, 37(5/6), 451–457.

Laclau, E. (1980). "Populist rupture and discourse." *Screen Education*, 34(99), 87–93.

Laclau, E., Mouffe, C. (2014). *Hegemony and Socialist Strategy: Towards a Radical Democratic Politics*. London: Verso Books.

Lai, C. H., & Fu, J. S. (2020). "Organizations' dialogic social media use and stakeholder engagement: Stakeholder targeting and message framing." *International Journal of Communication*, 14(1), 2246–2271.

Lakoff, G., Johnson, M. (1980/2008). *Metaphors We Live By*. Chicago: University of Chicago Press.

Lakoff, R. (1975). *Language and Woman's Place*. New York: Harper & Row.

Langer, R. (1998). "The concept of discourse in the analysis of complex communication events." *København: Institut for Interkulturel Kommunikation og Ledelse, IKL. Copenhagen Business School*, 1–39.

Lavin, T. (2020). *Culture Warlords: My Journey into the Dark Web of White Supremacy*. Boston: Legacy Lit.

Lazar, M. M. (2005). *Feminist Critical Discourse Analysis: Gender, Power and Ideology in Discourse*. London: Palgrave Macmillan.

Lazar, M. M. (2007). "Feminist critical discourse analysis: Articulating a feminist discourse praxis." *Critical Discourse Studies*, 4 (2), 141–164.

Leap, W.L. (1996). *Word's Out: Gay English in America*. Minneapolis: University of Minnesota Press.

Leap, W. L. (2015). "Lavender language." *The International Encyclopedia of Human Sexuality*, 649–719.

LeardMann, C. A., Pietrucha, A., Magruder, K. M., Smith, B., Murdoch, M., Jacobson, I. G. (2013). "Combat deployment is associated with sexual harassment or sexual assault in a large, female military cohort." *Women's Health Issues*, *23*(4), 215–223.

Lease, S. H. (2018). "Assertive behavior: A double-edged sword for women at work?." *Clinical Psychology: Science and Practice*, 25(1).

Leech, G. (1983). *The Principles of Pragmatics*. London: Longman

Lei, X. (2006). "Sexism in language." *Journal of Language and Linguistics*, 5(1), 87–94.

Lemke, J. L. (2002). "Travels in hypermodality." *Visual Communication*, 1(3), 299–325.

Lemke, J. (2009). "Multimodality, identity, and time." In: C. Jewitt (ed.). *The Routledge Handbook of Multimodal Analysis*. London: Routledge, 140–150.

Levy, I., Adam, K. M. (2018). "Online commenting about a victim of female-on-male rape: The case of Shia LaBeouf's sexual victimization." *Sex Roles*, 79(9), 578–593.

Lew-Starowicz, Z. (1988). "Cyclic impotence in male infertility." *Ginekologia polska*, 59(11), 690–694.

Lew-Starowicz, Z., Przyłuska-Fiszer, A., Stusiński J. (2014). *Normy i kontrowersje etyczne w seksuologii*. Gdańsk: Gdańskie Wydawnictwo Psychologiczne.

Lewis, S. C., Kaufhold, K., & Lasorsa, D. L. (2009). "Thinking about citizen journalism: Perspectives on participatory news production at community newspapers." *Journalism Practice*, 4(2), 1–25.

Lillian, D. L. (2008). "Modality, persuasion and manipulation in Canadian conservative discourse." *Critical Approaches to Discourse Analysis across Disciplines*, 2(1), 1–16.

Lindsey, L. L. (2015). "The sociology of gender theoretical perspectives and feminist frameworks." In: L. Lindsey (ed). *Gender Roles: A Sociological Perspective*. London: Routledge, 23–48.

Ling, R. (2005). "The sociolinguistics of SMS: An analysis of SMS use by a random sample of Norwegians." In: R. Ling, P. Pederson (eds). *Mobile Communications*. New York: Springer, 335–349.

Litosseliti, L. (2006). "Constructing gender in public arguments: the female voice as emotional voice." In: Baxter, J. (ed). *Speaking Out*. London: Palgrave Macmillan,40–58.

Livia, A., Hall, K. (1997). *Queerly Phrased: Language, Gender, and Sexuality*. Oxford: Oxford University Press.

Lopez, I. R. (2007). "The representation of women in teenage and women's magazines: Recurring metaphors in English." *Estudios Ingleses de la Universidad Complutense* 15, 15–42.

Lorber, J. (1994). " 'Night to his day': The social construction of gender." *Paradoxes of Gender*, 1, 1–8.

Lorber, J. (1997). "The social construction of gender." In: D. Kendall (ed). *Race, Class, and Gender in a Diverse Society: A Text Reader*. Boston: Ally and Bacon.

Lorber, J. E., Farrell, S. A. (1991). *The Social Construction of Gender*. London: Sage.

Lull, J. (1995). *Media, Communication, Culture: A Global Approach*. Cambridge: Polity Press.

Lyden, M. (2007). "Assessment of sexual consent capacity." *Sexuality and Disability*, 25(1), 3–20.

Łaziński, M. (2006). *O Panach i paniach: Polskie rzeczowniki tytularne i ich asymetria rodzajowo-płciowa*. Warsaw: Wydawnictwo Naukowe PWN.

Locher, M. A. (2010). "Introduction: Politeness and impoliteness in computer-mediated communication." *Journal of Politeness Research*, 6(1), 1–5.

Łukaszek M. (2013). *Szorstka młodość. Socjalizacyjne wyznaczniki zachowań seksualnych młodzieży (na podstawie badań wychowanków Ochotniczych Hufców Pracy)*, Rzeszów: Uniwersytet Rolniczy.

Łukaszek, M. (2014). "Ryzykowne zachowania seksualne mężczyzn odbywających karę pozbawienia wolności." *Rocznik Lubuski*, 40(1), 157–174.

Łysak, A., Zierkiewicz E. (2003). "Mitologia menstruacji w reklamie prasowej i telewizyjnej." In: M. Radkiewicz (ed.) *Gender w Kulturze Popularnej*. Kraków: Wydawnictwo Rabid, 63–80.

Łyś, A. E. (2015). "Mity i stereotypy na temat przemocy seksualnej–geneza, konsekwencje, wyzwania." *Nierówności Społeczne: W Trosce o Otwarcia Horyzontów Edukacji*. Gdańsk: Fundacja Instytut Równowagi Społeczno-Ekonomicznej, 117–133.

Macedo, D., Dendrinos, B., Gounari, P. (2015). *Hegemony of English*. London: Routledge.

Machin, D., Thornborrow, J. (2006). "Lifestyle and the depoliticisation of agency: Sex as power in women's magazines." *Social Semiotics* 16 (1), 173–188.

Machin, D., Mayr, A. (2007). "Antiracism in the British government's model regional newspaper: the talking cure." *Discourse & Society*, 18(4), 453–478.

Machin, D., Mayr, A. (2012). *How to do Critical Discourse Analysis: A Multimodal Introduction*. London: Sage.

MacKay, D. G. (1980). "Psychology, prescriptive grammar, and the pronoun problem." *American Psychologist*, 35(5), 444.

Macken-Horarik, M. (2003). "Appraisal and the special instructiveness of narrative." *Text & Talk*, 23(2), 285–312.

MacKinnon, C. A. (1983). "Not a moral issue." *Yale Legal & Political Review.*, 2, 321–333.

MacKinnon, C. A. (2016). "Points against Postmodernism" 75 *Chi.-Kent. L. Rev.* 687–690.

Maddux, W. W., & Yuki, M. (2006). "The 'ripple effect': Cultural differences in perceptions of the consequences of events." *Personality and Social Psychology Bulletin*, 32(5), 669–683.

Majer, A. (2016). *Dyskurs dyscyplinowania męskiego ciała w wybranych tekstach kultury popularnej.* Gdańsk: Katedra Wydawnictwo Naukowe.

Makara-Studzińska, M., Grzywa, A., Turek, R. (2005). "Przemoc w związkach między kobietą a mężczyzną." *Postępy Psychiatrii i Neurologii*, 14(2), 131–136.

Makin, D. A., Morczek, A. L. (2015). "The dark side of internet searches: A macro level assessment of rape culture." *International Journal of Cyber Criminology*, 9(1), 1–23.

Malamuth, N. M., & Briere, J. (1986). "Sexual violence in the media: Indirect effects on aggression against women." *Journal of Social Issues*, 42(3), 75–92.

Malamuth, N. M., & Check, J. V. (1980). "Penile tumescence and perceptual responses to rape as a function of victim's perceived reactions." *Journal of Applied Social Psychology*, *10*(6), 528–547.

Malamuth, N. M., Check, J. V. (1983). "Sexual arousal to rape depictions: Individual differences." *Journal of Abnormal Psychology*, 92(1), 55.

Malamuth, N. M., & Check, J. V. (1985). "The effects of aggressive pornography on beliefs in rape myths: Individual differences." *Journal of Research in Personality*, *19*(3), 299–320.

Maltz, D. N., Borker, R. A. (1982). "A cultural approach to male-female miscommunication." *A Cultural Approach to Interpersonal Communication: Essential Readings*, 168–185.

Małodzińska, W. (2017). "Wartość kształtowania kobiecości w procesie wychowania dziewcząt." *Edukacja Elementarna w Teorii i Praktyce*, (17–18/3–4), 22–28.

Marecek, J., Crawford, M., Popp, D. (2004). "On the construction of gender, sex, and sexualities." In: G. Wood (ed). *The Psychology of Gender.* London: Routledge, 192–216.

Markle, G. (2008). " 'Can women have sex like a man?': Sexual scripts in Sex and the City." *Sexuality & Culture*, 12(1), 45–57.

Marmaridou, S. (2011). "Pragmalinguistics and sociopragmatics." *Foundations of Pragmatics* 1, 77–106.

Martin, J.R. (2000). "Design and practice: enacting functional linguistics in Australia." *Annual Review of Applied Linguistics* 20, 116–126.

Martin, J. R. (2016). "Meaning matters: A short history of systemic functional linguistics." *Word*, 62(1), 35–58.

Martin, C. L., Wood, C. H., & Little, J. K. (1990). "The development of gender stereotype components." *Child Development*, *61*(6), 1891–1904.

Martin, J.R., Rose, D. (2003). *Working with Discourse: Meaning Beyond the Clause*. London: Continuum.

Martin, J. R., White, P. R. (2005). *The Language of Evaluation*, vol. 2. Basingstoke: Palgrave Macmillan.

Martínez, I. A. (2001). "Impersonality in the research article as revealed by analysis of the transitivity structure." *English for Specific Purposes*, 20(3), 227–247.

Martyna, W. (1978). "What does 'he' mean? Use of the generic masculine." *Journal of Communication*, 28, 131–138

Martyna, W. (1983). "Beyond the he/man approach: The case for nonsexist language." In: B. Thorne, C. Kramarae, N. Henley (eds), *Language, Gender and Society*. Rowley: Newbury House Publishers, 25–37.

Masser, B., Lee, K., McKimmie, B. M. (2010). "Bad woman, bad victim? Disentangling the effects of victim stereotypicality, gender stereotypicality and benevolent sexism on acquaintance rape victim blame." *Sex Roles*, 62(7), 494–504.

Masters, W. H., Johnson, V. E., Kolodny, R. C., Bergen, M. B. (1995). *Human Sexuality*. New York: HarperCollins College Publishers.

Matoesian, G. M. (2008). "You might win the battle but lose the war: Multimodal, interactive, and extralinguistic aspects of witness resistance." *Journal of English Linguistics*, 36(3), 195–219.

Matoesian, G., Gilbert, K. E. (2018). *Multimodal Conduct in the Law: Language, Gesture and Materiality in Legal Interaction*. Cambridge: Cambridge University Press.

Matthews, G. B. (1990). "Aristotelian essentialism." *Philosophy and Phenomenological Research*, 50, 251–262.

Matthiessen, C., Teruya, K., Lam, M. (2010). *Key Terms in Systemic Functional Linguistics*. London: Bloomsbury.

McCleary, C. M. (2014). "A not-so-beautiful campaign: A feminist analysis of the Dove campaign for real beauty." *TRACE: Tennessee Research and Creative Exchange*, 1–24.

McConnell-Ginet, S. (1984). "The origins of sexist language in discourse." *Annals of the New York Academy of Sciences*, 123–135.

McConnell-Ginet, S. (1989). "The sexual (re) production of meaning: A discourse-based theory." In: F. Wattman Frank and P.A. Treichler (eds), *Language,*

Gender, and Professional Writing: Theoretical Approaches and Guidelines for Nonsexist Usage. New York: Modern Language Association, 35–50.

McConnell-Ginet, S. (2011). *Gender, Sexuality, and Meaning: Linguistic Practice and Politics*. Oxford: Oxford University Press.

McDermott, R. C., Kilmartin, C., McKelvey, D. K., Kridel, M. M. (2015). "College male sexual assault of women and the psychology of men: Past, present, and future directions for research." *Psychology of Men & Masculinity*, 16(4), 355.

McDermott, R. C., Kilmartin, C., McKelvey, D. K., Kridel, M. M. (2015). "College male sexual assault of women and the psychology of men: Past, present, and future directions for research." *Psychology of Men & Masculinity*, 16(4), 355–370.

McKee, A. (2004). "Does size matter?: dominant discourses about penises in western culture." In: C. Healy, S. Muecke (eds). *Cultural Studies Review*, 10(2), 168–182.

McLaren, H. J., & Gatwiri, G. J. (2016). "Black women with vaginal fistula: The power to silence via internet imagery." *Social Alternatives*, 35(1), 47–52.

McMahon, S., Farmer, G. L. (2011). "An updated measure for assessing subtle rape myths." *Social Work Research*, 35(2), 71–81.

McNeill, L. (2005). "Genre under construction: The diary on the Internet." *Language@ Internet*, 1–10.

McPhillips, K., Braun, V., & Gavey, N. (2001). "Defining (hetero) sex: How imperative is the 'coital imperative'?." *Women's Studies International Forum* 24(2), Pergamon, 229–240.

Mead, M. (1949). *Male and Female: A Study of the Sexes in a Changing World*. New York: William Morrow.

Mendelsohn, B. (1963). "The origin of the doctrine of victimology." *Excerpta Criminal*, 3, 239–244.

Mendelsohn, G. (1976). "Victimology and contemporary society's trends." *Victiminology*, 1, 8–28.

Mendoza-Denton, N. (1995). "Pregnant pauses." In: K. Hall, M. Bucholtz (eds). *Gender Articulated: Language and the Socially Constructed Self*, London: Routledge, 51–66.

Merton, R. K. (1948). "The self-fulfilling prophecy." *The Antioch Review*, 8(2), 193–210.

Mey, J. (1979). *Pragmalinguistics: Theory and Practice*. The Hague & Paris: Mouton.

Michelson, K., Álvarez Valencia, J. A. (2016). "Study abroad: Tourism or education? A multimodal social semiotic analysis of institutional discourses of a promotional website." *Discourse & Communication*, *10*(3), 235–256.

Międzybrodzki, B. (2013). „Problematyka przestępczości seksualnej w latach 40. i 50. 'XX w. Trudności badawcze'" *Sensus Historiae* 10(1), 39–62.

Miemietz, B. (1997). "'Male person' vs. 'everything that is not a male person.'" In: Kotthoff, H., Wodak, R. (eds). *Communicating Gender in Context*. Amsterdam: John Benjamins Publishing Company, 31–50.

Milani, T. M. (2017). "Language and Sexuality." In: O. Garcia, N. Flores, M. Spotti (eds). *The Oxford Handbook of Language and Society*. Oxford: Oxford University Press, 403–422.

Millar, N., Hunston, S. (2015). "Adjectives, communities, and taxonomies of evaluative meaning." *Functions of Language*, 22(3), 297–331.

Miller, C., Swift, K. (2001). *The Handbook of Nonsexist Writing*. New York: Lipincott and Crowell.

Miller, P. (2003). "Gender and patriarchy in historical sociology." In: G. Delanty, E.F. Isin. *Handbook of Historical Sociology*, London: Sage, 337–348.

Mills, S. (1995). "Discontinuity and postcolonial discourse." *ARIEL: A Review of International English Literature*, 26(3), 73–88.

Mills, S. (2003). "Caught between sexism, anti-sexism and political correctness: feminist women's negotiations with naming practices." *Discourse & Society*, 14(1), 87–110.

Mills, S. (2002). *Feminist Stylistics*. London: Routledge.

Mills, S. (2008). *Language and Sexism*. Cambridge: Cambridge University Press.

Mills, S., Grainger, K. (2016). *Directness and Indirectness Across Cultures*. New York: Springer.

Miluska, J. (1993). "Stereotypy i uprzedzenia jako determinanty jakości życia kobiet" *Ruch Prawniczy, Ekonomiczny i Socjologiczny*, 145–156.

Mischel, W. (1973). "Toward a cognitive social learning reconceptualization of personality." *Psychological Review*, 80(4), 252–268.

Mohamed Haneef, M. S. (2019). "Multimodal social semiotic analysis of Delhi rape conviction news in 2013 in CNN IBN website." *Asian Journal of Communication*, 29(1), 92–107.

Mok, K., Chen, N. (2021). "Characteristics of online comments following high-profile celebrity suicide." *Crisis: The Journal of Crisis Intervention and Suicide Prevention*. Advance Online Publication. Accessed 3 March 2022, <https://psycnet.apa.org/doiLanding?doi=10.1027%2F0227-5910%2Fa000791>

Monelle, R. (2014). *Linguistics and Semiotics in Music*. London: Routledge.

Monro, S. (2019). "Non-binary and genderqueer: An overview of the field." *International Journal of Transgenderism*, 20(2–3), 126–131.

Moore, A., Reynolds, P. (2004). "Feminist approaches to sexual consent: A critical assessment." In: M. Cowling (ed). *Making Sense of Sexual Consent*. London: Routledge, 29–44.

Morgan, R., Wood, K. (1995). "The living room: Collusion." In: W.L. Leap (ed). *Beyond the Lavender Lexicon: Authenticity, Imagination, and Appropriation in Lesbian and Gay Languages*. London: Routledge: 235–250.

Moscovici, C. (2000). *Gender and Citizenship: The Dialectics of Subject-Citizenship in Nineteenth Century French Literature and Culture*. New York: Rowman & Littlefield Publishers.

Mosse, G. L. (2020). *Nationalism and Sexuality: Middle-class Morality and Sexual Norms in Modern Europe*. Madison: University of Wisconsin Press.

Mouffe, C. (2005). *The Return of the Political* (Vol. 8). London: Verso.

Mouzelis, N. (1995). *Sociological Theory: What Went Wrong?*. London: Routledge.

Mouzelis, N. (1997). "Social and System Integration: Lockwood, Habermas, Giddens." *Sociology*, 31(1), 111–119.

Mrozik, A. (2010). "Gender studies in Poland: prospects, limitations, challenges." *Dialogue and Universalism*, 20(5/6), 19–29.

Msibi, T. (2013). "Homophobic language and linguistic resistance in KwaZulu-Natal, South Africa." In: L. Atanga, S.E. Ellece, L. Litosseliti, J. Sunderland, *Gender and Language in Sub-Saharan Africa*. Amsterdam/Philadelphia: John Benjamins, 253–274.

Muehlenhard, C. L., Rodgers, C. S. (1998). "Token resistance to sex: New perspectives on an old stereotype." *Psychology of Women Quarterly*, 22(3), 443–463.

Mueller, C. M. (2006). "The US Women's Movement in Global Perspective," *Politics & Gender* 2(4): 539–541.

Muller, M., Ehrlich, K., Matthews, T., Perer, A., Ronen, I., Guy, I. (2012). "Diversity among enterprise online communities: collaborating, teaming, and innovating through social media." *Proceedings of the SIGCHI Conference on Human Factors in Computing Systems*. 2815–2824.

Murray, A. (2018). "Debt-bondage and trafficking: Don't believe the hype." *Global Sex Workers*. London: Routledge, 51–64.

Murugesan, S. (2007). "Understanding Web 2.0." *IT Professional*, 9(4), 34–41.

Myers, P. N., Biocca, F. A. (1992). "The elastic body image: The effect of television advertising and programming on body image distortions in young women." *Journal of Communication*, 108–133.

Naab, T., Naab, T., Brandmeier, J. (2021). "Uncivil user comments increase users' intention to engage in corrective actions and their support for authoritative restrictive actions." Journalism & Mass Communication Quarterly, 98(2), 566–588.

Nahajec, L. (2009). "Negation and the creation of implicit meaning in poetry." *Language and Literature*, 18(2), 109–127.

Nahajec, L. (2021). *Negation, Expectation and Ideology in Written Texts: A Textual and Communicative Perspective*. Amsterdam: John Benjamins Publishing Company.

Nasrullaeva, N. (2016). "The concepts 'man' and 'woman' in the English phraseology." *Scientific Enquiry in the Contemporary World: Theoretical Basics and Innovative Approach* 7, 74–82.

Nash, J. C. (2014). "Institutionalizing the margins." *Social Text*, 32(1), 45–65.

National Sexual Violence Resource Center. (2015). *Statistics about Sexual Violence*. National Sexual Violence Resource Center. Accessed: July 1 2019. https://www.nsvrc.org/sites/default/files/publications_nsvrc_factsheet_media-packet_statistics-about-sexual-violence_0.pdf

Noël, M. J. (2006). "Progressive polyamory: Considering issues of diversity." *Sexualities*, 9(5): 602–620.

Noelle-Neumann, E. (1974). "The spiral of silence a theory of public opinion." *Journal of Communication*, 24(2), 43–51.

Norgaard, R. B. (2010). "Ecosystem services: From eye-opening metaphor to complexity blinder." *Ecological Economics*, 69(6), 1219–1227.

Nowak, S. (2012). "Bądź Cosmo! Kolorowa prasa kobieca, popkultura i seksualność." *Studia Gejowsko Lesbijskie: Reaktywacja. Przegląd kulturoznawczy* 3(13): 273–286.

Nowakowska, A. (2008). "Konstruowanie męskości u źródeł przemocy interpersonalnej." In: R. Szczepanik, J. Wawrzyniak (eds.) *Różne Spojrzenia na Przemoc*. Łódź: Wydawnictwo Wyższej Szkoły Humanistyczno -Ekonomicznej w Łodzi, 153–168.

Nunan, D. (2008). "Exploring genre and register in contemporary English." *English Today*, 24(2), 56–61.

Nuyts, J. (2001). "Subjectivity as an evidential dimension in epistemic modal expressions." *Journal of Pragmatics*, 33(3), 383–400.

O'Barr, W. M., Atkins, B. K. (1980/2005). "'Women's Language' or 'Powerless Language'?" *Language, Communication and Education*, 202–217.

O'Reilly, T. (2009). *What is Web 2.0?*. Sebastopol: O'Reilly Media, Inc.

O'Reilly, T., & Battelle, J. (2009). *Web Squared: Web 2.0 Five Years On*. Sebastopol: O'Reilly Media, Inc.

O'Sullivan, P. B., Flanagin, A. J. (2003). "Reconceptualizing 'flaming' and other problematic messages." *New Media & Society*, 5(1), 69–94.

Oakley, A. (1972). *Sex, Gender and Society.* Maurice: Colophon Books.

Oakley, A. (1985). *Taking it Like a Woman.* London: Flamingo.

Ogiermann, E. (2009). "Politeness and in-directness across cultures: A comparison of English, German, Polish and Russian requests." *Journal of Politeness Research* 5, 189–216.

Oh, E., & Neville, H. (2004). "Development and validation of the Korean rape myth acceptance scale." *The Counseling Psychologist*, 32(2), 301–331.

Oliver, L. (1974). "Women in aprons: The female stereotype in children's readers." *The Elementary School Journal*, 74(5), 253–259.

Ostberg, J. (2010). "Thou shalt sport a banana in thy pocket: Gendered body size ideals in advertising and popular culture." *Marketing Theory*, 10(1), 45–73.

Pacuła, J. (2020). "Z historii polskiego słownictwa erotycznego–nazwy intymnych części ciała w dawnym socjolekcie przestępczym." *Annales Universitatis Paedagogicae Cracoviensis. Studia Linguistica*, (15), 163–178.

Palmer, F. (1986). *Mood and Modality.* Cambridge: Cambridge University Press.

Paolillo, J. C. (2015). "Computer-mediated communication: What a quantitative linguistic approach should do." *Revue Tranel (Travaux neuchâtelois de linguistique)*, 63, 49–69.

Park, J. S. Y., Bucholtz, M. (2009). "Public transcripts: Entextualization and linguistic representation in institutional." *Issue: Text and Talk,* 29 (5), 485–502.

Parks, J. B. (2004). "Attitudes toward women mediate the gender effect on attitudes toward sexist language." *Psychology of Women Quarterly*, 28(3), 233–239.

Parker, R. G., Gagnon, J. H. (2013). *Conceiving Sexuality: Approaches to Sex Research in a Postmodern World.* London: Routledge.

Pascual, D. (2020). "International participation and discursive choices in the digital genre of the travel blog comment." *LFE: Revista de Lenguas para Fines Específicos*, 26(1), 180–195.

Pauwels, A. (2003). "Linguistic Sexism and Feminist Linguistic Activism." In: J. Holmes, M. Meyerhoff (eds). *The Handbook of Language and Gender.* Oxford: Blackwell Publishing, 550–570.

Pérez Sabater, C., & Pérez Sabater, M. L. (2013). "Breaking gender stereotypes in technology education: Developing strategies in the English classroom." *English for Specific Purposes World*, 14(38), 1–14.

Pérez-Sabater, C. (2019). "Emoticons in relational writing practices on WhatsApp: Some reflections on gender." *Analyzing Digital Discourse*. London: Palgrave Macmillan, 163–189.

Persson, S., Dhingra, K., Grogan, S. (2018). "Attributions of victim blame in stranger and acquaintance rape: A quantitative study." *Journal of Clinical Nursing*, 27(13–14), 2640–2649.

Peters, C., Broersma M. J. (2013). *Rethinking Journalism: Trust and Participation in a Transformed News Landscape*. London: Routledge.

Peters, M. A., Besley, T. (2019). "Weinstein, sexual predation, and 'Rape Culture': Public pedagogies and Hashtag Internet activism." *Educational Philosophy and Theory*, 51(5), 458–464.

Peterson, S. (2015). "On slut shaming & rape culture." *Pamoja on: Interpersonal Violence* 1(5): 7–8.

Peterson, Z. D., Muehlenhard, C. L. (2004). "Was it rape? The function of women's rape myth acceptance and definitions of sex in labeling their own experiences." *Sex Roles, 51*(3), 129–144.

Philaretou, A. G., & Allen, K. R. (2001). "Reconstructing masculinity and sexuality." *The Journal of Men's Studies*, 9(3), 301–321.

Piechnik, A. (2019). „Określenia dzieci odnoszące się do ich wieku znane najmłodszym i najstarszym mieszkańcom pogórskich wsi." *SŁOWO. Studia Językoznawcze* 10, 168–177.

Piotrkowska, J. and A. Synakiewicz. (2011). *Dość milczenia: Przemoc seksualna wobec kobiet i problem gwałtu w Polsce.* Fundacja Feminoteka. Warszawa.

Pleck, J. (1981). *The Myth of Masculinity*. Cambridge: MIT Press.

Pleck, J. H., Sonenstein, F. L., Ku, L. C. (1993). "Masculinity ideology: Its impact on adolescent males' heterosexual relationships." *Journal of Social issues, 49*(3), 11–29.

Płonecka, M. (2017). "Negatywna seksualność jako bierna postawa społeczna." *Adeptus*, 9, 1–35.

Pollard, P. (1992). "Judgements about victims and attackers in depicted rapes: A review." *British Journal of Social Psychology*, 31(4), 307–326.

Porter, B. (2005). "Hetmanka and mother: Representing the virgin Mary in modern Poland." *Contemporary European History*, 14(2), 151–170.

Posteguillo, S. (2003). *Netlinguistics: An Analytical Framework to Study Language, Discourse and Ideology in Internet*. Jaume: Publicacions de la Universitat Jaume I.

Potts, C., Asudeh, A., Cable, S., Hara, Y., McCready, E., Alonso-Ovalle, L., Rajesh, B, Davis, C., Kratzer, A., Roepner, T., Walkow, M. (2009). „Expressives and identity conditions." *Linguistic Inquiry, 40*(2), 356–366.

Prihodko, G. (2018). "Specific nature of evaluative speech acts." *Advanced Education*, (9), 201–205.

Procházka, O. (2016). "Cohesive aspects of humor in Internet memes on Facebook: A multimodal sociolinguistic analysis." *Ostrava Journal of English Philology*, 8(1), 7–38.

Puda-Blokesz, M. (2016). "Jak nie ma w domu chłopa, zgłupieje i Penelopa–męskość i żeńskość w polskiej leksyce i frazeologii o proweniencji mitologicznej." *Socjolingwistyka* (30), 207–220.

Pryor, J. B. (1987). "Sexual harassment proclivities in men." *Sex Roles*, 17(5), 269–290.

Queen, R. (2014). "Language and Sexual Identities." In: S. Ehrlich, M. Meyerhoff, J. Holmes (eds). *The Handbook of Language, Gender, and Sexuality*. Hoboken: John Wiley and Sons, 201–219.

Quine, W. V. (1966). "Three grades of modal involvement." *The Ways of Paradox*. New York: Random House, 156–174.

Rafaeli, S. (1988). "From new media to communication." *Sage Annual Review of Communication Research: Advancing Communication Science, 16*, 110–134.

Raffnsøe, S., Gudmand-Høyer, M., Thaning, M. S. (2016). "Foucault's dispositive: The perspicacity of dispositive analytics in organizational research." *Organization*, 23(2): 272–298.

Rafi, M. S. (2010). "The sociolinguistics of SMS ways to identify gender boundaries." In: R. Taiwo (ed.) *Handbook of Research on Discourse Behavior and Digital Communication: Language Structures and Social Interaction*. Hershey: IGI Global, 104–111.

Rai, G. (2017). "Changing perceptions and meanings of cyberfeminism." *International Research Journal of Multidisciplinary Studies* 3(4), online, 1–10.

Raphael, J. D. (2013). *Rape is Rape: How Denial, Distortion, and Victim Blaming are Fueling a Hidden Acquaintance Rape Crisis*. Chicago: Lawrence Hill Books.

Raszewska-Żurek, B. (2011). „Kobieca cnota. Próba zrozumienia ewolucji znaczenia cnoty na przestrzeni wieków." *Studia z Filologii Polskiej i Słowiańskiej*, (46), 83–102.

Ray, O. (2016). *Sexual Violence in Popular Rap Music And Other Media*. Bachelor's Degree Dissertation. Tuscon: University of Arizona.

Reily, P. J. (1980). *Sexual Harassment in the Navy*. Thesis. Monterey: Naval Postgraduate School.

Reisigl, M. (2017). "The discourse-historical approach." In: J. Flowerdew, J.E. Richardson (eds). *The Routledge Handbook of Critical Discourse Studies*. London: Routledge, 44–59.

Reisigl, M., Wodak, R. (2009). "The discourse- historical approach (DHA)." In: R. Wodak, M. Meyer (eds), *Methods of Critical Discourse Analysis* (2). London: Sage, 87–121.

Rejter, A. (2013). „Władza płci w perspektywie komunikacyjnej." *Oblicza Komunikacji, 6*, 23–37.

Rickford, J. R. (2016). "Labov's contributions to the study of African American Vernacular English: Pursuing linguistic and social equity." *Journal of Sociolinguistics*, 20(4), 561–580.

Robinson, S. (2006). "Journalism and the Internet." *New Media & Society, 8*(5), 843–849.

Rodríguez, I. L. (2008). "The representation of women in teenage and women's magazines: Recurring metaphors in English." *Estudios Ingleses de la Universidad Complutense*, 15, 15–42.

Rogowska, B. (2018). „Ekonomia feministyczna jako podejście heterodoksyjne." *Studia Ekonomiczne*, 349, 201–209.

Rösner, L., & Krämer, N. C. (2016). "Verbal venting in the social web: Effects of anonymity and group norms on aggressive language use in online comments." *Social Media+ Society, 2*(3), 1–13.

Romaine, S. (2003). "Variation in language and gender." *The Handbook of Language and Gender*. Oxford: Blackwell, 98–118.

Rosewarne, L. (2013). *American Taboo: The Forbidden Words, Unspoken Rules, and Secret Morality of Popular Culture: The Forbidden Words, Unspoken Rules, and Secret Morality of Popular Culture*. Santa Barbara: ABC-CLIO.

Ross, K. L. (1996). "Against the theory of 'sexist language.'" *The Proceedings of the Friesian School, Fourth Series*, 3, 15–99.

Rossi, S. (2021). "Female onanism: Condemned pleasures, medical probes, and late-Victorian pornography." *Victoriographies*, 11(2), 148–164.

Roszak, J. (2008). "Kulturowe usankcjonowanie alkoholu i przemocy." In R. Szczepanik, & J. Wawrzyniak (eds.), *Różne spojrzenia na przemoc*. Łódź: Wydawnictwo WSHE, 167–183.

Rubin, G. (1984/2007). "Thinking sex: Notes for a radical theory of the politics of sexuality." *Culture, Society and Sexuality*. London: Routledge, 150–187.

Rubin, L. (1990). *Erotic Wars: What Happened to the Sexual Revolution?* New York City: Harper Perennial: A Division of Harper Publishers.

Ruiz, C., Domingo, D., Micó, J. L., Díaz-Noci, J., Meso, K., Masip, P. (2011). "Public sphere 2.0? The democratic qualities of citizen debates in online newspapers." *The International journal of press/politics*, 16(4), 463–487.

Russell, D. E. (1990). *Rape in Marriage*. Bloomington: Indiana University Press.

Ruth-Hirrel, L., Wilcox, S. (2018). "Speech-gesture constructions in cognitive grammar: The case of beats and points." *Cognitive Linguistics*, 29(3), 453–493.

Ryan, K. M. (2011). "The relationship between rape myths and sexual scripts: The social construction of rape." *Sex Roles*, 65(11), 774–782.

Rymes, B., Leone, A. R. (2014). "Citizen sociolinguistics: A new media methodology for understanding language and social life." *Working Papers in Educational Linguistics (WPEL)*, 29(2), 4.

Sabat, J. (2013, July 21). *Typologia zgwałceń*, accessed 19 June 2020 <http://www.psychologia.net.pl/artykul.php?level=692>

Sadock, J. (2004). "Speech acts." In: L. Horn, G. Ward (eds). *The Handbook of Pragmatics*, 53–73.

Saeed, J. L. (2003). *Semantics*. 2nd ed. Oxford: Blackwell Publishing.

Sahragard, R., & Davatgarzadeh, G. (2010). "The representation of social actors in interchange third edition series: A critical discourse analysis." *The Journal of Teaching Language Skills (JTLS)*, 2(1),67–89.

SAKI. (2015). "Victim or Survivor? Terminology From Investigation through Prosecution." *Sexual Assault Kit Initiative Toolkit*, 1–2.

Sampson, R. (2003). *Acquaintance Rape of College Students. Public Health Resources Guide*. Omaha: University of Nebraska.

Sanchez, D. T., Kiefer, A. K., Ybarra, O. (2006). "Sexual submissiveness in women: Costs for sexual autonomy and arousal." *Personality and Social Psychology Bulletin*, *32*(4), 512–524.

Sánchez-López, M. P., Flores, I. C., Dresch, V., Aparicio-Garcia, M. (2009). "Conformity to feminine gender norms in the Spanish population." *Social Behavior and Personality: An International Journal*, 37(9), 1171–1185.

Sanday, P.R. (1981). *Female Power and Male Dominance: On the Origins of Sexual Inequality*. Cambridge: Cambridge University Press.

Sanday, P. R. (2007). *Fraternity Gang Rape: Sex, Brotherhood and Privilege on Campus*. New York: New York University Press.

Santoro, G.M. (1995). "What is computer-mediated communication." In: Z.L. Berge, M.P. Collins (eds.), *Computer-Mediated Communication and The Online classroom 1: Overview and perspectives*. Cresskill: Hampton Press, 11–27.

Sapir, E. (1921). *Language*. New York: Harcourt.

Saporta, S. (1974). "Language in a sexist society." In: P.J. Hopper (ed). *Studies in Descriptive and Historical Linguistics: Festschrift for Winfred P. Lehmann*. Amsterdam: John Benjamins Publishing Company, 209–216.

Sauerland, U. (2008). "Implicated presuppositions." *The Discourse Potential of Underspecified Structures*, 8, 581–600.

Sauerteig, L. D. (2009). "Representations of Pregnancy and Childbirth in (West) German Sex Education Books, 1900s–1970s." In: L. Sauerteig, R. Davidson (eds), *Shaping Sexual Knowledge*. London: Routledge, 141–172.

Shchipitsina, L. Y. (2015). "Genre status of an online comment." *Vestnik Bashkirskogo Universiteta, 20*(2), 528–532.

Schleppegrell, M.J. (2004). *The Language of Schooling: A Functional Linguistics Perspective.* Mahwah, NJ: Erlbaum.

Schleppegrell, M. J. (2013). "Systemic functional linguistics." In *The Routledge Handbook of Discourse Analysis*. London: Routledge, 47–60.

Schulz, M. (1975). "The semantic derogation of women." *Language and Sex: Difference and Dominance*, 64(75), 134–147.

Scott, M. (2002). "Picturing the key words of a very large corpus and their lexical upshots or getting at the Guardian's view of the world." In: B. Ketteman, G. Marko (eds). *Proceedings of the Fourth International Conference on Teaching and Learning by Doing Corpus Analysis*. Leiden: Brill, 43–50.

Sczesny, S., Formanowicz, M., Moser, F. (2016). "Can gender-fair language reduce gender stereotyping and discrimination?." *Frontiers in Psychology*, 7, 25–35.

Seal, D. W., Ehrhardt, A. A. (2003). "Masculinity and urban men: Perceived scripts for courtship, romantic, and sexual interactions with women." *Culture, Health & Sexuality*, 5(4), 295–319.

Seals, C. A. (2021). "Interactional sociolinguistics in language and sexuality research." *The Routledge Handbook of Language, Gender, and Sexuality*. London: Routledge, 1–38.

Searle, J. R. (1975). "Indirect speech acts." In: P. Cole, J.L. Morgan (eds). *Speech Acts*. Leiden: Brill, 59–82.

Searle, J. R. (1976). "A classification of illocutionary acts." *Language in Society*, 5(1), 1–23.

Searle, J. R. (1979). "Intentionality and the use of language." In: A. Margalit (ed). *Meaning and Use*. Dordrecht: Springer, 181–197.

Seidler, V.J. (2003). *Rediscovering Masculinity: Reason, language and sexuality.* Milton Park: Taylor & Francis.

Shanahan, M. K. (2017). *Journalism, Online Comments, and the Future of Public Discourse*. London: Routledge.

Sheppard, M., & Mayo Jr, J. B. (2013). "The social construction of gender and sexuality: Learning from two spirit traditions." *The Social Studies*, 104(6), 259–270.

Sherif, C. W. (1982). "Needed concepts in the study of gender identity." *Psychology of Women Quarterly*, 6(4), 375–398.

Sherrick, B., & Hoewe, J. (2018). "The effect of explicit online comment moderation on three spiral of silence outcomes." *New Media & Society*, 20(2), 453–474.

Simon, W. Gagnon, J.H. (1986). "Sexual scripts : permanence and change." *Archives of Sexual Behavior*, 15(2): 97–120.

Simpson, P., Mayr, A. (2010). *Language and Power: A Resource Book for Students.* London: Routledge.

Sims, A.D. (2005). "Language and sexuality." *Language*, 81(3), 771–772.

Skowronek, B. (2014). "Językowe konceptualizacje czynności autoerotycznych. Rekonesans lingwistyczno-kulturowy." *Annales Universitatis Paedagogicae Cracoviensis| Studia de Cultura*, (135), 148–157.

Skrla, L. (2000). "The social construction of gender in the superintendency." *Journal of Education Policy*, 15(3), 293–316.

Slany, K. (2002). *Alternatywne formy życia małżeńsko-rodzinnego w ponowoczesnym świecie*. Kraków: Nomos.

Slany, K., Struzik, J., & Wojnicka, K. (2011). *Gender w społeczeństwie polskim.* Kraków: Nomos.

Slany, K., Kowalska, B., Śmietana, M. (eds.). (2005). *Homoseksualizm: Perspektywa interdyscyplinarna*. Kraków: Nomos.

Smith, K. (2019). "Lavender linguistics: Why words matter." In: L. Speidel, M. Jones (eds.) *The Edge of Sex: Navigating a Sexually Confusing Culture from the Margins*. London: Routledge, 83–88.

Sobyanina, V. A., Khokhlova, I. V. (2018). "Analysis Of immigration discourse metaphors in German mass media using the MaxQDA software." *Научный журнал*, 112–128.

Song, Z. (2013). "Transitivity analysis of A Rose for Emily." *Theory & Practice in Language Studies*, 3(12).

Spears, R., & Lea, M. (1994). "Panacea or panopticon? The hidden power in computer-mediated communication." *Communication Research*, 21(4), 427–459.

Spence, J. T., Helmreich, R., Stapp, J. (1975). "Ratings of self and peers on sex role attributes and their relation to self-esteem and conceptions of masculinity and femininity." *Journal of Personality and Social Psychology*, 32(1), 29–39.

Spence, J.T., Helmreich, R.L. (1978). *Masculinity and femininity: Their psychological dimensions, correlates, and antecedents.* Austin: University of Texas Press.

Spender, D. (1980). *Man Made Language*. London: Routledge.

Sprouse, J., Messick, T., Bobaljik, J. D. (2022). "Gender asymmetries in ellipsis: An experimental comparison of markedness and frequency accounts in English." *Journal of Linguistics*, 58(2), 345–379.

Stalnaker, R., Munitz, M. K., & Unger, P. (1977). "Pragmatic presuppositions." In: A. Rogers (ed). *Proceedings of the Texas Conference on Performatives, Presuppositions, and Implicatures.* Arlington, VA: Center for Applied Linguistics, 135–148.

Stamou, A. G. (2013). "Adopting a critical discourse analytical approach to the mediation of sociolinguistic reality in mass culture: The case of youth language in advertising." *Critical Studies in Media Communication*, 30(4), 327–346.

"Statutory rape." *West's Encyclopedia of American Law*, edition 2. (2008). The Gale Group 23 Aug. 2017

Stanko, B. and Williams, E. (2009). "Reviewing rape and rape allegations in London: What are the vulnerabilities of victims who report to the police?" In: M. Horvath, J. Brown (eds), *Rape: Challenging Contemporary Thinking.* Cullompton: Willan Publishing, 207–225.

Steele, C. M., Aronson, J. (1995). "Stereotype threat and the intellectual test performance of African Americans." *Journal of Personality and Social Psychology*, 69, 797–811.

Steinfeldt, J. A., Zakrajsek, R., Carter, H., Steinfeldt, M. C. (2011). "Conformity to gender norms among female student-athletes: Implications for body image." *Psychology of Men & Masculinity*, 12(4), 401–416.

Stępień, K. (2018). *Feminatywa w polskim dyskursie prasowym (na podstawie wybranych tygodników opinii).* Master's Degree Dissertation. Warsaw: University of Warsaw. Wydział Polonistyki Uniwersytetu Warszawskiego.

Stephens, D. P., Phillips, L. D. (2003). "Freaks, gold diggers, divas, and dykes: The sociohistorical development of adolescent African American women's sexual scripts." *Sexuality and Culture*, 7(1), 3–49.

Stoch, M. (2015). "Reprodukcja i reprezentacja–analiza związków w obrębie dyskursu feministycznego." *Annales Universitatis Paedagogicae Cracoviensis. Studia de Cultura*, (Re: Reprezentacja–Rekonstrukcja–Reinterpretacja"), 86–96.

Styśko, M. (2006). „O nietendencyjnym i tendencyjnie przychylnym osądzaniu winowajcy z negatywnie stereotypizowanej kategorii." *Psychologia Społeczna*, 2, 141–150.

Styśko, M. (2007). *Atrybucja winy: O roli stereotypów i odniesienia zdarzenia do Ja.* Warszawa: Wydawnictwa Uniwersytetu Warszawskiego.

Suarez, E., & Gadalla, T. M. (2010). "Stop blaming the victim: A meta-analysis on rape myths." *Journal of Interpersonal Violence*, *25*(11), 2010–2035.

Sugiera, M. (2003). "Lara Croft, córka Pandory: kobiecość i media." Małgorzata Radkiewicz (ed). *Gender w Kulturze Popularnej*. Kraków: Rabid, 103–116.

Sultana, A. (2010). "Patriarchy and women's subordination: A theoretical analysis." *Arts Faculty Journal*, 1–18.

Sunderland, J. (2006). *Language and Gender: An Advanced Resource Book*. London & New York: Routledge.

Sutherland, K. (2002). "From jailbird to jailbait: Age of consent laws and the construction of teenage sexualities." *William. & Mary Journal Race, Gender and Social Justice*, 9, 313–349.

Sutton, L. A. (1995). "Bitches and skankly hobags: the place of women in contemporary slang." In: K. Hall, M. Bucholtz (eds), *Gender Articulated: Language and the Socially Constructed Self*, New York: Routledge, 279–296.

Swann, J. (2000). "Gender and language use." In: R. Mesthrie, J. Swann, A. Deumert and W. L. Leap (eds). *Introducing Sociolinguistics*. Edinburgh: Edinburgh University Press, 216–247.

Sygit, E., & Ossowski, R. (2008). "Przemoc wobec osób starszych ze względu na ich wiek, płeć i wykształcenie." *Gerontologia Polska*, 16(3), 163–168.

Szczucki, K. (2011). "Rola zgody w strukturze przestępstwa na przykładzie przestępstwa zgwałcenia." *Czasopismo Prawa Karnego i Nauk Penalnych* (1), 31–58.

Szpakowska, M. (2004). "Seks i władza." *Konteksty: Polska sztuka ludowa: Antropologia kultury, etnografia, sztuka*, 58(1–2 (264–265)), 142–145.

Szpyra-Kozłowska, J. (2019a). "'Premiera', 'premierka' czy 'pani premier'? Nowe feminatywy w badaniu ankietowym." *Język Polski* (2), 22–40.

Szpyra-Kozłowska, J. (2019b). "Językowa 'zmiana płci.' Narracja męska i kobieca w wypracowaniach licealistów." *Poradnik Językowy*, (3), 17–34.

Szpyra-Kozłowska, J. (2021a). *Nianek, ministra i japonki. Eseje o języku i płci*. Warsaw: PWN.

Szpyra-Kozłowska, J. (2021b). "Rektorka, dziekana, kanclerka. Męskie i żeńskie nazwy kobiet zatrudnionych na stanowiskach uniwersyteckich w świetle badania ankietowego." *Acta Universitatis Lodziensis. Folia Linguistica*, (55), 37–55.

Szpyra-Kozłowska, J., Karwatowska M. (2004). "On, ona, seks i język polski." *Studia z Filologii Polskiej i Słowiańskiej*, 133–155.

Szwajcowska, J. (2006). "The myth of the Polish mother." In: E. Mazierska, J. Szwajcowska (eds). *Women in Polish Cinema*. New York: Berghahn Books.

Szydłowska, J. (2016). "Aside word and memory. Narration about sexual violence towards women from East Prussia in Polish memory discourse after the 1945." *Anthropos*, 25, 69–85.

Środa, M. (2007). "Kobiety, kościół, katolicyzm." In: C. Ockrent (ed). *Czarna Księga Kobiet*, 654–62.

Tabbert, U. (2015). *Crime and Corpus: The Linguistic Representation of Crime in the Press* (20). Amsterdam: John Benjamins Publishing Company.

Tabbert, U. (2016). *Language and Crime: Constructing Offenders and Victims in Newspaper Reports*. New York: Springer.

Taguchi, N. (2018). "Description and explanation of pragmatic development: Quantitative, qualitative, and mixed methods research." *System*, 75, 23–32.

Talbot, M. (2008). "Gender stereotypes: reproduction and challenge." In: J. Holmes, M. Meyerhoff (eds). *The Handbook of Language and Gender*. Malden: Blackwell, 468–486.

Talbot, M. (2010). *Language and Gender* (2nd Edition). Cambridge: Polity Press.

Tannen, D. (1981). "Indirectness in discourse: Ethnicity as a conversational style." *Discourse Processes*, 4(3), 221–238.

Tannen, D. (1986). *That's Not What I Meant! How Conversational Style Makes or Breaks Your Relations with Others*. New York: William Morrow, Ballantine

Tannen, D. (1990). *You Just Don't Understand: Women and Men in Conversation*. New York: William and Morrow and Co.

Tannen, D. (1994). *Gender and Discourse*. Oxford: Oxford University Press.

Tannen, D. (2013). "The medium is the metamessage." *Discourse*, 2, 99–117.

Tannen, D., Trester, A. M. (Eds.). (2013). *Discourse 2.0: Language and New Media*. Washington D.C.: Georgetown University Press.

Tantucci, V., Wang, A. (2018). "Illocutional concurrences: The case of evaluative speech acts and face-work in spoken Mandarin and American English." *Journal of Pragmatics*, *138*, 60–76.

Tarsiero, R. (2004). "Linguistics of computer-mediated communication." In. S. Kelsey, K. St. Amant (eds). *Handbook of Research on Computer-mediated Communication*. New York: Hershey, 983–1001.

Taylor, F. (2003). "Content analysis and gender stereotypes in children's books." *Teaching Sociology*, 300–311.

Tenorio, E. H. (2011). "Critical Discourse Analysis, an overview." *Nordic Journal of English Studies*, 10(1), 183–210.

Teo, P. (2000). "Racism in the news: A Critical Discourse Analysis of news reporting in two Australian newspapers." *Discourse and Society*, 11(1), 7–49.

Tharp, A. N. (2016). *Gender Spectrum Theory*. West Haven, CT: University of New Haven.

Thomas, J. (1983). "Cross-cultural pragmatic failure." *Applied Linguistics* 4, 91–112.

Thompson Jr., E. H., & Bennett, K. M. (2015). "Measurement of masculinity ideologies: A (critical) review." *Psychology of Men & Masculinity*, 16(2), 115.

Thompson, E. H., Pleck, J. H., Ferrera, D. L. (1992). "Men and masculinities: Scales for masculinity ideology and masculinity-related constructs." *Sex Roles*, 27(11), 573–607.

Thompson, G. (1996/2004/2013). *Introducing Functional Grammar*. London: Arnold.

Thornborrow, J. (2002/2014). *Power Talk: Language and Interaction in Institutional Discourse*. Harlow: Longman.

Thorne, B., Henley, N. (1975). *Language and Sex: Difference and Dominance*. Rowley: Newbury House Publishers.

Thurlow, C. (2007). "Fabricating youth: New-media discourse and the technologization of young people." In: S. Johnson, A. Ensslin (eds). *Language in the Media: Representations, Identities, Ideologies*. London: Continuum Publishing, 213–233.

Thurlow, C. (2018). "Digital discourse: Locating language in new/social media." In: J. Burgess, A. Marwick, T. Poell (eds). *The SAGE Handbook of Social media*. New York: Sage, 135–145.

Thurlow, C., Brown, A. (2003). "Generation Txt? The sociolinguistics of young people's text-messaging." *Discourse Analysis Online*, 1(1), 1–27.

Thurlow, C., Bell K. (2009). "Against technologization: Young people's new media discourse as creative cultural practice." *Journal of Computer-Mediated Communication*, 14(4). 1038–1049.

Thurlow, C., Mroczek K. (2011). *Digital Discourse: Language in the New Media*. Oxford: Oxford University Press.

Thurman, N. (2007). "The globalization of journalism online: A transatlantic study of news websites and their international readers." *Journalism*, 8(3), 285–307.

Tiefer, L. (1994). "Sex is not a natural act." *Sexualforsch*, 7, 36–42.

Titkow, A. (2003). *Szklany sufit: Bariery i ograniczenia karier kobiet. Monografia zjawiska*. Warsaw: Instytut Spraw Publicznych.

Titkow, A. (2007). *Tożsamość polskich kobiet*. Warsaw: Wydawnictwo IFiS PAN.

Tolman, D. L., Davis, B.R., Bowman, C.P. (2015). "'That's just how it is': A gendered analysis of masculinity and femininity ideologies in adolescent girls' and boys' heterosexual relationships." *Journal of Adolescent Research*, 1–29.

Tomaszewska, P., Krahé B. (2018). "Sexual aggression victimization and perpetration among female and male university students in Poland." *Journal of Interpersonal Violence*, 33(4), 571–594.

Tong, S., & Walther, J. B. (2011). "Relational maintenance and CMC." *Computer-Mediated Communication in Personal Relationships*, 53(9), 1689–1699.

Tranchese, A., Zollo, S. A. (2013). "The construction of gender-based violence in the British printed and broadcast media." *Critical Approaches to Discourse Analysis Across Disciplines*, 7(1), 131–163.

Tunstall, J. (1977). *The Media are American*. New York: Columbia University Press.

Turchik, J.A., Probst, D.R., Irvin, C.R., Chau, M., Gidycz, C.A. (2009). "Prediction of sexual assault experiences in college women based on rape scripts: A prospective analysis." *Journal of Consulting and Clinical Psychology*, 77(2): 361–366.

Turecka, M. (2005). "Czynniki zwiększające ryzyko i zapobiegające przemocy seksualnej." *Seksuologia Polska* 3(2): 43–51.

Tyler, M. (2011). *Selling Sex Short: the Pornographic and Sexological Construstion of Women's Sexuality in the West*. Cambridge: Cambridge Scholars.

Tyson, L. A. (2006). *Critical Theory Today. A User-Friendly Guide*. London: Routledge.

Unger, R. K. (1979). "Toward a redefinition of sex and gender." *American Psychologist* 34(11): 1085–1094.

Van Dijk, J. (2020). *The Network Society*. Newbury Park: Sage.

Van Dijk, T.A. (1984). *Prejudice in Discourse: An Analysis of Ethnic Prejudice in Cognition and Conversation*. Amsterdam: Benjamins.

Van Dijk, T. A. (1993). "Principles of Critical Discourse Analysis." *Discourse & Society* 4(2): 249–283.

Van Dijk, T. A. (1994). "Discourse and inequality." *Lenguas Modernas*, (21), 19–37.

Van Dijk, T. A. (1996). *Cognição, Discurso e Interação*. Sao Paulo: Editora Contexto.

Van Dijk, T. A. (1997). *Discourse as Social Interaction* (Vol. 2). Newbury Park: Sage.

Van Dijk, T. A. (1998). *Ideology: A Multidisciplinary Approach*. Newbury Park: Sage.

Van Dijk, T.A. (2001). "Discourse, ideology and context." *Folia Linguistica* 34(1–2), 11–40.

Van Dijk, T. A. (2005). *Discourse and Context: A Sociocognitive Approach*. Cambridge University Press.

Van Dijk, T.A. (2006). “Ideology and discourse analysis.” *Journal of Political Ideologies* 11(2): 115–140.

Van Dijk, T.A. (2007). *Discourse Studies*. London: Sage.

Van Dijk, T. A. (2017). “Socio-cognitive discourse studies.” In: J. Flowerdew, J.E. Richardson (eds.). *The Routledge Handbook of critical discourse studies*, 26–43.

Van Leeuwen, T. (1996/2013). “The representation of social actors.” *Texts and Practices: Readings in Critical Discourse Analysis*, 1, 32–70.

Van Leeuwen, T. (2005). *Introducing Social Semiotics*. New York: Routledge.

Van Leeuwen, T. (2008). *Discourse and Practice: New Tools for Critical Discourse Analysis*. Oxford: Oxford University Press.

Van Leeuwen, T. (2014). “Critical Discourse Analysis and multimodality.” *Contemporary Critical Discourse Studies*, 281–295.

Verbi Software. (2019/2022). *MAXQDA 2020* [computer software].

Vilar-Lluch, S. (2022). “Redefining attitude for studying explicit and indirect evaluations of human behaviour.” *Functions of Language* 29(2), 199–225.

Vincent, B. Y. (2009). “Computer-mediated language and corpus linguistics.” *Tokyo University of Foreign Studies (TUFS) Studies in Linguistics*, 103–120.

Virtanen, T. (2013). “Performativity in computer-mediated communication.” *Pragmatics of Computer-Mediated Communication,* Berlin: Mouton de Gruyter, 269–290.

Voloshinov, V. (1929/1973). *Marxism and the Philosophy of Language*. New York: Seminar Press.

Wall, C. J., Leary, P. (1999). “A sentence made by men: Muted group theory revisited.” *European Journal of Women's Studies*, 6(1), 21–29.

Walther, J. B. (1995). “Relational aspects of computer-mediated communication: Experimental observations over time.” *Organization Science*, 6(2), 186–203.

Walther, J. B. (1996). “Computer-mediated communication: Impersonal, interpersonal, and hyperpersonal interaction.” *Communication Research*, 23(1), 3–43.

Walther, J. B., Whitty, M. T. (2021). “Language, psychology, and new new media: The hyperpersonal model of mediated communication at twenty-five years.” *Journal of Language and Social Psychology*, 40(1), 120–135.

Ward, L. M. (2002). “Does television exposure affect emerging adults' attitudes and assumptions about sexual relationships? Correlational and experimental confirmation.” *Journal of Youth and Adolescence,* 31, 1–15.

Ward, L. M. (2003). “Understanding the role of entertainment media in the sexual socialization of American youth: A review of empirical research.” *Developmental Review,* 23, 347–388.

Ward, E. G. (2005). "Homophobia, hypermasculinity and the US black church." *Culture, Health & Sexuality*, 7(5), 493–504.

Wardhaugh, R. (2000). *An Introduction to Sociolinguistics* (3rd Ed.). Oxford: Blackwell Publishers.

Wareing, S. (1999). "Language and gender." In: J. Thomas, S. Wareing (eds.) *Language Society and Power*. London: Routledge, 65–81.

Wasilewski, J. S. (2010). *Tabu*. Warsaw: Wydawnictwa Uniwersytetu Warszawskiego.

Weeks, J. (2017). *Sex, Politics and Society: The Regulation of Sexuality since 1800*. London: Routledge.

Weitzman, L., Eifler, D., Hokada, E., Ross, C. (1972). "Sex-role socialization in picture books for preschool children." *American Journal of Sociology*, 77, 1125–1150.

Welskop, W. (2009). "Wykluczenie prostytutek z dyskursu społecznego. Sytuacja formalno-prawna zjawiska prostytucji w Polsce." *Pro Publico Bono* 5. Łódź: Wydawnictwo Atut, 225–233.

West, C., Lazar, M. M., Kramarae, C.. (1997). "Gender in discourse." In: T.A. Van Dijk (ed.) *Discourse as Social Interaction*, Newbury Park: Sage, 119–143.

West, C., Zimmerman, D. H. (1987). "Doing gender." *Gender & Society*, 1(2), 125–151.

Wetherell, M., Edley N. (1999). "Negotiating Hegemonic Masculinity: Imaginary Positions and Psycho-Discursive Practices." *Feminism and Psychology*, accessed 3 June 2021, <http://irep.ntu.ac.uk/id/eprint/4025/1/186657_4318%20Edley%20PostPrint.pdf>.

Wielgosz, M. (2015). "The persuasive function of commissive speech acts in Mexican and Portuguese homiletic discourse." *Kwartalnik Językoznawczy*, 1(2), 176–188.

Wierzbicka, A. (1985). "Different cultures, different languages, different speech acts: Polish vs. English." *Journal of Pragmatics* 9 (2–3), 145–178.

Wierzbicka, A. (1999). *Emotions Across Languages and Cultures: Diversity and Universals*. Cambridge: Cambridge University Press.

Wierzbicka, A. (2003). "Emotion and culture: Arguing with Martha Nussbaum." *Ethos*, 31(4), 577–600.

Williams, J. E. (1984). "Secondary victimization: Confronting public attitudes about rape." *Victimology*, 9(1), 66–81.

Williams, K., Crowston, M. (2000). "Reproduced and emergent genres of communication on the World Wide Web." *The Information Society*, 16(3), 201–215.

Willis, M., Jozkowski, K. N. (2018). "Sexual precedent's effect on sexual consent communication." *Archives of Sexual Behavior*, 48(6), 1723–1734.

Wisłocka, M. (1978). *Sztuka Kochania.* Warsaw: Iskry.

Wiśniewska, H. (2010). "Ekspansja wyrazu seks we współczesnych słownikach." In: M. Karwatowska, A. Siwiec (eds). *Przeobrażenia w Języku i Komunikacji Medialnej na Przełomie XX i XXI Wieku*, Lublin: Wydawnictwo Drukarnia Best Print, 197–205.

Witt, C. 2011. "What is gender essentialism?." *Feminist Metaphysics.* Dordrecht: Springer, 11–25.

Wittig, M. (1981/1993). "One is not born a woman." In: H. Abelove, M. A. Barale, D. M. Halperin (eds). *The Lesbian and Gay Studies Reader.* London: Routledge: 103–109.

Wodak, R. (1989). *Language, Power and Ideology: Studies in Political Discourse.* Amsterdam: John Benjamins Publishing Company.

Wodak, R. (2001a). "What CDA is about–a summary of its history, important concepts and its developments." *Methods of Critical Discourse Analysis* 1, 1–13.

Wodak, R. (2001b). "The discourse-historical approach." In: R. Wodak, M. Meyer (eds.). *Methods of Critical Discourse Analysis* 1, 63–94.

Wodak, R. (2004). „Critical Discourse Analysis." In: C. Seale, G. Gobo, J. Gubrium, D. Silverman (eds), *Qualitative Research Practice.* London: Sage, 197–213.

Wodak, R. and M. Meyer. (2001/2009/2015). *Methods of Critical Discourse Analysis.* Newbury Park: Sage.

Wodak, R., Krzyżanowski, M. (2008). *Qualitative Discourse Analysis in the Social Sciences.* London: Palgrave Macmillan.

Wolanski, B. (2013). "Taboo language and gender in Polish: A written text corpus analysis." *Social and Cultural Studies*, 34, 67–78.

Wolitzky-Taylor, K. B., Resnick, H. S., McCauley, J. L., Amstadter, A. B., Kilpatrick, D. G., Ruggiero, K. J. (2011). "Is reporting of rape on the rise? A comparison of women with reported versus unreported rape experiences in the National Women's Study-Replication." *Journal of Interpersonal Violence*, 26(4), 807–832.

Woodhams, J., Grant, T. (2006). "Developing a categorization system for rapists' speech." *Psychology, Crime & Law*, 12(3), 245–260.

Woolard, K. A. (1992). "Language ideology: Issues and approaches." *Pragmatics*, 2(3), 235–249.

Woolard, K. A., Schieffelin, B. B. (1994). "Language ideology." *Annual Review of Anthropology*, 55–82.

Worthen, M. G. (2021). "Categorically queer? An exploratory study of identifying queer in the USA." *Sexuality Research and Social Policy*, 1–24.

Wójcik, D. (2015). "Związki wyrazowe dotyczące seksualności człowieka nienotowane w ogólnych słownikach języka polskiego." *Od Redaktora*, 119–137.

Wynn, L. L., Foster, A. M., Trussell, J. (2010). "Would you say you had unprotected sex if…? Sexual health language in emails to a reproductive health website." *Culture, Health & Sexuality*, 12(5), 499–514.

Yong, C. (2011). "Does freedom of speech include hate speech?." *Res Publica*, *17*(4), 385–403.

Young, M., Penhollow, T. (2004). "Sexual desirability and sexual performance: Does exercise and fitness really matter." *Electronic Journal of Human Sexuality*, 7, accessed October 9, 2020, <http://www.ejhs.org/volume7/fitness.html>

Yu, G. (2006). "winMAX and MAXqda Workshop (half day)." *School of Language, Linguistics and Area Studies, University of West England*. University of West England, Online.

Yung, C. R. (2013). "How to lie with rape statistics: America's hidden rape crisis." *Iowa Law Review*, 99, 1197–1257.

Yung, C. R. (2015). "Rape Law Fundamentals." *Yale JL & Feminism*, 27, 1–47.

Yus, F. (2011). *Cyberpragmatics: Internet Mediated Communication in Context*. Amsterdam: John Benjamins Publishing Company.

Zafarovna, N. N. (2016). "Gender and gender stereotypes in the English phraseological system." *Восточно-европейский научный журнал*, 12(1), 111–114.

Zalewska, K. (2013). *Stereotypy męskości i kobiecości a zachowania agresywne mężczyzn chorujących na schizofrenię*. Doctoral Thesis. Katowice: University of Silesia.

Zaykowski, H. (2015). "Reconceptualizing victimization and victimization responses." *Crime & Delinquency*, 61(2), 271–296.

Zhou, L., Burgoon, J. K., Nunamaker, J. F., Twitchell, D. (2004). "Automating linguistics-based cues for detecting deception in text-based asynchronous computer-mediated communications." *Group Decision and Negotiation*, 13(1), 81–106.

Zimman, L. (2014). "The discursive construction of sex." In: L. Zimman, J. Davis, J. Raclaw. *Queer excursions: Retheorizing binaries in language, gender, and sexuality*, Oxford: Oxford University Press, 13–34.

Zimman, L., Davis, J., Raclaw, J. (2014). *Queer Excursions: Retheorizing Binaries in Language, Gender, and Sexuality*. Oxford: Oxford University Press.

Zimmerman, J., Morrison, A. S., Heimberg, R. G. (2015). "Social anxiety, submissiveness, and shame in men and women: A moderated mediation analysis." *British Journal of Clinical Psychology*, 54(1), 1–15.

Zimmerman, D.H., West, C. (1975). "Sex roles, interruptions and silences in conversation." In: B. Thorne, N. Henley. *Language and Sex: Difference and Dominance*. Rowley, MA: Newbury House, 105–129.

Zuber, S., Reed, A. M. (1993). "The politics of grammar handbooks: Generic he and singular they." *College English*, 55(5), 515–530.

Żebrowska, E. 2012. "Tekst w komunikacji zapośredniczonej komputerowo." *Lingwistyka Stosowana* (5), 145–154.

Żurowski, S. (2014). "Kontekstowa interpretacja wyrażeń o tzw. znaczeniu ogólnym." In W., Skit (ed.), *Semantyczne i pragmatyczne aspekty komunikacji. Od deminutywów do gestów*. Łódź: Wydawnictwo Uniwersytetu Łódzkiego, 27–50.

Text—Meaning—Context
Cracow Studies in English Language, Literature and Culture

Edited by Elżbieta Chrzanowska-Kluczewska and Władysław Witalisz

Vol. 1 Alicja Witalisz (ed.): Migration, Narration, Communication. Cultural Exchanges in a Globalised World. 2011.

Vol. 2 Bożena Kucała: Intertextual Dialogue with the Victorian Past in the Contemporary Novel. 2012.

Vol. 3 Cinta Zunino: *Mimesis* and the Representation of Experience: Dramatic Theory and Practice in pre-Shakespearean Comedy (1560–1590). 2012.

Vol. 4 Grzegorz Szpila: Idioms in Salman Rushdie´s Novels. A Phraseo-Stylistic Approach. 2012.

Vol. 5 Marta Gibińska / Władysław Witalisz (eds): Poetry and its Language. *Papers in Honour of Teresa Bela.* 2012.

Vol. 6 Peter Leese / Carly McLaughlin / Władysław Witalisz (eds.): Migration, Narration, Identity. Cross-Cultural Perspectives. 2012.

Vol. 7 Marta Dąbrowska: Variation in Language. Faces of Facebook English. 2013.

Vol. 8 From Sound to Meaning in Context. Studies in Honour of Piotr Ruszkiewicz. Edited by Alicja Witalisz. 2014.

Vol. 9 Anna Walczuk / Władysław Witalisz (eds.): Old Challenges and New Horizons in English and American Studies. 2014.

Vol. 10 Bożena Kucała / Robert Kusek (eds.): Travelling Texts: J.M. Coetzee and Other Writers. 2014.

Vol. 11 Maria Jodłowiec: The Challenges of Explicit and Implicit Communication. A Relevance-Theoretic Approach. 2015.

Vol. 12 Anna Jankowska: Translating Audio Description Scripts. Translation as a New Strategy of Creating Audio Description. Translated by Anna Mrzygłodzka and Anna Chociej. 2015.

Vol. 13 Robert Kiełtyka: Various Faces of Animal Metaphor in English and Polish. 2016.

Vol. 14 Elżbieta Chrzanowska-Kluczewska / Olga Vorobyova (eds.): Language – Literature – the Arts: A Cognitive-Semiotic Interface. 2017.

Vol. 15 Henrik Gottlieb: Echoes of English. Anglicisms in Minor Speech Communities—with Spe- cial Focus on Danish and Afrikaans. 2020.

Vol. 16 Anna Paluchowska-Messing: Frances Burney and Her Readers. The Negotiated Image. 2020.

Vol. 17 Dorota Mihułka: In Search of Identity and Spirituality in the Fiction of American Jewish Female Authors at the Turn of the 21st Century. 2020.

Vol. 18 Ewa Rusek / Władysław Witalisz (eds.): Across Borders. Cultural and Linguistic Shifts in the 21st Century. 2020

Vol. 19 Andrzej Pawelec / Aeddan Shaw / Grzegorz Szpila (eds.): Text-Image-Music: Crossing the Borders. Intermedial Conversations on the Poetics of Verbal, Visual and Musical Texts In Honour of Prof. Elżbieta Chrzanowska-Kluczewska. 2021.

Vol. 20 Joanna Szczepańska-Włoch: Playing Discourse Games. The Political TV Interview in Great Britain and Poland. 2022.

Vol. 21 Olga O'Toole: (De-)constructing Rape Culture and Victim Blaming Online. 2025.

www.peterlang.com

www.ingramcontent.com/pod-product-compliance
Ingram Content Group UK Ltd.
Pitfield, Milton Keynes, MK11 3LW, UK
UKHW011005120926
8556IPUK00027B/15

9 783631 92230